1994

Teaching Writing:
Balancing Process and Product

SECOND EDITION

Teaching Writing: Balancing Process and Product

GAIL E. TOMPKINS
California State University, Fresno

Merrill, an imprint of
Macmillan College Publishing Company
New York

Maxwell Macmillan Canada
Toronto

Maxwell Macmillan International
New York   Oxford   Singapore   Sydney

Cover art: © 1993 by Tom Post
Editor: Linda James Scharp
Production Editor: Jonathan Lawrence
Art Coordinator: Ruth A. Kimpel
Text Designer: Anne Flanagan
Cover Designer: Cathleen Norz
Production Buyer: Patricia A. Tonneman
Illustrations: Steve Botts

This book was set in Korinna and Kaufman by Compset, Inc., and was printed and bound by R.R. Donnelley & Sons Company. The cover was printed by Phoenix Color Corp.

Macmillan College Publishing Company
866 Third Avenue
New York, NY 10022

Macmillan College Publishing Company is part of the
Maxwell Communication Group of Companies.

Maxwell Macmillan Canada, Inc.
1200 Eglinton Avenue East, Suite 200
Don Mills, Ontario M3C 3N1

Library of Congress Cataloging-in-Publication Data
Tompkins, Gail E.
  Teaching writing : balancing process and product / Gail E.
Tompkins.—2nd ed.
      p.   cm.
  Includes bibliographical references and index.
  ISBN 0-02-420843-4
  1. English language—Composition and exercises—Study and teaching
(Elementary) 2. Creative writing (Elementary education) I. Title.
LB1576.T66   1994
372.6'23'044—dc20   93-26793
                                                              CIP

Printing: 1 2 3 4 5 6 7 8 9   Year: 4 5 6 7 8

Photo credits: All photos were provided by the author.

To the teachers and students of
Western Hills Elementary School, Lawton, Oklahoma,
and their principal, Jenny Reno

Preface

More than 50 years ago, Alvina Burrows and her colleagues (1938) recognized that students "all want to write," but not until Donald Graves's pioneering work in process writing (1975, 1983) did the movement to empower children in the elementary grades through writing take hold. In the last two decades, teachers and researchers have extended Graves's work in different contexts, with varied types of writing, and at all grade levels. *Teaching Writing: Balancing Process and Product* integrates this recent research and theory about the writing process, collaborative learning, reading and writing connections, and writing across the curriculum to assist teachers who teach students in kindergarten through eighth grade to write.

This book is unique because of its attention to both the process that children use as they write and the quality of their compositions. The text provides practical strategies for teaching writing—with step-by-step directions—and presents more than 100 student samples to illustrate the teaching strategies. The current edition emphasizes two instructional approaches: writers' workshop and thematic writing. In writers' workshop, students use the writing process to write about self-selected topics in a supportive classroom community of writers. Thematic writing projects are connected to literature focus units and social studies and science theme cycles.

Individual chapters focus on eight writing forms: journal writing, descriptive writing, letter writing, biographical writing, expository writing, narrative writing, poetry writing, and persuasive writing. These chapters begin with a vignette illustrating how students and the teacher in an elementary classroom learn about the writing form and apply what they have learned in writers' workshop and thematic writing projects. Then information about the writing form is presented, including reading-writing connections and applications across the curriculum, and the steps involved in teaching students to write using the form are explained. Suggestions for assessing students' writing are also included.

SPECIAL FEATURES OF THE SECOND EDITION

Numerous features have been included to increase this second edition's usability:

▼ *Focus on Writers' Workshop.* Writers' workshop is presented as one of two approaches for teaching writing. It is introduced in the second chapter and elaborated on in the chapters on writing forms.

▼ *Focus on Thematic Writing.* Writing in connection with literature focus units and social studies and science theme cycles is the second of two approaches for teaching writing emphasized in this edition.

▼ *Emphasis on Portfolio Assessment.* An entire chapter focuses on assessment and how students develop portfolios to reflect on and showcase their writing.

▼ *Chapter on Descriptive Writing.* A new chapter on descriptive writing describes how to help student writers become more observant and create more vivid images and comparisons in their writing.

▼ *The Reading-Writing Connection.* Lists of children's literature that exemplify each writing form are presented, and strategies are suggested to demonstrate the connections between reading and writing.

▼ *Writing Across the Curriculum.* Throughout the book, examples demonstrate how to use writing as a response to literature and in writing across the curriculum.

▼ *Reorganization of Chapters.* Letter writing, biographical writing, and expository writing are treated in separate chapters, and a new chapter on instructional approaches introduces writers' workshop and thematic writing.

▼ *Chapter Overviews.* One-page overviews summarize the purposes, audience, forms, topics, and approaches for teaching each writing form in Chapters 3–10. These overviews can be found at the beginning of the chapters.

SUGGESTIONS FOR USING THIS BOOK

Teaching Writing: Balancing Process and Product can be used as a text for undergraduate or graduate writing courses or as one of a collection of texts for reading and language arts courses. It can be coordinated with *Teaching Reading with Literature* by Gail E. Tompkins and Lea M. McGee (Macmillan) for literacy seminars. Also, teachers participating in in-service workshops will find it useful.

Instructors can proceed through *Teaching Writing* chapter by chapter or choose an order that fits the instructor's preferences or teaching style. For instructors who wish to vary the sequence of the chapters, it might be useful to think of the book in three parts. The first two chapters are the foundation for the rest of the book and should be read in order. Chapters 3 through 10 deal with how to teach elementary students to write stories, poems, reports, letters, and other forms of writing. These chapters can be taught in any order, based on personal preference. The last two chapters can be read at any time, but they will be more easily understood when read after the preceding ten chapters because they refer to concepts presented earlier.

ACKNOWLEDGMENTS

My heartfelt thanks go to the many people who have encouraged me and provided invaluable assistance as I wrote the first edition of *Teaching Writing: Balancing Process and Product* and revised it for this second edition. This text is a reflection of what the teachers and students I have worked with in Oklahoma, California, and across the United States have taught me, and it is a testimony to their excellence. In particular, I want to acknowledge the teachers at Western Hills Elementary School in Lawton, OK, and their principal, Jenny Reno, who opened their school to me. This school has blazed a new direction for literacy instruction in Oklahoma and the teachers, principal, and students deserve special recognition. Many of the teachers I describe in the vignettes teach at Western Hills School, and many of the photos and samples of student writing also come from this exceptional school. I also want to highlight contributions to this edition from Carol Ochs, Jackson Elementary School, Norman, OK; Whitney Donnelly, Pleasant Valley School, Pleasant Valley, CA; Judy Reeves and Betty Jordan, Western Hills Elementary School, Lawton, OK; and Kimberly Clark, Aynesworth Elementary School, Fresno, CA.

I want to express my appreciation to the children whose writing samples and photographs appear in this text and to the teachers, administrators, and parents who shared writing samples with me: Max Ballard, Nicoma Park Intermediate School, Nicoma Park, OK; Anita Beard, Norman, OK; Marc Bell, Monroe Elementary School, Norman, OK; Kathy Bending, Highland Elementary School, Downers Grove, IL; Linda Besett, Sulphur Elementary School, Sulphur, OK; Gracie Branch, Eisenhower Elementary School, Norman, OK; Juli Carson, Jefferson Elementary School, Norman, OK; Shirley Carson, Wayne School, Wayne, OK; Pam Cottom, James Griffith Intermediate School, Choctaw, OK; Kimberly Crider, Ewing Elementary School, Fresno, CA; Jean Davis, James Griffith Intermediate School, Choctaw, OK; Deanie Dillen, Putnam City Schools, Oklahoma City, OK; Polly Dwyer, University of Oklahoma, Norman, OK; Charlotte Fleetham, Pioneer Intermediate School, Noble, OK; Parthy Ford, Whittier Elementary School, Lawton, OK; Debbie Frankenberg, Purcell, OK; Chuckie Garner, Kennedy Elementary School, Norman, OK; Mendy Gipson, Eisenhower Elementary School, Norman, OK; Peggy Givens, Watonga Middle School, Watonga, OK; Teri Gray, James Griffith Intermediate School, Choctaw, OK; Garett Griebel, Chickasha, OK; Carole and Bill Hamilton, Stillwater, MN; Debbie Hamilton, Irving Middle School, Norman, OK; Lori Hardy and Kay Hughes, James Griffith Intermediate School, Choctaw, OK; Ernestine Hightower, Whittier Elementary School, Lawton, OK; Linda Hopper, Wilson Elementary School, Norman, OK; Annette Jacks, Blanchard Elementary School, Blanchard, OK; Suzie Jennings, Lindsay, OK; Merry Kelly, Thomas Oleata School, Atwater, CA; Helen Lawson, Deer Creek School, Oklahoma City, OK; Diane Lewis, Irving Middle School, Norman, OK; Mark Mattingly, Central Junior High School, Lawton, OK; Pam McCarthy, Hubbard Elementary School, Noble, OK; Tissie McClure, Nicoma Park Intermediate School, Nicoma Park, OK; Gina McCook, Whittier Middle School, Norman, OK; Joyce Mucher, Penryn Elementary School, Penryn, CA; Mary Oldham, University of Oklahoma, Norman, OK; Teresa Ossenkop, Eisenhower Elementary School, Norman, OK; Sandra Pabst, Monroe Elementary School, Norman, OK; Alice Rakitan, Highland Elementary School, Downers Grove, IL; Jelta Reneau, Lincoln Elementary School, Norman, OK; Martha Rhynes, Stonewall, OK; Bobby Russell, Seiling Schools, Seiling, OK; Becky Selle, Bethel School, Shawnee, OK; Linda Shanahan, Nicoma Park Intermediate School, Nicoma Park, OK; Jo Ann Steffen, Nicoma Park Junior High School, Nicoma Park, OK; Gail Warmath, Longfellow Middle School, Norman, OK; MaryBeth Webeler, Highland Elementary School, Downers Grove, IL; Lynnda Wheatley, Briarwood Elementary School, Moore, OK; Linda White, University of Oklahoma, Norman, OK; Vera Willey, Lincoln Elementary School, Norman, OK; Jean Winters, Irving Middle School, Norman, OK; and Susie Wood, Marlow, OK.

Very special thanks go to my husband, Dick Osterberg, for understanding how important writing is to me and for making it possible for me to have the time and space to write. It's one of the reasons why I love you. Special thanks, too, go to my stepchildren, Todd and Linnea, and my parents for understanding my preoccupation with this project.

I also want to thank the colleagues who served as reviewers, carefully reading and critically reacting to the manuscript: Linda B. Amspaugh, University of Cincinnati; Jill Fitzgerald, University of North Carolina; Shirley Haley-James, Georgia State University; James L. Hoot, University of Buffalo; and Ruth Justine Kurth, University of North Texas.

Finally, I want to express my sincere appreciation to my editors at Macmillan in Columbus, Ohio. I offer very special thanks to Linda James Scharp for her creative inspiration and nurturing encouragement through both editions of *Teaching Writing.* Jeff Johnston originally provided the opportunity for me to pursue this project and I appreciate his support. I also want to thank Jonathan Lawrence for moving the second edition so efficiently through the maze of production details and for his patient manner with me. Thanks, too, to Martha Morss for asking the tough questions and for smoothing out the rough spots in the manuscript.

Gail E. Tompkins

Brief Contents

Contents

Teaching Writing: Balancing Process and Product

1

Teaching Children to Write

Writing About Weather

Mrs. Winston's second and third graders are learning about weather, and they use writing as a learning tool. They begin the theme cycle by making a KWL chart (Ogle, 1986, 1989). Mrs. Winston divides the chart into three columns; the first is K: What We *Know,* the second is W: What We *Want to Learn,* and the third is L: What We *Learned.* Students begin by brainstorming things they already know about weather, and Mrs. Winston writes them in the K column. The list includes "Weather is different in summer and winter," "Lightning is very dangerous," "You tell the temperature on a thermometer," and "Snow is frozen rain." Then a child asks, "How does it rain?" and Mrs. Winston writes the question in the W column. Other questions about tornadoes and different types of clouds are asked, and Mrs. Winston adds them to the W column. The discussion continues, and other information and questions are added to the K and W columns. During the theme study, students continue to add questions to the W column, and as they learn more about weather, they write what they are learning in the L column to complete the chart.

Mrs. Winston also talks with students about the kinds of activities they might pursue during the theme cycle. The students decide they want to keep daily weather calendars, interview a television weather forecaster, do weather experiments, and write an ABC book on weather, as they did on plants earlier in the school year. They also want to keep learning logs, read weather books, make posters about weather, and do self-selected projects. Writing will be an important tool in these activities, and Mrs. Winston uses their ideas together with the learner outcomes specified by her school district to plan the theme.

Mrs. Winston and several students hang a long sheet of butcher paper on the wall to make a "word wall." All interesting and unfamiliar words about weather will be added to the word wall during the theme. Students refer to the list as they write and work on projects. As soon as the paper is hung several students suggest words, including *tornado, thermometer, hurricane, freezing,* and *thunderstorm,* to be written on the word wall. By the end of the four-week theme, more than 100 words will have been added to the word wall.

Mrs. Winston collects weather books and displays them on a special rack in the classroom library. She gives a book talk about each, briefly mentioning something of interest about the book. Among the books she introduces are *Cloudy with a Chance of Meatballs* (Barrett, 1978), *The Cloud Book* (de Paola, 1975), and *Weather Forecasting* (Gibbons, 1987). In addition, earlier she copied a collection of weather poems from *Sing a Song of Popcorn: Every Child's Book of Poems* (de Regniers, 1988), and ten copies of the poetry booklet are in the library center. Students will read one book together as a class and other books during reading workshop (independent reading of self-selected books).

Students write about what they read in learning logs. They make their own logs, at the beginning of the theme, by compiling 20 sheets of notebook paper and construction paper covers, punching holes, and adding brads. During the theme, students decorate the covers with weather-related illustrations and diagrams. At the end of the theme, they number the pages and add a table of contents. In the logs students write quickwrites (short informal writings), draw pictures, and add clusters (diagrams shaped like spider webs), charts, and other information. Two entries from students' learning logs are presented in Figure 1-1. The first entry is a cluster about clouds

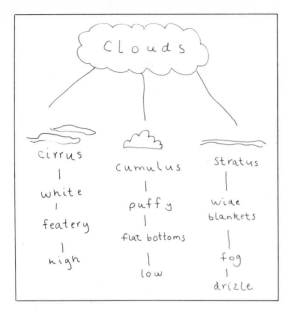

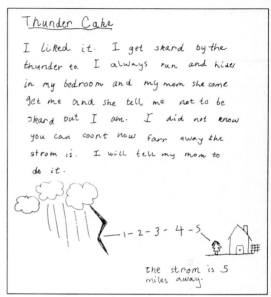

FIGURE 1-1   *Excerpts from Students' Learning Logs*

written after reading *The Cloud Book,* and the second is a quickwrite written after Mrs. Winston read Patricia Polacco's *Thunder Cake* (1990), a story about how a young girl overcame her fear of thunderstorms.

These writings are informal. Mrs. Winston views students' learning logs as a place to experiment with new concepts and vocabulary. She checks to see that the various assignments have been completed but does not correct misspelled words or mark other mechanical errors. She does, however, make comments, ask questions, and correct inaccurate weather facts. If, for example, on the cloud cluster, a student had confused cirrus and cumulus clouds, she would make a correction.

Mrs. Winston's students use writing as a part of many science activities. One example is when the local television weather forecaster, Mr. Reed, visited the class for an interview. A small group of students wrote a letter inviting Mr. Reed to visit the class and answer their questions. Next the class brainstormed a list of questions to ask him, and Mrs. Winston wrote the questions on a chart. Then students each chose a question to ask and wrote it on an index card. During Mr. Reed's visit, students took turns asking questions and taking notes about the answers on the backs of the cards.

Afterwards, students discussed the weather forecaster's visit and shared the notes they had made. They decided to make a class book to share what they had learned. On each page a student wrote the question he or she had asked Mr. Reed and his answer. Students used the writing process to draft, revise, and edit their writing. Since the book was being published and would be shared with parents and other classes, it was important for students to write in complete sentences using capital letters and punctuation marks. They also wanted to spell all words correctly. A page from the class book is presented in Figure 1-2 (left).

FIGURE 1-2   *Excerpts from Students' Weather Books*

Mrs. Winston's students used the writing process again to write another class book on weather written in an ABC format. They began by hanging a strip of paper beside the word wall and writing the alphabet on it. Then students identified words and phrases beginning with each letter on the first list and wrote them on the second list. For example, they wrote *forecasters, flurries,* and *fog* under F and *thermometers, temperature, thunder,* and *thunderstorms* under T. As a class students decided on the page layout featuring the letter highlighted, an illustration, and accompanying text (a sentence or two). Then students, individually or in pairs, selected a letter to do. After creating rough drafts of their pages, they met in writing groups to share their drafts and get feedback on the accuracy of their illustrations and text and suggestions on additional information they might add. After making revisions, Mrs. Winston met with students in small groups for editing. She helped them proofread their sentences and correct spelling, capitalization, punctuation, and any other factual or mechanical errors. Then students made their final copies on special drawing paper and arranged the pages in alphabetical order. Several students worked together to make the title page and the cover. Mrs. Winston punched holes in the pages and used ribbon to bind the book. The D page from the class ABC weather book is shown in Figure 1-2 (right).

Students also choose individual projects to do that relate to weather. Their projects included

▼ drawing weather maps
▼ painting a mural about weather

Snowy Thoughts,

the best thing about Snow is a Swon man

When it stats to snow I think about having a snow ball fight

When it's snowing I like to play with my brother.

My favorite swon-day food is hot sup.

FIGURE 1-3 *A Second Grader's Weather Book* Snowy Thoughts

▼ making weather safety posters
▼ performing a skit about weather forecasting
▼ constructing weather instruments
▼ retelling a favorite weather story such as *Cloudy with a Chance of Meatballs*
▼ making a weather can (a coffee can decorated with a picture and filled with 5 facts about or a particular type of weather such as tornadoes)
▼ writing a weather book

Mrs. Winston sets aside 45-minute chunks of time for students to work on these projects. They work individually or in small groups, and Mrs. Winston circulates around the classroom to supervise their work. She meets with students briefly in conferences to keep track of their work and solve problems as needed. After they complete their projects, students share them with classmates during a special sharing time.

Most projects involve some writing as students write signs and labels. Other projects such as making a can or writing a book require more writing. Students refer to the word wall for help in spelling words, and Mrs. Winston encourages them to make and share rough drafts before working on their final copies. One student's project, a weather book called *Snowy Thoughts,* is presented in Figure 1-3. This child began by drawing the pictures on each page and then went back and wrote the text to accompany each illustration. After writing, he shared his book with Mrs. Winston and a small group of students. He made a few revisions and then met with Mrs. Winston again for an editing conference. He corrected several spelling and punctuation errors and then shared his book with his classmates. Even though several spelling errors remain, he was very proud of his book!

*T*his vignette about Mrs. Winston's second and third graders and their writing about weather demonstrates children's ability to write. Notions that children in the elementary grades cannot write, that they must learn to read before learning to write, or that they must learn to write letters, words, and sentences before writing longer texts are antiquated. Classroom teachers as well as writing researchers have discovered that even young children communicate through writing, and they begin writing as they are learning to read or even before they read (Bissex, 1980; Chomsky, 1971; Graves, 1983).

M. A. K. Halliday (1980) identified learning language, learning about language, and learning through language as the three components in the language arts curriculum. These components can be rephrased slightly to describe the role of writing in the elementary grades:

1. *Learning to Write.*   Through experiences with writing, students learn to write. Informal writing activities, such as making clusters and quickwriting, provide opportunities for students to acquire writing fluency. For more formal writing activities, such as stories, reports, and poems, students use the writing process. This is a multistep process through which students gather and organize ideas, write rough drafts, and refine and polish their writing before publishing it.

2. *Learning About Written Language.*   As students learn to write, they discover the uniqueness of written language and the ways in which it differs from oral language and other types of graphics. They develop an appreciation for the interrelations of purpose, audience, and form in writing and learn to consider these three elements as they write. In addition, students learn about the mechanics of writing, including standard spelling and usage, capitalization, and formatting.

3. *Learning Through Writing.*   Writing is a valuable learning tool that has many applications across the curriculum. Students write informally to analyze and synthesize their learning, and they write formally and apply their knowledge when they write books and other reports.

Mrs. Winston's second- and third-grade students exemplified all three components as they used writing during their theme on weather. They learned to write by writing and practiced the writing process as they drafted, revised, and edited class books and individual projects. Mrs. Winston's students learned about written language as they revised and edited their writing when it was to be published. They also used writing as a tool for learning about weather through both informal writing and more formal writing projects.

Frank Smith (1988) reflected that "the first time I explored in detail how children learn to write, I was tempted to conclude that it was, like the flight of bumblebees, a theoretical impossibility" (p. 17). The writing samples in the vignette about Mrs. Winston's students show that just as bumblebees really do fly elementary students really do write, even though it may seem improbable that second and third graders who are just becoming literate can be fluent and expressive writers.

In this chapter, you will read about the process and product dimensions of writing instruction. The writing process approach to writing instruction is based on how real writers write. While this approach is the foundation for teaching children to write, product considerations are also important. Students will not always use the writing process, for example, when they write informally using brainstorming, KWL charts, clustering, and quickwriting. Furthermore, there are many writing forms students need to become acquainted with, including letters, poems, journals, and advertisements. This book focuses on eight of these writing forms. Finally, elementary students frequently write when they study literature, social studies, science, and math, in addition to writing about experiences in their lives and their own special interests. Using writing across the curriculum helps students learn the subject matter better as they develop their writing abilities.

THE WRITING PROCESS

The writing process is a way of looking at writing instruction in which the emphasis is shifted from students' finished products to what students think and do as they write. James Britton (1970) and Janet Emig (1971) were two of the first researchers to examine students' writing processes. In her study, Emig interviewed 12th graders as they wrote and studied the writing processes that one student used in depth. At the same time, Britton and his colleagues examined 2,000 essays written by British high school students and found that students' writing processes differed according to the type of writing. Several years later, Donald Graves (1975) examined young children's writing and documented that 7-year-olds, like high school students, used a variety of strategies as they wrote.

These researchers generally divided the writing process into three activities, processes, or stages. Britton (1970) labeled them as conception, incubation, and production. In the conceptual stage, writers choose topics and decide to write; in the incubation stage, they develop the topic by gathering information; and in the production stage they write, revise, and edit the composition. Donald Graves (1975) described a similar process of prewriting, composing, and postwriting. In prewriting, writers choose topics and gather ideas for writing; in the composing stage, they write the composition; and in the postwriting stage, they share their writing.

Linda Flower and John Hayes (1977, 1981, 1986) studied college students' writing and asked students to talk about their thought processes while they composed. They then analyzed students' talk to examine the strategies writers use and developed a model that describes writing as a complex problem-solving process. According to the model, the writing process involves three activities: planning, as writers set goals to guide the writing; translating, as writers put the plans into writing; and reviewing, as writers evaluate and revise the writing. These three activities are not linear steps, according to Flower and Hayes, because writers continually monitor their writing and move back and forth among the activities. This monitoring might be considered a fourth component of the writing process. An important finding from their research is that writing is recursive. Using this monitoring mechanism, writers jump back and forth from one process to another as they write.

Some researchers have examined particular aspects of the writing process. Nancy Sommers (1980, 1982) described writing as a revision process in which writers develop their ideas, not polish their writing. Less experienced writers, according to Sommers, focus on small word-level changes and error-hunting. This emphasis on mechanics rather than content may be due to teachers' behavior. Sondra Perl (1979, 1980) examined how the writing process is used in high school and college classrooms and concluded that teachers place inordinate importance on mechanical errors. Flower and Hayes found that less successful writers have a limited repertoire of alternatives for solving problems as they write, and Bereiter and Scardamalia (1982) found that even though children participated in writing process activities, they were less capable of monitoring the need to move from activity to activity.

This research has confirmed the importance of the process approach to writing and that what writers do as they write is at least as important as the products they produce. Even though there is much more to study about the writing process and the social contexts of composing, the conclusions drawn from the research can guide instructional practice today. The following four precepts guide the presentation of the writing process in this chapter:

1. *Elementary students can write.*   Research on first graders' writing demonstrates that elementary students, even at the primary grade level, can write and that they use the writing process.

2. *Elementary students develop a repertoire of writing strategies.* According to research findings, less experienced writers have a smaller repertoire of writing strategies and monitor their use of these strategies less effectively than do more experienced writers. In a process approach to writing, students learn a variety of writing strategies, including ways to gather and organize ideas about a topic, develop introductions or leads that grab the reader's attention, read a rough draft critically, make revisions, and proofread to identify mechanical errors.

3. *Elementary students separate revising and editing.* The three-stage versions of the writing process combine revising and editing activities, even though research has shown that when they are grouped together, the emphasis of both teachers and students is on editing, or the error-hunting activity. The two activities should be separated so that neither is neglected.

4. *Elementary students use a problem-solving approach.* Writing is a form of problem solving in which students experiment with alternative activities as they try to communicate effectively. These activities can be organized into a multicomponent model of the writing process that researchers have described in various ways. While there is no consensus on the names of the stages or the activities involved in each stage, there is agreement that writers use a variety of activities and move back and forth among them.

The five-stage writing process presented in this chapter incorporates activities identified through the research. The stages are prewriting, drafting, revising, editing, and publishing. The key features of each stage are presented in Figure 1-4. The labeling and numbering of the stages does not mean that this writing process is a linear series of discrete activities. Research has shown that the process is cyclical, involving recurring cycles, and labeling is only an aid for identifying and discussing writing activities. In the classroom, the stages merge and recur as students write. Moreover, students personalize the process to meet their own needs and vary the process according to the writing assignment.

Stage 1: Prewriting

Prewriting is the getting-ready-to-write stage. The traditional notion that writers have thought out their topic completely is ridiculous. If writers wait for the ideas to be fully developed, they may wait forever. Instead, writers begin tentatively talking reading, and writing to see what they know and what direction they want to go. Pulitzer prize-winning writer Donald Murray (1985, 1987) calls this stage the discovery of writing. You begin writing to explore what you know and to surprise yourself.

Prewriting has probably been the most neglected stage in the writing process; however, it is as crucial to writers as a warm-up is to athletes. Donald Murray (1982) believes that 70% or more of writing time should be spent in prewriting. During the prewriting stage, the activities are

▼ choosing a topic
▼ considering purpose, form, and audience
▼ generating and organizing ideas for writing

FIGURE 1-4   Overview of the Writing Process

Stage 1: Prewriting

Students choose a topic.
Students gather and organize ideas.
Students identify the audience to whom they will write.
Students identify the purpose of the writing activity.
Students choose an appropriate form for their compositions based on audience and
    purpose.

Stage 2: Drafting

Students write a rough draft.
Students write leads to grab their readers' attention.
Students emphasize content rather than mechanics.

Stage 3: Revising

Students share their writing in writing groups.
Students participate constructively in discussions about classmates' writing.
Students make changes in their compositions to reflect the reactions and comments
    of both teacher and classmates.
Between the first and final drafts, students make substantive rather than only minor
    changes.

Stage 4: Editing

Students proofread their own compositions.
Students help proofread classmates' compositions.
Students increasingly identify and correct their own mechanical errors.

Stage 5: Publishing

Students publish their writing in an appropriate form.
Students share their finished writing with an appropriate audience.

Choosing a Topic.   Choosing topics for writing can be a stumbling block for students who have become dependent on teachers to supply their topics. In the traditional approach, teachers supplied the topics by suggesting gimmicky story starters and relieving students of the "burden" of topic selection. Often, this tactic stymied students, who were forced to write on topics they knew little about or were not interested in. Donald Graves (1976) calls this traditional approach of supplying topics for students "writing welfare." Instead, students need to take responsibility for choosing their own topics for writing.

At first, dependent students will argue that they do not know what to write about; however, teachers can help them brainstorm a list of three, four, or five topics and then identify the one topic they are most interested in and know the most about. Students who feel they cannot generate any writing topics are often surprised that they have so many options available. Then through prewriting activities, students can talk, draw, read, and even write to develop information about their topics.

Asking students to choose their own topics for writing does not mean that the teachers never give writing assignments. Rather, teachers provide general guidelines. Teachers may specify the writing form—journal, story, poem, report, and so on. At other times they may establish the purpose—for example, to share what students have learned about life in ancient Egypt—while students choose the specific content and possibly the form of presentation. For instance, students can demonstrate what they have learned about life in ancient Egypt by writing a report about how people were mummified; by assuming the persona of a person who lived in ancient Egypt and writing a simulated journal; by writing a biography of Queen Nefrititi; by writing an acrostic poem on the word *pyramid;* or by writing a story set in ancient Egypt.

Considering Purpose.　As students prepare to write, they need to identify their purpose for writing. Are they writing to entertain? To inform? To persuade? This decision about purpose influences other decisions students make about audience and form. M. A. K. Halliday (1973, 1975) has identified seven language functions that apply to both oral and written language:

1. *Instrumental Language.* Language to satisfy needs, such as in business letters.
2. *Regulatory Language.* Language to control the behavior of others, such as in directions and rules.
3. *Interactional Language.* Language to establish and maintain social relationships, such as in pen pal letters and dialogue journals.
4. *Personal Language.* Language to express personal opinions, such as in learning logs and letters to the editor.
5. *Imaginative Language.* Language to express imagination and creativity, such as in stories, poems, and scripts.
6. *Heuristic Language.* Language to seek information and to find out about things, such as in learning logs and interviews.
7. *Informative Language.* Language to convey information, such as in reports and biographies.

Frank Smith (1977) has observed that these language functions are learned through genuine communication experiences rather than through practice activities that lack functional purposes. Moreover, skill in one function does not generalize to other functions, so students need to learn to use each one. Language is rarely used for just one function, according to Smith; typically, two or more functions are involved in any composition.

Considering Audience.　Students may write primarily for themselves to express and clarify their own ideas and feelings or they may write for others. Possible audiences include classmates, younger children, parents, foster grandparents, children's authors, and pen pals. Other audiences are more distant and less well known. For example, students may write letters to businesses to request information, write articles to be published in the local newspaper, or submit stories and poems to be published in literary magazines.

Children's writing is influenced by their sense of audience. James Britton (Britton et al., 1975) defines sense of audience as "the manner in which the writer expresses a relationship with the reader in respect to the writer's understanding" (pp. 65–66). When students write for others, they adapt their writing to fit their audience, just as they vary their speech to fit the audience. This variance is called "register" (Smith, 1982). Students must be aware of their audience while writing in order to choose the appropriate register. In contrast, when students write only to complete assignments, they lack a sense of audience.

Elementary students demonstrate their relationship with the audience in a variety of ways, often by adding parenthetical information or an aside. For example, a seventh grader begins "George Mudlumpus and the Mystery of the Golden Spider," his sixth mystery featuring George Mudlumpus, the detective with the outrageous rates, this way:

▽ *I had decided to take my vacation, as you already know from the last story I told you. So, I packed, got my airplane ticket, and got on a 747 jetliner. I was off to San Francisco!*

This student feels a close relationship, that of a storyteller, with his unknown audience. He often includes asides in his stories, and George sometimes comments to his readers, "I know! You think I should have recognized that clue!"

Also, there are times when students need to learn a new register, one they may not have been exposed to through oral language or through previous writing experiences. For example, children recognize that the closings "Love" or "Your friend" may not be appropriate to end a business letter, but they may not be familiar with a more appropriate way to close the letter.

When students write for others, teachers are the most common audience and they can assume several roles. How writers perceive these roles is crucial. Teachers can assume the role of trusted adult, a partner in dialogue, or judge (Britton et al., 1975). In writing to a trusted adult, students feel secure because they can rely on their reader to respond sympathetically. When writing a dialogue with a teacher, students are secure in the teacher's presence and assume that the teacher will be interested in the writing, responding to *what* has been written, not to *how* it has been written. Unfortunately, the teacher's most common role is that of judge, and this role is least conducive to good writing. When a teacher acts as a judge, students produce writing only to satisfy a teacher's requirement or to receive a grade.

Considering Form.   One of the most important considerations is the form the writing will take. A story? A letter? A poem? A journal entry? A writing project could be handled in any one of these ways. As part of a science theme on hermit crabs, for instance, students could write a story about a hermit crab, draw a picture of a hermit crab and label body parts, write an explanation of how hermit crabs obtain shells to live in, or keep a log of observations about live hermit crabs kept in the classroom. There is an almost endless variety of forms that children's writing may take, but too often the choices are limited to writing stories, poems, and reports. Instead, students need to experiment with a wide variety of writing forms and to explore the purposes and formats of these forms. Through reading and writing, students develop a strong sense of these forms and how they are structured. Langer (1985) found that by third grade, students responded in different ways to story and report writing assignments. They organized compositions differently and varied the kinds of information and elaboration they used depending on the form. Similarly, Hidi and Hildyard (1983) found that elementary students could differentiate between stories and persuasive essays. Because children are clarifying the distinctions between various writing forms during the elementary grades, it is very important that teachers use the correct terminology and not label all children's writing as "stories."

While most writing forms look like the text on this page does—block form written from left to right and from top to bottom—some writing forms require a special arrangement on a page or special language patterns. For example, scripts, recipes, poems, and letters are four writing forms that have very recognizable formats. Examples of writing forms that use special language patterns would be a story that begins with "Once upon a time . . ." or letters that require "Dear . . ." and "Sincerely." As children are introduced to these writing forms and have opportunities to experiment with them, they will learn about the unique requirements of the formats.

Teaching children to make decisions about purpose, audience and form is an important component of writing instruction. In each case, children need to learn to know the range of options available to writers. Decisions about these aspects of writing have an impact on each other. For example, if the purpose is to entertain, a form such as a story, poem, or script might be selected. These three forms look very different on a piece of paper. While a story is written in the traditional block format, scripts and poems have unique arrangements on the page. For example, in a script, the character's name appears first and is followed by a colon and then the dialogue. Action and dialogue, rather than description, carry the storyline in a script. In contrast, poems have unique formatting considerations and words are used judiciously. Each word and phrase is chosen to convey a maximum amount of information.

Audience also plays an important role. Audiences for stories, scripts, and poems are often unknown or large, while the audience for a letter is usually one particular person. While the purpose of a letter may be to request information or share personal information, it is customized according to audience. Children might share the same information with their pen pal and with their grandparents, but the way they present the information varies according to their familiarity.

While these decisions may change as students write and revise, writers must begin with at least a tentative concept of purpose, audience, and form as they move into the drafting stage.

Gathering and Organizing Ideas.   Students gather and organize ideas for writing by drawing, talking, reading, interviewing, dramatization, and writing. Graves (1983) calls these strategies and activities that help students prepare for writing "rehearsal" activities.

Drawing is the way young children gather and organize ideas for writing. Kindergarten and first-grade teachers often notice that students draw before they write. When young children are asked to write before drawing, for example, they explain that they can't write yet because they don't know what to write until they see what they draw. As young children become writers, they use drawing and other symbol systems as they grapple with the uniqueness of writing (Dyson, 1982, 1983, 1986).

Too often the value of talk is ignored in the classroom, but as students write, talk is necessary. Students talk with their classmates to share ideas about possible writing topics, try out ways to express an idea, and ask questions. They read and react to each other's writing. They also participate in class discussions about writing forms, elements of story structure, and other writing-related issues. Talk continues throughout the writing process as students discuss their compositions in conferences and proofread each other's work.

Reading and writing are symbiotic, mutually beneficial processes. Through reading, children gather ideas for writing and investigate the structure of various written forms. Reading is a form of experience, and writers need a variety of experiences to draw on as they write. Often students will retell a favorite story in writing, write new adventures for favorite story characters, or experiment with repetition, onomatopoeia, or another poetic device used in a poem they have read. Reading informational books also provides the raw material necessary for writing. For example, if students decide to write about polar bears, they need to gather background information about the animal, its habitat, and predators. If they are interested in Olympic athletes, they may read biographies of Jesse Owens or Mary Lou Retton and then share what they learn by writing a collection of biographical sketches.

Students can interview people in the community who have special knowledge about the topic they will write about. Interviewing involves three steps: planning the interview, conducting the interview, and sharing the results. In the first step, students arrange for the interview and develop a list of questions to ask during the interview. Next, students conduct the interview and take notes or tape-record the answers. Last, students share the information they gathered in the interview. This sharing can take many different forms, ranging from newspaper articles to reports to books.

Through dramatization, children discover and shape ideas that they will use in their writing (Wagner, 1983). According to Mills (1983), having students role-play an experience provides energy and purpose for writing. Often writing comes more easily after performing a dramatic play or role-playing stories. For example, dramatizing can help children learn to write directions. Typically, when writing directions for an activity, such as making a peanut butter sandwich, children omit crucial steps, such as opening the jar of peanut butter. However, when they write directions after dramatizing the activity, the directions are better organized and more complete. Students can also assess the effectiveness of their directions by having a classmate try to follow the directions. In this way, children learn about the steps they have omitted.

Similarly, after reading stories, students can reenact events to bring the experience to life. British educator Dorothy Heathcote (Wagner, 1976, 1983) recommends that teachers choose a dramatic focus, or a particular critical moment for students to reenact, and that the teacher becomes a character too. During the role-play, questions are used to draw students' attention to certain features and to prove their understanding. For example, after reading *Sarah, Plain and Tall* (MacLachlan, 1985), the story of a mail-order bride, children might reenact the day that Sarah took the wagon to town. This is the critical moment in the story: Does Sarah like the family and their prairie home well enough to stay? Through role-playing, students become immersed in the event, and by reliving it they are learning far more than mere facts.

Writing is another way for students to gather and organize ideas before beginning to draft their compositions. They may brainstorm words and images, make and sequence lists of events, cluster main ideas and details, or quickwrite to discover what they know about a topic and what direction their writing might take. Outlining is another form of prewriting, but this traditional prewriting activity is less effective than clustering and not recommended for elementary students.

Stage 2: Drafting

In the process approach to writing, students write and refine their compositions through a series of drafts. During the drafting stage, students focus on getting their ideas down on paper. Because writers do not begin writing with their compositions already composed in their minds, they begin with tentative ideas developed through prewriting activities. The drafting stage is the time to pour out ideas, with little concern about spelling, punctuation, and other mechanical errors. The activities in this stage are

▼ writing a rough draft
▼ writing leads
▼ emphasizing content, not mechanics

Writing a Rough Draft. Students skip every other line as they write their rough drafts to leave adequate space for revising. They use arrows to move sections of text, cross-outs to delete sections, and scissors and tape to cut apart and rearrange text just as adult writers do. Similarly, students should only write on one side of a sheet of paper so that the paper can be cut apart or rearranged. As word processors become more available in elementary classrooms, revising, with all its shifting and deleting of text, will be much easier. However, for students who handwrite their compositions, the wide spacing of lines is crucial. Make small Xs on every other line of young children's papers as a reminder to skip lines as they draft their compositions.

Students label their drafts by writing "rough draft" in ink at the top of their papers or by stamping the papers with a "rough draft" stamp. This label indicates to the writer, other students, parents, and administrators that the composition is a draft in which emphasis has been placed on content, not mechanics. It also explains why teachers have not graded the paper or marked mechanical errors. Also, if some students who are just learning the writing process plan to make the rough draft their final draft by writing carefully, the label "rough draft" at the top of the paper negates this idea and further emphasizes that writing involves more than one stage.

As students draft their compositions, they may need to modify their earlier decisions about purpose, audience, and especially the form their writing will take. For example, a composition that began as a story might be transformed into a report, letter, or a poem. The new format may allow the student to communicate more effectively. This process of modifying earlier decisions also continues into the revising stage.

It is important in the drafting stage not to emphasize correct spelling and neatness. In fact, when teachers point out mechanical errors during the drafting stage, they send a false message to students that mechanical correctness is more important than content (Sommers, 1982). Later, during editing, students can clean up mechanical errors and put their composition into a neat, final form.

Writing Leads.   The lead, or opening sentences, of a composition is crucial. Think of the last time you went to a library to choose a book to read. Several titles or book jacket pictures may have caught your eye, but in making your selection you opened the book and read the first paragraph or two. Which one did you choose? Probably the one that hooked you, or grabbed your attention. The same is true for children's writing. Students who consider audience as they write will want to grab the attention of the audience. Children may use a variety of techniques to appeal to their audience, such as questions, facts, dialogue, brief stories, and problems. Donald Graves (1983) and Lucy Calkins (1986) recommend that students create several leads and try them out on classmates before choosing one. As students write these leads they gain valuable knowledge about how to manipulate language and how to vary viewpoint or sequence in their writing.

Stage 3: Revising

During the revising stage, writers refine ideas in their compositions. Often students terminate the writing process as soon as they complete a rough draft, believing that once their ideas are jotted down the writing task is complete. Experienced writers, however, know they must turn to others for reactions and revise on the basis of these comments. Revision is not just polishing writing; it is meeting the needs of readers by adding, substituting, deleting, and rearranging material. The word *revision* means "seeing again," and in this stage writers see their compositions again with their classmates and the teacher helping them. The activities in the revising stage are

▼ rereading the rough draft
▼ sharing the rough draft in a writing group
▼ revising on the basis of feedback received from the writing group

Rereading the Rough Draft.   Writers are the first to revise their compositions. Some revision occurs during drafting when writers make choices and changes as they write. After finishing the rough draft, writers need to distance themselves from the draft for a day or two and then reread the draft from a fresh perspective, as a reader might. As they reread, students make changes—adding, substituting, deleting, and moving—and place question marks by sections that need work. It is these trouble spots that students ask for help with in their writing group.

Writing Groups[1]. Students meet in writing groups to share their compositions with small groups of classmates. Because writing cannot occur in a vacuum and must meet the needs of readers, feedback is crucial. Mohr (1984) has identified four general functions of writing groups: to offer the writer choices, to give the writers responses, feelings, and thoughts, to show different possibilities in revising, and to speed up revising. Writing groups provide a scaffold, or supportive environment, in which teachers and classmates can talk about plans and strategies for writing and revising (Applebee & Langer, 1983; Calkins, 1983).

Writing groups can form spontaneously when several students have completed drafts and are ready to share their compositions, or they can be formal groupings with identified leaders. In some primary classrooms, for example, writing groups may form spontaneously; when students finish writing, they go to the reading rug and sit in a chair designated as the "author's chair" (Graves & Hansen, 1983). As soon as a child with writing to share is sitting in the chair, others who are available to listen and respond to the writing sit on the floor in front of the author's chair. When three or four children have arrived for the writing group, the writer reads the writing and the other children listen and respond to it, offering compliments and relating this piece of writing to their own experiences and writing. Sometimes the teacher joins the listeners on the rug to participate in the writing group; at other times the children work independently. In other classrooms, writing groups are more formal. Writing groups meet when all children have completed a rough draft and are ready to share their writing with classmates and the teacher. The teacher participates in these groups, providing feedback with the students. In some classrooms, writing groups may function independently. Four or five students are assigned to each group, and a list of the groups and their members is posted in the classroom. On the list, the teacher puts a star by one student's name, and that student serves as a group leader. Every quarter the leader changes.

Once writing group arrangements are set, students meet in writing groups to share their writing through these activities:

Step by Step

1. *The writer reads.* Students take turns reading their compositions aloud to writing group members. Everyone listens politely, thinking about compliments and suggestions for improvement they will make after the writer has finished reading. Typically, only the writer looks at the composition as it is read, because when classmates and the teacher look at it, they quickly notice and comment on mechanical errors even though the emphasis during revising is on content. Listening to the writing without looking at it keeps the focus on content.

2. *Listeners offer compliments.* After reading, writing group members state what they liked about the writing. These positive comments should be specific, focusing on strengths rather than the often-heard "I like it" or "It was good." Even though

---

[1] Adapted from Tompkins & Friend, 1988, pp. 4–9.

these are positive comments, they do not provide effective feedback because they are not specific. When teachers first introduce revision, they should model appropriate types of responses because students may not know how to offer specific and meaningful responses. Working together, the teacher and students might brainstorm a list of acceptable comments and post it in the classroom for students to refer to. Comments may focus on organization, leads, word choice, voice, sequence, dialogue, theme, and other elements of writing.

3. *The writer asks questions.*   After a round of positive comments, writers ask their classmates for assistance on trouble spots they identified earlier when they reread their writing, or they may ask questions that reflect more general concerns about how well they are communicating. Admitting that they need help from their classmates is a major step in learning to revise. Encourage students to ask for help using a specific context, as these students did:

> "When I was trying to explain that the dinosaurs all died off, well I didn't know what to say. What's that word that means they all died off?"

> "Well, I put this part first, about how lions are the giraffe's main enemy. I don't know if that part should go before where giraffes live. Or I could say that male giraffes are 18 feet tall. Is it better to start there?"

> "I don't have very much information to put in this first chapter about Betsy Ross's childhood. It seems so short. What can I do?"

The teacher can model some of these questions, prefacing them with "If I were the writer, I might ask. . . ." Many students find it difficult to ask questions about their writing, but when they work with their writing to the extent that they ask questions as in the examples above, they have become writers who look to their classmates for assistance.

4. *Listeners offer suggestions.*   Next, members of the writing group ask questions about things that were unclear to them and make suggestions about how to revise the composition. Almost any writer resists constructive criticism, and it is especially difficult for elementary students to appreciate these comments and suggestions. However, this approach is far more constructive than the traditional approach in which the teacher grades the paper and covers it with comments and corrections. Listeners may ask the same types of questions that writers ask about their own trouble spots, for example:

> "Up here at the top you said that birds migrate. But later on you said that ducks live at ponds in our town all year long. Well, ducks are birds, aren't they? What did you mean?"

> "You say 'It is . . .' 'It is . . .' 'It is . . . .' I think that you could put all of those together because it is boring to read the same words over and over."

> "Here you tell why junk food is bad for you. Then you say 'Junk food is fun to eat.' That doesn't really go there. You need to put it somewhere else. Maybe where you talk about why junk food is good."

It is important to take time to teach students what kinds of comments and suggestions are acceptable so that students can phrase their comments in a helpful rather than a hurtful way.

5. *Repeat the process.*   After everyone in the writing group has offered feedback, the process is repeated as each student reads his or her composition and receives feedback. This is the appropriate time for teachers to provide input as well. They should react to the piece of writing as any other listener would, not with red pen in hand, hunting for errors (Sommers, 1982). In fact, most teachers prefer to listen to students read their compositions aloud rather than read them themselves and become frustrated by numerous misspelled words and nearly illegible handwriting common in rough drafts.

6. *Writers plan for revision.*   At the end of the writing group session, students each make a commitment to revise their writing based on the comments and suggestions of their writing group members. The final decision on what to revise always rests with the writers themselves, but with the understanding that their rough drafts are not perfect comes the realization that some revision will be necessary. When students verbalize their planned revisions, they are more than likely to complete the revision stage. Some students also make notes for themselves about their revision plans. After the group disbands, students make the revisions.

Students' Revisions.   As they make revisions, students add words, substitute sentences, delete paragraphs, and move phrases. They cross out, draw arrows, and write in the space they left between the lines of writing when they double-spaced their rough drafts. Students move back and forth into prewriting to gather additional information, into drafting to write a new paragraph, and into revising to replace an often-repeated word. Messiness is inevitable, but despite the scribbles, students are usually able to decipher what they have written.

Students' changes can be classified as to the kind of change (e.g., additions, substitutions, deletions, and movements) and the level of change (e.g., a word, a phrase or clause, a sentence, a paragraph, or the entire text) (Faigley & Witte, 1981). This revision hierarchy is illustrated in Figure 1-5. The least complex change is the change of a word, and the most complex change is at the text level. Elementary students often focus at the word and phrase/clause level and make more additions and substitutions than deletions and movements.

Teachers can determine the types and levels of revisions that students are making by examining their revised rough drafts. The revisions that students make are one gauge of their growth as writers. Teachers also might want to share this hierarchy with upper-grade students so they know the revision options that are available. Students should be encouraged to record their revisions on a chart and track the types of revisions they make. Even though some revisions might be considered more sophisticated than others, students should make the change that is most effective for their writing. They should not move a paragraph when adding a sentence is the more effective revision.

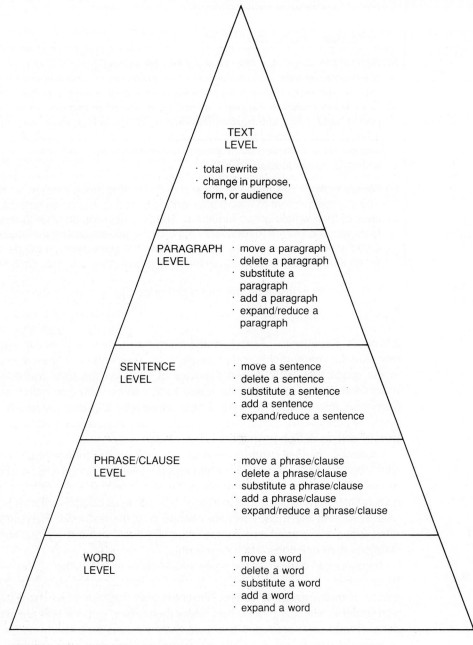

FIGURE 1-5 *A Revision Hierarchy*

Stage 4: Editing

Editing is putting the piece of writing into its final form. Until this stage, the focus has been primarily on the content of students' writing. Once the focus changes to mechanics, students polish their writing by correcting spelling and other mechanical errors. The goal here is to make the writing "optimally readable" (Smith, 1982). Writers who write for readers understand that if their compositions are not readable, they have written in vain because their ideas will never be read.

Mechanics refers to the commonly accepted conventions of written standard English. They include capitalization, punctualization, spelling, sentence structure, usage, and formatting considerations specific to poems, scripts, letters, and other writing forms. The use of these commonly accepted conventions is a courtesy to those who will read the composition.

The most effective way to teach mechanical skills is during the editing stage of the writing process rather than through workbook exercises. When editing a composition that will be shared with a genuine audience, students are more interested in using mechanical skills correctly so they can communicate effectively. In a study of two third-grade classes, Calkins (1980) found that the students in the class who learned punctuation marks as a part of editing could define or explain more marks than the students in the other class who were taught punctuation skills in a traditional manner with instruction and practice exercises on each punctuation mark. In other words, the results of this research as well as other studies (Bissex, 1980; Elley et al., 1976; Graves, 1983) suggest that a functional approach to teaching the mechanics of writing is more effective than practice exercises.

Students move through three activities in the editing stage:

▼ getting distance from the composition
▼ proofreading to locate errors
▼ correcting errors

Getting Distance. Students are more efficient editors when they set the composition aside for a few days before beginning to edit. After working so closely with the piece of writing during drafting and revising, they are too familiar with it to be able to locate many mechanical errors. After a few days, children are better able to approach editing with a fresh perspective and gather the enthusiasm necessary to finish the writing process by making the paper optimally readable.

Proofreading. Students proofread their compositions to locate and mark possible errors. Proofreading is a unique form of reading in which students read word by word and hunt for errors rather than for meaning (King, 1985). Concentrating on mechanics is difficult because of our natural inclination to read for meaning. Even experienced proofreaders often find themselves reading for meaning and overlooking errors that do not inhibit meaning. It is important, therefore, to take time to explain proofreading and to demonstrate how it differs from regular reading.

To demonstrate proofreading, teachers take a piece of student writing and copy it on the chalkboard or display it on an overhead projector. The teacher reads it several times, each time hunting for a particular type of error. During each reading, the composition is read slowly, with the teacher softly pronouncing each word and touching the word with a pencil or pen to focus attention on it. The teacher marks possible errors as they are located.

Errors are marked or corrected with special proofreaders' marks. Students enjoy using these marks, the same ones that adult authors and editors use. A list of proofreaders' marks that elementary students can learn and use in editing their writing is presented in Figure 1-6.

Editing checklists also help students focus on particular categories of error as they proofread their compositions. Teachers can develop these checklists with two to six items appropriate for the students' grade level. A first-grade checklist, for example, might include only two items, one about using a capital letter at the beginning of a sentence and a second about using a period at the end of a sentence. In contrast, a

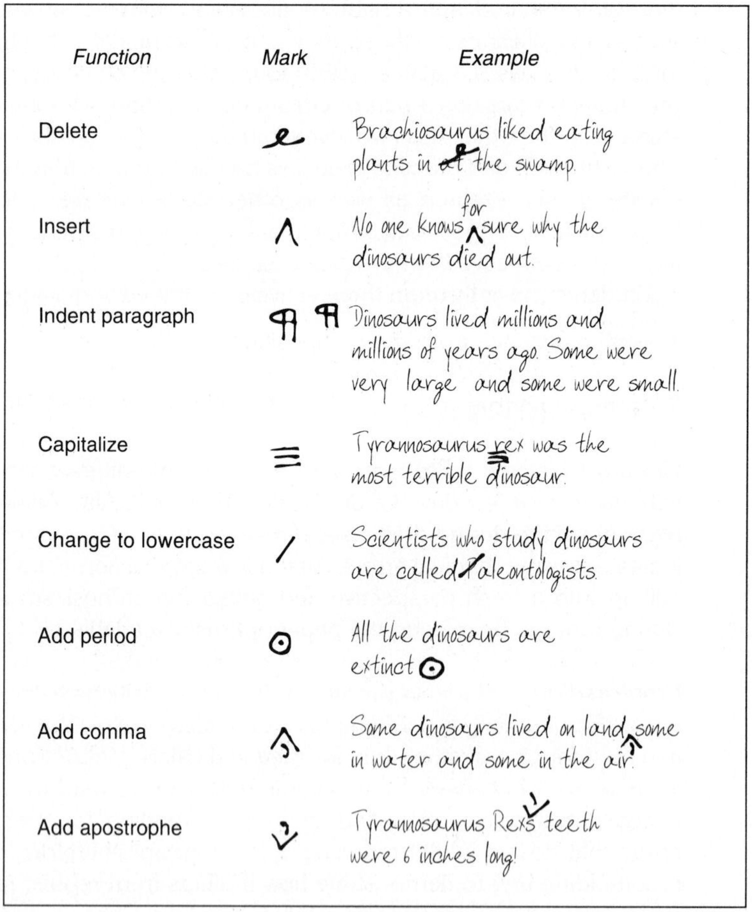

Function	Mark	Example
Delete	ℓ	Brachiosaurus liked eating plants in at the swamp.
Insert	∧	No one knows for sure why the dinosaurs died out.
Indent paragraph	¶ ¶	Dinosaurs lived millions and millions of years ago. Some were very large and some were small.
Capitalize	≡	Tyrannosaurus rex was the most terrible dinosaur.
Change to lowercase	/	Scientists who study dinosaurs are called Paleontologists.
Add period	⊙	All the dinosaurs are extinct ⊙
Add comma	˄	Some dinosaurs lived on land some in water and some in the air.
Add apostrophe	˅	Tyrannosaurus Rexs teeth were 6 inches long!

FIGURE 1-6   Proofreaders' Marks

middle-grade checklist might include items on using commas in a series, paragraph indentation, capitalizing proper nouns and adjectives, and spelling homonyms correctly. During the school year, teachers revise the checklist to focus attention on skills that have recently been taught. A sample third-grade editing checklist is presented in Figure 1-7. Using this checklist, the writer and a classmate work together as partners to edit their compositions. First, students proofread their own compositions, searching for errors in each category listed on the checklist and after proofreading check off each item. After completing the checklist, students sign their names and trade checklists and compositions. Now they become editors and complete each other's checklist. Having the writer and editor sign the checklist helps them to take the activity seriously.

Correcting Errors.   After students proofread their compositions and locate as many errors as possible, they correct these errors individually or with an editor's assistance. Some errors are easy to correct, some require the use of a dictionary, and others involve instruction from the teacher. It is unrealistic to expect students to locate and correct every mechanical error in their compositions. Not even published books are error-free! Once in a while, students may even change a correct spelling or punctua-

---

EDITING CHECKLIST

Author   Editor

☐   ☐   1. I have circled the words that might be misspelled.

☐   ☐   2. I have checked that all sentences begin with capital letters.

☐   ☐   3. I have checked that all sentences end with punctuation marks.

☐   ☐   4. I have checked that all proper nouns begin with a capital letter.

Signatures:

Author: _____   *Editor:* _____

FIGURE 1-7   *A Third-Grade Editing Checklist*

tion mark and make it incorrect, but overall they correct far more errors than they create.

Editing can end after students and their editors correct as many mechanical errors as possible, or students may meet with the teacher in a conference for a final editing. When mechanical correctness is crucial, this conference is important. The teacher proofreads the composition with the student and assists in identifying and correcting the remaining errors, or the teacher makes checkmarks in the margin to note errors that the student corrects independently.

Stage 5: Publishing

In the final stage of the writing process, students publish their writing and share it with an appropriate audience. As they share their writing with real audiences of their classmates, other students, parents, and the community, students come to think of themselves as authors.

Concept of Author.   As students use the writing process, they develop an understanding of what it means to be an author. They begin to think of themselves as authors as they compile their writing into books and share these books with classmates and other audiences. The burgeoning awareness of the concept of author motivates students to be more interested in writing and to take greater pride in their compositions.

Donald Graves and Jane Hansen (1983) suggest that one way to help students develop the concept of author is to have a special chair in the classroom designated as the "author's chair." Whenever someone, either the teacher or a child, reads a book, that person sits in the author's chair. At the beginning of the year, most of the books read from that chair are picture books written by Dr. Seuss, Steven Kellogg, and other authors of children's books. However, as children begin to write and construct their own books, they sit in that chair to share the books they write. Through sitting in the special author's chair and sharing their books, children gradually realize that they too are authors! Graves and Hansen describe children's transition from student to author in three steps:

1. *Replication: Authors write books.* Students develop the concept that authors are the people who write books after hearing many books read to them and reading books themselves.
2. *Transition: I am an author.* Students view themselves as authors as they sit in the author's chair and share with classmates the books they have written.
3. *Option awareness: If I wrote this published book now, I wouldn't write it this way.* Students learn that they have options when they write, and this awareness grows after experimenting with various writing functions, forms, and audiences.

In classrooms where reading, writing, and sharing writing are valued activities, students become authors. Often they recopy a story or other piece of writing into a stapled booklet or hardcover book. These published books are added to the classroom or the school library. Sometimes students form a classroom publishing company and add the name of the publishing company and the year the book was made to the title page. In addition, students can add an "All About the Author" page with a photograph at the end of their books, similar to the author bio included on the jackets of books written by adult authors. A fifth grader's "All About the Author" page from a collection of poetry he wrote is presented in Figure 1-8. Notice that Brian used the third-person pronoun *he* in writing about himself, as in an adult biographical sketch.

> ## All About the Author
>
> Brian was born on August 22, 1976 in Woodward, Ok. He is going to be a USAF pilot and Army L.T., and a college graduate. He is also wanting to be a rockstar singer. He is going to write another book hopefully about the Air Force or Army. In his spare time he likes to run, ride his motorcycle, skate board, and play with his dogs. He also wrote "How the Hyena Got His Laugh."

FIGURE 1-8 *A Fifth Grader's "All About the Author" Page*

Ways to Share Writing.   Students read their writing to classmates, or share it with larger audiences through hardcover books that are placed in the class or school library, class anthologies, letters, newspaper articles, plays, filmstrips and videotapes, or puppet shows. Ways to share children's writing include the following:

- ▼ Read the writing aloud in class.
- ▼ Submit the piece to writing contests.
- ▼ Display the writing as a mobile.
- ▼ Contribute to a class anthology.
- ▼ Contribute to the local newspaper.
- ▼ Make a shape book.
- ▼ Record the writing on a cassette tape.
- ▼ Submit it to a literary magazine.
- ▼ Read it at a school assembly.
- ▼ Share at a read-around party.
- ▼ Share with parents and siblings.

- ▼ Produce a videotape of it.
- ▼ Display poetry on a "poet-tree."
- ▼ Send it to a pen pal.
- ▼ Make a hardbound book.
- ▼ Produce it as a roller movie.
- ▼ Display it on a bulletin board.
- ▼ Make a filmstrip of it.
- ▼ Make a big book.
- ▼ Design a poster about the writing.
- ▼ Read it to foster grandparents.
- ▼ Share it as a puppet show.
- ▼ Display it at a public event.
- ▼ Read it to children in other classes.

Through this sharing, students communicate with genuine audiences who respond to their writing in meaningful ways.

Sharing writing is a social activity, and through sharing, children develop sensitivity to the audience and confidence in themselves as authors. When students share writing, Dyson (1985) advises that teachers consider the social interpretations—students' behavior, teacher's behavior, and interaction between students and the teacher—within the classroom context. Individual students will naturally interpret the sharing event differently. More than just providing the opportunity for students to share writing, teachers need to teach students how to respond to their classmates. Also, teachers themselves offer a model for responding to students' writing without dominating the sharing.

One of the most popular ways for children to share their writing with others is by making and binding books. Simple booklets can be made by folding a sheet of paper into quarters like a greeting card. Students write the title on the front and have three sides remaining for their compositions. They can also construct booklets by stapling sheets of writing paper together and adding construction-paper covers. Sheets of wallpaper cut from old sample books also make good, sturdy covers. These stapled booklets can be cut into various shapes too. Students can make more sophisticated hardcover books by covering cardboard covers with contact paper, wallpaper samples, or cloth. Pages are sewn or stapled together, and the first and last pages (endpapers) are glued to the cardboard covers to hold the book together. The directions for making one type of hardcover book are presented in Figure 1-9.

Responding to Student Writing.   The teacher's role should not be restricted to that of evaluator. Again and again researchers report that although teachers are the most common audience for student writing, they are often one of the worst because many teachers read with a red pen in their hands (Lundsteen, 1976). Teachers should read

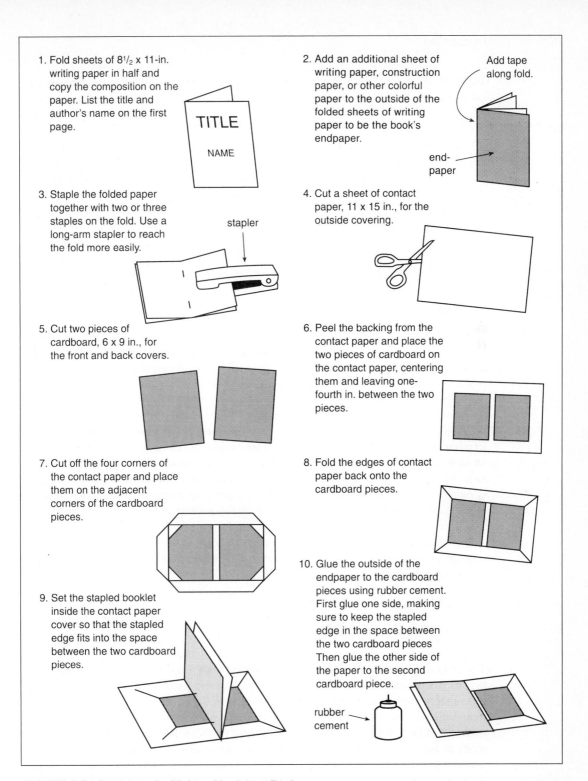

1. Fold sheets of 8½ x 11-in. writing paper in half and copy the composition on the paper. List the title and author's name on the first page.

TITLE

NAME

2. Add an additional sheet of writing paper, construction paper, or other colorful paper to the outside of the folded sheets of writing paper to be the book's endpaper.

Add tape along fold.

endpaper

3. Staple the folded paper together with two or three staples on the fold. Use a long-arm stapler to reach the fold more easily.

stapler

4. Cut a sheet of contact paper, 11 x 15 in., for the outside covering.

5. Cut two pieces of cardboard, 6 x 9 in., for the front and back covers.

6. Peel the backing from the contact paper and place the two pieces of cardboard on the contact paper, centering them and leaving one-fourth in. between the two pieces.

7. Cut off the four corners of the contact paper and place them on the adjacent corners of the cardboard pieces.

8. Fold the edges of contact paper back onto the cardboard pieces.

9. Set the stapled booklet inside the contact paper cover so that the stapled edge fits into the space between the two cardboard pieces.

10. Glue the outside of the endpaper to the cardboard pieces using rubber cement. First glue one side, making sure to keep the stapled edge in the space between the two cardboard pieces Then glue the other side of the paper to the second cardboard piece.

rubber cement

FIGURE 1-9 *Directions for Making Hardcover Books*

students' writing for information, for enjoyment, and for all of the other purposes that other readers do. Much of students' writing does not need to be assessed; instead it should simply be shared with the teacher as a trusted adult (Martin, D'Arcy, Newton, & Parker, 1976).

When children use a process approach to writing, there is less chance that students will plagiarize, or copy work from another source and pass it off as their own. The reason is that students will have developed their compositions, step by step, from prewriting and drafting to revising and editing. However, almost every teacher has come across a composition that they fear is not the student's own work. Jackson, Tway, and Frager (1987) cite several reasons why children may plagiarize. First, some students may simply internalize a piece of writing through repeated readings so that they do not realize that it is not their own work, months or years later, when they write it. Second, some students may plagiarize because of the competition to succeed. Third, some students plagiarize by accident, not realizing the consequences of their actions. A final reason that some students plagiarize is that they have not been taught how to write using a process approach, and they may not know how to synthesize information from published sources. There are two excellent ways to prevent plagiarism. One is to teach students how to write using the writing process, and the second is to have students write at school rather than at home. When students write at school and move through the various writing process activities, they know how to complete a writing project.

To measure students' growth in writing, it is not always necessary to assess their finished products (Tway, 1980). Teachers make judgments about students' progress in other ways. One of the best ways is by observing students as they write and noting whether they are prewriting, whether they are focusing on content rather than mechanics in their rough drafts, and whether they are participating in writing groups.

When an assessment of students' writing is necessary, teachers can judge whether students have completed all components of the writing project and can assess the quality of the final product. Information about how to assess stories, poems, reports, and other forms of writing is included in the chapters discussing these forms, and a more complete description of assessment alternatives is provided in Chapter 12, "Assessing Students' Writing."

THE PRODUCT: OTHER CONSIDERATIONS IN TEACHING WRITING

The writing process is the foundation for writing instruction today, but there are other factors to consider in teaching writing in the elementary grades. Three of these factors are informal writing, writing forms, and connecting writing across the curriculum. Mrs. Winston's students, in the vignette at the beginning of the chapter, did a lot of writing, but they did not always use the writing process; sometimes they wrote informally in learning logs. Her students used a variety of writing forms, including ABC books and interview reports, and their writing was connected with a weather theme. At other times during the school day, the second and third graders wrote on self-selected topics, but as part of the weather theme they wrote about what they were learning in science.

Informal Writing

Not all of children's writing moves through the five stages of the writing process. Many times students brainstorm lists of words and ideas, create a KWL chart, make clusters and other diagrams to organize what they are learning, and quickwrite by jotting down reactions to what they are reading or learning without taking time to refine and polish their writing. In these informal types of writing, students record experiences and opinions and use writing as a tool for learning. The emphasis is on content, not spelling, punctuation, and capitalization.

Brainstorming. One good way to generate ideas is through brainstorming, a strategy that includes the following steps:

1. Choose a topic.
2. Quickly list all words and phrases that come to mind in response to the topic.
3. Make no value judgments about items in the list; instead, look for unusual relationships among the items.

Brainstorming is used to generate ideas for writing. For example, students use brainstorming to develop a list of signs of spring to prepare for writing a poem about spring, they list the causes of the American Revolution before writing a chapter in a report about that war, or they list the characteristics of mysteries before writing their own mystery stories. Brainstorming takes only a few minutes but helps students generate many ideas and words to use in their writing.

Similarly, students use brainstorming when they are identifying a writing topic. For example, after reading Judith Viorst's *Alexander and the Terrible, Horrible, No Good, Very Bad Day* (1972), students might be asked to write about a very bad day they have had. Students begin by listing some bad days they have had. They then choose from the list the most promising recollection for their topic. Or, after studying community helpers, students might brainstorm a list of all the helpers they have learned about and then select one helper to write about.

Students also use brainstorming before they write in social studies, science, or other content area units. For example, on the day that a class of upper-grade students began a social studies unit on Egypt, the teacher asked the students to brainstorm a list of all the words they knew about Egypt to put in their newly decorated Egypt learning logs. The students suggested *mummy, Africa, Nile River, pyramids, slaves, tomb, hieroglyphics,* and *desert.* Students continued to add to their list until, five weeks later, their lists contained more than 100 words. The brainstormed list provided one measure of students' learning about Egypt, and students used the list to provide ideas for posters, journal entries, spelling words, acrostic poems, and research projects. While students used the brainstormed list of words for many activities, the list itself was a piece of informal writing that students used to help them learn, not a polished piece of writing that was graded by the teacher. The teacher required that students have a list of words about Egypt in their Egypt learning logs, and it was graded simply as done or not done.

KWL Charts.   A special type of brainstorming is the KWL strategy (Ogle, 1986, 1989) that students use to take a more active role in learning social studies or science. KWL stands for *K*now, *W*ant to know, and *L*earned. Teachers can use this strategy at the beginning of a theme cycle, before watching a film or reading an informational book. The steps are as follows:

*Step
by
Step*

1. The teacher asks students to brainstorm what they know about a topic and records the information in the K, or What We Know, column on a class chart as shown in Figure 1-10. As students are suggesting information, conflicts and confusions usually arise, and the teacher adds these in the W, or What We Want to Find Out, column. Brainstorming information in the K column helps students activate prior knowledge, and developing questions in the W column provides students with specific purposes for reading or learning. Next teachers ask students to look for ways to categorize the information in the Know and Want to Know columns. It is important to take time to categorize the information so that students will have a system for organizing what they are learning, as they watch a film, read a book, or make other investigations.

2. As students are involved in activities related to the theme cycle, they look for new information and for answers to questions in the W column. They may also suggest additional questions to add to the W column.

3. Toward the end of the theme cycle, for example, after viewing a particular film or reading a certain book, students reflect on what they have learned and complete the L, or What We Learned, column of the class chart.

When students develop KWL charts, they can work together as a class with a student recording the information on a large chart. Or students can work in a small group to make a KWL chart or they can work individually.

Clustering.   Another technique that students use to help them start writing is clustering (Rico, 1983). The process is similar to brainstorming except that all the words generated are circled and linked to a nucleus word. The result is a weblike diagram rather than a list. This strategy includes the following steps:

1. Choose a topic.
2. Write a topic or nucleus word in a circle centered on a sheet of paper.
3. Draw rays from the circle and add main ideas.
4. Add branches with details and examples to flesh out each main idea.

Clustering is designed to capture as many associations as possible in a short amount of time. This strategy helps students discover what they know about a topic. In clustering, ideas are triggered by associating one idea with another.

FIGURE 1-10 *KWL Chart*

Note. Adapted from "K-W-L: A Teaching Model That Develops Active Reading of Expository Text" by D. M. Ogle, 1986, *The Reading Teacher, 39*, p. 565. Reprinted by permission.

K What We Know	**W** What We Want to Find Out	**L** What We Learned

The main ideas in a cluster are the same as main ideas in an outline, and the details in a cluster are the same as details in the outline. A cluster about Florence Nightengale is presented in Figure 1-11 with the same information presented in an outline. While upper-grade elementary students often feel outlining is a meaningless activity, these same students enjoy clustering and recognize its usefulness in organizing ideas before writing. Outlining has outlived its usefulness. Too many older students, when required to have an outline as part of a high school or college writing assignment, construct the outline *after* writing the composition. In contrast to clustering, which helps students become better writers, outlining is often perceived as an unrelated task. Whenever possible, students should use clustering rather than outlining to organize ideas before writing. When outlining must be taught, it should be described as the formal rewriting of a cluster. Once students have made a cluster to gather and organize ideas for writing, the cluster can be rewritten as an outline, with the main ideas and details sequenced in the outline as they will be in the composition.

Clusters take many different forms. A cluster for a story might include three rays, one for the beginning of the story, one for the middle, and one for the end, and a cluster for a research report on an animal might have five rays, one ray to answer each of the following questions:

▼ What does the animal look like?
▼ Where does the animal live?
▼ What does the animal eat?
▼ How does the animal protect itself?
▼ What is special about the animal?

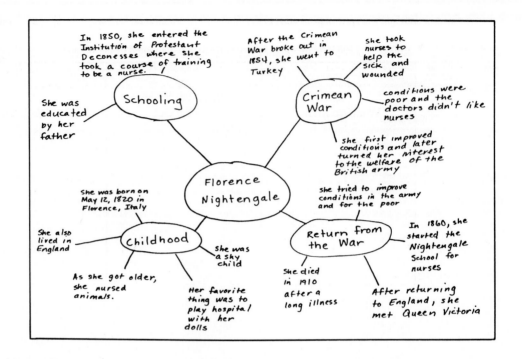

Florence Nightengale

I. Childhood
   A. She was born on May 12, 1820 in Florence, Italy.
   B. She also lived in England.
   C. She was a shy child.
   D. As she got older, she nursed animals.

II. Schooling
   A. She was educated by her father.
   B. In 1850, she entered the Institution of Protestant Deconesses where she took a course of training to be a nurse.

III. Crimean War
   A. After the Crimean War broke out in 1854, she went to Turkey.
   B. She took nurses to help the sick and wounded.
   C. Conditions were poor and the doctors didn't like the nurses.
   D. She first improved conditions and later turned her interest to the welfare of the British army.

IV. Return from the War
   A. She tried to improve conditions in the army and for the poor.
   B. In 1860, she started the Nightengale School for nurses.
   C. After returning to England, she met Queen Victoria.
   D. She died in 1910 after a long illness.

FIGURE 1-11   *Information Presented as a Cluster and as an Outline*

A third type of cluster is a five-senses cluster in which each of the senses is used as a main idea. Sensory clusters are useful for descriptive writing. A fourth type of cluster is the 5Ws Plus One cluster that journalists and student reporters use. In this cluster, the words *Who? What? Where? Why? When?* and *How?* are used as the main ideas. This type of cluster is useful in writing newspaper articles as well as describing historical and autobiographical events. Examples of these four types of clusters are presented in Figure 1-12.

These clusters are an example of informal writing because students are writing for themselves. Students may develop the cluster to help them understand what they are learning or to use as information in a writing activity. Sometimes the writing process is used and the cluster is revised, edited, and published. For instance, the biographical cluster presented in Figure 1-11 was refined and recopied on a large sheet of pos-

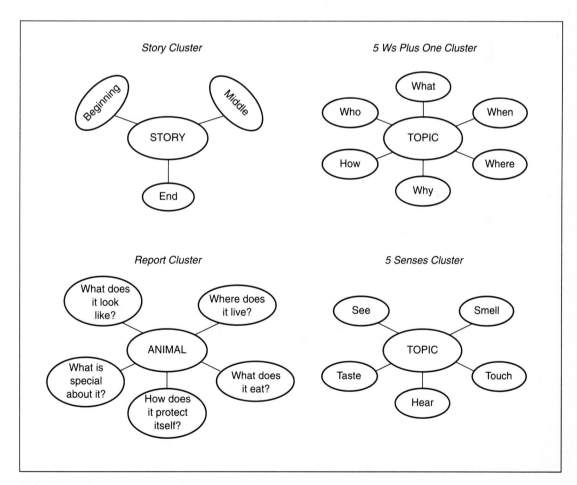

FIGURE 1-12 *Four Types of Clusters*

terboard as a book report. The student added the title of the book, illustrations, and a quotable quote from the book.

Students can make clusters to explore the meaning of an unfamiliar or interesting word from a book they are reading or a word related to a social studies or science theme cycle. Figure 1-13 presents the format for word clusters and a sample cluster for the word *mongrel* made by a third grader who listened to the story *Bunnicula* (Howe & Howe, 1979) read aloud. To create a word cluster students each choose a word from the word wall and write the word in the center of a sheet of paper. Then they draw a circle around the word and draw out four rays from the center circle. On one ray students write a category for the word, on a second ray they write a brief defini-tion, on a third ray they draw a picture or write a sentence, and on the fourth ray they

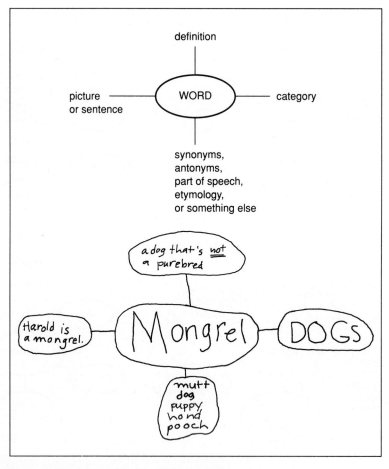

FIGURE 1-13   *Word Cluster (format and example)*

write synonyms, antonyms, part of speech, etymology, or something else related to the word.

Clusters can also be developed that do not have a hierarchical arrangement. In these clusters, all words radiate out from the nucleus word, like rays from the sun. Creating this type of cluster is much like brainstorming notes in that the words are not organized into main ideas and details. A nonhierarchical cluster can be used any time you might use brainstorming. Examples of two nonhierarchical clusters are presented in Figure 1-14. Fourth graders developed these two clusters describing the hare and the tortoise after reading Paul Galdone's retelling of the familiar fable *The Hare and the Tortoise* (1962).

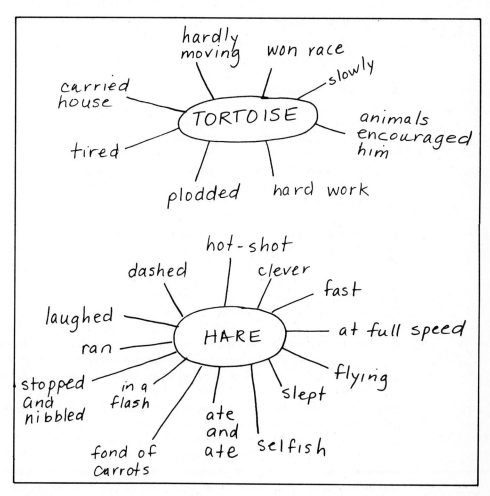

FIGURE 1-14   *Two Nonhierarchical Clusters*

Quickwriting.   *Quickwriting* is just what the name suggests, a strategy in which students simply begin to write and let their thoughts flow freely without focusing on mechanics or revisions. Quickwriting includes the following steps:

1. Choose a topic.
2. Write for 5 to 10 minutes without pausing to think, reread the writing, make corrections, or for any other reason.
3. Write "I don't know what to write about" or a similar phrase over and over until an new idea comes.
4. Share writing with a classmate or a small group of classmates.
5. *Optional:* At the end of the writing time, reread the writing and circle a specific and promising idea that can be expanded in another quickwriting session.
6. *Optional:* Write again for another 5 to 10 minute period on the circled idea without pausing for any reason.

Through quickwriting, students ramble on paper, generating words and ideas and developing writing fluency. This strategy, popularized by Peter Elbow (1973), helps students focus on content rather than mechanics. Even by second or third grade, students have learned that many teachers and parents prize correct spelling and careful handwriting over the content of a composition. Elbow explains that focusing on mechanics makes writing "dead" because it does not allow students' natural voices to come through. In quickwriting, students focus on content, and later, if they choose, they can revise and polish their compositions using the writing process.

Student and adult writers often suffer from "blank-page syndrome," or an inability to start writing. When they look at the clean, blank sheet of writing paper, writers freeze. Or they discard sentence after sentence as they try to create a perfect first sentence, an imposing task for any writer! Quickwriting is a good prescription for the blank-page syndrome because writers begin to write imperfectly with the confidence that after three or four sentences, a usable sentence will emerge (Elbow, 1981). Experienced writers often return to quickwriting whenever they are stuck for ideas or words. They know that it gives them writing power.

Elbow has developed two types of quickwriting—unfocused and focused. In unfocused quickwriting, students let their thoughts ramble from topic to topic. Quickwriting can end after the first quickwrite, or students can write a second, more focused quickwrite that develops and expands one of the ideas mentioned in the first attempt. If students are going to continue with a second quickwrite, they reread what they have written and choose one idea to develop in the second try. Students should circle a word, phrase, or sentence in the first quickwrite to specify the topic for the second quickwrite. Then students write again for a period of 5 to 10 minutes, following the guidelines presented for unfocused quickwriting. This time students try to write on a single topic, probing as many dimensions of the topic as possible.

A set of unfocused and focused quickwrites written by a seventh grader is presented in Figure 1-15. In the first quickwrite, the student mentioned a variety of topics and then selected one topic, the upcoming project on Beowulf, as the topic for the second quickwrite.

FIGURE 1-15 *Unfocused and Focused Quickwrites by a Seventh-Grader*

Unfocused Quickwrite

I am doing a quickwrite. We are about to start doing things on Beowulf the warrior and Grendel the werewolf monster. We can do reports, comic books, magazines, newspapers, movies, soap operas, and many other things. I just got through with my report on the snake-killing mongoose. It was a fun report to write. My hand and arm are starting to ache. Today is the last day of school for the week—T.G.I.F. day! Well, I almost got everything down. I am in my third hour Language Arts class. My next class is Science, then Band, and then lunch. I wonder what I am going to do on the (Beowulf) project. Surely I'll find something to do. In science there's a hard report I need to get started on soon. It is on the planet Uranus.

Focused Quickwrite
Beowulf

In Language Arts we are listening to the teacher read *Beowulf.* I have heard about Beowulf before this book. I have read several of the Time-Life books. Beowulf was into dragons and night creatures. He was killed fighting a cave-dwelling dragon. In *Dragons and Night Creatures,* he battled with Grendel and his wife (two werewolfs). Although the book *Beowulf* is based mainly on the fight between the valiant warrior and Grendel, he is more famous as a dragonslayer, having destroyed many menacing dragons. Both books are quite different from each other. To know the truth, you would have to have lived in the seventh century.

Young children and older students who are not fluent writers can quickly quick-draw or sketch a picture in much the same way that they would quickwrite. Later, students can add words or a sentence to label their pictures. As in quickwriting, students share their completed quickdraws with classmates. Students can make quickdraws in response to literature or as a part of theme cycles. Figure 1-16 presents two quickdraws. The first quickdraw was done by Rajdeep after listening to his teacher read aloud *If You Give a Mouse a Cookie* (Numeroff, 1985). Rajdeep has drawn a picture of a chocolate chip cookie, and using "kid writing" he has written, "I like to eat cookies and the mouse likes to eat cookies."

The second quickdraw by first-grade William is about his favorite part of P. D. Eastman's *Are You My Mother?* (1960), the story of a baby bird who sets out to find his mother and asks everything it meets, "Are you my mother?" In the picture William has drawn the steam shovel called Snort that puts the baby bird back in its nest and the mother bird returning to the nest with a big, fat worm for the baby. In three lines across the bottom of the page, William has written, "The baby bird said, 'Are you my mother, you big ole Snort?'" Starting directly under the bird with the worm in its mouth, William has written, "The mom said," and he finishes the thought writing clockwise out of the mother bird's mouth, "Here's a worm here. I'm here." He wrote the three lines across the bottom of the page first, and after sharing and seeing other students' quickdraws, he added the part about the mother bird.

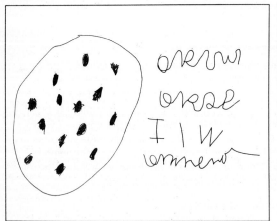
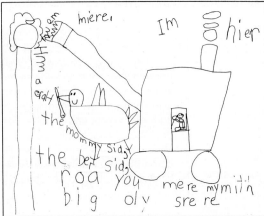

FIGURE 1-16   *Quickdraws by Two Primary-Grade Students*

Students quickwrite for a variety of purposes. First, they can quickwrite as they do in personal journal entries, letting their minds wander from topic to topic as they write. This develops writing fluency because, in far too many classrooms, students rarely fill up a page with writing. After these quickwrites, students are often amazed at how much they have written. Often when the timer rings, students sigh and ask, "Do we have to stop?"

Second, teachers can assign specific topics for students to explore in quickwriting. Before starting a new theme cycle, teachers might ask students to quickwrite on the theme. This activity has several purposes: to check students' knowledge about the topic, to relate students' personal experiences to the topic, and to stimulate students' interest in the topic. For example, students can participate in the following quickwrites in connection with current events, literature, social studies, and science units:

▼ Quickwrite on freedom or a geographic location before discussing a current events topic
▼ Quickwrite on the theme of friendship before reading *Bridge to Terabithia* (Paterson, 1977)
▼ Quickwrite on a trip students have taken before studying the Oregon Trail
▼ Quickwrite on snakes before studying reptiles
▼ Quickwrite on junk food before studying nutrition

After completing the theme, students quickwrite again on the same topic, applying what they have learned in the second quickwrite, and compare the two quickwrites as one measure of what they have learned in the theme.

Through this informal and unstructured writing, students collect and explore ideas and words that eventually may be used in a polished composition. Even if the writing is never developed, however, the quickwriting experience is valuable because students are developing writing fluency, learning a strategy to use when they don't know how to start a writing assignment, and learning that they usually *do* have something to say on almost any topic.

Writing Forms

Students often write personal narratives about experiences in their own lives. They may write about a vacation to Yellowstone National Park, a time when they broke an arm, or a pet dog or cat. Sometimes they may choose to report information about dinosaurs, making candles, or other topics they are knowledgeable about. Many other forms of writing are available to elementary students, and later chapters in this book are devoted to the following forms:

▼ *Journal Writing.* Students write in personal journals about events in their lives, in dialogue journals to converse with classmates and the teacher, in learning logs to document learning in content area classes, in reading logs to reflect on literature, and in simulated journals in the role of a historical personality or literary character.
▼ *Descriptive Writing.* Students use observation, sensory words, and comparisons to write descriptions of objects, people, and events.
▼ *Letter Writing.* Students write friendly letters to pen pals and authors, courtesy letters, and business letters to request and share information.
▼ *Biographical Writing.* Students write biographies of well-known contemporary and historical personalities, personal narratives about experiences in their own lives, and autobiographies to document their own lives.
▼ *Expository Writing.* Students write reports and other forms of expository writing to share information about social studies, science, and familiar topics.
▼ *Narrative Writing.* Students retell familiar stories, write stories with a well-developed structure, rewrite stories from different points of view.
▼ *Poetic Writing.* Students play with words, create word pictures, and write poems.
▼ *Persuasive Writing.* Students use persuasion techniques and propaganda devices to write persuasive essays and letters and create advertisements and commercials.

Elementary students use these forms for a variety of writing activities. They also read books of children's literature that model these forms, such as the Ahlbergs' *The Jolly Postman or Other People's Letters* (1986), a collection of letters written to fairy tale characters.

Writing Across the Curriculum

Students write across the curriculum in math, social studies, science, and other content area classes as well as in language arts. Anne Gere (1985) explains that when students write about what they are learning and what they want to learn in content area classes, they are learning that writing is a tool for learning. Using the writing-to-learn strategy allows students to assume responsibility for and ownership of their own learning. Writing across the curriculum has at least three significant benefits for elementary students (Henbrow, 1986). It encourages learning of content area information, develops writing fluency, strategies and skills, and activates critical thinking skills. Writing makes a significant contribution to learning because through writing students develop their own knowledge of the subject. As students write in all of their subjects across the curriculum, they write more easily and the writing makes their thinking more concrete. As they write, students discover, organize, classify, connect, and evaluate information.

Writing is a powerful learning tool because it fosters critical thinking through the creation of a language scaffold. (Britton, Burgess, Martin, McLeod, & Rosen, 1975; Emig, 1977). In the vignette at the beginning of the chapter, the learning logs and other writing activities served as a scaffold for the second and third graders' learning about weather. Through writing, learning becomes interactive and students become engaged and personally involved in what they are learning.

Students also use writing as they reflect on their reading and experiment with various writing forms. For example, after reading *Jamberry* (Degen, 1983), a delightful wordplay book using many invented "berry" words, a first grade class became wordsmiths and added *berry* to almost every word they said. With such a high level interest in inventing new words, the class decided to write their own berry verse. The first graders chose a space theme and dictated "Spaceberry" which their teacher recorded on chart paper. The children followed the same numerical sequence in their version that Degen used in his:

▽   *One berry*   *Five berries*
      Two berries   *Six berries*
      In my rocketshipberry   *Going to moonberry*
      Zoom-zoomberry   *To pick strawberries.*
      Going to Plutoberry.   *Never to crashberry!*

      Three berries   *Seven berries*
      Four berries   *Eight berries*
      Landing at Plutoberry   *Returning to Earthberry*
      Floating out of the doorberry   *To eat chocolate berries*
      To pick blueberries.   *Yumberry! Yumberry!*
                                  Yumberry!

Another way students connect literature and writing is by writing comparisons. After a class of fifth graders listened to their teacher read aloud the award-winning book *Sounder* (Armstrong, 1969) and viewed the film version of the book, students made charts in their reading logs to compare the two versions. Then they wrote an essay about the version they liked better. One student's comparison chart and essay are presented in Figure 1-17. It's interesting to note that the student incorporated the "thumbs up–thumbs down" technique used by a well-known pair of movie critics.

After reading a children's version of the Anglo-Saxon epic *Beowulf* retold by Charles Keeping (1982), a class of seventh graders created projects to respond to the book. One student wrote and videotaped a television interview with Beowulf in which he asked the hero about his battle with Grendel. This is his script:

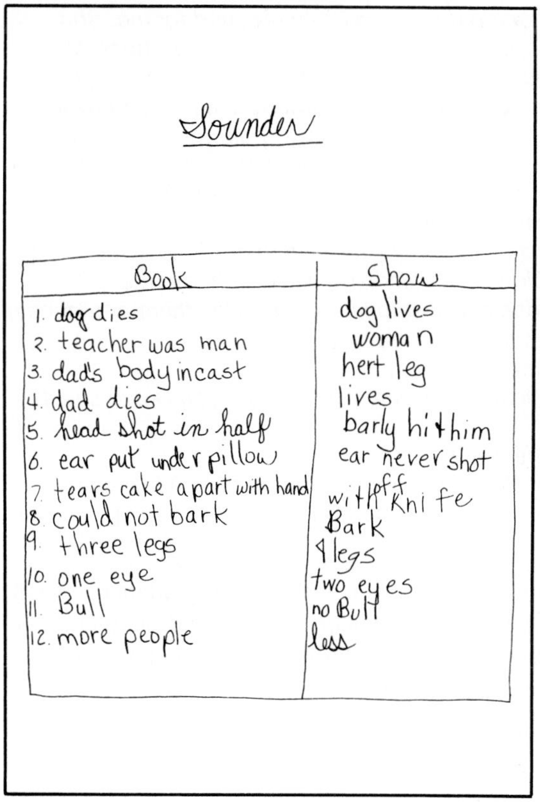

Sounder

Book	Show
1. dog dies	dog lives
2. teacher was man	woman
3. dad's body in cast	hert leg
4. dad dies	lives
5. head shot in half	barly hit him
6. ear put under pillow	ear never shot
7. tears cake apart with hand	with off knife
8. could not bark	Bark
9. three legs	4 legs
10. one eye	two eyes
11. Bull	no Bull
12. more people	less

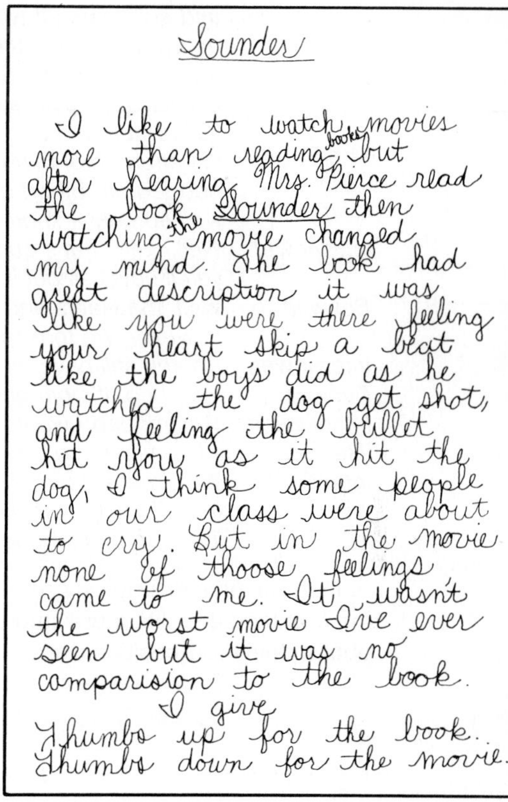

Sounder

I like to watch movies more than reading books but after hearing Mrs. Pierce read the book Sounder then watching the movie changed my mind. The book had great description it was like you were there feeling your heart skip a beat like the boy's did as he watched the dog get shot, and feeling the bullet hit you as it hit the dog. I think some people in our class were about to cry. But in the movie none of thoose feelings came to me. It wasn't the worst movie I've ever seen but it was no comparision to the book. I give Thumbs up for the book. Thumbs down for the movie.

FIGURE 1-17 *A Student's Comparison Chart and Essay*

▽ **Interviewer:** Today is May 10, 587 A.D. and our guest today is Beowulf, the greatest of the Geats. Welcome Mr. Wulf. I'm sure there are a lot of people out in the world who would like to know about your battle with Grendel.

Beowulf: Well, it all started when Grendel came to the palace one night a long time ago. The blasted creature broke thirty Thanes' necks! Well, this was totally intolerable, so I got together a group of my best Geats and set out to find Grendel! That night after we had all set up our camp and gone to sleep I was suddenly awakened by a rustling in the bushes. I opened my eyes but I didn't even move a muscle. Then I saw him, the most sickening thing I had ever seen. It was Grendel. Grendel slowly moved toward a Geat. He never had a chance. Grendel grabbed the Geat and before he could even scream, his head was gone! It rolled down beside me. I actually thought I was going to see my supper again. Grendel then turned the Geat upside-down and drank and ate all of his internals. Really sickening. He then saw the head laying beside me and moved towards it. He picked the head up and swallowed it with one big gulp. He then reached for me. Suddenly, faster than the eye could see I jumped up and grabbed him by the arm. I yelled, "Surprise Grendel! Your days of terror are over. This is your day—your end." Grendel yelled in agony like he had never yelled before. For the first time he was feeling pain. He was feeling the strength of thirty men in one. I twisted his right arm until it finally popped off. Blood dripped from his body and his arm. The beast walked only a short distance and then died.

Interviewer: Well, well, that's quite a scary story you have told, Mr. Wulf. I'm sure you'll never forget it. Did you do anything with the body or arm?

Beowulf: Well, the Geats and I decided just to let the body lay there and decay; however, we took the arm back for a souvenir.

Interviewer: Do you still have the arm?

Beowulf: Yes, I do. It's hanging in the souvenir room. Would you like to see it?

Interviewer: Yes, indeed I would.

[Beowulf takes Interviewer to view the arm.]

Interviewer: Well, that's the story of Beowulf's greatest adventure. A few years later Beowulf was killed by a great dragon. It was the end of Beowulf. The end of a legend!

In these three examples, first graders, fifth graders, and seventh graders used writing to extend their literature study. They used the writing process to draft, refine, and publish their compositions, and they shared their writings with genuine audiences.

Answering Teachers' Questions About . . . Teaching Children to Write

1. Is the writing process and writers' workshop the same thing?

The writing process and writers' workshops are related, but they are not the same thing. Writers' workshop is one classroom application of the writing process, and it will be discussed in Chapter 2, "Instructional Approaches."

2. The writing process is just for older students, isn't it?

No, the writing process is for all students. Kindergartners and first graders participate in prewriting activities just as older students do, and they share their composi-

tions in writing groups and use the author's chair. At first young children may write only one draft, but they like hearing compliments about their writing, and before long a suggestion for improvement is intermingled with a series of compliments. For example, "I really liked all the facts you told about gerbils, but you didn't say that they are mammals." And the writer responds, "Oh, I forgot. I think I can put it here. Thanks!" With the realization that readers provide worthwhile suggestions and that students need to revise their writing, these youngsters become full-fledged members of the writing process club.

3. *I don't feel comfortable with the writing process. Really, I'm afraid I'll lose control.*

A writing process classroom is different from a traditional classroom. There is more noise as students work in groups and move around the classroom for different activities. This environment stimulates learning because students are actively involved and assuming responsibility for their own learning. To ensure that students are learning, teachers can move about the classroom, observing and talking with students as they write, talk, revise, and share their writing. If the noise or movement becomes too great, teachers can stop students for a class meeting. At the meeting, they discuss the problem and consider ways to solve it.

To become more comfortable with the writing process approach, teachers might observe in a classroom that is already using the approach. They will observe a teacher who serves as a guide or a facilitator and students who know how to use the writing process and are actively involved in a writing project. In spite of the freedom to talk, move, and work independently, there is discipline and there are techniques for monitoring students' behavior and the work they complete.

4. *I am a middle school math teacher. Are you saying that my students will learn math better when they write about what they are learning?*

Yes, your students will learn mathematics better through writing. Researchers have documented the value of having students write in learning logs and do other writing activities to clarify their knowledge, apply specialized vocabulary, and reflect on their own learning.

REFERENCES

Ahlberg, J., & Ahlberg, A. (1986). *The jolly postman or other people's letters.* Boston: Little, Brown.

Applebee, A. L., & Langer, J. A. (1983). Instructional scaffolding: Reading and writing and natural language activities. *Language Arts, 60,* 168–175.

Armstrong, W. M. (1969). *Sounder.* New York: Harper & Row.

Barrett, J. (1978). *Cloudy with a chance of meatballs.* New York: Macmillan.

Bereiter, C., & Scandemalia, M. (1982). From conversation to composition: The role of instruction in the developmental process. In R. Glaser (Ed.), *Advances in Instructional Psychology* (vol. 2, pp. 1–64). Hillsdale, NJ: Erlbaum.

Bissex, G. L. (1980). *Gnys at wrk: A child learns to write and read.* Cambridge, MA: Harvard University Press.

Britton, J. (1970). *Language and thought.* Harmondsworth: Penguin.

Britton, J., Burgess, T., Martin, N., McLeod, A., & Rosen, H. (1975). *The development of writing abilities (11–18).* London: Schools Council Publications.

Calkins, L. M. (1980). When children want to punctuate: Basic skills belong in context. *Language Arts, 57,* 567–573.

Calkins, L. M. (1983). *Lessons from a child: On the teaching and learning of writing.* Portsmouth, NH: Heinemann.

Calkins, L. M. (1986). *The art of teaching writing.* Portsmouth, NH: Heinemann.

Chomsky, C. (1971). Write now, read later. *Childhood Education, 47,* 296–299.

Degen, B. (1983). *Jamberry.* New York: Harper & Row.

de Paola, T. (1975). *The cloud book.* New York: Holiday House.

de Regniers, B. S. (1988). *Sing a song of pop-corn: Every child's book of poems.* New York: Scholastic.

Dyson, A. H. (1982). The emergence of visible language: Interrelationships between drawing and early writing. *Visible Language, 6,* 360–381.

Dyson, A. H. (1983). *Early writing as drawing: the developmental gap between speaking and writing.* Presentation at the Annual Meeting of the American Educational Research Association, Montreal, CA.

Dyson, A. H. (1985). Second graders sharing writing: The multiple social realities of a literacy event. *Written Communication, 2,* 189–215.

Dyson, A. H. (1986). The imaginary worlds of childhood: A multimedia presentation. *Language Arts, 63,* 799–808.

Eastman, P. D. (1960). *Are you my mother?* New York: Random House.

Elbow, P. (1973). *Writing without teachers.* Oxford: Oxford University Press.

Elbow, P. (1981). *Writing with power.* New York: Oxford University Press.

Elley, W. B., Barham, I. H., Lamb, H., & Wyllie, M. (1976). The role of grammar in a secondary school English curriculum. *Research in the Teaching of English, 10,* 5–21.

Emig, J. (1971). *The composing processes of twelfth graders.* Champaign, IL: National Council of Teachers of English.

Emig, J. (1977). Writing as a mode of learning. *College Communication and Composition, 28,* 122–128.

Faigley, L., & Witte, S. (1981). Analyzing revision. *College Composition and Communication, 32,* 400–410.

Flower, L. S., & Hayes, J. R. (1977). Problem-solving strategies and the writing process. *College English, 39,* 449–461.

Flower, L. S., & Hayes, J. R. (1981). A cognitive process theory of writing. *College Composition and Communication, 32,* 365–387.

Galdone, P. (1962). *The hare and the tortoise.* New York: Seabury.

Gere, A. R. (1985). Introduction. In A. R. Gere (Ed.), *Roots in the sawdust: Writing to learn across the disciplines* (pp. 1–8). Urbana, IL: National Council of Teachers of English.

Gibbons, G. (1987). *Weather forecasting.* New York: Four Winds Press.

Graves, D. H. (1975). An examination of the writing processes of seven-year-old children. *Research in the Teaching of English, 9,* 227–241.

Graves, D. H. (1976). Let's get rid of the welfare mess in the teaching of writing. *Language Arts, 53,* 645–651.

Graves, D. H. (1983). *Writing: Teachers and children at work.* Exeter, NH: Heinemann.

Graves, D. H., & Hansen, J. (1983). The author's chair. *Language Arts, 60,* 176–183.

Halliday, M. A. K. (1973). *Explorations in the functions of language.* London: Edward Arnold.

Halliday, M. A. K. (1973). *Learning how to mean: Explorations in the development of language.* London: Edward Arnold.

Halliday, M. A. K. (1980). Three aspects of children's language development: Learning language, learning through language, learning about language. In Y. M. Goodman, M. M. Haussler, & D. S. Strickland (Eds.), *Oral and written language development research: Impact on the schools* (pp. 7–19). Proceedings from the 1979–1980 IMPACT Conferences sponsored by the International Reading Association and the National Council of Teachers of English.

Hayes, J. R., & Flower, L. S. (1986). Writing research and the writer. *American Psychologist, 41,* 1106–1113.

Henbrow, V. (1986). A heuristic approach across the curriculum. *Language Arts, 63,* 674–679.

Hidi, S., & Hildyard, A. (1983). The comparison of oral and written productions in two discourse modes. *Discourse Processes, 6,* 91–105.

Howe, D., & Howe, J. (1979). *Bunnicula: A rabbit-tale of mystery.* New York: Atheneum.

Jackson, L. A., Tway, E., & Frager, A. (1987). Dear teacher, Johnny copied. *The Reading Teacher, 41,* 22–25.

Keeping, C. (1982). *Beowulf.* Oxford: Oxford University Press.

King, M. (1985). Proofreading is not reading. *Teaching English in the Two-year College, 12,* 108–112.

Langer, J. A. (1985). Children's sense of genre. *Written Communication, 2,* 157–187.

Lundsteen, S. W. (Ed.). (1976). *Help for the teacher of written composition: New directions in research.* Urbana, IL: National Conference on Research in English and ERIC Clearinghouse on Reading and Communication Skills.

MacLachlan, P. (1985). *Sarah, plain and tall.* New York: Harper and Row.

Martin, N., D'Arcy, P., Newton, B., & Parker, R. (1976). *Writing and learning across the curriculum, 11–16.* London: Schools Council Publication.

Mills, B. S. (1983). Imagination: The connection between writing and play. *Educational Leadership, 41,* pp. 50–53.

Mohr, M. M. (1984). *Revision: The rhythm of meaning.* Upper Montclair, NJ: Boynton/Cook.

Murray, D. H. (1982). *Learning by teaching.* Montclair, NJ: Boynton/Cook.

Murray, D. H. (1985). *A writer teaches writing* (2nd ed.). Boston: Houghton Mifflin.

Murray, D. H. (1987). *Write to learn* (2nd ed.). Boston: Houghton Mifflin.

Numeroff, L. (1985). *If you give a mouse a cookie.* New York: Harper & Row.

Ogle, D. M. (1986). K-W-L: A teaching model that develops active reading of expository text. *The Reading Teacher, 39,* 564–570.

Ogle, D. M. (1989). The know, want to know, learn strategy. In K. D. Muth (Ed.), *Children's comprehension of text: Research into practice* (pp. 205–223). Newark, DE: International Reading Association.

Paterson, K. (1977). *Bridge to Terabithia.* New York: Crowell.

Perl, S. (1979). The composing processes of unskilled college writers. *Research in the Teaching of English, 13,* 317–336.

Perl, S. (1980). Understanding composition. *College Composition and Communication, 31,* 363–369.

Polacco, P. (1990). *Thunder cake.* New York: Philomel.

Rico, G. L. (1983). *Writing the natural way.* Los Angeles: Tarcher.

Smith, F. (1977). The uses of language. *Language Arts, 54,* 638–644.

Smith, F. (1982). *Writing and the writer.* New York: Holt.

Smith, F. (1988). *Joining the literacy club: Further essays in education.* Portsmouth, NH: Heinemann.

Sommers, N. (1980). Revisions strategies of student writers and experienced writers. *College Composition and Communication, 31,* 378–388.

Sommers, N. (1982). Responding to student writing. *College Composition and Communication, 33,* 148–156.

Tompkins, G. E., & Friend, M. (1988). After your students write: What's next? *Teaching Exceptional Children, 20,* 4–9.

Tway, E. (1980). Teacher responses to children's writing. *Language Arts, 57,* 763–772.

Viorst, J. (1972). *Alexander and the terrible, horrible, no good, very bad day.* New York: Atheneum.

Wagner, B. J. (1976). *Dorothy Heathcote: Drama as a learning medium.* Washington, DC: National Education Association.

Wagner, B. J. (1983). The expanding circle of informal classroom drama. In B. A. Busching and J. I. Schwartz (Eds.), *Integrating the language arts in the elementary school* (pp. 155–163). Urbana, IL: NCTE.

2

Instructional Approaches

Reading and Writing About Families

Mrs. Reeves's third graders spend an hour and a half in the morning reading and talking about books that are about families, including *Ramona Quimby, Age 8* (Cleary, 1981) and *A Chair for My Mother* (Williams, 1982), during readers' workshop. Later in the day, they spend an hour and a half in writers' workshop, writing about their own families. Mrs. Reeves's schedule for writers' workshop is

1:30–1:50 Class meeting
1:50–2:45 Writing
2:45–3:00 Sharing

Mrs. Reeves begins with a class meeting. She brings the class together for a variety of reasons: Sometimes they write a class composition together with Mrs. Reeves taking the students' dictation, sometimes she shares information about a favorite author of children's books, and at other times she teaches minilessons about writing skills and strategies, such as proofreading or writing leads.

Next, students spend almost an hour writing and working on their compositions. Students are working at different stages of the writing process. Some students are drawing pictures to illustrate their completed compositions, and others are meeting with Mrs. Reeves in a writing group to revise their compositions. Students' desks are arranged in five groups, and Mrs. Reeves keeps track of her students' activities by briefly conferencing with students during each writing period and making notes on a clipboard she carries. She describes the activities students are involved in and records her observations about students' progress. An excerpt from a chart she uses for these notes is presented in Figure 2-1.

Students sign up on the chalkboard when they are ready to meet in revising groups, and after four students have signed up, a group is formed. Mrs. Reeves has another sign-up list for students who want to have a conference with her. Mrs. Reeves has found it easier than she expected to juggle the activities of students working at different writing process stages. Because her students are working independently on their own projects, some students are drafting or writing final copies when others need her assistance in writing groups or for proofreading.

Mrs. Reeves and her students use the last 15 minutes of writers' workshop to meet together as a class to share their completed compositions. Students sit in the author's chair, a place of honor, to read their published writings to the class. After reading, students clap and offer compliments. Sometimes a student offers a suggestion or asks for further information, but writers do not have to go back into their compositions to make further revisions.

Mrs. Reeves' students are writing about themselves and their own families. They began by brainstorming a list of questions about families, family histories, and memorable family events. Students interviewed their parents and sometimes their brothers, sisters, and other relatives. These are some of the questions they asked:

What family event do you remember best?

What things did we do when I was a baby?

What was one of your most embarrassing moments?

Did you have any arguments with your parents when you were a child?

WRITERS' WORKSHOP TRACKING SHEET

Week ___ October 23 ___

P = Prewriting
D = Drafting
R = Revisions
E = Editing
P/S = Publishing/Sharing

Names	M	T	W	Th	F
Brad "My Dog Smokey"	Starting over again. Having difficulty choosing a topic he cares about (P)	Clusters about his dog. Finally a good topic! (P)	Begins drafting "My Dog Smokey" (D)	Finishing draft. — 3pp. Signs up for writing group (D)	Writing group w/ Josh, Michael, Paula, and Rebel (R)
Maria "The Longest Day"	Proofreading with Jodee. Wants to conference with me. (E)	Making final copy "The Longest Day"	Taking great care with illustrations →	Helping Chris with proofreading (P)	Planning next book (P)
Rebel "Washington, DC"	absent	Begins draft about trip to Wash. DC Working hard (D)	Continue drafting. Brings photos for illustrations (D)	Very organized. Has spread papers across table to match text and photos → (D)	Writing group w/ Josh, Brad, Michael and Paula (R)
Lori "The Accident"	Drafting—on 8th page! Begins writing group with Colin, Brian, and Megan (D/R)	Writing group continued. Group working well together—supportive (R)	Making revisions (R)	Proofreading with Megan (E)	Conferences with me —few spelling errors —minilesson needed on run-on sentences Working on final copy (E)

FIGURE 2-1 A Tracking Sheet Used During Writers' Workshop

49

Who taught you how to swim?

What do you remember about when you went to elementary school?

What pets do you like?

Students also brainstormed lists of their own memories. Mrs. Reeves showed a collection of objects including a dog biscuit, a postcard, a teddy bear, a camera, a book, a slice of pizza, a bandage, and a package wrapped as a gift. As she shared each object, she asked students to jot down a phrase about a memory that the object brought to mind. She also asked students to list other memories that occurred to them.

Armed with this information, students sorted through the information and picked memorable events to write about. They made a cluster about the event to collect and organize information before beginning to write. Some students drew pictures, and others chose a book about a family to use as a model. Other students had more developed ideas in mind and immediately began to write. Mrs. Reeves does not try to keep the students together, with everyone drafting or revising at the same time. Instead, they prewrite, draft, revise, edit, and publish at their own speed. Some students write two compositions in the time it takes one child to complete one piece, and sometimes students decide to start over after spending a week or two on a topic. Although the students do not work at the same pace, all students are involved in the same type of assignment.

During the month that students spend reading and writing about families, all students are expected to do the prewriting activities and complete at least one composition, most likely a personal narrative about a memorable family event. Children can also experiment with other writing forms—a newspaper account of the event, a letter recounting the event, or a poem.

Many students wrote about their pets. One wrote about his dog:

▽
My Dog Smokey

My dog Smokey always loves to play. One of my friends gets Smokey and holds him. There's this blanket and I scoot back with the blanket. Then my friend lets him go. Then Smokey runs real fast for the blanket. Then he gets it and I let go. Then he tries to stop and he does a flip!

Another student wrote about an unusual pet he found on a vacation:

▽
Found and Lost and Found

When I went on my vacation I found a soldier crab in my aunty's backyard in St. Thomas. I climbed a tree and looked down and I saw a shell first. I thought it was a snail shell. Then I picked it up and it was not a snail shell. It was a soldier crab. I put him in a paper bag. I carried him home on the airplane when I was coming back to Lawton. When we got home he was still in a little paper bag and he went to sleep. In the morning he was gone. Two weeks passed and I found him in between my two couches. I put him in a round glass fish bowl. He eats lettuce but he does not like water. Now he is safe.

The grades students receive for their work are based on the accumulated information they present in their reading and writing folders. In the writing folder, students place their brainstorming lists of memorable events, notes from their interviews of family members, prewriting, drafting, and final copies of compositions, and an evaluation letter they have written to Mrs. Reeves at the end of the month reflecting on their writing and work habits.

---

*T*eachers implement the writing process in their classrooms in various ways. The two basic instructional approaches for teaching writing are writers' workshop and thematic projects. In the writers' workshop approach, students write on self-selected topics and work independently, employing the writing process as they work. In the thematic projects approach, students write in response to literature or as part of social studies and science theme cycles. For example, students might work with partners to write sequels after reading *Jumanji* (Van Allsburg, 1981), or they might write reports or poems about the planets as part of a science theme on the solar system. In the vignette at the beginning of the chapter, Mrs. Reeves used the writers' workshop approach. Her students worked independently on their writing projects during a regularly scheduled writing time even though they all wrote compositions about their families.

This chapter develops the information on the writing process presented in Chapter 1 and describes two ways to teach the writing process to elementary students. Both writers' workshop and thematic projects are educationally valid approaches and can be used with primary, middle, and upper-grade students. Neither approach is better than the other; the two approaches serve different purposes and complement each other. Through writers' workshop, children become familiar with the ebb and flow of the writing process and experience the exhilaration that all authors feel as they share their view of the world with readers. Through thematic projects, on the other hand, students use writing to explore and extend their learning about literature, social studies, and science. Through both approaches, students learn how to use the writing process to write autobiographies, poems, persuasive essays, and other writing forms.

INTRODUCING THE WRITING PROCESS

Introducing students to the writing process, whether they are first graders or eighth graders, and helping them learn the activities involved in each stage are crucial. Certainly students learn about the writing process as they write, but an introduction to the process and activities involved in each stage is in order. Teachers begin by explaining the process approach, describing and demonstrating each stage, and guiding students as they develop several brief compositions to experience the writing process. Guidelines for introducing the writing process are presented in Figure 2-2.

1. **Use the writing process terminology.** As teachers introduce the writing process, they should use the names of each stage and related terms. Students, even young children, learn to use *proofread, leads, compliments, cluster, writing groups,* and other terms quickly and easily.

2. **Develop charts listing the stages of the writing process.** Charts listing the stages of the writing process and activities involved at each stage should hang in classrooms. The chart is a useful reminder for students and emphasizes the importance of writing. Students should help make the charts. Teachers might begin by listing the five stages and then have students add information about the activities involved in each stage.

3. **Demonstrate the writing process.** Teachers demonstrate the writing process by writing a composition with the class. Teachers choose a topic related to a literature focus unit or a social studies or science theme and work through the five stages of the writing process with the class to prewrite, draft, revise, edit, and publish the composition.

4. **Keep first writings short.** Students' first writings should be short pieces so that they can move through the writing process rather quickly. First graders might write a four-page "All about _____" book with a sentence or two on each page; fourth graders might write a paragraph or two about an experience. A detailed, seven-page biography of a sports personality or a historical figure is not a good first time project for students at any grade level because of the time and effort involved in gathering and organizing the information, writing the rough draft, sharing it in writing groups, revising the piece, locating and correcting mechanical errors, and recopying the final draft.

5. **Demonstrate revising and editing activities in minilessons.** Because revising and editing activities are unfamiliar to most students, teachers need to demonstrate the activities in minilessons. For a minilesson on revision, teachers might read aloud a composition and invite students to take turns giving compliments, asking questions, and making suggestions for revising the piece. Then teachers make revisions and duplicate copies to share with the class during another minilesson. Students see how sections are crossed out, moved, and new sections are added. For a minilesson on editing, students proofread the revised composition to identify mechanical errors and correct them.

6. **Use writing folders.** Students use writing folders to hold their prewriting, illustrations, rough drafts, writing group notes, and editing checklists. When the writing project is completed, all materials are organized, stapled together and clipped to the final copy. The folder is used again for the next writing project.

Students need to learn the procedures and activities involved in each stage of the writing process and the terminology associated with the writing process. In particular, they need to learn how to make clusters, participate in writing groups, revise, and proofread. Teachers use minilessons to demonstrate each procedure and then provide many opportunities for students to practice each procedure and activity through writers' workshop and thematic projects.

Learning the writing process takes time. Students need to work through the entire process again and again using writers' workshop and thematic projects until the stages and activities become automatic. Once students understand the writing process, they can manipulate the activities of each stage to meet the differing demands of particular writing projects and modify the process to accommodate their personal writing styles.

It is often useful to hang charts outlining the writing process and related activities in the classroom, and these charts should be developed with students rather than made in advance by the teacher. Five writing process charts are presented in Figure 2-3. Chart A, "We Use the Reading and Writing Processes," was developed in a first-grade classroom. Even though the two processes are briefly stated, the first graders recognize the similarities between them. Chart B, "The Writing Process," was developed by sixth graders and lists the five stages and activities involved in each one. Fourth graders developed "Your Jobs in a Writing Group" (chart C) to identify the responsibilities and duties of each person in a revising group. The same group of fourth graders also developed "Proofreading Reminders" (chart D) as part of a minilesson on proofreading. Chart E, "Things to Say in Writing Groups," is from a third-grade classroom. In the first part, students listed polite sentence stems for making comments, and they identified important things to look for in a piece of writing in the second part of the chart. Students refer to this chart when they are thinking of comments to make in writing groups.

Class Collaborations

One way to demonstrate the writing process is through a class collaboration. A class collaboration is a composition that students write together with the teacher, using all five stages of the writing process. Students practice the writing process within a supportive environment, and the teacher reviews concepts and clarifies misconceptions as the group piece is written. Students supply the ideas for writing and offer suggestions for how to tackle common writing problems.

The teacher begins by introducing the idea of writing a group composition and discussing the project. Almost any type of writing project can be written as a class collaboration including poems, letters, stories, reports, and persuasive essays. What is most important is that all students are familiar with the topic and writing form. If, for example, students are writing an impassioned letter to the editor of the local newspaper about a community ecological problem, they should be knowledgeable about the problem and about how to write a persuasive letter.

Students compose the composition together, moving through the prewriting, drafting, revising, editing, and publishing stages of the writing process. The teacher

```
We Use the Reading and Writing Processes

READING                    WRITING

1. Make predictions.       1. Draw a picture or
                              make a cluster.

2. Read the book.          2. Write the book.

3. Respond by talking,     3. Share your book
   drawing, or writing.       in the Author's
                              Chair.
```

A.

```
THE WRITING PROCESS

1. PREWRITING:    Gather and organize ideas.

2. DRAFTING:      Write a sloppy copy.

3. REVISING:      Share your draft in a writing group.
                  Then make at least three changes.

4. EDITING:       Proofread and correct errors.

5. PUBLISHING:    Write the final copy and illustrate
                  it. Share with an audience.
```

B.

```
YOUR JOBS IN A WRITING GROUP

1. Bring your rough draft and blue revising pen.

2. Share your rough draft.

3. Talk about your rough draft and listen for compliments, questions, and
   suggestions.

4. Take notes on your rough draft.

5. Make a plan for revising your rough draft.

6. Be a good listener when other people share their rough drafts.

7. Give compliments, ask questions, and make suggestions about other
   people's rough drafts.
```

C.

FIGURE 2-3 *Five Writing Process Charts*

```
┌─────────────────────────────────────────────┐
│            Proofreading Reminders            │
│                                              │
│   1. Say every word as you proofread.        │
│                                              │
│   2. Point with your pencil.                 │
│                                              │
│   3. Proofread three times:                  │
│      a. for spelling errors                  │
│      b. for capitalization and punctuation   │
│      c. for homonyms                         │
│                                              │
│   4. Ask someone else to proofread your      │
│      paper.                                  │
└─────────────────────────────────────────────┘
```

D.

```
┌─────────────────────────────────────────────────────────┐
│              Things to Say in Writing Groups              │
│                                                           │
│  1. Be polite. Say things that will not hurt anyone's     │
│     feelings.                                             │
│                                                           │
│     • I like . . .                                        │
│                                                           │
│     • I got confused when . . .                           │
│                                                           │
│     • Tell me more about . . .                            │
│                                                           │
│     • Your writing reminds me of . . .                    │
│                                                           │
│     • My favorite part is . . .                           │
│                                                           │
│     • Could you try to . . .                              │
│                                                           │
│                                                           │
│  2. These are important things to say about someone's     │
│     writing:                                              │
│       • LEADS                • BEGINNING–MIDDLE–END        │
│       • DESCRIPTIVE WORDS    • SPECIAL $10 WORDS           │
│       • DETAILS              • SOUND WORDS                 │
│       • DIALOGUE             • CHARACTERS                  │
│       • EXCITEMENT           • VOICE                       │
│       • LOTS OF FACTS        • SEQUENCE                    │
│       • ORGANIZATION         • REPEATED WORDS              │
│       • SETTING              • POINT OF VIEW               │
│       • COMPARISONS          • PAINTS A PICTURE            │
└───────────────────────────────────────────────────────────┘
```

E.

FIGURE 2-3, continued

does the actual writing, taking students' dictation on chart paper or on the chalkboard or using an overhead projector. The teacher is alert for any misunderstandings students may have about writing or the writing process and, when necessary, reviews concepts and offers suggestions.

Students prewrite to gather and organize ideas. The teacher records students' ideas in a cluster or another appropriate form. Then students dictate a rough draft which the teacher writes, taking care to double-space the writing and label it "rough draft." Students take turns dictating sentences, suggesting words and sentences.

Then the students and teacher move on to the third stage, revising. The class becomes a writing group. The teacher or a student reads the rough draft aloud several times. Next, students comment on the strong points of the composition, ask questions, and make suggestions about how to fine-tune the composition. Some parts may be reworked; other parts may be deleted or moved. More specific words will be substituted for less specific ones, and redundant words and sentences will be deleted. Also, students may want to add new parts to the composition. After making the necessary content changes, students proofread the composition, identifying mechanical errors, checking paragraph breaks, and combining sentences as needed. Students take turns making changes. The teacher clarifies any questions students have about mechanics such as spelling homophones or using commas in a series.

Finally, the composition is published. The teacher or several students copy the completed composition on sheets of chart paper and compile them into a big or regular-size book or copy them on sheets of writing paper and duplicate copies of the composition for each student. Students add illustrations to a class book or personalize the individual copies they receive.

A first-grade class wrote this collaborative retelling of *Where the Wild Things Are* (Sendak, 1963):

▽ Page 1: *Max got in trouble. He scared his dog and got sent to bed.*
Page 2: *His room turned into a jungle. His room grew more and more.*
Page 3: *A boat came for Max. It was his private boat.*
Page 4: *He came to where the wild things lived. They made him king.*
Page 5: *The wild things had a wild rumpus. They danced and hung on trees. Max sent them to bed without any supper.*
Page 6: *Max waved good-bye and went back home.*
Page 7: *His dinner was waiting for him. It was still hot from the microwave.*

This version is very revealing. The children clearly understand the beginning, middle, and end of the story, and their explanation on page 7 of why Max's dinner was still hot is an interesting rationalization. The teacher was disappointed that the children chose not to include Sendak's vivid descriptions of the wild things "roaring their terrible roars" and "gnashing their terrible teeth"; their choices indicate a focus on the plot rather than literary language.

The students divided their retelling into pages, and students took turns copying the final copy onto large sheets of chart paper which were compiled in a big book. The first graders enjoyed the book so much that several days later the teacher made smaller individual copies of the pages which the children illustrated and bound into books. Students read and reread their versions, and many wrote other books about wild things and other things that might have happened to Max.

In "Marbles Lost, Marbles Found: Collaborative Production of Text," Esther Fine (1987) described how her middle grade class of students with behavior disorders wrote a novel collaboratively. All of the students contributed to the writing and through the experience learned that they could write and that they had valuable contributions to make. Fine summed up the experience this way: "Collaboration is learning to learn and to work together . . . Collaboration is a great solution" (p. 487).

In another type of class collaboration students divide the writing project into small segments, and each student or small group completes one part. If students are writing a report, for example, they divide into small groups, and each group writes one chapter. Or, if the class is writing a retelling of a favorite story, each student or pair of students writes and illustrates one page or chapter of the book. Often the class does the first page or chapter together to review the writing process and procedure for the particular writing project. Then students work independently on their own parts. Students come back together to revise and edit their writing and finally to compile and publish their writing as a book.

Figure 2-4 presents an excerpt from a class book "California: The Golden State" written by fourth graders as the culmination of a yearlong study of the state. Students brainstormed topics and divided into pairs and small groups to write the sections. This book is interesting because students wrote the chapters from the viewpoint of Californians in each setting. The chapter about the gold rush was written from a miner's viewpoint, and the chapter on Yosemite National Park was written from naturalist John Muir's viewpoint. The excerpt in Figure 2-4, "A Tour of San Francisco," was written from the viewpoint of a tour guide. This perspective makes the writing more interesting to read and allows students to add personal experiences to the information they present. There is no doubt that these students have visited San Francisco and been on tours themselves. Students participated in all five stages of the writing process as they prepared the book. As the final step, the chapters were compiled, and a cover, title page, dedication, and a table of contents were added. Then copies were made for each student.

Collaborative compositions give students a dry run at the writing process and give teachers a chance to respond to students' questions and misconceptions. Teachers also use class collaborations when introducing writing forms or when students would have trouble doing the writing independently either because of the large size of the project or students' limited writing experience.

USING THE WRITING PROCESS IN ELEMENTARY CLASSROOMS

Two approaches to teaching writing in elementary classrooms are writers' workshop and thematic projects. Writers' workshop is an established daily period of time, usually an hour or hour and a half, in which students write and publish compositions on topics of their own choosing. Students work through the stages of the writing process at their own pace. Thematic projects are compositions that students do as part of

FIGURE 2-4   *An Excerpt from a Fourth-Grade Class Book on California*

A Tour of San Francisco

Clang! Clang! Clang! go the bells on the cable cars. The cable cars go up and down the hills of San Francisco. Let's take a ride. It's a good way to learn about this city. San Francisco is the third largest city in California and the population is 678,974. It is located on a peninsula next to the Pacific Ocean.

San Francisco is an old city. Spanish missionaries founded it in 1776. The city really began to grow in 1848 with the Gold Rush. It was an important mining supply center. People who made a lot of money came back to live in San Francisco, and they built beautiful homes on Nob Hill. Most of the homes are gone now because of the Great San Francisco Earthquake in 1906.

Our first stop is at Chinatown. There are many people from China that live in San Francisco. Some Chinese people came to America to work in the gold rush and some came to work on the First Transcontinental Railroad that was built in the 1860's. Now some of their great grandchildren live in one area that is called China-town. Look on the street signs. You see the names written in Chinese and in English. Do you hear people talking Chinese in the stores and on the street? We can stop and eat Chinese food and buy little gifts that come from China. Did you know there is a fortune cookie factory here, too?

Our second stop is at Fisherman's Wharf. Many, many fishing boats used to dock here. They caught fish in the ocean. Then they came here to sell the fish. Now there are only a few boats but there are good seafood restaurants here. We will walk over to two fun shopping centers. One shopping center is called the Cannery. It used to be a factory that made canned food. That's why it's called the Cannery. The other one is Ghirardelli Square, and it used to be a chocolate factory. You can eat Ghirardelli chocolates at a store there.

Now we will take a boat tour of San Francisco Bay and see the sights. Look straight ahead and you will see the Golden Gate Bridge. It is very tall and you can see the two towers and the cables that hang down to hold the bridge up. It is called a suspension bridge and it is 8,981 feet long. Many people drive across the bridge every day and you can even walk across it. There is a sidewalk. Over here you can see Alcatraz Island. It used to be a military fort and prison. The most dangerous criminals in America used to be put here, but it is closed now.

Thank you for taking this tour. I hope you have learned that San Francisco is a great and interesting city. There is much, much, much more to see and you can take more of our tours. I want you to leave your heart in San Francisco and come back soon. Good bye!

---

literature focus units or social studies and science theme cycles. Teachers provide chunks of time during language arts, social studies, or science periods in which students use the writing process to draft, revise, edit, and publish compositions.

These two approaches incorporate certain basic principles of writing instruction:

▼ *The Writing Process.* Students use the writing process in both approaches.
▼ *Time.* Students have ample time for writing in both approaches. In writers' workshop, time is regularly scheduled; for thematic projects, students have a set number of days to complete the writing.

▼ *Choice.* Students make choices about topic, form, purpose, and audience in both approaches. While the writers' workshop approach allows for more choice, students make choices when they work on thematic projects too.

▼ *Community.* In both approaches, students are members of a supportive classroom community in which they write and share their writing with classmates.

The two approaches differ with respect to schedule and organization. Writing is a time-consuming process, and it is very difficult to start and stop it according to a schedule. How convenient it would be if the five-stage model of the writing process equated to prewriting on Monday, drafting on Tuesday, revising on Wednesday, editing on Thursday, and sharing on Friday—but it does not. In fact, it is difficult to predict how long a writing project will last because of differences in how students write.

Thematic projects are organized and scheduled in connection with literature focus units and social studies and science themes, while writers' workshop is an ongoing part of the classroom schedule with regularly scheduled whole-class and individual activities. A comparison of the two approaches to writing instruction is presented in Figure 2-5.

FIGURE 2-5 *A Comparison of the Two Approaches to Writing*

	Writers' Workshop	**Thematic Projects**
Purpose	To let students experience the process that writers use and learn to write by writing about self-selected topics.	To respond to literature and extend learning about social studies and science through writing projects.
Topics	Students choose their own topics. They often choose to write about events in their own lives, their hobbies, and things that interest them.	Students write on topics related to literature they are reading or social studies and science themes they are involved in.
Time	Students spend 60–90 minutes each day in writer's workshop.	Students spend 30–60 minutes (or more) a day working on writing projects until the project is completed.
Schedule	Writing is an ongoing and regularly scheduled part of the school day.	Writing time is part of literature focus units or themes. It continues until the project is completed, usually a week or two.
Organization	Writers' workshop includes minilessons, independent writing time, and sharing.	Students write during language arts focus units or social studies and science theme cycles.

The Writers' Workshop Approach

The writers' workshop approach is a new way of implementing the writing process (Calkins, 1986, 1991; Graves, 1983; Parry & Hornsby, 1985). According to Lucy McCormick Calkins (1986), in this approach students write about what is vital and real for them, and their writing becomes the curriculum. They assume ownership of their learning and choose what they write and how they will write. At the same time, the teacher's role changes from being a provider of knowledge and writing topics to serving as a facilitator and guide. The classroom becomes a community of writers who write and share their writing. Alan Ziegler (1981) calls writers' workshop a state of mind.

In a writers' workshop classroom, students have writing folders in which they keep all papers related to the writing project they are working on. They also keep writing notebooks in which they jot down images, impressions, dialogue, and experiences that they can build upon for writing projects (Calkins, 1991). Students have access to different kinds of paper, some lined and some unlined, and writing instruments, including pencils and red and blue pens. Art supplies for illustrating books and book-making supplies are also available in the classroom. Students also have access to a well-stocked classroom library. Many times a student's writing project will grow out of a favorite book. The student may write a sequel to a book or retell a story from a different point of view. Primary grade students often use patterns from a book they have read to structure a book they are writing.

Students sit at desks or tables arranged in small groups as they write. The teacher circulates around the classroom, conferencing briefly with students, and the classroom atmosphere is free enough that students converse quietly with classmates and move around the classroom to assist classmates or share ideas. There is space for students to meet together for writing groups, and often a sign-up sheet for writing groups is posted in the classroom. A table is available for the teacher to meet with individual students or small groups for conferences, writing groups, proofreading, and minilessons.

Components of Writers' Workshop.   Writers' workshop is an hour to hour-and-a-half period scheduled each day. During this time students are involved in three activities:

1. *Minilessons.* During this 5- to 15-minute period, teachers provide brief lessons on writing workshop procedures, literary concepts, and writing strategies and skills.
2. *Independent Writing.* Students spend 30 to 45 minutes working on writing projects.
3. *Sharing.* For the last 10 to 15 minutes of writers' workshop, the whole class gathers together to share their new publications.

It is important to have a clear, simple structure for writers' workshop so that students can anticipate the writing activities they will be involved in.

Minilessons are brief discussions or demonstrations of writers' workshop procedures, literary concepts, and writing strategies and skills (Atwell, 1987). A list of pos-

FIGURE 2-6   *Topics for Minilessons*

Writers' Workshop Procedures

Writing rough drafts	Making and binding books
Participating in writing groups	Using word processing programs
Conferencing	Writing reflections
"All About the Author" pages	Choosing compositions for portfolios

Literary Concepts

Plot	Comparisons (metaphors and similes)
Characters	Personification
Setting	Alliteration
Theme	Repetition
Point of view	Wordplay

Writing Strategies and Skills

Clustering	Adding details
Proofreading	Writing dialogue
Making revisions	Distinguishing between homophones
Choosing titles	Sentence combining
Making tables of content	Capitalization
Writing leads	Punctuation

sible topics for minilessons is shown in Figure 2-6. The purpose of minilessons is to highlight the topic, not to isolate it or provide drill-and-practice (Crafton, 1991). Worksheets are not used in minilessons; instead, students apply the lesson to their own writing. Minilessons can be conducted with the whole class, small groups of students who have indicated that they need to learn more about a particular topic, and individual students. Minilessons can be held whenever teachers see a need as they observe students writing and talk with students. Teachers can also plan minilessons on a regular basis to introduce topics.

The steps in teaching a minilesson are as follows:

1. Introduce the writers' workshop procedure, literary concept, or writing strategy or skill.
2. Share examples of the topic using children's writing or books written for children.
3. Provide information about the topic and make connections to literature or to writing.
4. Have students make notes about the topic on a poster to be displayed in the classroom or in their writers' notebook.
5. Ask students to reflect on or speculate on how they can use this information in their reading and writing.

A description of a minilesson on revising for a small group of sixth graders is presented in Figure 2-7.

Frequent and regular times to write are needed for students to write well. During independent writing time, students spend 30 to 45 minutes working on writing proj-

FIGURE 2-7 *A Minilesson on Revising for a Small Group of Sixth Graders*

[1]In Donald M. Murray, *Shoptalk: Learning to Write with Writers* (p. 182). Portsmouth, NH: Heinemann, 1990. Reprinted with permission.

1. **Introduce revising.** Mrs. Hernandez gathers together seven students and explains they will spend approximately 15 minutes in a minilesson on revising. She reminds them that revising is the third stage of the writing process and it is the stage when students revisit their rough drafts. They reread and make revisions to make their writing better. By the word *better* she means both clearer and more complete. She shares this quote from children's author Roald Dahl about revision: "By the time I am nearing the end of a story, the first part will have been reread and altered and corrected at least 150 times. I am suspicious of both facility and speed. Good writing is essentially rewriting. I am positive of this."[1] 150 times! The students are shocked, but Mrs. Hernandez assures them that she does not expect that much revision.

2. **Share examples of revision using students' writing samples.** Mrs. Hernandez shares a classmate's rough draft and final copy of a piece of writing (with that classmate's permission, of course). She asks students to identify changes they noted between the drafts. They also look at the classmate's rough draft to see how the changes were made by crossing out and adding words and phrases and using arrows to move text. They also notice that the classmate's rough draft was double-spaced and written in pencil. The revisions were written in the spaces between lines in blue pen. (They also notice the editing corrections made in red pen.)

3. **Provide information about revising.** Mrs. Hernandez explains that there are four kinds of revisions students can make in their writing: adding, deleting, substituting, and moving. She points to a wall chart with this information. Then students look at the classmate's rough draft and classify his revisions into the four categories.

4. **Have students make notes about revising in their writers' notebooks.** Mrs. Hernandez asks students to list the four kinds of revisions in their writers' notebooks. She also asks them to return the next day with a composition (rough draft and final copy) that they have written so that they can analyze their own revisions.

5. **Ask students to reflect on how they revise and how they can use this information in revising.** The next day the small group of students gathers together for another 15-minute minilesson and they examine their own revisions. Students notice that they have made only one or two revisions and most changes are either adding or deleting. One student finds an example of moving text. Mrs. Hernandez asks students to write a plan of action in their writers' notebooks under the list of kinds of revisions they added yesterday. She wants students to recognize the value of revising and plan to pay more attention to revisions they make in the writing they are doing now. Mrs. Hernandez also notes in her conference notebook to check with these seven students next week during independent writing time about their revising.

ects. They move through all five stages of the writing process—prewriting, drafting, revising, editing, and publishing—at their own pace.

During prewriting, students create lists of topics they would like to write on, write brief statements they might want to expand, and note other ideas in their writing notebooks. They also draw pictures and reread favorite books when they are looking for a topic. They might also write a short retelling of a favorite story, write out the verses of a familiar song or poem, or play with the sentence pattern from a favorite book. Drawing pictures, making clusters, and reviewing the pattern structure of a favorite story are all ways to gather and organize ideas for writing.

Teachers help students learn to identify their own topics for writing. Instead of suggesting topics, teachers ask students to talk about things that interest them, stories they have enjoyed, ideas they might want to share with classmates. Out of these conversations topics emerge. Sometimes classmates can help students identify topics to write about. Donald Graves (1983) explains that children come to school wanting to write, but too often teachers ignore children's urge to show what they know.

Once students have gathered and organized their ideas, they begin to draft their compositions. Students work independently but often share their ideas with the teacher or classmates working nearby. They focus on the development of their piece rather than worrying about spelling each word correctly or making sure to capitalize and punctuate correctly. Students understand that in the drafting stage writers pour out their ideas. They double-space their writing and mark their papers as "rough drafts" or "sloppy copies."

As they are writing, students often stop to think of ideas, reread their piece, or ask a classmate a question. Sometimes students decide to make changes or start over if the piece is not working. The teacher walks around the classroom stopping to say, "Tell me about your piece." Through brief conferences, teachers provide support for young writers and are available to help students when their writing is not going smoothly. Teachers and students must recognize that writing rarely does go smoothly; it develops with stops and starts, and a few dead ends.

Students are constantly revising. They revise in their minds, before they even write a word, and they revise as they write, often stopping to reread what they have written, making changes and adding words, phrases, and sentences. After students finish their first draft, they reread it at least once to themselves and make some appropriate revisions. They may notice that some words were omitted as they wrote hastily or that too many sentences start with the word *It.* They may think of a better way to express an idea or discover that they need to check their facts. They make necessary changes before meeting with a writing group.

In the writing group, students share their rough drafts with a small group of classmates and get compliments and other comments from the students. These comments give students ideas for revising. Sometimes the teacher meets with the group; at other times students meet by themselves. It is crucial that students know how to conduct a writing group and how to give constructive suggestions to classmates. Many teachers have found that is is more effective for students to meet in a small group rather than with a partner because a group can provide more feedback than a single student can.

After sharing their compositions in a writing group, students make some revisions. They may choose to make revisions based on feedback they received from classmates in the writing group, or other ideas may come to mind. Some teachers have students use a blue pen to make revisions so that the revisions will stand out. Students should cross out and make revisions, not erase the original, so that the student and the teacher can track the child's use of revision strategies. Sometimes the revising stage leads to more prewriting and drafting; at other times, students move on to editing after they have made revisions.

During editing, students proofread their compositions to locate mechanical errors and then correct as many of the errors as they can. Many teachers have students use a red pen to make the corrections. Classmates can help proofread each other's papers, and students often meet with the teacher for an editing conference so the teacher can identify and correct any remaining errors.

After students' rough drafts have been edited, they make their final copies. Many times students compile their final copies to make books during writers' workshop, but sometimes they attach their writing to artwork, make posters, write letters that are mailed, or perform scripts as skits or puppet shows.

For the last 10 to 15 minutes of writers' workshop, the class gathers together to share their new publications and make other related announcements. A student who has just finished writing a puppet show script and making puppets may ask for volunteers to help perform the puppet show, which could be held several days later during sharing time. Younger students often sit in a circle or gather together on a rug for sharing time. If an author's chair is available, each student sits in the special chair to read his or her composition. After reading, classmates clap and offer compliments. They may also make other comments and suggestions, but the focus is on celebrating completed writing projects, not on revising the composition to make it better.

Sometimes teachers add a fourth component to writers' workshop in which they talk about authors of children's literature and read literature aloud to share examples of good writing with students. This activity also helps students to feel part of a community of writers. Teachers can also connect readers' workshop with writers' workshop.

Connecting with Readers' Workshop.   Teachers often use writers' workshop in conjunction with readers' workshop, as Mrs. Reeves did in the vignette at the beginning of the chapter. In readers' workshop, students have large chunks of time for reading and responding to literature and a choice about what they read. The components of readers' workshop often include the following:

1. *Independent Reading.* Students spend 30–60 minutes reading and responding to books and other reading materials.
2. *Minilessons.* The teacher spends 10–20 minutes teaching brief lessons on readers' workshop procedures, literary concepts, and reading strategies and skills.
3. *Sharing.* For the last 15 minutes of readers' workshop, the class gathers together to share books and response projects.

Just as writers' workshop fosters real writing for genuine purposes and authentic audiences, readers' workshop fosters real reading of self-selected stories, poems, and informational books. Teachers often connect the two, and students participate in many of the same types of activities.

The Thematic Approach

The second way elementary students use the writing process is during literature focus units and in social studies and science theme cycles. In these thematic projects, students respond to literature or apply what they are learning about social studies or science. Sometimes students choose their own writing projects related to a particular theme, or they might work on a project chosen by the class. For example, during an author study on Eric Carle, students might choose projects related to the author and his books; as part of a science theme on insects, the class might decide to make models of insects and write an encyclopedia with an entry about each insect. In either case, students use the writing process to develop and refine their compositions.

For thematic writings, a specific period of time is set aside for writing. After students read books or are introduced to concepts in social studies and science, students begin work on these writings. If students are working on different, self-selected projects, a period of time each day, usually 30 minutes to an hour, is set aside for students to work through the project. During this time, students move through the stages of the writing process. Teachers help students identify projects, keep track of students' progress, and provide information on the various types of activities students have selected; for example, the teacher might show the student how to write a description to accompany a diorama or how to format a letter being written to a favorite author.

If all students are working on the same project, the writing proceeds in a more uniform fashion. The teacher works with students to plan the writing project. Together they decide on the design of the project and the amount of time allowed for each stage of the writing process. The teacher keeps track of students' progress and helps students follow the design and keep up with the time schedule. The teacher also guides students as they move from one stage to the next in the writing process.

Components of the Thematic Approach. Writing projects usually span a week or two in which students move through all five stages of the writing process. The projects usually begin part way through the theme, after students have read relevant books or learned some key concepts. The preceding activities that are related to the theme serve as prewriting for the writing project. Then students work during the time allocated for the project to create a composition. Writers' workshop activities, including mini-lessons, independent writing, and sharing, are not set out; instead, students use the time period to work their way through the writing project, from prewriting to publishing and sharing.

Step
by
Step

1. *Prewriting.*   Students prepare for the writing project in several ways. The focus unit or theme activities provide students with background information. They also use words listed on the word wall and their literature journal or learning log entries as they gather ideas for writing. After the writing projects are identified, students choose a specific topic and writing form. Then they gather and organize ideas for writing, often using clusters and other charts or diagrams.

   After they have gathered and organized their ideas for writing, students usually conference with the teacher to share their plans. After the teacher approves them, students begin drafting.

2. *Drafting.*   Students use the ideas they developed during prewriting to pour out their ideas as they write their rough drafts. They focus on content rather than me- chanical correctness as they write, and they double-space their writing and mark their drafts as "rough drafts" or "sloppy copies." The teacher circulates during this stage, providing support and encouragement, often asking, "Tell me about your writing." The teacher monitors students' understanding of the project, including the purpose, audience, form, and topic.

3. *Revising.*   After students complete a draft of their writing projects, they move into the revising stage. Students reread their writing and add words they inadvertently omitted, delete redundant phrases, and make other revisions. Then they meet in writing groups to share their writing. Classmates listen to students read their rough drafts aloud and give compliments, comments, and suggestions on how well they are communicating. Students use this feedback to revise their composi- tions and make other changes to improve the quality of their rough drafts.

   Teachers often use a sign-up sheet on which students list their names when they are ready to meet in a writing group. When five or six students have signed up, they form a writing group. These groups are often formed on the basis of writ- ing speed, but sometimes students meet in already established writing groups. In that case, classmates help each other finish their rough drafts and get ready to meet because the whole group is held up until the last group member finishes drafting. Sometimes the teacher meets with the writing group, and sometimes not. It usually depends on whether the groups are meeting simultaneously or whether the teacher is busy working with individual students when the group is meeting.

4. *Editing.*   Next students turn their attention to identifying and correcting spelling, capitalization, punctuation, and other mechanical errors. Students proofread their own papers to identify errors and correct as many as they can. Teachers often have students use a red pen because it makes the job more fun and so correc- tions will stand out. Students frequently trade papers with a partner and proofread each other's papers to locate and correct more of the remaining errors. Then stu- dents usually meet with the teacher for a final editing.

5. *Publishing.*   Students make a final copy of their compositions, and the final cop- ies might be compiled into books, printed from a computer, or handwritten onto art projects. After students complete their projects, they share them with an appropri- ate audience. Often the audience is their classmates, but letters are mailed to in- dividuals, posters are displayed in the school lobby, and puppet shows are performed for other classes in the school.

Students move through the writing process stage by stage as a class when they are working on thematic projects, and teachers keep the process moving along. While the more lockstep nature of the approach has some drawbacks, it does have several significant benefits. Probably the most important benefit is that teachers have additional opportunities to teach writing forms and review writing procedures. Also, this approach ensures that students are more likely to finish their projects, and they have opportunities to apply what they are learning about literature, social studies, and science in meaningful writing projects.

Writing about Literature.   After reading, students explore and extend their response to literature through writing. A list of some of the ways that students can write in response to literature is presented in Figure 2-8. Young children often work in activity centers to complete a response-to-literature project selected from four or five differ-

FIGURE 2-8   *Some Ways of Responding to Literature Through Writing Projects*

1. Write a prequel (a book set earlier) or a sequel (a book that follows).
2. Build a table-top diorama of the book's setting, label it, and write an explanation.
3. Write a letter to a favorite author or illustrator.
4. Write an essay to compare the book and film made from it.
5. Make a map of the book's setting and write an explanation.
6. Write a poem about a character.
7. Identify a favorite quote from the book and explain why it was chosen.
8. Write a biographical sketch of the author or illustrator.
9. Write a rap about the book.
10. Rewrite the story from another point of view or in another setting.
11. Compare two characters using a Venn diagram and write an explanation.
12. Write an original book patterned on the structure of the book that was read.
13. Change a story into a script for a play or puppet show.
14. Write about an event in your life that is like an event in the book.
15. Research a topic related to the book and share the information in a report or poster.
16. Collect five items related to the book, put the collection in a box or can, and write an explanation.
17. Write a simulated letter to a character or subject of a biography to persuade him or her to take a certain action.
18. Write a poem using the chapter titles of the book.
19. Make a mural of the book and add captions.
20. Write several journal entries as one of the book's characters.
21. Write a newspaper with articles about events from the book.
22. Write a series of letters between two or more of the characters.
23. Create a series of pictures to use in retelling the book's story.
24. Construct a mobile about the book's theme.
25. Design your own writing project.

ent projects. Students choose which response project they want to pursue—for example, writing a book, constructing puppets, writing a character sketch, or writing a poem—and then they spend one, two, or three periods on the project. By second or third grade, students will have had experience with many different types of response activities, some that involve writing and others that do not, and are able to choose their own projects.

One generally successful response project is for students to write their own version of a favorite book. Books with repetitive patterns work well for this project. After a class of second graders read John Burningham's *Would You Rather . . .* (1978), students made their own books in which they offered readers a series of outrageous choices. One student's "Would You Rather . . ." book is presented in Figure 2-9. Like the original, this second grader's book spurs audience participation.

Sometimes several students work together on a project, but at other times every student in the class is working on a different project. Students in a sixth-grade class chose different projects to pursue after reading *Tuck Everlasting* (Babbitt, 1975). One boy chose to put together a story box. He brought a shoe box from home and decorated it with the title, scenes, and characters from the book. Then he collected four items related to the story and placed them in the box: a small bottle of water, Winnie's tombstone made from construction paper, a picture of a Ferris wheel, and a small music box. He wrote a paragraph-length composition explaining the book and the items in his box, and glued the final copy of the explanation into the inside of the box top. Here is his explanation:

▽   *Tuck Everlasting is an awesome book, and everyone should read it. The story is about life and how life is like a wheel. The wheel is supposed to keep turning from birth to death. But what happens if the wheel stops? It could if you drank magic water and you stopped getting any older. You would keep on living the same old way year after year after year. You would keep going back to the same old places while the rest of the world lived and died. You would finally learn that the lucky ones are the people who live and love and then grow old and die.*

This project demonstrates the depth of understanding that students can develop and display through writing projects. Writing is a powerful way of learning.

Writing as Part of a Theme.   Students use writing to extend learning in social studies or science theme cycles. They apply what they are learning by creating poems, reports, posters, and other projects. A list of projects is presented in Figure 2-10. As with literature focus unit projects, a class may choose to work on the same project, or students may choose different projects to work on in small groups or individually.

In an eighth-grade science class, students wrote picture books about scientific concepts and planned to donate the books to an elementary school. To develop these picture books, students used the writing process and worked through each of the five stages. Because they were publishing their books as picture books, students had an additional step. They had to break their revised and edited compositions into pages and design illustrations to accompany each page. They kept their audience in mind

FIGURE 2-9 *A Second Grader's "Would You Rather..." Book*

as they planned their books and were careful to explain concepts simply and draw easily interpreted illustrations. Figure 2-11 presents an excerpt from one student's picture book about solstices and equinoxes.

Variations for Young Children

Many teachers of young children find it necessary to adapt writers' workshop and the thematic project approach for use with their students. The three most important steps in the writing process for emerging writers are prewriting, drafting, and publishing. The revising and editing stages can be added when students begin to see value in

FIGURE 2-10 *Some Ways of Extending Understanding of Social Studies and Science Themes Through Writing Projects*

1. Write an "All about _____" book related to the theme.
2. Make a poster to share information.
3. Construct a mobile about important concepts.
4. Make a cluster, Venn diagram, or other chart to share important information.
5. Write a rap about the theme.
6. Build a table-top diorama related to the theme, label it, and write an explanation.
7. Write a letter to an organization, historical society, state tourism office, or business.
8. Read a biography about a personality and share information in a poem, poster, lifeline, or report.
9. Collect five items related to the theme, put the collection in a box or can, and write an explanation.
10. Write a simulated letter to the subject of a biography to persuade him or her to take a certain action.
11. Draw, color, and cut out a life-size picture of a scientific or historical personality and write a speech that person might give.
12. Make a mural about some aspect of the theme and add captions.
13. Write an essay to compare two concepts.
14. Make a map and write an explanation.
15. Write a poem about a topic or personality related to the theme.
16. Write several simulated journal entries as a person who lived during the time period studied.
17. Write a newspaper with articles about events related to the theme.
18. Create a series of pictures to tell about an event or teach a key concept.
19. Write and illustrate a picture book to teach an important concept.
20. Write a story set during the period studied or applying concepts learned during the theme study.
21. Interview someone with special knowledge about some aspect of the theme and share what is learned through the interview in a report, newspaper article, or poster.
22. Write a script for a play or puppet show.
23. Write about an event in your life that is like an event that was studied.
24. Research a topic related to the theme and share the information in a report or poster.
25. Design your own writing project.

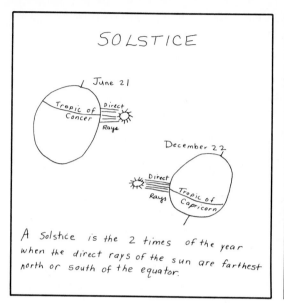

SOLSTICE

June 21

Tropic of Cancer
Direct Rays

December 22

Direct Rays
Tropic of Capricorn

A solstice is the 2 times of the year when the direct rays of the sun are farthest north or south of the equator.

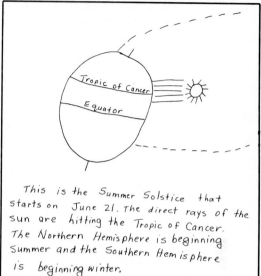

Tropic of Cancer
Equator

This is the Summer Solstice that starts on June 21. The direct rays of the sun are hitting the Tropic of Cancer. The Northern Hemisphere is beginning summer and the Southern Hemisphere is beginning winter.

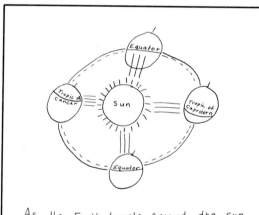

Equator

Tropic of Cancer

Sun

Tropic of Capricorn

Equator

As the Earth travels around the sun, the sun's rays hit the Earth's surface more directly in some places than others. This causes equinoxes and solstices.

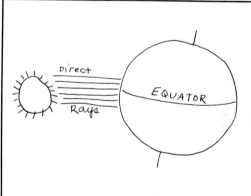

Direct Rays

EQUATOR

On March 21st the direct rays of the sun strike the equator. In the Northern Hemisphere spring begins.

FIGURE 2-11   *An Excerpt from an Eighth-Grader's Picture Book on Solstices and Equinoxes*

revising their writing to make it better, when they have moved from invented spelling toward more conventional spelling, and when they have been introduced to capitalization and punctuation rules.

Two ways to use the writing process with kindergartners and first graders (and older students who are emerging writers) is for students to write single-draft books using invented spelling and for teachers to transcribe books for students. Which procedure teachers use depends on their purpose for writing and the time and resources that are available.

Books with Invented Spelling.   Young children write single-draft books using invented spelling (spelling words according to the phonetic principles that the student knows). Students draw a series of pictures for a booklet and then write the text to accompany the pictures. The student may be able to read the book, but classmates and the teacher may have have difficulty deciphering the words or sentences, which may be strings of letters without any spaces between words. As students become more fluent writers, these books are easier for the writer and the rest of the class to read and reread.

The emphasis in these books is on encouraging students to be independent writers. Students sit in an author's chair to share their books with classmates, but because students use idiosyncratic invented spelling strategies, the books are not widely read by classmates. An excerpt from a child's book about dinosaurs which was written with invented spelling is presented in Figure 2-12. On the page shown in the figure, the

FIGURE 2-12   *An Excerpt from a First Grader's Book About Dinosaurs Written Using Invented Spelling*

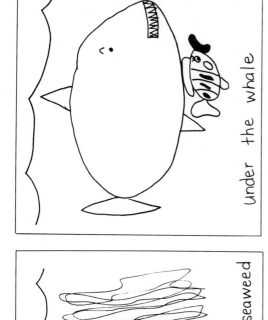

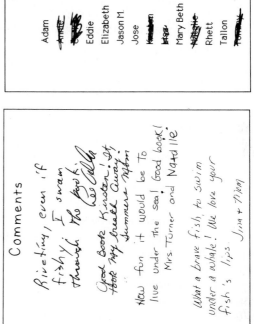

FIGURE 2-13 A First Grader's Transcribed Book Lisa the Fish

child wrote "Baby dinosaurs hatch from eggs." The drawing and the spacing between words make it easier to decipher the child's invented spellings.

Transcribed Books.   In transcribed books, young children write books that the teacher transcribes into conventional English for the final copy. Students draw pictures and write the first draft using invented spelling. Then the teacher (or another adult) prints or types the final copy, changing the invented spelling into conventional spelling and adding appropriate capital letters and punctuation marks. Sometimes teachers type the final copy using a word processor and print out very professional looking pages. Students bind the pages into a book and make new drawings for each page.

This approach is useful if students place the completed books in the class library for classmates to read or if the books are used as part of the reading program. A first grader's transcribed book, "Lisa the Fish," is presented in Figure 2-13. The teacher transcribed the student's invented spelling for the final copy and then the student added the illustrations. Two pages have been added to the back of the book. Next to the last page is a "Comments" page. Students and parents who read the book write compliments and other comments to the author. The last page is a list of the students in the class. After students read the book or take the book home to read with their parents, they cross off their name.

This second approach is much more time-consuming for both students and teachers. Students have to draw the illustrations twice and sometimes the second set of drawings is not as detailed as the first because students are tired or losing interest in the project. Also, teachers spend a lot of time preparing the final copies of the books.

As students' writing becomes more fluent and their spelling approaches conventional forms, students begin to make the transition to the five-stage writing process. Students show their readiness in several ways. They may want to do all the writing on both the rough draft and the final copy themselves, if the teacher has been writing the final copy, or if they have been doing their own writing, they may begin to squeeze revisions into their writing. Sometimes students mention how they might change part of a book and ask if they should start over. When students demonstrate an awareness of the need to refine the ideas in their writing and to correct mechanical errors, they are ready to move into the five-stage writing process. It is important that students see value in working through the process; otherwise, revision and editing will seem meaningless to them.

Answering Teachers' Questions About...
Instructional Approaches

1. *My students just aren't mature enough to use writers' workshop. What should I do?*

Some teachers complain that their students are uninterested in writing, inattentive in writing groups, or irresponsible about completing assignments. The best way to help these students become interested in and feel responsible for their writing is to use writers' workshop. When students make decisions about their writing, choose topics that are important to them, and share their writing with classmates, their behavior changes.

2. *Which instructional approach is better—writers' workshop or the thematic approach?*

Neither approach is better than the other. Both approaches are effective ways to teach writing, but they serve different purposes. Students need writers' workshop to become fluent writers and to have a chance to write about their own lives, experiences, and interests. Through thematic projects, students use writing to learn and to apply what they are learning in a specific class. It is important that teachers understand the purpose of each approach and plan activities to fit their goals.

3. *Can you use both approaches at the same time or should you pick one or the other?*

Yes, you can use both approaches at the same time. A regularly scheduled writers' workshop can be part of your language arts program, and you can also provide time for students to do projects as part of literature focus units and social studies and science theme cycles.

REFERENCES

Atwell, N. (1987). *In the middle: Writing, reading, and learning with adolescents.* Portsmouth, NH: Heinemann.

Babbitt, N. (1975). *Tuck everlasting.* New York: Farrar, Straus, & Giroux.

Burningham, J. (1978). *Would you rather . . .* New York: Crowell.

Calkins, L. M. (1986). *The art of teaching writing.* Portsmouth, NH: Heinemann.

Calkins, L. M. (1991). *Living between the lines.* Portsmouth, NH: Heinemann.

Cleary, B. (1981). *Ramona Quimby, age 8.* New York: Morrow.

Crafton, L. K. (1991). *Whole language: Getting started . . . moving forward.* Katonah, NY: Richard C. Owen.

Fine, E. S. (1987). Marbles lost, marbles found: Collaborative production of text. *Language Arts, 64,* 474–487.

Graves, D. (1983). *Writing: Teachers and children at work.* Portsmouth, NH: Heinemann.

Murray, D. M. (1990). *Shoptalk: Learning to write with writers.* Portsmouth, NH: Boynton/Cook.

Parry, J., & Hornsby, D. (1985). *Write on: A conference approach to writing.* Portsmouth, NH: Heinemann.

Sendak, M. (1963). *Where the wild things are.* New York: Harper & Row.

Van Allsburg, C. (1981). *Jumanji.* Boston: Houghton Mifflin.

Williams, V. B. (1982). *A chair for my mother.* New York: Mulberry.

Ziegler, A. (1981). *The writing workshop* (Vol. 1). New York: Teachers & Writers Collaborative.

3

Journal Writing

Overview of Journal Writing

Purpose   Students use journals to record personal experiences, explore reactions and interpretations, and record and analyze information.

Audience   The audience for journal writing is usually very limited. Sometimes the writer is the only audience. When the writer shares journal entries with others, these readers are typically well known and trusted.

Forms   Journal forms include personal journals, dialogue journals, reading logs, learning logs, and simulated journals. Students often write personal and dialogue journal entries in spiral-bound notebooks and other types of journal entries in small stapled booklets.

Topics   Topics for personal journals and dialogue journals come from students' own lives and are chosen by students themselves. Topics for reading logs come from books students are reading, and topics for learning logs are drawn from social studies, science, math, and other content areas. Students write simulated journals as characters in books they are reading and as historical personalities.

Approaches   Students write in personal and dialogue journals as part of writers' workshop and in reading logs as part of readers' workshop. They also write in journals as part of theme studies. They write in learning logs and simulated journals during theme cycles and in reading logs and simulated journals during literature focus units.

Responding in a Reading Log

Mrs. Wheatley asks her sixth graders, "Would you like to live forever?" After a lively discussion of the advantages and disadvantages of immortality, she becomes more specific and asks students to write their answers to this question: "If I offered you a drink of water from a magic spring that would allow you to stay the same age you are right now forever, would you drink it?" Veronica answers:

▽ *I think I would save the water until I finish college and started my career. Then I would drink it because I would like to know how the world would be in about 200 years, and if I lived forever I could become a very important person.*

After Veronica and her classmates share their writings, Mrs. Wheatley introduces the book she will read aloud to them, Natalie Babbitt's *Tuck Everlasting* (1975), the story of the Tuck family who unknowingly drank from a magic spring that stopped them from growing any older, a condition they found to have some surprising disadvantages. As the story begins, a young girl named Winnie comes upon the spring, and the Tucks kidnap her to keep her from drinking from it. Later, the Tucks explain to Winnie why they took her away from the spring, and their story is overheard by an evil man who plans to expose them and make a profit from selling the magic spring water. The Tucks must prevent the man from doing this or risk having everyone find out about them and their immortality.

Mrs. Wheatley explains that *Tuck Everlasting* is a "think-about" story, and she suggests that the students make reading logs in which they can write their thoughts about the story. Students then compile individual booklets of paper stapled together with construction paper covers which they decorate as Mrs. Wheatley begins reading the story. What the students have already written about drinking from the magic spring will become the first page in their logs. Like their impromptu writing about immortality, their other writings in this log will be informal and personal, written for and about themselves rather than for the teacher. They will be thinking on paper, she explains, because by writing about the story, they will understand it better.

Each day Mrs. Wheatley reads one or two chapters aloud, and after she reads students spend approximately 10 minutes writing an entry in their logs. Rather than having them simply summarize the chapter, she asks them to relate the story to their own lives and gives them this list of possible writing topics:

▼ Who is your favorite or least favorite character?
▼ Does one character remind you of a friend or family member?
▼ Does one character remind you of yourself?
▼ Do any of the events in this story remind you of your own life?
▼ What event would you have handled differently if you were the character?
▼ Does anything puzzle you about the story? If so, explain.
▼ Does the setting remind you of somewhere you have been?
▼ What do you like best or least about the story?
▼ How does this story make you feel?
▼ What other stories that you have read does this story remind you of?
▼ What would you change about this story, if you could?

After writing, some students will eagerly share their entries with the class, while others will keep their entries private. Excerpts from Veronica's reading log are presented below:

▽ Chapter 1:   I found the book quite boring although the author did use a lot of imagination in making the animals seem like real people.

Chapter 4:   At this point of the story I am beginning to like it a lot. My favorite character right now is Winnie. She seems like quite a little girl and the elf music I think is coming from Mae's music box. Winnie's grandmother seems pretty funny also.

Chapter 6:   Winnie has been kidnapped by the Tucks and you can tell she has a big imagination when you think about how she imagined the kidnappers. In a way I think she kind of enjoys this but as they go farther she begins to become more scared. Mae started playing the music box and the music was the same music her grandmother had told her was elf music.

Chapter 8:   indomitable—unstoppable
eddies of dust—small whirlpools or swirls
mirage—illusion, trick of eyes
I did notice the food they ate is rarely eaten today. I never really thought about chewing but now that I do think about it, it is kind of a personal thing. I don't really like people watching me chew.

Chapter 18: Right now in the story I like Jesse the best because he has big dreams and seems intent on making them come true. He's always looking at the bright side of things.

Chapter 22: Winnie is feeling really guilty about Mae so she is going to help them get her out of jail. If I was Winnie I think I might run away with them because they are really nice people and she has grown to love them. She would probably miss her family a lot but if she drank the water, they wouldn't have to worry about her getting hurt.

Chapter 24: I wish I was more like Winnie in a way. She is a very brave person and would do anything to help someone. "Stone walls do not a prison make" means there are other kinds of prisons besides rock walls and you can put yourself in a prison by shutting out others and not helping other people.

Epilogue: I think Tuck is happy that Winnie died and didn't have to live forever. I think it was neat that they saw the toad that lived forever. I liked the way the story ended but I kind of wanted Winnie to find Jesse and the Tucks and to drink the water and live forever.

Veronica's use of the first person pronoun *I* in this log demonstrates that she wrote about what she thought, what she liked, and what was meaningful to her. She didn't try to second-guess what author Natalie Babbitt intended or what Mrs. Wheatley thought. She wrote for herself. Also, Veronica used the log to note unfamiliar words and phrases (e.g., "eddies of dust" in Chapter 8) and sayings (e.g., "Stone walls do not a prison make" in Chapter 24).

After finishing the story, Mrs. Wheatley asks the students to respond again to the question, "If I offered you a drink of water from a magic spring that would allow you to stay the same age you are right now forever, would you drink it?" and Veronica writes:

▽ *If someone offered me some magic water that would let me live forever, I wouldn't take it because I believe if the Lord wanted us to live forever he would let us. And I wouldn't want to because forever is an awful long time.*

The about-face in Veronica's second response demonstrates the power of a reading log to stimulate thinking and verifies Toby Fulwiler's statement that "when people write about something they learn it better" (1987, p. 9). Having thought about immortality, Veronica has become less egocentric and more perceptive in her response.

*A*ll sorts of people—artists, scientists, dancers, politicians, writers, assassins, and children—keep journals (Mallon, 1984). In most of these journals, people record the everyday events of their lives and the issues that concern them. These journals, typically written in notebook form, are personal records, not intended for public display. Other journals might be termed "working journals" in which writers record observations and other information that will be used for another purpose. For example, farmers might record weather or crop data or gardeners the blooming cycle of their plants.

The journals of some well-known public figures have survived for hundreds of years and provide a fascinating glimpse of their authors and the times in which they lived. For example, the Renaissance genius Leonardo da Vinci recorded his daily activities, dreams, and plans for his painting and engineering projects in more than 40 notebooks. In the 1700s, Puritan theologian Jonathan Edwards documented his spiritual life in his journal. In the late 1700s, American explorers Meriwether Lewis and George Rogers Clark kept a journal of their travels across the North American continent, more for geographical than personal use. In the nineteenth century, the American writer Henry David Thoreau filled 39 notebooks with his essays. French author Victor Hugo carried a small pocket notebook to record ideas as they came to him, even at inopportune moments while talking with friends. American author F. Scott Fitzgerald filled his notebooks with snippets of conversation that he overheard, many of which he later used in *The Great Gatsby* and other novels. Anne Frank, who wrote while hiding from the Nazis during World War II, is the best-known child diarist.

Elementary students use journals for a variety of purposes, just as adults do. The focus is on the writer, and the writing is personal and private. Students' writing is spontaneous, loosely organized, and often contains many mechanical errors because students are focusing on thinking, not on spelling, capitalization, and punctuation. James Britton and his colleagues (1975) compare this type of writing to a written conversation, and that conversation may be with oneself or with trusted readers who are interested in the writer. Some of the purposes of a journal are to

▼ record experiences
▼ stimulate interest in a topic
▼ explore thinking

▼ personalize learning
▼ develop interpretations
▼ wonder, predict, and hypothesize
▼ engage the imagination
▼ ask questions
▼ activate prior knowledge
▼ assume the role of another person
▼ share experiences with trusted readers

Veronica and the other students in Mrs. Wheatley's sixth-grade class wrote for many of these purposes in their reading logs. Students wrote to activate prior knowledge when they wrote in response to Mrs. Wheatley's question about immortality before listening to a reading of the book; they wrote to record experiences, explore thinking, and develop interpretations when they made entries in their logs. In addition, they wrote to make learning personal as they related the experiences in *Tuck Everlasting* to their own lives.

This chapter focuses on the five types of journals that elementary students can write. In personal and dialogue journals, students record and share personal experiences and interests. They respond to books they read and write interpretations in reading logs and make notes in connection with social studies and science themes in learning logs. In simulated journals, students assume the role of a literary character or historical figure and write journal entries from that person's viewpoint. The chapter concludes with a section on teaching students to write in journals and ways to assess students' writing.

PERSONAL JOURNALS

Students can keep personal journals in which they recount the events in their lives and write about topics of their own choosing. These third graders' entries show the variety of topics students may choose. Kerry reviews the events of a school day:

▽   *I came to school and cleaned out my desk and got my work all done and put a layer on a pumpkin and went to lunch. On recess me, Rex, Ray and Tray got chased and then we came in and worked.*

Andrea tells about Thanksgiving vacation:

▽   *Yesterday was the end of Thanksgiving break. I went to the church crafts fair and they served soup. I got a gingerbread cookie and it was about 6 inches long. We had for Thanksgiving dinner: mashed potatoes, turkey, stuffing, sweet potatoes, pumpkin pie, Dutch apple pie, oregano beans, and water. We put up our Christmas tree. So far it has almost drunk a gallon of water and we have some presents.*

Micah describes a grandparent's death:

▽   *My PaPa had a heart attack by sitting down and he could not get up. My Grandma called the ambulance and I saw the people in the ambulance help. And he died.*

Michael shares a problem:

▽   *Today I made a friend an enemy, and I am glad of it, too. It all started about the beginning of the year. My brother and somebody else and me started a club, so the person that I am mad at was jealous. He started hanging around us and we didn't like it so we didn't pay attention to him. So yesterday he started a club. Today I talked some of his people in his club into being in my club. That's why he is mad at me and I am mad at him.*

Micah writes about his plans for the future:

▽   *I am going to be a golfer when I grow up. Now I can hit a golf ball almost 80 yards. My dad can hit a golf ball almost 300 yards. I go golfing almost every 2 months. And I might be a baseball player or a basketball player.*

And Jenna writes about a disappointment:

▽   *My class all got pen pals. My pen pal's name is Eric. He is 8½ years old and lives in Washington. See I wanted a girl but when I went up to Mrs. Carson she was fresh out of girls.*

An excerpt from another third grader's personal journal is presented in Figure 3-1. In this journal, Mandy ends each entry by saying good-bye as many children do; her arrangement of entries on the page seems unusual unless you know that her class writes a monthly newspaper which is formatted the same way.

Toby Fulwiler (1985) shared excerpts from his daughter Megan's third-grade journal in *Language Arts,* demonstrating how she used writing for many of these purposes. Then Megan Fulwiler (1986), now a teenager, reflected on her journal writing experience, and her reasons for writing are like those listed earlier. Most importantly, Megan described her journal as "an extension of my mind" that she used to "work out my feelings, ask questions, and find answers and write down and organize all my floating thoughts" (p. 809). She noted that as she grew up, her entries grew more personal and became a record of her growing up. Like Megan, students can gain valuable practice in writing through journal writing. They gain fluency and confidence that they can write. They also can experiment with new writing styles and formats without worrying too much about the conventions of writing that must be considered in more public writing. If they decide to make an entry "public," students can later revise and edit their writing.

Topics for Personal Journals

It is often helpful to list possible journal-writing topics on a chart in the classroom or on sheets of paper clipped inside each student's journal notebook. A list of possible journal-writing topics developed by a class of fourth and fifth graders is presented in Figure 3-2. Throughout the year, students may add topics to their list, which may include more than one hundred topics by the end of the school year. In personal journals students choose their own topics. Although they can write about almost

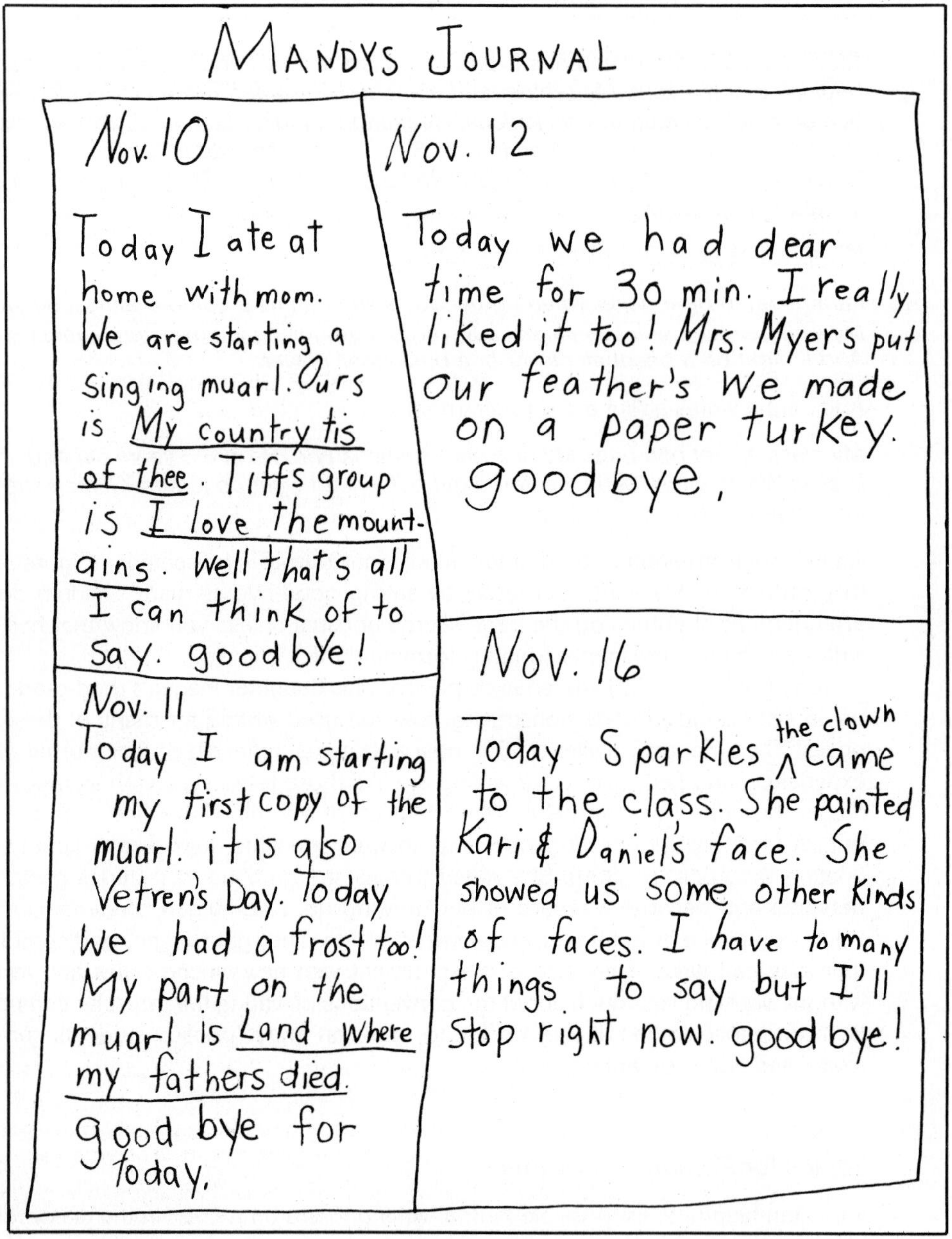

MANDYS JOURNAL

Nov. 10

Today I ate at home with mom. We are starting a singing muarl. Ours is <u>My country tis of thee</u>. Tiffs group is <u>I love the mountains</u>. Well thats all I can think of to say. good bye!

Nov. 11

Today I am starting my first copy of the muarl. it is also Vetren's Day. Today we had a frost too! My part on the muarl is <u>Land where my fathers died.</u> good bye for today,

Nov. 12

Today we had dear time for 30 min. I really liked it too! Mrs. Myers put our feather's we made on a paper turkey. good bye,

Nov. 16

Today Sparkles _{the clown} came to the class. She painted Kari & Daniel's face. She showed us some other kinds of faces. I have to many things to say but I'll stop right now. good bye!

FIGURE 3-1 *Entries from a Third Grader's Personal Journal*

FIGURE 3-2 *A List of Possible Personal Journal Topics*

my favorite place in town	if I had three wishes
boyfriends/girlfriends	my teacher
things that make me happy or sad	TV shows I watch
music	my favorite holiday
an imaginary planet	if I were stranded on an island
cars	what I want to be when I grow up
magazines I like to read	private thoughts
what if snow were hot	how to be a super hero
dreams I have	dinosaurs
cartoons	my mom/my dad
places I've been	my friends
favorite movies	my next vacation
rock stars	love
if I were a movie/rock star	if I were an animal or something else
poems	books I've read
pets	favorite things to do
football	my hobbies
astronauts	if I were a skydiver
the president	when I get a car
jokes	if I had a lot of money
motorcycles	dolls
things that happen in my school	if I were rich
current events	wrestling and other sports
things I do on weekends	favorite colors
a soap opera with daily episodes	questions answered with "never"
or ANYTHING else I want to write about	

anything, some students will complain that they don't know what to write about. A list of topics provides a crutch for students who believe they have nothing to write about. Referring students to the list or asking them to brainstorm a list of topics encourages them to become more independent writers and discourages them from becoming too dependent on teachers for writing topics.

Privacy is an important issue as students grow older. Most primary grade students are very willing to share what they have written, but by third or fourth grade some students become reluctant to share their writing with classmates. Usually they are willing to share their personal journal entries with a trusted teacher. Teachers must be scrupulous about protecting students' privacy and not insist that students share their writing. It is also important to require students to respect each other's privacy and not read each other's journals. To protect students' privacy, many teachers keep personal journals on a shelf out of the way when they are not being used.

When students share personal information with teachers through their journals, a second issue also arises. Sometimes teachers may learn details about students' problems and family life that they may not know how to deal with. Entries about child abuse, suicide, or drug use may be the child's way of asking for help. While teachers are not counselors, they do have a legal obligation to protect their students and report possible problems to appropriate school personnel. Occasionally a student may invent a personal problem in a journal entry as an attention-getting tactic. However, asking the student about the entry or having a school counselor do so will help to ensure that the student's safety is being fully considered.

DIALOGUE JOURNALS

Another approach to journal writing is the dialogue journal. In this approach, students and teachers, at any grade level, carry on a private conversation with each other through writing (Bode, 1989; Gambrell, 1985; Staton, 1980, 1987; Staton & Shuy, 1987). Dialogue journals are interactive, conversational in tone, and provide the opportunity for real student-teacher communication, something that is too often missing in elementary classrooms (Shuy, 1987). Each day students write informally to the teacher about something of interest or a concern, and the teacher responds. Students choose their own topics for writing and usually control the direction that the writing takes. Staton (1987) offers these suggestions for responding to students' writing and continuing the dialogue:

1. Acknowledge students' ideas and encourage them to continue to write about their interests.
2. Support students by complimenting their behavior and school work.
3. Provide new information about topics, so that students will want to read your responses.
4. Write less than the students do.
5. Avoid nonspecific comments like "good idea" or "very interesting."
6. Ask few questions; instead, encourage students to ask you questions.

Teachers' responses do not need to be lengthy; a sentence or two is often enough. Even so, it is very time-consuming for teachers to respond to 25 journal entries every day. Often teachers read and respond to students' journal entries on a rotating basis. They might respond to one group of students' writing one week and another group the next week.

In this fifth grader's dialogue journal, Daniel shares the events and problems in his life with his teacher, and she responds sympathetically. Daniel writes:

▽   *Over spring break I went down to my grandma's house and played basketball in their backyard and while we were there we went to see some of my uncles who are all Indians. Out of my whole family down there they are all Indians except Grandpa Russell.*

And Daniel's teacher responds:

▽   *What a fun spring break! That is so interesting to have Indians in your family. I think I might have some Indian ancestors too. Do you still plan to go to Padre Island for the summer?*

The next day Daniel writes:

▽ *My family and I plan to go to Padre Island in June and I imagine we will stay there for quite a while. I think the funnest part will probably be swimming or camping or something like that. When we get there my mom says we will probably stay in a nice motel.*

Daniel's teacher responds:

▽ *That really sounds like a fun vacation. I think swimming is the most fun, too. Who will go with you?*

Daniel continues to talk about his family, now focusing on the problems he and his family are facing:

▽ *Well, my mom and dad are divorced so that is why I am going to court to testify on Tuesday but my mom, me, and my sister, and brother are all going and that kind of makes me sad because a couple of years ago when my mom and dad were to-gether we used to go a lot of places like camping and hiking but now after what happened we hardly go anywhere.*

His teacher responds:

▽ *I am so sorry your family is having problems. It sounds as if your mom and dad are having problems with each other, but they both love you and want to be with you. Be sure to keep talking to them about how you feel.*

Daniel replies:

▽ *I wish my mom and dad did not have problems because I would have a lot more fun and get to go and do a lot more things together, but since my mom and dad are divorced I have to take turns spending time with both of them.*

His teacher offers a suggestion:

▽ *I'm sure that is hard. Trevor and Carla have parents who are divorced, too. Maybe you could talk to them. It might help.*

This journal is not a series of teacher questions and student answers. Instead, Daniel and his teacher are having a dialogue or conversation, and the interchange is built on mutual trust and respect. Another series of entries from a dialogue journal is presented in Figure 3-3. These entries are written by a second-grade learning disabled student and the student teacher working in her classroom.

Dialogue journals can also be used effectively to deal with students who are misbehaving or having any a problem in school (Staton, 1980). The teacher and student write back and forth about the problem. To begin, the teacher may ask the student to explain the problem and identify ways to solve it. In later entries, the student reflects on progress made toward solving the problem. The teacher responds to the student's message, asks clarifying questions, or offers sympathy and praise.

Joy Kreeft (1984) suggests that the greatest value of dialogue journals is that they bridge the gap between talking and writing; they are literally written conversations. A second value is the strong bond that develops between student and teacher as a

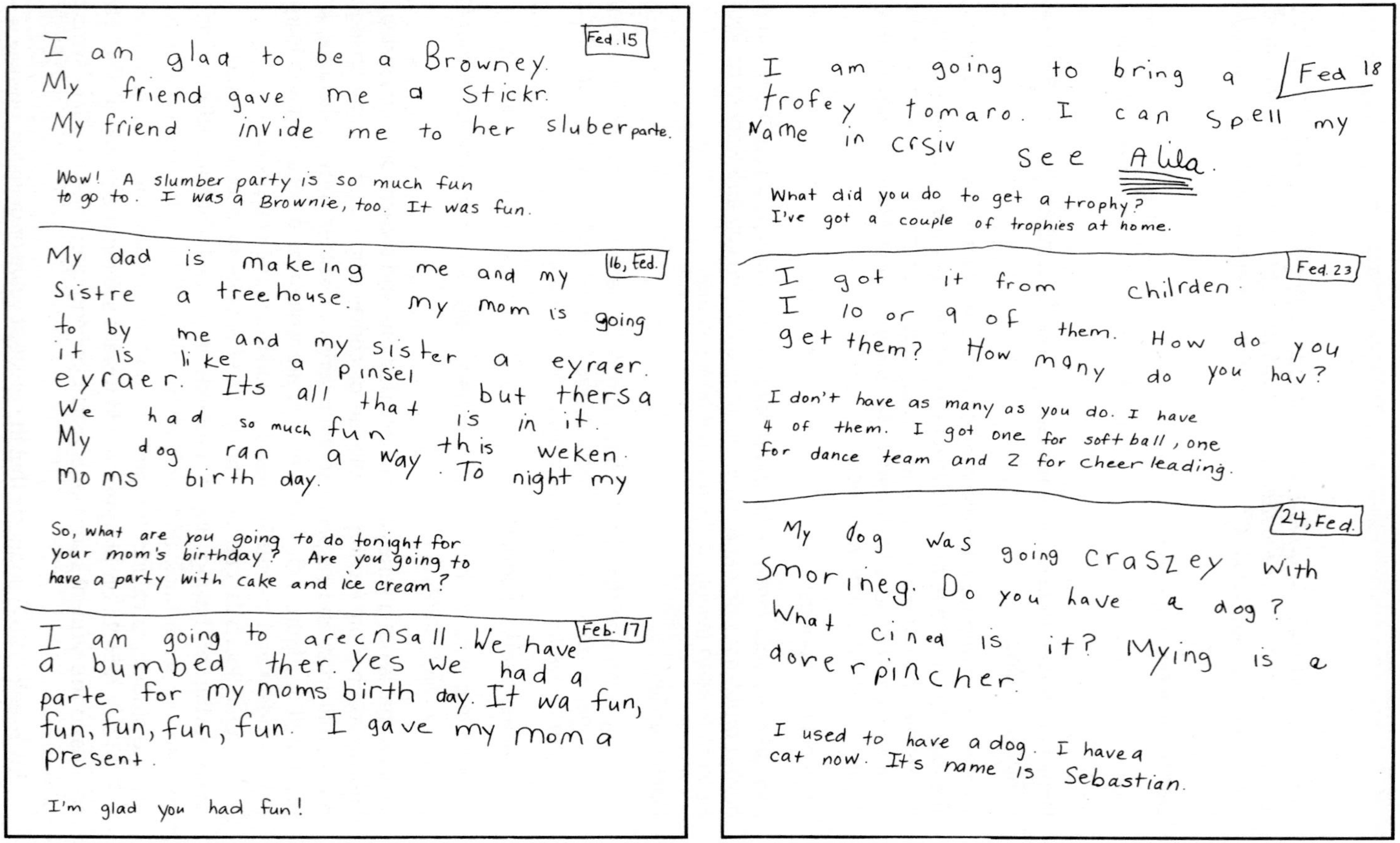

Feb. 18

I am going to bring a trofey tomaro. I can spell my name in crSiv See Alila

What did you do to get a trophy? I've got a couple of trophies at home.

Feb. 23

I got it from chilren. I 10 or 9 of them. How do you get them? How many do you hav?

I don't have as many as you do. I have 4 of them. I got one for soft ball, one for dance team and 2 for cheer leading.

24, Feb.

My dog was going craszey with smorineg. Do you have a dog? What cined is it? Mying is a dover pincher.

I used to have a dog. I have a cat now. It's name is Sebastian.

Feb. 15

I am glad to be a Browney. My friend gave me a stickr. My friend invide me to her sluberparte.

Wow! A slumber party is so much fun to go to. I was a Brownie, too. It was fun.

16, Feb.

My dad is makeing me and my Sistre a treehouse. My mom is going to by me and my sister a eyraer. It is like a pinsel eyraer. Its all that but thersa is in it. We had so much fun. My dog ran away this weken. To night my moms birth day.

So, what are you going to do tonight for your mom's birthday? Are you going to have a party with cake and ice cream?

Feb. 17

I am going to arecnsall. We have a bumbed ther. yes we had a parte for my moms birth day. It wa fun, fun, fun, fun. I gave my mom a present.

I'm glad you had fun!

FIGURE 3-3 Excerpts from a Second Grader's Dialogue Journal

result of writing to each other. Peyton and Seyoum conclude that "the success of the dialogue journal interaction lies precisely in the teacher's participation as an active partner in a meaningful, *shared* communication" (1989, p. 330).

Dialoguing with Limited English Proficient Students

Dialogue journals are especially effective in promoting the writing development of limited English proficient (LEP) students. Researchers have found that LEP students are more successful writers when they choose their own topics for writing and their teachers contribute to the dialogue with requests for a reply, statements, and other comments (Peyton & Seyoum, 1989; Reyes, 1991). Not surprisingly, students wrote more in response to teachers' requests for a reply than when teachers made comments which did not require a response. Peyton and Seyoum found that when a student was particularly interested in a topic, it was less important what the teacher did, and when the teacher and student were both interested in a topic, the topic seemed to take over as they shared and built on each other's writing. Reyes also found that bilingual students were much more successful in writing dialogue journal entries than in writing in response to books they had read.

Figure 3-4 presents an excerpt from a fourth grader's dialogue journal. This student is a native speaker of Lao and is learning English as a second language. In this entry, the fourth grader writes fluently about a trip to a county fair, recounting his activities there, and his teacher responds briefly to the account.

Dialoguing about Literature

Students can use dialogue journals to write to classmates or the teacher about books they are reading (Atwell, 1987; Barone, 1990; Dekker, 1991). In these journal entries, students write about the books they are reading, compare the books to others by the same author or others they have read, and offer opinions about the book and whether a classmate or the teacher might enjoy reading it.

This approach is especially effective in readers' workshop classrooms when students are each reading a different book independently. Students are often paired and they write back-and-forth to their reading buddies; this activity provides the socialization that independent reading does not. Depending on whether students are reading relatively short picture books or longer chapter books, students write dialogue journal entries every day or two or once a week, and then classmates write back.

READING LOGS

Students write in reading logs about the stories and other books they are reading during literature focus units and readers' workshop. As students read or listen to books read aloud, they respond to the book or relate it to events in their own lives as Veronica did in the *Tuck Everlasting* reading log described at the beginning of the chapter. Students can also list unfamiliar words, jot down quotable quotes, and take notes about characters, plot, or other elements of the story, but the primary purpose

Yesterday I went to the fair
with my brother-in-law and my brother,
sister my sister tell me to use the
three doller to get that big
miorrow so I use the three doller
but I only got one dart to
throw at the balloon then I hit
the balloon and I got a big
miorrow for my sister my brother-
in-law tell me to get one for my
brother-in-law so I got a biger one
then I give to my sister and
I got my self some tiket to
ride I went on the super sidle
and I got scard then I was
sitting and I jump up hight when
I was going down.
    You must have good aim to be able to
throw a dart and hit a balloon. I'm glad
you won some mirrors. Was this your first
trip to the fair?

FIGURE 3-4 *An Excerpt from a Fourth-Grade LEP Student's Dialogue Journal*

of these journals is for students to think about the book, connect literature to their lives, and develop their own interpretations. These journals go by a variety of names, including story journals (Farris, 1989), literature response journals (Hancock, 1992), literature journals (Five, 1986), and reading journals (Wollman-Bonilla, 1989), but no matter what they are called their purpose remains the same.

Teachers and researchers (Barone, 1990; Dekker, 1991; Hancock, 1992) have examined students' reading log entries and have identified these categories of response:

▼ Questions related to understanding the text
▼ Interaction with characters
▼ Empathy with characters

▼ Prediction and validation
▼ Personal experiences
▼ Personal feelings and opinions
▼ Simple and elaborated evaluations
▼ Philosophical reflections
▼ Retellings and summaries

For example, a primary grade student wrote this evaluative reading log entry (Barone, 1990, p. 39):

▽ *I just read* In a Dark, Dark Room [*Schwartz, 1984*]. *I like the story called "The Green Ribbon." I like the part where her head fell off.*

A middle grade student wrote this entry after reading the third chapter of *Summer of the Swans* (Byars, 1970); the focus is on personal opinions:

▽ *I think looks are not the most important thing because the way you act is. When some people look good and still act good—that's when people are really lucky, but I just think you should go ahead and appreciate the way you look.*

When students begin writing entries in reading logs, their first entries are often literal retellings and plot summaries, but as students gain experience reading and responding to literature, their entries become more interpretive and personal. Teachers can model writing "I think" reactions, share student entries that are interpretive, and respond to students' writing by asking questions.

Double-Entry Journals

A special type of reading log is the double-entry journal (Barone, 1990; Berthoff, 1981). Students divide their journal pages into two columns; in the left column they write quotes from the story or other book they are reading, and in the right column they relate each quote to their own life and literature they have read. Through this type of reading log, students become more engaged in what they are reading, note sentences that have personal connections, and become more sensitive to the author's language.

Students in a fifth-grade class kept a double-entry journal as they read C. S. Lewis's classic *The Lion, the Witch, and the Wardrobe* (1950). After they read each chapter, they reviewed the chapter and selected one, two, or three brief quotes. They wrote these excerpts in the left columns of their journals, and they wrote reactions beside each quote in the right columns. An excerpt from a fifth grader's journal is presented in Figure 3-5. This student's responses indicate that she is engaged in the story and connecting the story to her own life as well as to another story she has read.

Double-entry journals can be used in several other ways. Instead of recording quotes from the book, students can write "Reading Notes" in the left column and then add "Reactions" in the right column. In the left column students write about the events they read about in the chapter. Then they make personal connections to the events in the right column.

FIGURE 3-5   *An Excerpt from a Fifth Grader's Double Entry Journal about* The Lion, the Witch, and the Wardrobe

In the Text	My Response
Chapter 1 I tell you this is the sort of house where no one is going to mind what we do.	I remember the time that I went to Beaumont, Texas to stay with my aunt. My aunt's house was very large. She had a piano and she let us play it. She told us what we could do whatever we wanted to.
Chapter 5 "How do you know?" he asked, "that your sister's story is not true?"	It reminds me of when I was little and I had an imaginary place. I would go there in my mind. I made up all kinds of make-believe stories about myself in this imaginary place. One time I told my big brother about my imaginary place. He laughed at me and told me I was silly. But it didn't bother me because nobody can stop me from thinking what I want.
Chapter 15 Still they could see the shape of the great lion lying dead in his bonds.	When Aslan died I thought about when my Uncle Carl died.
They're nibbling at the cords.	This reminds me of the story where the lion lets the mouse go and the mouse helps the lion.

As an alternative, students can use the heading "Reading Notes" for one column and "Discussion Notes" for the second column. Students write reading notes as they read or immediately after reading. Later, after students discuss the story or chapter of a longer book, they add discussion notes. As with the other types of double-entry journals, it is in the second column that students make more interpretive comments.

Younger students can use the double-entry format for a prediction journal. They label the left column "Predictions" and the right column "What Happened." In the left column they write or draw a picture of what they predict will happen in the chapter before reading it. Then after reading, they draw or write what actually happened in the right column.

LEARNING LOGS

Students use learning logs to record or react to what they are learning in social studies, science, or math (Fulwiler, 1985). Students write in these journals to reflect on their learning, to discover gaps in their knowledge, and to explore relationships between what they are learning and their past experiences. According to Paulo Freire (1973), learning logs help students develop "critical consciousness"; they learn that knowledge must be constructed by learners, not passively received from teachers.

In Social Studies

Students often keep learning logs as a part of theme cycles in social studies. In their logs, students write in response to informational books, write vocabulary related to the theme, create timelines, and draw diagrams and maps. For example, as part of a study of the Pilgrims, middle grade students might include the following in their learning logs:

▼ Informal quickwrites about Pilgrims
▼ List of words related to the theme
▼ Chart comparing the Pilgrims of 1620 to modern-day pilgrims
▼ Timeline showing when groups of Pilgrims came to America
▼ Brainstormed list of questions to ask parents about how each student's family came to America
▼ Answers to these questions
▼ Map showing how family came to America
▼ Picture of the Statue of Liberty with labels for the various parts
▼ Notes from interviewing a recent immigrant to America
▼ Response to *Molly's Pilgrim* (Cohen, 1983)
▼ Response to *The Long Way to a New Land* (Sandin, 1981)
▼ Response to *. . . If You Sailed on the Mayflower in 1620* (McGovern, 1969)

Through these learning log activities, students explore concepts they are learning and record information they want to remember about the Pilgrims.

In Science

Science-related learning logs can take several different forms. One type of learning log is an observation log in which students make daily entries to track the growth of a plant or animal. Figure 3-6 presents first-grade Tyler's seed journal. In this journal, Tyler makes each entry on a new page. Drawing is as important as writing, and Tyler uses invented spelling. Because several pages are difficult for adults to decipher, the text on each page has been translated into standard orthography.

A second type of learning log is one in which students make daily entries during a unit of study. Students may take notes during a presentation by the teacher or a classmate, after viewing a film, or at the end of each class period. Sometimes students make entries in list form, sometimes in clusters or charts, and at other times in paragraphs.

A lab report is a third type of learning log. In these logs, students list the materials and procedures used in the experiment, present data on an observation chart, and then discuss the results. A fourth grader's lab report for an experiment with hermit crabs is presented in Figure 3-7.

3—27

we PlAt DIAlPlAt

(We planted a plant.)

3—30

we dUPthe PlAt
itは fAt

(We dug up the plant.
It is fat.)

4-1

we D u GUP
the UPThe
PAt it dIAl Not
CACAEC

(We dug up the plant.
It did not crack open.)

4—2

we DAG
UPThePLUt
itDID Mot
GRo

(We dug up the plant.
It did not grow.)

FIGURE 3-6 *A First Grader's Seed Log*

4-3

iT CRAt
OPN

(It cracked open.)

(We dug up the seed.
It grew a root.)

4 — 7

iT GoT F AtR
iTGR RoS

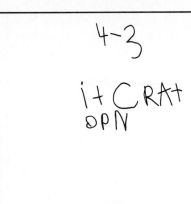

(It got fatter.
It grew roots.)

(The plant grew roots.
It grew leaves.)

FIGURE 3-6. continued

Lab Report

Do hermit crabs prefer a wet or dry habitat?

Materials
- trough
- trough cover
- 2 paper towels
- water sprinkler

Procedures
1. Put one wet and one dry paper towel in the trough.
2. Place the hermit crab in the center of the trough and put on the cover.
3. Wait 60 seconds.
4. Open the cover and observe the location of the hermit crab.
5. Mark the location on the observation chart.
6. Do the experiment 6 times.

Observation Chart

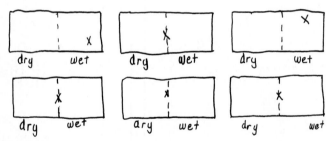

Results

Wet: 2
Dry: 0
Center 4

Our hermit crab liked the center part best. 4 out of 6 times it stayed in the center. Then it liked the wet part next best. It didn't like the dry part at all.

FIGURE 3-7 *A Fourth Grader's Lab Report*

In Math

Students also use learning logs to write about what they are learning in math (Salem, 1982). They record explanations and examples of concepts presented in class and react to any problems they may be having. Some upper-grade teachers allow students the last 5 minutes of math class to summarize the day's lesson and react to it in their learning logs (Schubert, 1987). Students write about what they have learned during class, the steps involved in solving a problem, definitions of mathematical terms, and things that confuse them. Writing in learning logs has several advantages over class discussion (Greesen, 1977). All students participate simultaneously in writing, and teachers can review written responses more carefully than oral ones. Also, students use mathematical vocabulary and become more precise and complete in their answers. They also learn how to reflect on and evaluate their own learning (Stanford, 1988).

Figure 3-8 presents an entry from a sixth grader's learning log in which she describes how to change improper fractions. Notice that after she describes the steps in sequence, she includes a review of the six steps.

In addition to the benefits to students, teachers use learning logs to informally assess student's learning. Through students' math entries, teachers

▼ assess what students already know about a concept before teaching
▼ help students integrate what they are learning and make the knowledge a part of their lives
▼ discover what students are really learning
▼ check on confusions and misconceptions
▼ monitor students' self-images and attitude toward math
▼ assess students' learning of a concept after teaching (McGonegal, 1987)

Sometimes teachers simply read these entries, and at other times the learning logs become dialogue journals as teachers respond to students by clarifying misconceptions and offering encouragement.

SIMULATED JOURNALS

In simulated journals students assume the role of another person and write from that person's viewpoint. As students read biographies or study social studies units, they can assume the role of a historical figure. As they read stories, they can assume the role of a character in the story. In this way, students gain insight into the lives of other people and into historical events. A series of diary entries written by fourth-grade Lisa, who has assumed the role of Betsy Ross, is presented below. Lisa chose the date for each entry carefully. She picked important dates in Betsy's life and wove factual information into each entry.

▽ *May 15, 1773*
Dear Diary,
    This morning at 5:00 o'clock I had to wake up my husband John to get up for work but he wouldn't wake up. I immediately called the doc. He came over as fast

Changing to Improper Fractions

To Change a mixed number such as: $5\frac{2}{3}$, you must must multiply the denominator, which is the bottom number, times the whole number which is 5. So now we have: $3 \times 5 = 15$, Next you add the numerator to the problem like this! $15 + 2 = 17$. Put the same denominater, the bottom number, and it should look like this! $\frac{17}{3}$. To check your answer, find out how many times 3, the bottom number, goes into the top number, 17. It goes in 5 times. There are two left over, so the answer is $5\frac{2}{3}$, It is correct.

6 Steps!

1. $5\frac{2}{3}$
2. $3 \times 5 = 15$
3. $15 + 2 = 17$
4. $\frac{17}{3}$
5. $3\overline{\smash{)}17}^{\,5\,\,2} = 5\frac{2}{3}$
6. $5\frac{2}{3}$ — Correct

FIGURE 3-8 *A Sixth Grader's Math Learning Log*

as he could. He asked me to leave the room so I did. An hour later he came out and told me he had passed away. I am so sad. I don't know what to do.

June 16, 1776
Dear Diary,
   Today General Washington visited me about making a flag. I was so surprised. Me making a flag! I have made flags for the navy, but this is too much. But I said yes. He showed me a pattern of the flag he wanted. He also wanted six-pointed stars but I talked him into having five-pointed stars.

July 8, 1776
Dear Diary,
   Today in front of Carpenter Hall the Declaration of Independence was read by Tom Jefferson. Well, I will tell you the whole story. I heard some yelling and shouting about liberty and everyone was gathering around Carpenter Hall. So I went to my next door neighbors to ask what was happening but Mistress Peters didn't know either so we both went down to Carpenter Hall. We saw firecrackers and heard a bell and the Declaration of Independence being read aloud. When I heard this I knew a new country was born.

June 14, 1777
Dear Diary,
   Today was a happy but scary day. Today the flag I made was adopted by Congress. I thought for sure that if England found out that a new flag was taking the old one's place something bad would happen. But I'm happy because I am the maker of the first American flag and I'm only 25 years old!

   Ira Progoff (1975) uses a similar approach, called "dialoging," in which students converse with a historical figure or other character in a journal by writing both sides of the conversation. He suggests focusing on a milestone in the person's life and starting the journal at an important point. A dialogue with Martin Luther King, for instance, might take place the day he gave his "I Have a Dream" speech in Washington, D.C.

YOUNG CHILDREN'S JOURNALS

   Teachers have used journals effectively with preschoolers, kindergartners, and other young children who are emergent readers or who have not yet learned to read (Elliott, Nowosad, & Samuels, 1981; Hipple, 1985; Nathan, 1987). Young children's journal entries include drawings as well as some type of text. Children may write scribbles, random letters and numbers, simple captions, or extended texts using invented spelling. These invented spellings often seem bizarre by adult standards but are reasonable in terms of children's knowledge of phoneme-grapheme correspondences and spelling patterns. Other children want parents and teachers to take their dictation and write the text. After the text is written, children can usually read it immediately, and they retain recognition of the words several days later.
   Four journal entries made by kindergartners are presented in Figure 3-9. In his journal entry, Brandon focuses on the illustration, drawing a detailed picture of a football game (note that the player in the middle right position has the ball), and adds

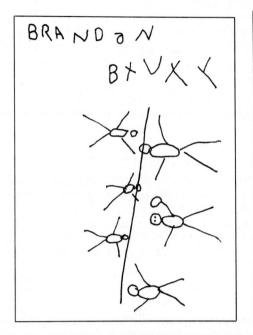

FIGURE 3-9 *Entries from Young Children's Journals*

five letters for the text so his entry will have some writing. Becky's entry is about her dog, and she writes a text vertically to accompany her illustration. She writes the first letter (or an important letter) in each word, except that she writes the entire word *dog* because she knows how to spell it. Becky reads her text this way: "My mother would like our black dog very much." Jessica and Marc's entries are more similar to personal journal entries because they describe events in the five-year-olds' lives. Jessica writes, "I spent the night at my dad's," and her picture shows her sleeping at her dad's house. Marc writes that "I'm going to be a phantom for Halloween" and draws a picture of himself in his Halloween costume going trick-or-treating.

Journal writing takes a variety of different forms and can be used for a number of purposes, but through each type of journal elementary students discover the power of writing in recording information and exploring ideas. Students usually cherish their informal journals and are amazed by the amount of writing they contain.

TEACHING STUDENTS TO WRITE IN JOURNALS

Journals are typically written in notebooks. Spiral-bound notebooks are used for long-term personal and dialogue journals and writing notebooks, while small booklets of paper stapled together are more often used for learning logs and simulated journals. Students often decorate the covers of these short-term journals as Mrs. Wheatley's students did with their reading logs for *Tuck Everlasting.* Most teachers prefer to keep the journals in the classroom so they will be available for students to write in each day.

Students usually write in journals at a particular time each day. Many teachers have students make personal or dialogue journal entries while they take attendance or immediately after recess. Learning logs and simulated journals can be written in as part of a daily assignment or as part of social studies or science class. For example, students may go over to an incubator of quail eggs, observe them, and then make an entry in their learning log during their daily language arts time. Students who are writing simulated journals as part of a social studies unit on the Crusades might make their entries during language arts time or during social studies class.

Introducing Students to Journal Writing

Teachers introduce students to journal writing using minilessons in which they explain the purpose of the journal-writing activity and procedures for gathering ideas, writing in a journal, and sharing with classmates. Teachers often model the procedure by writing a sample entry on the chalkboard or on chart paper as students observe. This sample demonstrates that the writing is to be informal, with content being more important than mechanics. Then students make their own first entries, and several read their entries aloud. Through this sharing, students who are still unclear about the writing activity have additional models on which to base their own writing.

Similar procedural minilessons are used to introduce each type of journal. While all journals are informal, the purpose of the journal, the information included in the entry, and the point of view of the writer vary according to the type of journal.

FIGURE 3-10 *Books in Which Characters and Historical Personalities Keep Journals*
P = primary grades (K–2); M = middle grades (3–5); U = upper grades (6–8)

Anderson, J. (1987). *Joshua's westward journal.* New York: Morrow. (M)

Avi. (1991). *Nothing but the truth.* New York: Orchard. (M–U)

Blos, J. (1979). *A gathering of days: A New England girl's journal, 1830–1832.* New York: Scribner. (U)

Bourne, M. A. (1975). *Nabby Adams's diary.* New York: Coward. (U)

Cleary, B. (1983). *Dear Mr. Henshaw.* New York: Morrow. (M)

Cleary, B. (1991). *Strider.* New York: Morrow. (M)

Conrad, P. (1991). *Pedro's journal: A voyage with Christopher Columbus (August 3, 1492–February 14, 1493).* Honedale, PA: Boyds Mills Press. (M–U)

Crusoe, R. (1972). *My journals and sketchbooks.* New York: Harcourt Brace Jovanovich. (U)

Fisher, L. E. (1972). *The death of evening star: Diary of a young New England whaler.* New York: Doubleday. (M–U)

Fitzhugh, L. (1964). *Harriet the spy.* New York: Harper & Row. (M)

Frank, A. (1952). *Anne Frank: The diary of a young girl.* New York: Doubleday. (U)

George, J. C. (1959). *My side of the mountain.* New York: Dutton. (M–U)

Glaser, D. (1976). *The diary of Trilby Frost.* New York: Holiday House. (U)

Harvey, B. (1986). *My prairie year: Based on the diary of Elenore Plaisted.* New York: Holiday House. (M)

Harvey, B. (1988). *Cassie's journey: Going west in the 1860s.* New York: Holiday House. (M)

Leslie, C. W. (1991). *Nature all year long.* New York: Greenwillow. (M)

Lowry, L. (1986). *Anastasia has the answers.* Boston: Houghton Mifflin. (M)

Mazer, N. F. (1971). *I, Trissy.* New York: Delacorte. (U)

Oakley, G. (1987). *The diary of a church mouse.* New York: Atheneum. (M)

Orgel, D. B. (1978). *The devil in Vienna.* New York: Dial. (U)

Reig, J. (1978). *Diary of the boy king Tut-Ankh-Amen.* New York: Scribner. (M)

Roop, P., & Roop, C. (Eds.). (1990). *I Columbus: My journal 1492–1493.* New York: Avon Books. (M–U)

Roth, S. L. (1990). *Marco Polo: His notebook.* New York: Doubleday. (M–U)

Sachs, M. (1975). *Dorrie's book.* New York: Doubleday. (M)

Smith, R. K. (1987). *Mostly Michael.* New York: Delacorte Press. (M)

Van Allsburg, C. (1991). *The wretched stone.* Boston: Houghton Mifflin. (M–U)

Wilder, L. E. (1962). *On the way home.* New York: Harper & Row. (M)

Williams, V. B. (1981). *Three days on a river in a red canoe.* New York: Greenwillow. (P–M)

Journal writing can also be introduced with examples from literature. Characters in children's literature, such as Harriet in *Harriet the Spy* (Fitzhugh, 1964), Leigh in *Dear Mr. Henshaw* (Cleary, 1983), and Catherine Hall in *A Gathering of Days* (Blos, 1979), keep journals in which they record the events in their lives, their ideas, and dreams. A list of books in which characters and historical personalities keep journals is presented in Figure 3-10. In these books, the characters demonstrate the process of journal writing and illustrate both the pleasures and difficulties of keeping a journal (Tway, 1981). A good way to introduce journal writing is by reading one of these books.

Sustaining Journal Writing

Students write in journals on a regular schedule, usually daily. Once students know how to write the type of entry, they write independently. While some children prefer to write private journals, others will volunteer to read their journal entries aloud each day no matter what type of journal they are writing. Young children share their picture journal entries and talk about them. If the sharing becomes too time-consuming, several children can be selected each day on a rotating basis to share. Teachers and classmates may offer compliments about the topic, word choice, humor, and so on.

Students can select entries from their journals and develop them into polished compositions if they wish. However, the journal entries themselves are rarely revised and edited because the emphasis is on writing fluency and self-expression rather than on correct spelling and neat handwriting.

Students may continue to write in personal journals throughout the school year while their writing in other types of journals starts and stops with particular literature focus units and theme cycles. Sometimes students seem to lose interest in personal journals. If this happens, many teachers find it useful to put the journals away for several weeks and substitute another type of journal or free reading in lieu of personal journals.

Assessing the Journals Students Write

Students can write in journals independently with little or no sharing with the teacher, or they can make daily entries that the teacher monitors or reads regularly (Tway, 1984). Typically, students are accustomed to having teachers read all or most of their writing, but the quantity of writing that students produce in their journals is often too great for teachers to keep up with. Some teachers try to read all entries, while others read selected entries and monitor remaining entries. Still others rarely check their students' journals. These three management approaches can be termed private journals, monitored journals, and shared journals. When students write private journals, they write primarily for themselves, and sharing with classmates or the teacher is voluntary. The teacher does not read the journals unless invited to do so by students. When students write monitored journals, they write primarily for themselves, but the teacher monitors the writing to ensure that entries are being made on a regular basis. The teacher may simply check that entries have been made and not read the entries unless they are specially marked "Read me." When students write shared journals, they write primarily for the teacher. The teacher regularly reads all entries except for those personal journal entries marked "Private" and offers encouragement and suggestions.

How to grade journal entries is a concern. Because the writing is informal and usually not revised and edited, teachers should not grade the quality of the entries. One option is to give points for each entry made, especially with personal journals. For learning logs and simulated journals, though, some teachers grade the content because they can check to see if particular pieces of information are included in the entries. For example, when students write simulated journals about the Crusades, students can be asked to include five pieces of historically accurate information in their entries. (It is often helpful to ask students to identify the five pieces of information by underlining or highlighting them.) Rough draft journal entries should not be graded for mechanical correctness. Students need to complete the writing process and revise and edit their entries if they are to be graded for mechanical correctness.

Answering Teachers' Questions About . . . Journal Writing

1. *Sometimes my fourth graders get tired of writing in their personal journals. What can I do?*

Many teachers report this problem. During the first month or two of the school year, students are eager to write in their journals and then they get tired of it. There are several things you might try. First, you can alternate journal-writing with independent reading activities so that students only write every other day in their journals, or give students a choice of reading a book or writing in their journal during this time. Second, change from personal journals to dialogue journals. Corresponding with you might add new interest to journal-writing activities. Third, read aloud a book in which the main character keeps a journal, such as Beverly Cleary's *Dear Mr. Henshaw* (1983) (check the list of suggested books in Figure 3-10), and ask students to reflect on their journal-writing activities by comparing them to the character's.

2. *How does quickwriting differ from personal journals? They seem like the same thing to me.*

You're right. These two types of personal writing are very similar, and the differences between them can be confusing. Quickwriting is a specific strategy that students use to write more fluently. They can use quickwriting to write a journal entry, but they can use it for other informal writing activities as well. In contrast, a personal journal is a place where students write informally for themselves about almost any topic. They may use quickwriting or any other approach to writing these entries.

3. *Which type of journal should I use with my fifth-grade class?*

Choosing a type of journal depends on your purpose for having your students keep journals. If you want your students to develop writing fluency, or if this is your students' first experience with journals, the personal journal is a good choice. If you want your students to gain writing practice and you also want to get to know your students better, you might try dialogue journals. In connection with your literature focus units, try reading logs. If you want to use journals in content area classes, learning logs or simulated journals are two options. Many teachers have students keep personal (or dialogue) journals and reading logs in separate notebooks throughout the school year and have them staple together booklets of paper for learning logs and simulated journals for theme cycles or other units.

4. *I have to disagree with you about not correcting errors in students' journals. I'm a teacher and it's my job to correct students' spelling, capitalization, punctuation, and other errors.*

Many teachers agree with you, and it's difficult for me to ignore many of the errors I see in students' journal entries. But what

good would the corrections do? Would the effect of your corrections be to teach students how to spell or use punctuation marks correctly; or would your overemphasis on correctness convince students that they're "no good at this writing thing," a conclusion that causes many students to stop writing? Many teachers have found that focusing on students' mechanical errors rather than on the content of their writing teaches students that correctness is more important than meaning, and that is just not true. Journal entries are a form of personal and private writing, in contrast to public writing in which mechanical correctness counts. In more formal types of writing, mechanics do count, and through the writing process students learn to identify and correct their mechanical errors. If you focus on errors in students' journals, you are defeating the purpose of informal writing.

REFERENCES

Atwell, N. (1987). *In the middle: Writing, reading, and learning with adolescents.* Portsmouth, NH: Heinemann.

Babbitt, N. (1975). *Tuck everlasting.* New York: Farrar.

Barone, D. (1990). The written responses of young children: Beyond comprehension to story understanding. *The New Advocate, 3,* 49–56.

Berthoff, A. (1981). *The making of meaning.* Upper Montclair, NJ: Boynton/Cook.

Blos, J. (1979). *A gathering of days: A New England girl's journal, 1830–1832.* New York: Scribner.

Bode, B. A. (1989). Dialogue journal writing. *The Reading Teacher, 42,* 568–571.

Britton, J., Burgess, T., Martin, N., McLeod, A., & Rosen, H. (1975). *The development of writing abilities (11–18).* London: Macmillan.

Byars, B. (1970). *Summer of the swans.* New York: Viking.

Cleary, B. (1983). *Dear Mr. Henshaw.* New York: Morrow.

Cohen, B. (1983). *Molly's pilgrim.* New York: Lothrop, Lee & Shepard.

Dekker, M. M. (1991). Books, reading, and response: A teacher-researcher tells a story. *The New Advocate, 4,* 37–46.

Elliott, S., Nowosad, J., & Samuels, P. (1981). "Me at home," "me at school": Using journals with preschoolers. *Language Arts, 58,* 688–691.

Farris, P. J. (1989). Story time and story journals: Linking literature and writing. *The New Advocate, 2,* 179–185.

Fitzhugh, L. (1964). *Harriet the spy.* New York: Harper and Row.

Five, C. L. (1986). Fifth graders respond to a changed reading program. *Harvard Educational Review, 56,* 395–405.

Freire, P. (1973). *Education for critical consciousness.* New York: Continuum.

Fulwiler, M. (1986). Still writing and learning, grade 10. *Language Arts, 63,* 809–812.

Fulwiler, T. (1985). Writing and learning, grade 3. *Language Arts, 62,* 55–59.

Fulwiler, T. (1987). *The journal book.* Portsmouth, NH: Boynton/Cook.

Gambrell, L. B. (1985). Dialogue journals: Reading-writing interaction. *The Reading Teacher, 38,* 512–515.

Greeson, W. E. (1977). Using writing about mathematics as a teaching technique. *Mathematics Teacher, 70,* 112–115.

Hancock, M. R. (1992). Literature response journals: Insights beyond the printed page. *Language Arts, 69,* 36–42.

Hipple, M. L. (1985). Journal writing in kindergarten. *Language Arts, 62,* 255–261.

Kreeft, J. (1984). Dialogue writing—Bridge from talk to essay writing. *Language Arts, 61,* 141–150.

Lewis, C. S. (1950). *The lion, the witch, and the wardrobe.* New York: Macmillan.

Mallon, T. (1984). *A book of one's own: People and their diaries.* New York: Ticknor & Fields.

McGonegal, P. (1987). Fifth-grade journals: Results and surprises. In T. Fulwiler (Ed.), *The journal book* (pp. 201–209). Portsmouth, NH: Boynton/Cook.

McGovern, A. (1969). *. . . If you sailed on the Mayflower in 1620.* New York: Scholastic.

Nathan, R. (1987). I have a loose tooth and other unphotographic events: Tales from a first-grade journal. In T. Fulwiler (Ed.), *The journal book* (pp. 187–192). Portsmouth, NH: Boynton/Cook.

Peyton, J. K., & Seyoum, M. (1989). The effect of teacher strategies on students' interactive writing: The case of dialogue journals. *Research in the Testing of English, 23,* 310–334.

Progoff, I. (1975). *At a journal workshop: The basic text and guide for using the intensive journal process.* New York: Dialogue House.

Reyes, M. de la L. (1991). A process approach to literacy using dialogue journals and literature logs with second language learners. *Research in the Teaching of English, 25,* 291–313.

Salem, J. (1982). Using writing in teaching mathematics. In M. Barr, P. D'Arcy, & M. K. Healy (Eds.), *What's going on? Language/learning episodes in British and American classrooms, grades 4–13,* (pp. 123–134). Montclair, NJ: Boynton/Cook.

Sandin, J. (1981). *The long way to a new land.* New York: Harper & Row.

Schubert, B. (1987). Mathematics journals: Fourth grade. In T. Fulwiler (Ed.), *The journal book* (pp. 348–358). Portsmouth, NH: Boynton/Cook.

Schwartz, A. (1984). *In a dark, dark room.* New York: Harper & Row.

Shuy, R. W. (1987). Research currents: Dialogue as the heart of learning. *Language Arts, 64,* 890–897.

Stanford, B. (1988). Writing reflectively. *Language Arts, 65,* 652–658.

Staton, J. (1980). Writing and counseling: Using a dialogue journal. *Language Arts, 57,* 514–518.

Staton, J. (1987). The power of responding in dialogue journals. In Toby Fulwiler (Ed.), *The journal book* (pp. 47–63). Portsmouth, NH: Boynton/Cook.

Staton, J., & Shuy, R. W. (1987). Talking our way into writing and reading: Dialogue journal practice. In B. Rafoth & D. Rubin (Eds.), *The social construction of written communication.* Norwood, NJ: Ablex.

Tway, E. (1981). Come, write with me. *Language Arts, 58,* 805–810.

Tway, E. (1984). *Time for writing in the elementary school.* Urbana, IL: ERIC Clearinghouse on Reading and Communication Skills and the National Council of Teachers of English.

Wollman-Bonilla, J. E. (1989). Reading journals: Invitations to participate in literature. *The Reading Teacher, 43,* 112–120.

4

Descriptive Writing

Overview of Descriptive Writing

Purpose Students use descriptive writing to paint word pictures and to make writing more concrete or vivid by adding specific information, sensory images, comparisons, and dialogue.

Audience Students use descriptive writing when they write for themselves in learning logs and when they use the writing process to write compositions for wider audiences.

Forms Students use descriptive writing in learning logs and quickwrites, and they use descriptive techniques in more sophisticated compositions, including stories, reports, and poems.

Topics Description is used in writing about a variety of topics. Students write descriptions of events in their own lives, characters from literature, results of experiments, observations of classroom animals, art prints, historical events and personalities, and current events.

Approaches Students use descriptive techniques to make their writing more interesting in both theme studies and writers' workshop. As part of theme studies, they write lists of attributes and observations in science learning logs and character descriptions in reading logs. Students incorporate descriptions into reports and essays, and many times, they carefully craft specific information and sensory images into the poems they write. Students also use description in personal narratives and other compositions they write during writers' workshop.

Writing Vivid Descriptions

The sixth graders in Mrs. Ochs's class are studying life in ancient Egypt. Their study occupies much of the school day because language arts and social studies are integrated into a theme cycle. The students in Mrs. Ochs's class read books about life in ancient Egypt, and they write in response to their reading. The type of response varies—it may be a simulated journal or learning log, an essay or report, a biography, or a simulated letter. Students work cooperatively in small groups on projects that may involve reading, writing, talking, art, music, and drama in addition to social studies. Students learn language arts and writing strategies and skills as they need them to respond to their reading or work on their projects. These are some of the specific activities:

▼ Students read informational books and keep a reading log.
▼ Each student researches an Egyptian god or goddess and makes a poster to share the information.
▼ Mrs. Ochs reads *The Egypt Game* (Snyder, 1967) aloud to the students, a chapter or two a day.
▼ Students work in small groups on various projects. One group creates a salt map of ancient Egypt; one dresses dolls in clothes like those worn by ancient Egyptians; one makes a timeline, chronicling the major events in the period; another designs a chart of hieroglyphic symbols.

One day several students share with the class what they have learned about Howard Carter's discovery of King Tut's tomb in 1922 from *In Search of Tutankhamun* by Piero Ventura and Gian Paolo Ceserani (1985). Mrs. Ochs capitalizes on the class's interest and shows a videotaped film of Carter's discovery that she rented from a local video store. Several students express the wish that they could have been with Carter when the tomb was discovered. They discuss what this would have been like. The students' interest gives Mrs. Ochs an idea: She asks if the students would like to write a first-person "I was with Howard Carter" narrative of the discovery. Are the students interested? You bet they are!

Mrs. Ochs suggests that their writing, like the film, evoke a strong mood and focus on the description of the tomb. To gather words and ideas for writing, she and the students create a five senses cluster on the chalkboard in which they brainstorm words for the sights, sounds, smells, tastes, and feelings they might have experienced as they entered the tomb. A copy of this collaborative cluster is presented in Figure 4-1. Taste was the most difficult sense for the students because the explorers did not eat in the tomb, but students recognized that the explorers might have tasted dryness, sandy grit, and even fear. The feel sense evoked perhaps the most powerful images as students suggested that the explorers might have felt guilt about their trespassing.

With the background of knowledge gained from the unit on ancient Egypt and the clustering experience, students write the rough draft of their first-person narratives. After students finish their rough drafts, they meet in groups to share their writing. Mrs. Ochs asks students to focus on the mood created in the writing and the use of description as writing-group members comment about each other's writings.

In his writing group, Josh reads first:

▽ *It was November 1922 and I was in Egypt with Howard Carter. We had uncovered one step in the Sahara Desert and then 15 more leading downward. As Howard and I walked down we heard the echo of our footsteps. When we got to the bottom we*

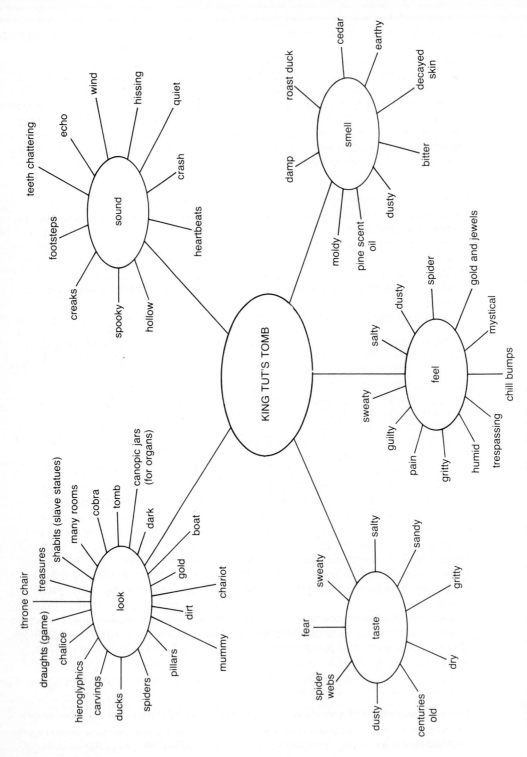

FIGURE 4-1 A Collaborative Cluster Describing King Tut's Tomb

could not see our hands nor each other. I called, "Are you there, Howard?" And he called, "Yes." Both our voices echoed.

As we waited for our eyes to adjust to the darkness we listened. It was quiet, so quiet. I could hear my heartbeat, and I think Howard could hear his too.

My eyes had adjusted and I was amazed at what I saw. There was gold and jewels everywhere. There was a boat and a chariot. There were canopic jars, statues, tools, some kind of gameboards that looked like chess, and a child-size throne chair.

Suddenly it hit me. I turned around and there it was—Tut's tomb!

There is a silence and then his writing group members beg, "Read it again." Josh willingly reads his piece a second time, this time more dramatically. When he finishes, Matt says, "I've got chill bumps like I was with Howard Carter. That's my compliment." Then Amber tells Josh she liked the part about hearing his heartbeat, and Becky Lee says she liked the dialogue.

Next it is Josh's turn, as the writer, to ask a question. He asks if his classmates think he included enough details as Mrs. Ochs suggested. They count the details from the cluster that he included and after they reach 10, they quit counting and conclude that he did.

Finally, Josh asks the writing group members for suggestions to improve his writing. "I think you should keep writing and get to the part about the cobra," suggests Matt. "That's the best part and you could give it a lot of mood!" Becky Lee suggests that Josh call the game by its real name *draughts* instead of describing it and saying it was like chess. Josh agrees to continue writing but explains to Becky Lee that he didn't name the game on purpose because if he was just exploring with Howard Carter, not studying Egypt in sixth grade, he might not know the name!

The other students take turns sharing their rough drafts, listening to compliments and suggestions from the writing-group members, and asking questions themselves. After everyone in the group has shared, they move back to their desks to make revisions. Later, they will edit and recopy their "I was with Howard Carter" writings and add them to a bulletin board display about King Tut.

D escriptive writing is painting pictures with words. Students need to be keen observers, attentive to sensory images, as Mrs. Ochs' students were when they wrote about King Tut's tomb. Her students added specific details, such as the number of steps at the entrance to King Tut's tomb, and used the sensations of sound, touch, smell, and taste to paint a vivid picture for readers. Sometimes descriptive writing is a phrase, sentence, or paragraph embedded within a composition, and sometimes it is an entire composition.

Ken Macrorie (1985) advises writers to show, not tell, as they write. When writers show, they paint word pictures with details, dialogue, sensory images. Telling, in contrast, keeps readers at a distance, not as involved as they might be because they are observers on the sideline rather than actively experiencing what the writing is describing. Readers have to supply the missing details and create their own sensory images.

However, it does little good to simply admonish students to "show, don't tell." Macrorie's advice must be translated into practice by teaching students how to write descriptively and encouraging them to revise their compositions to paint more vivid word pictures.

The first part of the chapter explains four important descriptive techniques, and the second part offers teaching strategies. Teachers introduce these descriptive writing techniques during minilessons, and then students practice the techniques as they use the writing process in thematic studies and writers' workshop.

DESCRIPTIVE TECHNIQUES

Writers use specific techniques in descriptive writing to create vivid, multisensory word pictures. Four of these techniques are

▼ adding specific information
▼ creating sensory images
▼ making comparisons (metaphors and similes)
▼ writing dialogue

These techniques help writers make their writing come alive for readers because they help writers shift from telling to showing.

Specific Information

Writers make their writing more descriptive when they add specific information and details. Rather than saying something is noisy, the writer identifies the specific noise: a thunderstorm, a baby crying, a car engine roaring, or six dogs barking. Each of these noisy examples conjures up a distinct mental picture. Young writers can provide specific information in several ways:

1. *Identify specific activities and behaviors.* Instead of writing that "The bear was busy in the woods," the writer identifies the bear's activities: It climbed a tree, hunted for food, slept in its cave. Writers provide a wealth of information for readers when they identify specific activities rather than generalize with a word like *busy*.

2. *Name the characters.* Instead of writing about "a little girl," the writer gives the character a name and provides details about the character's appearance and personality.

3. *Identify the setting.* Instead of writing "In a little town . . . ," the writer names the town or describes where it is located. The writer also identifies other aspects of setting, including weather, season, time of day, date, or day of the week.

4. *List attributes.* Rather than writing only that "The boy walked on the beach," the writer continues with details about the beach: noisy seagulls flying overhead, seashells spread across the sand like stars in the night sky, cold waves splashing against the boy's ankles. These attributes, or details, help the reader visualize the boy's walk on the beach.

FIGURE 4-2   *Children's Books That Use Good Descriptions*
P = primary grades (K–2); M = middle grades (3–5); U = upper grades (6–8)

Babbitt, N. (1978). *Tuck everlasting.* New York: Farrar, Straus & Giroux. (U)
Barrett, J. (1987). *Cloudy with a chance of meatballs.* New York: Atheneum. (P–M)
Baylor, B. (1982). *The best town in the world.* New York: Aladdin Books. (M–U)
Cooney, B. (1982). *Miss Rumphius.* New York: Viking. (M)
Fox, M. (1988). *Wilfred Gordon McDonald Partridge.* Brooklyn, NY: Kane/Miller.
     (M–U)
Houston, G. (1992). *My great-aunt Arizona.* New York: HarperCollins. (M)
Kalan, R. (1987). *Rain.* New York: Mulberry. (P)
King, E. (1990). *The pumpkin patch.* New York: Dutton. (P–M)
Martin, B., Jr., & Archambault, J. (1985). *The ghost-eye tree.* New York: Holt, Rine-
     hart & Winston. (M)
Polacco, P. (1988). *The keeping quilt.* New York: Simon & Schuster. (M–U)
Ringgold, F. (1991). *Tar beach.* New York: Crown. (M–U)
Rylant, C. (1985). *The relatives came.* New York: Bradbury Press. (P–M)
Say, A. (1989). *The lost lake.* Boston: Houghton Mifflin. (M–U)
Showers, P. (1991). *The listening walk.* New York: HarperCollins. (P)
Siebert, D. (1989). *Heartland.* New York: Crowell. (M–U)
Soto, G. (1992). *Neighborhood odes.* San Diego: Harcourt Brace Jovanovich. (U)
Van Allsburg, C. (1984). *The mysteries of Harris Burdick.* Boston: Houghton Mifflin.
     (M–U)
Van Allsburg, C. (1985). *The polar express.* Boston: Houghton Mifflin. (M)
Wood, A. (1984). *The napping house.* San Diego: Harcourt Brace Jovanovich. (P)
Yolen, J. (1987). *Owl moon.* New York: Philomel. (M–U)
Zolotow, C. (1967). *Summer is . . .* New York: Crowell. (P–M)

As children write, they need to incorporate specific information into their writing. Many books of children's literature can be used as examples of descriptive writing, and a list of useful books is presented in Figure 4-2. For example, in *The Best Town in the World* (1982), Byrd Baylor describes the town where her father grew up. Even though she does not name the town other than to say that it is in the Texas hills and that people called it "The Canyon," she shows, not tells, how the people lived and what the land was like. She writes about celebrations on the fourth of July, going swimming in the creek, the toys the children played with, and the foods the people ate.

Sensory Images

Writers incorporate the senses into their writing to create stronger images and make their word pictures more vivid. When Jane Yolen wrote about a father and child going owling on a cold winter night in *Owl Moon* (1987), she described how cold it was (touch), how the snow looked in the moonlight (sight), how the snow sounded as it crunched under their boots (hearing), how the wool scarf tied around the child's neck smelled (smell), and even how the fuzz from the scarf tasted (taste). Writers do not always use all five senses as Jane Yolen did; sometimes they include information about only one or two senses. Even so, the added sensory information makes the writing more memorable.

Too often children's writing is limited to one sense—sight. Elementary students often write a narrative of what they have seen, as though their writing were a home movie without any sound. Teachers should teach minilessons about writing sensory images and encourage children to incorporate more than one sense to enrich their writing. If a student is writing about a camping experience, for example, information about how things looked and sounded at night, how the food tasted, or how it felt sleeping in a sleeping bag on the ground might be included.

Comparisons

One of the most powerful techniques that writers use to describe something is to compare it to something else. Good comparisons go beyond the conventional uses of words. In Alfred Noyes's poem "The Highwayman," the moon is called *a ghostly galleon* and the road *a ribbon of moonlight* (Noyes, 1983), and in Lois Lowry's *Anastasia Krupnik* (1979), Anastasia's nervousness when she begins to read a poem she has written to the class is compared to having ginger ale in her knees. These are fresh and unexpected comparisons.

Two types of comparisons are metaphors and similes. Metaphors are the more powerful because the comparison is made directly as in "The toddler was a clown." Similes are less direct and are often signaled by the use of the words *like* or *as,* as in "The toddler acted like a clown." Another form of simile introduces an attribute to connect the subject and the thing it is compared to, as in "The toddler seemed as silly as a clown." Here the attribute that connects *toddler* and *clown* is *silly.*

Students often have difficulty interpreting comparisons in their reading. Readence, Baldwin, and Head (1987) explain that metaphors and similes can be difficult to understand because they are nonliteral comparisons. Students must be knowledge-able about the meanings of the two things being compared their shared attribute to interpret the statement. Sometimes students recognize that the phrase they are read-ing is a comparison and that two words are being compared, but they cannot figure out the relationship between them.

During the elementary grades, children grow in their understanding of figurative language and their ability to say, read, and write metaphors (Geller, 1984). Books, such as *Quick as a Cricket* (Wood, 1982), are a good way to introduce primary grade children to traditional comparisons. In this book, a child is described using 22 com-parisons, including "loud as a lion" and "wild as a chimp." From this introduction to traditional comparisons, middle- and upper-grade students begin to notice traditional comparisons and then fresh comparisons in the books and poems they are reading. Figure 4-3 presents a list of poems with fresh comparisons that are appropriate for middle- and upper-grade students. At the same time, students begin writing their own comparisons, as these third graders did about their classmates:

▽   *Eleanor's bangs are as curly as the ocean waves.*

Joey is as smart as a computer.

FIGURE 4-3 *Poems That Use Interesting Comparisons*

Bennett, R. (1988). "The steam shovel." In B. S. de Regniers (Ed.), *Sing a song of popcorn: Every child's book of poems.* New York: Scholastic. (A steam shovel is compared to a dinosaur.)

Conkling, H. (1983). "Dandelion." In J. Prelutsky (Ed.), *The Random House book of poetry for children: A treasury of 572 poems for today's child.* New York: Random House. (A dandelion is compared to a soldier.)

Francis, R. (1983). "The base stealer." In J. Prelutsky (Ed.), *The Random House book of poetry for children: A treasury of 572 poems for today's child.* New York: Random House. (A base stealer is compared to a tightrope walker.)

Hughes, L. (1983). "Dreams." In J. Prelutsky (Ed.), *The Random House book of poetry for children: A treasury of 572 poems for today's child.* New York: Random House. (Broken dreams are compared to an injured bird and a barren field.)

Lawrence, D. H. (1989). "Bat." In E. Carle (Illus.), *Eric Carle's animals animals.* New York: Philomel. (The bat is compared to a glove.)

Moore, L. (1988). "Dragon smoke." In B. S. de Regniers (Ed.), *Sing a song of popcorn: Every child's book of poems.* New York: Scholastic. (A person's cold breath is described as "dragon smoke.")

Morrison, L. (1983). "Air traveler." In J. Prelutsky (Ed.), *The Random House book of poetry for children: A treasury of 572 poems for today's child.* New York: Random House. (An airplane is called "a silver cigar.")

Noyes, A. (1983). *The highwayman* (C. Mikolaycak, Illus.). New York: Lothrop, Lee & Shepard. (The moon is called "a ghostly galleon," the road "a ribbon of moonlight.")

O'Neill, M. (1983). "What is red?" In J. Prelutsky (Ed.), *The Random House book of poetry for children: A treasury of 572 poems for today's child.* New York: Random House. (The color red is described as many things, including blood, embarrassment, and a valentine heart.)

O'Neill, M. (1983). "What is orange?" In J. Prelutsky (Ed.), *The Random House book of poetry for children: A treasury of 572 poems for today's child.* New York: Random House. (The color orange is described as many things, including a parrot's feather, zip, and a marigold.)

Rossetti, C. G. (1988). "Clouds." In B. S. de Regniers (Ed.), *Sing a song of popcorn: Every child's book of poems.* New York: Scholastic. (Clouds are called white sheep and the sky a blue hill.)

Sandburg, C. (1983). "Fog." In J. Prelutsky (Ed.), *The Random House book of poetry for children: A treasury of 572 poems for today's child.* New York: Random House. (Fog is compared to a cat.)

Smith, W. J. (1983). "The toaster." In J. Prelutsky (Ed.), *The Random House book of poetry for children: A treasury of 572 poems for today's child.* New York: Random House. (A toaster is called a dragon.)

Tennyson, A. (1983). "The eagle." In J. Prelutsky (Ed.), *The Random House book of poetry for children: A treasury of 572 poems for today's child.* New York: Random House. (An eagle is compared to a thunderbolt.)

Thurman, J. (1983). "Zebra." In J. Prelutsky (Ed.), *The Random House book of poetry for children: A treasury of 572 poems for today's child.* New York: Random House. (A fire escape on a city building is compared to a zebra.)

Worth, V. (1989). "Tiger." In E. Carle (Illus.), *Eric Carle's animals animals.* New York: Philomel. (The tiger's black stripes are compared to flames from a black sun.)

Sanjay is as quiet as a burning candle.

Tim is as big as King Kong.

Sandra's hair shines like a black corvette.

Dialogue

Another way writers show, not tell, is by adding dialogue to their writing instead of summarizing what the characters talked about. For example, instead of writing "The boy hesitantly asked Veronica for a date," the student writes, "The boy asked, 'Veronica, I, um, will you go to the dance with me?'" In this way the student shows the boy's hesitation through the dialogue. Macrorie (1985) notes that dialogue gives force to writing and introduces a tension between characters.

Many examples of dialogue can be found in children's literature. In *The Ghost-Eye Tree* (Martin & Archambault, 1985), for example, a recounting of two children's spooky trip to get a pail of milk, the dialogue of the children is realistic. They use childlike language, with the big sister calling her little brother "a fraidy cat" and the boy's hat "dumb." The lines of talk are short, highlighting the children's fear. The anxious feeling created by the book would not be as strong without the dialogue.

TEACHING STUDENTS TO WRITE DESCRIPTIVELY

Students learn about descriptive techniques through minilessons. Teachers explain the techniques, share examples of descriptive writing in stories and poems, and then encourage students to practice the techniques in their own writing. After lessons on the descriptive techniques, students focus on making their writing more descriptive, especially during the revising step of the writing process, whether they are writing in connection with theme studies or in writers' workshop.

Teaching Minilessons

In the lessons on the four descriptive techniques, teachers provide basic information about the technique, share examples from literature, and involve students in writing activities. Teachers may want to refer to the list of books in Figure 4-2 and poems in Figure 4-3 for these minilessons. Six descriptive writing activities are described below:

▼ Creating five-senses clusters
▼ Listing attributes
▼ Building sentences
▼ Crafting comparisons
▼ Creating dialogue
▼ Adding words to wordless picture books

These activities can be incorporated into minilessons on the descriptive writing techniques.

Creating Five-Senses Clusters. To help students focus on the senses, they can create five-senses clusters. In this activity, students focus on each of the five senses as they explore an object or a concept and brainstorm words related to each sense. A class of first graders examined apples as part of a study of Johnny Appleseed and created a five-senses cluster for apples as shown in Figure 4-4. The teacher drew the cluster on a large piece of chart paper and then added the attributes that the children suggested. Later, words and phrases from the cluster can be used in writing about apples.

Food is a very effective stimulus for a five-senses cluster because it evokes a response for each sense. Students can write about apples, pumpkins, popcorn, and other foods. For example, a fourth grader wrote this paragraph after doing a five-senses cluster about popcorn:

▽ *I love to see popcorn pop. It looks like little white firecrackers. Sometimes it looks like a little white bunny. And it feels like bumpy little clouds shooting toward the sky. And they all get together and make one big smooth soft cloud. I like to hear it pop-*

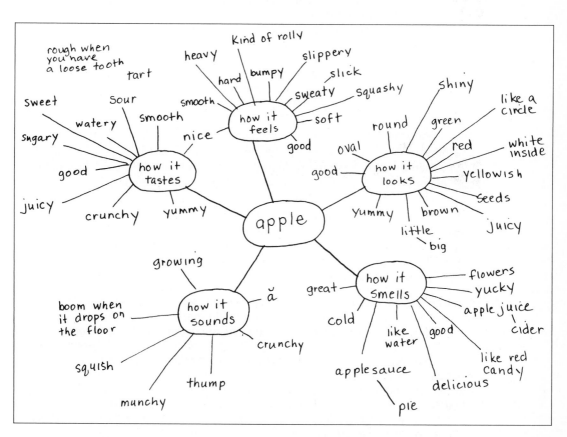

FIGURE 4-4 *A First-Grade Class's Five-Senses Cluster for Apples*

*ping. It sounds like little stars falling from the sky and when they land it makes a
whole bunch of popcorn for you to share with your friends. I love to eat it, too.*

In this paragraph, the student incorporated three senses—sight, touch, and hearing—
and made several comparisons. A seventh grader wrote this poem about popcorn
after making a five-senses cluster:

Life Span of Popcorn

*In the beginning, I was a golden teardrop.
An ancient, petrified, golden teardrop.
I was tosssed into a fountain of youth
where I became a sizzling teenager.
Suddenly, the ground beneath me
became hot—unbearably hot.
I jumped into the air and P O P
my dull, indifferent shape
became unique—individual.
I was fluffy and almost weightless.
Filled with life,
I jumped into the air again and again
until I suddenly felt tired.
I could jump no more,
exhausted and old.
Now I lay in a bowl awaiting my inevitable fate—
the human being.*

This sophisticated poem contains a metaphor; the popping of popcorn is compared
to a person's life. The sensory images come from the words this student wrote on
her five-senses cluster as she examined a few kernels of unpopped corn, observed
the popcorn being popped, and ate some of the popped popcorn.

The class can gradually move on to more sophisticated sensory writings. For example, after reading a story about courage, students can try to cluster sensory details
related to this abstract concept. Or, a social studies theme cycle on freedom, students
can ask, What does freedom look like? Sound like? Feel like? Smell like? Taste like?
A class of fifth graders wrote this class collaboration about freedom and what it
means to them, incorporating sensory details:

*The men and women who fought in the American Revolution made America a free
country, but many people today take freedom for granted. They shouldn't, but they
do. Freedom is hard to explain, but when you see people pledging allegiance to the
flag, going to the church they want to go to, and writing letters to the editor of the
newspaper, you are seeing freedom. On the fourth of July, freedom tastes like hot
dogs and apple pie and it sounds like bands and fireworks. But every day, it smells
like fresh air and sounds like people speaking their minds. George Washington and
Abraham Lincoln and Martin Luther King, Jr. symbolize freedom for many people,
but we think we do, too. The pride and love we feel for the United States of America
is our expression of freedom.*

Listing Attributes. Writers are careful observers of life. They incorporate the attributes of people, places, and events in their writing so that readers feel as though they are eyewitnesses. Students need opportunities to develop observational skills and learn how to give eyewitness quality to their writing. They can observe classroom pets and list attributes from their observations, cut pictures from magazines and list attributes from the picture, or watch a film or video about a historical event and write a description of it.

Another way to help students develop observational skills and the words they need to express these observations is through examining art prints. A sixth-grade class brainstormed these attribute words and phrases as they looked at a large print of Vincent van Gogh's famous painting *The Starry Night*:

whirlwinds of light	lonely town
bursting out	darkness
cypress trees dancing	stars sparkle
frustration	glittering moon
anger	swirling
dark	round and round
few lights	scary
empty	frightening

Then students wrote quickwrites describing the print, trying to incorporate many of the attributes from the brainstormed list. They shared their quickwrites with a classmate and highlighted favorite descriptive sentences using highlighter pens. Then in a class read-around students took turns reading their highlighted descriptive sentences, including the following:

▽ *In the sky above, stars are bursting with light.*

The stars are whirlwinds of light.

Clouds are swirling round and round.

Sparkles of brightness shoot out of the moon as it gleams in the sky.

The wind swiftly swings through the darkness.

Cypress trees on a hillside are dancing in the wind.

The coldness of the air puts ice into my bones.

All I can see is the frustration of the sky on a gusty night.

The sky above a small lonely town shatters the darkness.

The sky waves good night.

These sentences are powerful because the students were studying descriptive writing. They focused on how authors use description in books and practiced the descriptive techniques themselves.

Building Sentences. Students can practice building sentences to see the power of specific information, sensory images, and comparisons. Teachers present an outline for a sentence, such as A _____ horse _____ _____ . Students brainstorm a list of words and phrases for each blank and then choose words and phrases from the three lists to create descriptive sentences. Here are some sentences that a fifth-grade class created using sentence building:

▽   *A startled horse reared up into the air when he heard the crash of thunder.*

The white stallion ran like the wind.

The ancient chestnut horse snoozed contentedly in his stall in the barn.

The hungry colt gobbled the oats in his feed bucket.

The black and white horse pranced jauntily as he pulled the carriage down the drive.

The mare gently licked her foal dry.

These sentences demonstrate some of the possible images that students can create about a horse in a single sentence. Students are often amazed by the variety of sentences their classmates create. Other topics for sentences might include an actor, a tree, a car, a space capsule, a cat, and other nouns that can inspire a range of images.

Crafting Comparisons.   Teachers should be alert to figurative language and provide opportunities for children to craft comparisons. After reading the folktale *Jack and the Beanstalk,* for instance, the teacher can encourage students to identify other things that grow as quickly as a beanstalk or things that are as big as a giant. Building on a shared experience and providing the attribute for the comparison (e.g., *fast* or *big*) is a good way to help elementary students practice inventing comparisons. Even young children can create comparisons (Geller, 1981, 1984, 1985). For example, after petting a bunny and remarking on how soft the tail was, a kindergartner said, "My blue sweater is as soft as a bunny's tail." Then classmates began to name other things that were as soft as a bunny's tail.

To help students say and write comparisons once they have a subject, ask: What does _____ make you think of? What is it like? Students brainstorm several comparisons and then select the one that seems most powerful to them. Children exploring a Hershey's Kiss have compared it to a teepee, a mountain, a pyramid, an upside-down raindrop or tornado, a bell, the nosecone of a rocket, a volcano, and a castle. As they write, students add a phrase to complete the comparison or build a piece of writing around the comparison as this second grader did:

▽
Hershey's Kiss

I like to eat Hershey's kisses.
It is a chocolate mountain.
My teeth climb up the mountain
and my tongue sits on the pointy tip.
Then I eat it.
I like to eat Hershey's kisses.

Another second grader wrote:

▽

Yummy Little Chocolate Kiss

A little brown raindrop
Good, chocolate, and sweet.
A yummy chocolate kiss
Dressed in silver.
The little brown raindrop
Melting in my mouth.
Yummy, yummy in my tummy!

In the first poem the Hershey's Kiss is called a mountain, and in the second it is called a raindrop. These second graders are using comparison (metaphor) effectively in crafting their poems.

Poet Kenneth Koch (1970) has taught elementary students to write poems using metaphors and similes. To begin, Koch asked the students to pretend something was like something else and compare the two things using *like* or *as.* One child wrote "An octopus looks like a table and chair" (p. 104). Some students wrote a different and unrelated comparison in each line of their poems, and others took one comparison and expanded on it in each line of the poem. After experience with similes, students tried metaphors. Koch asked them to think of a comparison and instead of saying one thing was like the other, to say that one thing *was* the other. Examples of students' poems are collected in *Wishes, Lies and Dreams: Teaching Children to Write Poetry* (Koch, 1970). For more information about wordplay and writing poetry, see Chapter 9, "Poetic Writing."

Creating Dialogue.   Elementary students gain experience in creating dialogue by drawing a picture of a scene from a favorite story and adding talk balloons for the characters they show. A fifth grader's drawing inspired by Chris Van Allsburg's fantasy *Jumanji* (1981), featuring a dialogue between two children (and a warning from a friendly sun), is shown is Figure 4-5.

Students can also practice writing dialogue on story boards. Story boards can be made by cutting pages from two copies of a picture book, backing the pictures with posterboard, and then laminating them. Students examine the story boards and write dialogue for the characters on stick-on notes which they then attach to the story boards. The next step is for students to write about the story by referring to the pictures and adding the dialogue they have written on the notes, as well as other descriptions, to the composition. Students can collect all the writings, arrange them in sequence, and compile them to make a class retelling of the book.

Adding Words to Wordless Picture Books.   In wordless books, authors tell the entire story using only pictures. A variety of wordless books are available today, and students at all levels enjoy "reading" these books and making up a text to accompany the pictures. A favorite book is *Frog Goes to Dinner* (Mayer, 1974), a hilarious story of a frog who goes to a fancy restaurant hidden in a small boy's jacket pocket. At the

FIGURE 4-5   *A Fifth Grader's Dialogue Picture Based on Van Allsburg's* Jumanji

restaurant, the frog jumps out of the boy's pocket and causes all sorts of mayhem. A list of wordless picture books is presented in Figure 4-6.

Students can practice the descriptive writing techniques they are learning with wordless books. They brainstorm descriptive words and phrases on small stick-on notes and attach a note to each page in the book, or they can write dialogue on the notes. Then they incorporate the notes they have written into their retelling of the book. Here an excerpt from a third grader's retelling of *Frog Goes to Dinner*:

▽ Page 3: *The boy is dressed in his Sunday best clothes. He bends over to pat his dog's head. "Good-bye and I will be home from the restaurant very soon," he says. He does not see the silly frog jump into his pocket.*

Page 15: *The lady wearing a flower hat puts a fork full of lettuce into her mouth. Then she looks down to the plate, and she sees the silly frog sitting in her salad. He has a smile on his face, but the woman screams anyway.*

FIGURE 4-6 *Wordless Picture Books*

Alexander, M. (1968). *Out! Out! Out!* New York: Dial. (P)
Alexander, M. (1970). *Bobo's dream.* New York: Dial. (P)
Anno, M. (1978). *Anno's Italy.* New York: Collins. (M–U)
Anno, M. (1978). *Anno's journey.* New York: Philomel. (M–U)
Anno, M. (1982). *Anno's Britain.* New York: Philomel. (M–U)
Anno, M. (1983). *Anno's USA.* New York: Philomel. (M–U)
Aruego, J. (1971). *Look what I can do.* New York: Scribner. (P)
Bang, M. (1980). *The grey lady and the strawberry snatcher.* New York: Four
    Winds. (M–U)
Briggs, R. (1980). *The snowman.* New York: Random House. (P)
Carle, E. (1971). *Do you want to be my friend?* New York: Crowell. (P)
Carroll, R. (1965). *What whiskers did.* New York: Walck. (P)
Day, A. (1985). *Good dog, Carl.* New York: Green Tiger Press. (M)
de Groat, D. (1977). *Alligator's toothache.* New York: Crown. (P–M)
de Paola, T. (1978). *Pancakes for breakfast.* New York: Harcourt Brace Jovanovich.
    (P)
de Paola, T. (1979). *Flicks.* New York: Harcourt Brace Jovanovich. (P)
de Paola, T. (1981). *The hunter and the animals: A wordless picture book.* New
    York: Holiday House. (P–M)
de Paola, T. (1983). *Sing, Pierrot, sing.* New York: Harcourt Brace Jovanovich. (M)
Dupasquier, P. (1988). *The great escape.* Boston: Houghton Mifflin. (M–U)
Goodall, J. S. (1975). *Creepy castle.* New York: Macmillan. (M)
Goodall, J. S. (1979). *The story of an English village.* New York: Atheneum. (M–U)
Goodall, J. S. (1980). *Paddy's new hat.* New York: Atheneum. (M)
Goodall, J. S. (1983). *Above and below stairs.* New York: Atheneum. (U)
Goodall, J. S. (1987). *The story of a high street.* London: Andre Deutsch. (M–U)
Goodall, J. S. (1988). *Little red riding hood.* New York: McElderry Books. (P–M)
Henstra, F. (1983). *Mighty mizzling mouse.* New York: Lippincott. (P–M)
Hoban, T. (1971). *Look again.* New York: Macmillan. (P)
Hoban, T. (1988). *Look! Look! Look!* New York: Greenwillow. (P)
Hutchins, P. (1971). *Changes, changes.* New York: Macmillan. (P)
Keats, E. J. (1973). *Psst! Doggie.* New York: Franklin Watts. (P)
Krahn, F. (1970). *A flying saucer full of spaghetti.* New York: Dutton. (P–M)
Krahn, F. (1977). *The mystery of the giant footprints.* New York: Dutton. (P–M)
Krahn, F. (1978). *The great ape.* New York: Penguin. (P–M–U)
Mayer, M. (1967). *A boy, a dog, and a frog.* New York: Dial. (P–M)
Mayer, M. (1973). *Bubble, bubble.* New York: Parents. (P–M)
Mayer, M. (1974). *Frog goes to dinner.* New York: Dial. (P–M)
Mayer, M. (1976). *Ah-choo.* New York: Dial. (P–M)
Mayer, M. (1977). *Oops.* New York: Dial. (P–M)
McCully, E. A. (1984). *Picnic.* New York: Harper & Row. (P)
McCully, E. A. (1985). *First snow.* New York: Harper & Row. (P)
McCully, E. A. (1987). *School.* New York: Harper & Row. (P)
McCully, E. A. (1988). *New baby.* New York: Harper & Row. (P)
Monro, R. (1987). *The inside-outside book of Washington, D.C.* New York: Dutton.
    (M–U)

FIGURE 4-6, *continued*

Prater, J. (1987). *The gift.* New York: Viking. (P–M)
Spier, P. (1977). *Noah's ark.* New York: Doubleday. (P–M–U)
Spier, P. (1982). *Rain.* New York: Doubleday. (P–M–U)
Tafuri, N. (1985). *Rabbit's morning.* New York: Greenwillow. (P)
Tafuri, N. (1986). *Have you seen my duckling?* New York: Viking. (P)
Turkle, B. (1976). *Deep in the forest.* New York: Dutton. (P–M)
Ward, L. (1973). *The silver pony.* Boston: Houghton Mifflin. (P–M)
Wiesner, D. (1988). *Free fall.* New York: Lothrop, Lee & Shepard. (M–U)
Winters, P. (1976). *The bear and the fly.* New York: Crown. (P–M–U)
Winters, P. (1980). *Sir Andrew.* New York: Crown. (P–M)
Young, E. (1984). *The other bone.* New York: Harper & Row. (P–M)

This is a very effective retelling because the student clearly conveys the plot and has incorporated descriptive words and dialogue.

Using the Writing Process

As students work in writers' workshop or on writing projects connected with theme studies, they apply the descriptive writing techniques they are learning. Students gather descriptive words and phrases during prewriting and incorporate these words during drafting, but the revising stage is probably the most important for descriptive writing. During the revising stage, students compliment classmates on their use of description—vivid sensory images, specific details, dialogue, and comparisons—and they suggest that writers add more description to their writing. Students then have the opportunity to return to their rough drafts to make changes.

In Theme Studies

In literature, social studies, or science theme studies, students often use descriptive writing. A fourth-grade class, for example, was reading *Bunnicula: A Rabbit-Tale of Mystery* (Howe & Howe, 1979). In a minilesson students learned about the roles of characters in a story and then chose their favorite character from *Bunnicula* to examine. They began by making a character map, or cluster. The character's name was written in a circle in the middle of a piece of paper, and then rays or lines were drawn out from the center circle. At the end of each ray, students wrote specific bits of information about the character. One student's character map for Harold, the literary dog in *Bunnicula,* is shown in Figure 4-7. The activity can end with the character map, or the student can use the information to write a paragraph-length description of Harold.

Another example is from a sixth-grade class that was involved in an author study of Chris Van Allsburg. Students each chose one of the illustrations from *The Mysteries of Harris Burdick* (1984), a collection of fantastic, surrealistic illustrations, and

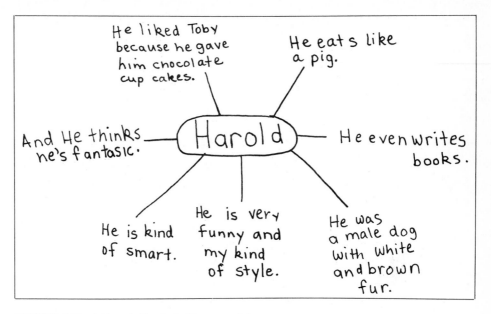

FIGURE 4-7 *A Fourth Grader's Character Map*

wrote a description of it. The teacher had taught several minilessons on descriptive writing before students wrote the descriptive, and students were encouraged to experiment with descriptive techniques. One student wrote about the illustration titled "Under the Rug":

▽ *It was Tuesday evening and Harold Grimsley had had his dinner. He'd put on an old, comfortable sweater and his favorite leather slippers. He was in the family room reading the* People *magazine when he thought he heard a squeaky noise in the living room. So he went in to investigate. There was a round lump under the gray wall-to-wall carpet. It was the same thing that happened two weeks ago. Now it was back? Harold grabbed a chair from the dining room and hit the lump over and over. The lump squeaked louder and louder and grew larger and larger. Finally it broke through the carpet and a kind of fog spread throughout the room. Harold threw the chair down and ran out of the room and kept on running. He slammed the front door closed as he ran out of the house.*

In Writers' Workshop

As students write on self-selected topics and work on projects during writers' workshop, they often use description, whether they are describing a trip to New York City, the pizza they had for dinner last night, or the hermit crab living in a terrarium in the classroom. During a fourth-grade theme cycle on Antarctica, for instance, two students chose to write a poem about penguins during writers' workshop. This is the procedure they followed. Their work at each stage is shown in Figure 4-8.

Prewriting	Feathers rock orange chubby belly feet yellow gray black black wing black penguin funny beak white red likens
Drafting	① The penguins belly is white its back is black. ② The penguin has yellow and orange head feathers sticking out of its head. ③ The rock is covered with likens. ④ The penguin is up on a rock ledge in the sunshine.
Revising	The Penguin White belly and black back yellow and orange head feather sticking out of the side of its head. Up on a liken rock in the sunshine.
Final Copy	The Penguin White chubby belly. yellow and orange head feathers sticking out of the side of its head Up on a lichen-covered rock Standing in the sunshine.

FIGURE 4-8 *The Writing Process Used by Two Fourth Graders in Writing a Poem about Penguins*

1. *Prewriting.* The students collected books about penguins from the class library and looked at the pictures. They brainstormed a list of words as they looked at the illustrations.
2. *Drafting.* Drawing on the words in their list, the students wrote four sentences about penguins.
3. *Revising.* Students shared the sentences with their writing group and decided to "unwrite" (delete unnecessary words) to make a poem from the sentences. After

unwriting, they met with their writing group again to share their poem. Classmates complimented the students on the word picture they had created and commented that the first line was the weakest one, offering commonly known information. Afterwards, the students revised their poem by strengthening the first line and making several other changes.

4. *Editing.* The students proofread their poem and noted that they had misspelled *lichen*. They made the correction and met with the teacher for a final editing. Then they wrote their final copy, which is shown at the bottom of Figure 4-8.

5. *Sharing.* The students pasted the final copy of their poem on a picture of a penguin they had drawn, colored, and cut out. At the class sharing time, the two students showed their final product and read their poem aloud to the class.

Assessing Students' Writing

Teachers assess students' descriptive writing in several ways. Informally, as they observe and conference with students, teachers can note whether or not students are familiar with and use the descriptive techniques. They can examine students' use of specific information, sensory images, comparison, and dialogue to show, not tell, in their writings.

Teachers can also provide more formal minilessons to teach students about the descriptive techniques. Then they assess whether or not students applied the technique effectively. Teachers might want to ask students to focus on these techniques as they offer suggestions for revision in their writing group, as Mrs. Ochs did in the vignette at the beginning of the chapter.

Answering Teachers' Questions About . . . Descriptive Writing

1. *When should I teach descriptive writing?*

There is no specific sequence for teaching particular writing forms, or specific grade levels at which each writing form should be taught. Descriptive writing should be taught at all grade levels beginning in kindergarten. Five- and six-year-olds can dictate lists of attributes, learn about the five senses, and use informal drama and puppets to create dialogue. Older students continue to write lists of attributes, develop five-senses clusters, and write dialogue, and they learn about other techniques as well. Through the elementary grades, children become increasingly capable of incorporating description into their writing.

2. *When students are writing dialogue, how important is it that they use quotation marks correctly?*

When students begin to include dialogue in their writing, teachers should focus on the achievement, rather than criticizing them for not marking the dialogue with punctuation marks. However, teachers should build on students' interest in dialogue and give a series of minilessons on how to use quotation marks. Also, you can introduce quotation marks during the editing stage of the writing process and demonstrate their use by marking them on the student's rough draft.

3. *What about students' trite expressions— pretty and nice? They use those words over and over!*

Teaching students about descriptive writing will help them find alternatives for *pretty* and *nice.* As students brainstorm lists of

words and draw five-senses clusters, they will realize that there are many better alternatives for these overworked words. Another way to combat the problem is to suggest to students in their writing groups (during the revising stage) that they substitute more descriptive words.

REFERENCES

Baylor, B. (1982). *The best town in the world.* New York: Aladdin Books.

Geller, L. (1981). Riddling: A playful way to explore language. *Language Arts, 58,* 669–674.

Geller, L. G. (1984). Exploring metaphor in language development and learning. *Language Arts, 61,* 151–161.

Geller, L. G. (1985). *Wordplay and language learning for children.* Urbana, IL: National Council of Teachers of English.

Howe, D., & Howe, J. (1979). *Bunnicula: A rabbit-tale of mystery.* Boston: Houghton Mifflin.

Koch, K. (1970). *Wishes, lies and dreams: Teaching children to write poetry.* New York: Vintage Press.

Lowry, L. (1979). *Anastasia Krupnik.* Boston: Houghton Mifflin.

Macrorie, K. (1985). *Telling writing* (4th ed.). Upper Montclair, NJ: Boynton/Cook.

Martin, B., Jr., & Archambault, J. (1985). *The ghost-eye tree.* New York: Holt, Rinehart & Winston.

Mayer, M. (1974). *Frog goes to dinner.* New York: Dial.

Noyes, A. (1983). *The highwayman* (C. Mikolaycak, Illus.). New York: Lothrop, Lee & Shepard.

Readence, J. E., Baldwin, R. S., & Head, M. H. (1987). Teaching young readers to interpret metaphors. *The Reading Teacher, 40,* 430–443.

Snyder, Z. K. (1967). *The Egypt game.* Boston: Atheneum.

Van Allsburg, C. (1981). *Jumanji.* Boston: Houghton Mifflin.

Van Allsburg, C. (1984). *The mysteries of Harris Burdick.* Boston: Houghton Mifflin.

Ventura, P., & Cesarani, G. P. (1985). *In search of Tutankhamun.* Morristown, NJ: Silver Burdett.

Wood, A. (1982). *Quick as a cricket.* London: Child's Play.

Yolen, J. (1987). *Owl moon.* New York: Philomel.

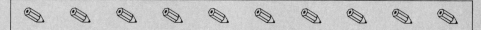

5

Letter Writing

Overview of Letter Writing

Purpose Students write friendly letters to develop relationships and share information. They write business letters to conduct business and to offer opinions. In simulated letters, students use their imaginations to assume the role of another person and to reflect on their learning.

Audience Students usually write friendly letters to known audiences and business letters to more distant known or unknown audiences. Simulated letters are often written for a more limited audience—students themselves, teachers, and classmates.

Forms The two basic forms of letters are friendly and business letters. Students write friendly letters to pen pals, family members, teachers, classmates, favorite authors and illustrators, and other known audiences. Students also use the friendly letter form to write simulated letters in which they assume the role of a historical personality or literary character. They write business letters to companies, nonprofit organizations, and political leaders.

Topics Students write about their families, friends, and school activities in friendly letters. They may also write about books they are reading. Students often write business letters to request information or express an opinion as part of social studies and science theme cycles.

Approaches Students usually write letters as part of theme studies, but they may write letters to pen pals or favorite authors during writers' workshop.

Writing About Favorite Books

The students in Mrs. Donnelly's third-grade classroom spend 45 minutes after lunch in readers' workshop reading self-selected books from the classroom library. After reading two, three, or four books, students identify and work on a project to extend their reading of one of the books. One of the most popular projects in Mrs. Donnelly's classroom is to make and mail a picture postcard to share information about a favorite book with a friend or relative. Students make the postcard using a piece of poster board. On the front they draw and color a picture of a scene from the book, and on the reverse they write a message.

When Mrs. Donnelly introduced this project at the beginning of the school year, she taught three brief minilessons. One minilesson was about drawing pictures on postcards. The class examined Mrs. Donnelly's collection of picture postcards. Some were vacation postcards she had received from friends, and others were postcards advertising books of children's literature she had picked up at a convention. Together the class developed guidelines for the pictures they would draw on postcards: the picture should be about something special in the book, the picture should touch all four sides of the card, and the title and author should be listed. These three guidelines were recorded on a chart about postcards that was hung in the classroom.

The second minilesson was about how to address a postcard. The information about writing an address was added to the poster so that students could refer to the poster when they addressed their postcards. The third minilesson was on writing the message on the postcard. The students decided to include both personal information and information about the book in the message. Mrs. Donnelly also reviewed how to begin and end the message. This information was added to the chart.

Students use the writing process to create postcards. They begin by reviewing the book to choose a high point or favorite episode for the illustration. They also plan what they will write on the postcard. Next, students draft the message for the postcard on scratch paper and draw the picture on the postcard. Mrs. Donnelly encourages students to begin the message with personal information but to also include information about the book. Many times students' messages are persuasive, saying that they are sure this is a book the recipient of the postcard would enjoy reading.

Students meet briefly with Mrs. Donnelly to revise and edit their messages before they make the final copy on the postcard. They also share the picture they have drawn on the postcard with Mrs. Donnelly. Then students copy their message on the postcard and address the card.

Students share their completed cards with the class during sharing time (the last five minutes of readers' workshop), and then they are mailed.

One student's postcard about *Iktomi and the Berries* (Goble, 1989) is presented in Figure 5-1. Both sides of the postcard, showing the picture and the message, are included in the figure. This postcard exemplifies many of the characteristics that Mrs. Donnelly taught through the series of three minilessons on postcard projects. The picture is about the book, it covers the entire postcard, and the title and author are included. The student focuses on information about the book in the message and begins and ends the message appropriately for a letter to his parents. The address is also written correctly.

Writing and mailing postcards is an example of an authentic writing activity because the cards are written for real people to read, not just for the teacher to grade. Mrs. Donnelly reports that her students really enjoy making the postcards and that

IKTOMI aND THE BErrIES By Paul Goble

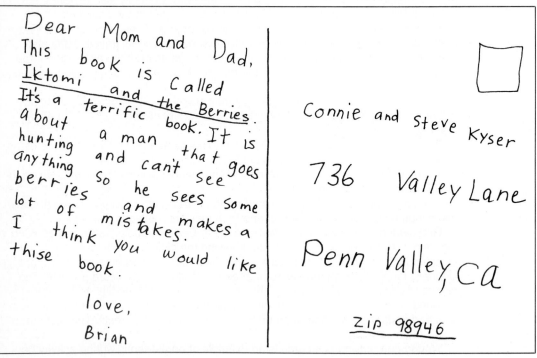

Dear Mom and Dad,
This book is Called
Iktomi and the Berries.
It's a terrific book. It is
about a man that goes
hunting and can't see
anything so he sees some
berries and makes a
lot of mistakes.
I think you would like
thise book.

love,
Brian

Connie and Steve Kyser

736   Valley Lane

Penn Valley, Ca

Zip 98946

FIGURE 5-1   *A Third Grader's Postcard About* Iktomi and the Berries

community response to this project has been enthusiastic. Parents and grand-parents are pleased to see this evidence of their children's reading and writing abil-ity, and the children's friends also show more interest in reading after receiving these postcards.

*P*eople write postcards and other types of letters for genuine communicative pur-poses. Mrs. Donnelly's students wrote to get someone's attention, to sustain friendships, to share information, to persuade, and to recount events. Other purposes for letter writing include to ask questions, to ask permission, to apologize, to remind, and to request information (Karelitz, 1988).

Children's interest in letter writing often begins with writing notes. Young children often write "I love you" notes to their parents and messages to Santa Claus. Some-times parents continue the practice by writing "Have a good day" notes to primary grade children and then tucking the notes into lunch boxes for children to find and read at school. Reta Boyd (1985) is a firm believer in the value of note writing, and she encourages her elementary students to write notes and post them on a special message board in the classroom. The children write notes for a variety of purposes, but Boyd emphasizes their educational value. Children practice reading and writing skills, and they recognize the functional and social nature of writing. An added benefit is that through note writing Boyd stays in touch with all students even though she may be working with a small group.

Letter writing is the logical extension of these informal notes. As with note writing, audience and function are important considerations, but in letter writing form is also important. While letters may be personal, they involve a genuine audience of one or more persons. Not only do students have the opportunity to sharpen their writing skills through letter writing, but they also increase their awareness of audience. Because letters are written to communicate with a specific and important audi-ence, students think more carefully about what they want to say; are more inclined to use spelling, capitalization, and punctuation conventions correctly; and write more legibly.

Letters written by elementary students are typically classified as friendly or busi-ness letters. The forms for friendly letters and business letters are presented in Fig-ure 5-2. The choice of format depends on the function of the letter. When students write informal, chatty letters to pen pals or thank you notes to a television newscaster who has come to the classroom to be interviewed, they use the friendly letter form. When they write letters to a cereal company requesting information about the nutri-tional content of breakfast cereals or letters to the mayor expressing an opinion about current events, they use the more formal, business letter form. Before students write either type of letter, they need to learn how to format the letter.

Friendly and business letter formats are accepted writing conventions, and most teachers simply explain the formats to students and prepare a set of charts to illus-

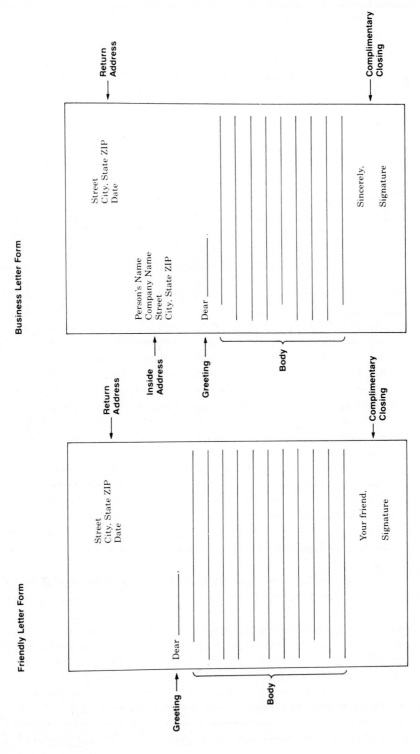

FIGURE 5-2 Forms for Friendly and Business Letters

trate them. This attention to format should not suggest that form is more important than content; rather, it highlights the fact that elementary students are typically unfamiliar with the formatting aspects of letter writing.

FRIENDLY LETTERS

Children write friendly letters to classmates, friends who live out of town, relatives, and pen pals. Students may want to list addresses of people to whom they can write friendly letters on a special page in their journals or in address booklets. In these casual letters, they share news about events in their lives and ask questions to learn more about the person to whom they are writing and to encourage that person to write back. Receiving mail is the real reward of letter writing!

After being introduced to the friendly letter format, students need to choose a real person to write to. Writing authentic letters that are delivered is a much more valuable experience than writing practice letters to be graded by the teacher. Students may draw names and write letters to classmates; to pen pals, by exchanging letters with students in another class in the same school or in a school in another town; or to friends and relatives.

Students use the writing process in letter writing. In the prewriting stage of the writing process, they decide what to include in their letters. Brainstorming and clustering are effective strategies to help students choose types of information to include and questions to ask in their letters. A cluster with four rays developed by a third-grade class for pen pal letters they were writing is presented in Figure 5-3. As a class, the students brainstormed a list of possible topics and finally decided on the four main idea rays (me and my family, my school, my hobbies, and questions for my pen pal). Then each student completed a cluster by adding details to each main idea. As they wrote their rough drafts, students incorporated the information from one ray in the first paragraph, information from a second ray in the second paragraph, and so on for the body of their letters. After writing their rough drafts, students met in writing groups to revise the content of their letters, and they edited their letters to correct mechanical errors with a classmate and later with the teacher. Finally, they recopied the final draft of their letters, addressed envelopes, and mailed them. A sample letter is also presented in Figure 5-3. By comparing each paragraph of the letter with the cluster, you can see that by using the cluster the student wrote a well-organized and interesting letter that was packed with information.

Pen Pal Letters

Teachers can arrange for their students to exchange pen pal letters with students in another class by contacting a teacher in a nearby school, through local educational associations, or by answering advertisements in educational magazines. Sometimes teachers arrange for students to write to pen pals who are the same age, and sometimes they arrange for cross-age groups. Both arrangements have benefits. When students write to same-age children, they have many things in common on which to

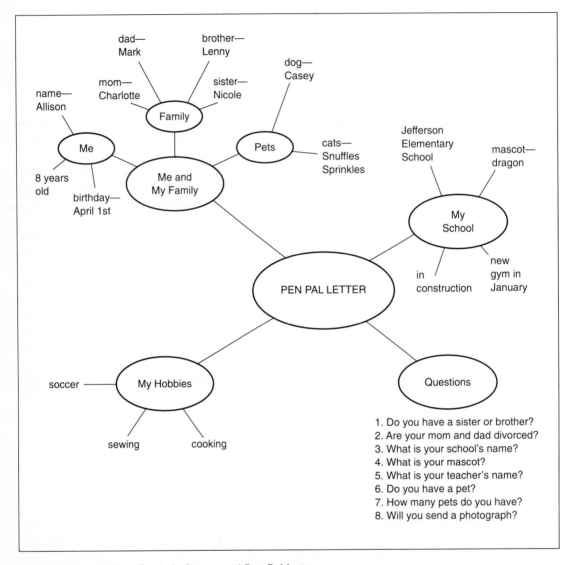

FIGURE 5-3 *A Third Grader's Cluster and Pen Pal Letter*

build relationships. When they write to older or younger children, the relationship changes. Younger children work to impress the older children, and older children assume a parental regard for their pen pals.

Students usually write about school activities and their families and friends in pen pal letters, but they can also write to pen pals about the literature they are reading. In an innovative reading-writing program in Houston, third graders write to pen pals about their thoughts and reactions to books they are reading (Dorotik & Betzold, 1992).

December 10

Dean Annie,

I'm your pen pal now. My name is Allison and I'm 8 years old. My birthday is on April 1st.

I go to Jefferson Elementary School. Our mascot is a dragon. We are in construction because we're going to have a new gym in January.

My hobbies are soccer, sewing, and cooking. I play soccer, sewing I do in free time, and I cook dinner sometimes.

My pets are two cats and a dog. The dog's name is Casey and he's a boy. He is two years old. The cat is a girl and her name is Snuffles. She is four years old. The kitten is a girl and her name is Sprinkles. She is two months old.

My dad's name is Mark and my mom's name is Charlotte. Her birthday is the day after Mother's Day. My brother's name is Lenny. He is 13 years old. My sister's name is Nicole. She is 3 years old.

I have some questions for you. Do you have a sister or a brother? Are your mom and dad divorced? Mine aren't. What is your school's name? What is your mascot? What is your teacher's name? Do you have a pet? How many pets do you have? Will you send me a photograph of yourself?

Your friend,
Allison

FIGURE 5-3, *continued*

Individual students can also arrange for pen pals by contacting one of the following organizations:

International Friendship League, 22 Batterymarch, Boston, MA 02109

League of Friendship, PO Box 509, Mt. Vernon, OH 43050

Student Letter Exchange, 308 Second St. NW, Austin, MN 55912

World Pen Pals, 1690 Como Avenue, St. Paul, MN 55108

Students should write to one of the organizations, describing their interests and including their name, address, age, and sex. Also, they should inquire if a fee is required and enclose a self-addressed, stamped envelope (identified by the acronym SASE) for a reply.

Another pen pal arrangement is for a class of elementary students to become pen pals with college students in a language arts methods class. Over a semester, the elementary students and preservice teachers write to each other four, five, or six times and might arrange to meet each other at the end of the semester. The child has the opportunity to be a pen pal, and the college student has the opportunity to get to know an elementary student and examine the student's writing. In one study (Greenlee, Hiebert, Bridge, & Winograd, 1986), a class of second graders became pen pals with a group of preservice teachers. The researchers investigated whether having a genuine audience would influence the quality of the letters the young students wrote. Second graders' letters were compared with letters written by a control group of students who wrote letters to imaginary audiences and received traditional teacher comments on their letters. The researchers found that the students who wrote pen pal letters wrote longer and more complex letters once they received responses to their letters. The results of this study emphasize the importance of providing real audiences for student writing.

In another study (Crowhurst, 1992), sixth graders corresponded with preservice teachers, and students' letters showed similar growth. The sixth graders wrote increasingly longer letters, and their later letters were syntactically more complex with more adverbials and more embedded clauses. Only a few students wrote more than one paragraph in their first letters, but many used a series of paragraphs in later letters. Over the semester, students also experimented with more mature ways of beginning and ending letters and became more skillful in introducing new topics. In addition, the students themselves changed as writers. As they developed a sense of purpose and audience, they became more eager to write and more concerned about expressing themselves clearly.

Courtesy Letters

Invitations and thank you notes are two other types of friendly letters that elementary students write. They may write to parents to invite them to an after school program, to the class across the hall to ask to visit a classroom exhibit, or to a community person to be interviewed as part of a content area unit. Similarly, children write letters to thank persons who have been helpful.

A sixth-grade social studies class developed a multimedia presentation about the United States Constitution and shared their presentation with a fourth-grade class. The fourth graders wrote a thank you note to each sixth grader, and they included a question in their letters so that the sixth graders would write back. One of the thank you notes is presented in Figure 5-4 together with the sixth grader's response.

Letters to Authors and Illustrators

Students write letters to favorite authors and illustrators to share their ideas and feelings about the books they read. They ask questions about how a particular character was developed or why the illustrator used a certain art medium. Students also describe the books they have written. A first grader's letter to Dr. Seuss is presented in Figure 5-5. Most authors and illustrators will reply to children's letters; however, they receive thousands of letters from children every year and cannot be pen pals with students.

Beverly Cleary's award-winning book *Dear Mr. Henshaw* (1983) provides a worthwhile lesson about what students (and their teachers) can realistically expect from

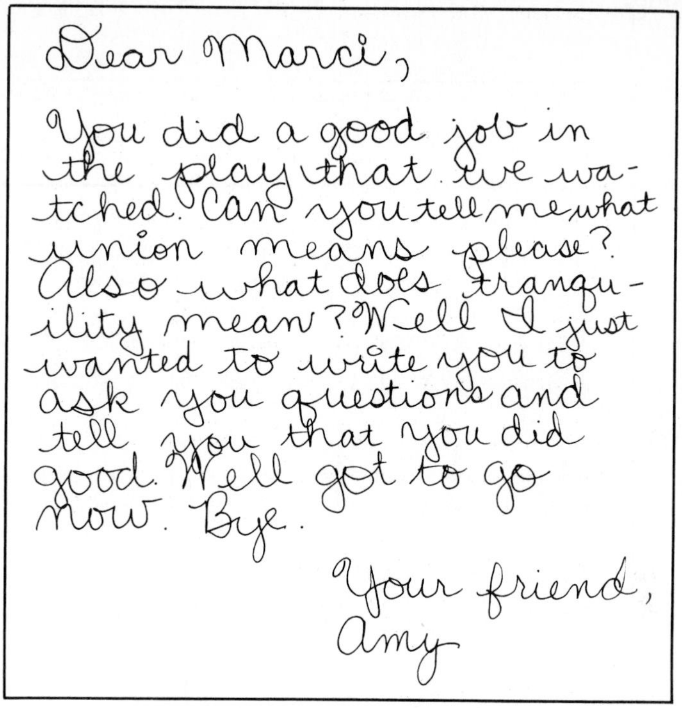

Dear Marci,

You did a good job in the play that we watched. Can you tell me what union means please? Also what does tranquility mean? Well I just wanted to write you to ask you questions and tell you that you did good. Well got to go now. Bye.

Your friend,
Amy

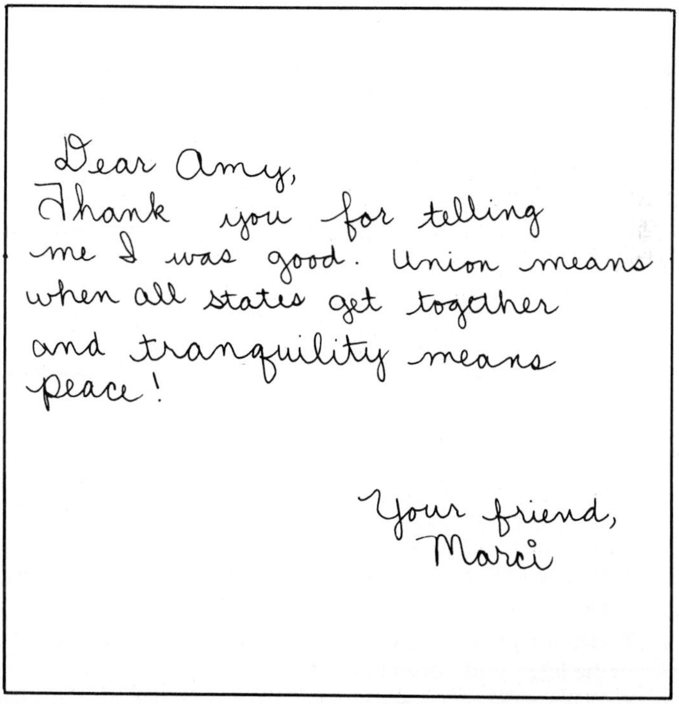

Dear Amy,
Thank you for telling me I was good. Union means when all states get together and tranquility means peace!

Your friend,
Marci

FIGURE 5-4 *A Fourth Grader's Thank You Note and Response by a Sixth Grader*

Dear Dr. Seuss,
I like the SLEEP Book
Becos it is contagus
Amd the illustrations
Are the best of all.
I hav fourde Books
of yours and I have
rede them all.
                    Love, Sara

FIGURE 5-5   *A First Grader's Letter to an Author*

authors and illustrators. The following guidelines are suggested when writing to authors and illustrators:

▼ Follow the correct letter format with return address, greeting, body, closing, and signature.
▼ Use the process approach to write, revise, and edit the letter. Be sure to proofread the letter and correct errors.
▼ Recopy the letter as a courtesy to the reader so that it will be neat and easy to read.
▼ Write the return address on the envelope and on the letter.

▼ Include a stamped, self-addressed envelope for a reply.

▼ Be polite in the letter, and use the words *please* and *thank you.*

▼ Write meaningful letters to share thoughts and feelings about the author's writing or the illustrator's artwork. Students should write only to authors and illustrators with whose work they are familiar.

Avoid these pitfalls:

▼ Do not include a long list of questions to be answered.

▼ Do not ask personal questions, such as how much money he or she earns.

▼ Do not ask for advice on how to become a better writer or artist.

▼ Do not send stories for the author or artwork for the illustrator to critique.

▼ Do not ask for free books because authors and illustrators do not have copies of their books to give away.

▼ Send letters to the author or illustrator in care of the publisher.

Publishers' names are listed on the book's title page, and addresses are usually located on the copyright page, the page following the title page. If the complete mailing address is not listed, check *Books in Print* or *Literary Market Place,* reference books that are available in most public libraries. The suggestions in this list were adapted from Cleary (1983, 1985).

Young Children's Letters

Young children can write individual letters, as the first grader's letter to Dr. Seuss in Figure 5-5 illustrates. They prewrite as older students do, by brainstorming or clustering possible ideas before writing. A quick review of how to begin and end letters is also helpful. In contrast to older children's letters, kindergartners' and first graders' letters may involve only a single draft in which invented spellings and the artwork may carry much of the message.

Primary grade students also compose class letters. The children brainstorm ideas that the teacher records on a large chart. After the letter is finished, children add their signatures. They might write these collaborative letters to thank persons from the community who have visited the class, to invite another class to attend a puppet show, or to compliment a favorite author. Class collaboration letters can also be used as pen pal letters to another class.

Two books have been published that are very useful in introducing young children to letter writing. The Ahlbergs' *The Jolly Postman; or, Other People's Letters* (1986) is a fantastic storylike introduction to reasons why people write letters, and Lillian Hoban's story *Arthur's Pen Pal* (1982) is a delightful way to explain what it means to be a pen pal. Through books like these, kindergartners and other young children can be introduced to different letter formats and the types of information included in a letter. A list of books about letter writing is presented in Figure 5-6. Some of the books demonstrate how to write letters or be a pen pal; others present letters written to real people or to literary characters.

FIGURE 5-6   *Books about Letter Writing*

P = primary grades (K–2); M = middle grades (3–5); U = upper grades (6–8)

Adkins, J. (1981). *Letterbox: The art and history of letters.* New York: Walker. (M)

Ahlberg, J., & Ahlberg, A. (1986). *The jolly postman or other people's letters.* Boston: Little, Brown. (P–M)

Cleary, B. (1983). *Dear Mr. Henshaw.* New York: Morrow. (M–U)

Dupasquier, P. (1985). *Dear daddy . . .* New York: Bradbury Press. (P–M)

Hoban, L. (1982). *Arthur's pen pal.* New York: Harper & Row. (P)

James, S. (1991). *Dear Mr. Blueberry.* New York: McElderry. (P)

Lasky, K. (198). *Sea swan.* New York: Macmillan. (P–M)

Lewis, C. S. (1985). *Letters to children.* New York: Macmillan. (M–U)

Lindsay, E. (1988). *A letter for Maria.* New York: Orchard Books. (P)

MacLachlan, P. (1985). *Sarah, plain and tall.* New York: Harper & Row. (M)

Rocklin, J. (1988). *Dear baby.* New York: Macmillan. (M–U)

Taylor, J. (1992). *Letters to children from Beatrix Potter.* New York: Warne. (M)

Turner, A. (1987). *Nettie's trip south.* New York: Macmillan. (M–U)

BUSINESS LETTERS

Students write business letters to seek information, to complain and compliment, and to transact business. These more formal letters are used to communicate with businesses, local newspapers, and governmental agencies. Students write to businesses to order products, ask questions, and complain about or praise specific products. Students write letters to the editors of local newspapers and magazines to comment on recent articles and to express their opinions on a particular issue. It is important that students support their comments and opinions with facts if they hope to have their letters published. Students can also write to local, state, and national government leaders to express their concerns, make suggestions, or seek information.

Addresses of local elected officials are listed in the telephone directory, and the addresses of state officials are available in the reference section of the public library. The addresses of the President and United States senators and representatives are

President's name, The White House, Washington, DC 20500

Senator's name, Senate Office Building, Washington, DC, 20510

Representative's name, House of Representatives Office Building, Washington, DC 20515

Students may also write other types of business letters to request information and free materials. One source of free materials is *Free Stuff for Kids* (Lansky, 1993), which lists more than 250 free or inexpensive materials that elementary students can write for. This book is updated yearly. In addition, children can write to NASA, the

National Wildlife Federation, publishers, state tourism bureaus, and businesses to request materials.

As part of an author unit on Laura Ingalls Wilder and her series of *Little House* books, a fourth-grade class decided to write a letter to the Laura Ingalls Wilder–Rose Wilder Lane Memorial Museum and Home in Missouri to request some information about the author and the museum. The class discussed what information needed to be included in the letter, and one child was selected to write the letter. A copy of this business letter is presented in Figure 5-7.

SIMULATED LETTERS

Students can also write simulated letters, in which students assume the identity of a historical or literary figure. They write letters as though they were Davy Crockett or another man defending the Alamo or as Thomas Edison, inventor of the electric light. Students can write from one book character to another. For example, after reading Patricia MacLachlan's *Sarah, Plain and Tall* (1985), students can assume the per-

Horace Mann Elementary School
1201 Whisenant Street
Duncan, Oklahoma 73533
February 23, 1993

Ms. Irene V. Lichty, Director
Laura Ingalls Wilder-Rose Wilder Lane
   Memorial Museum and Home
Mansfield, Missouri 65704

Dear Ms. Lichty:

My fourth grade class has been studying about Laura Ingalls Wilder because February is the month of her birthday. We even have a learning center about her. Our teacher has put a few chapters on tape of *The Little House in the Big Woods*. It is a very good book.

We'd like to learn more about Laura. If you wouldn't mind, could you please send our class some brochures about the museum and any other information about her?

Thank you.

Sincerely,

Kyle Johnson and
Mrs. Wilkins's Class

FIGURE 5-7   *A Fourth-Grade Class Letter to a Nonprofit Organization*

sona of Sarah and write a letter to her brother William, as third-grade Adam did in this letter:

▽   *Dear William,*
    I'm having fun here. There was a very big storm here. It was so big it looked like the sea. Sometimes I am very lonesome for home but sometimes it is very fun here in Ohio. We swam in the cow pond and I taught Caleb how to swim. They were afraid I would leave. Maggie and Matthew brought some chickens.
    Love,
    Sarah

Even though these letters are never mailed, they give students an opportunity to focus on a specific audience as they write. After students write simulated letters, they can exchange letters with a classmate who assumes the role of the respondent and replies to the letter.

TEACHING STUDENTS TO WRITE LETTERS

Students write letters as part of theme studies as well as during writers' workshop. They use the process approach to write both friendly and business letters, following these basic steps:

Step by Step

1. *Gather and organize information for the letter.*   Students identify the purpose, audience, and form for their letters and participate in prewriting activities, such as brainstorming or clustering, to decide what kinds of information to include in their letters. For friendly letters and pen pal letters in particular, they also identify several questions to include in their letters.

2. *Review the friendly or business letter form.*   Before writing the rough drafts of their letters, the teacher reviews the friendly or business letter form in a minilesson.

3. *Write the letter using a process approach.*   Students write a rough draft, incorporating the information developed during prewriting and following either the friendly or business letter form. Next, students meet in a writing group to share their rough drafts, receive compliments, and get feedback about how to improve their letters. Then they make changes in their letters based on the feedback they have received. Students edit their letters with a partner, proofread to identify errors, and then correct as many errors as possible. They also check that they have used the appropriate letter format. After all mechanical corrections have been made, students recopy their letters and address envelopes for mailing their letters. As the crucial last step, students mail their letters.

Assessing Students' Letters

Traditionally, students wrote letters that were turned in to the teacher to be graded. After they were graded, the letters were returned to the students, but they were never mailed. Educators now recognize the importance of having a real audience for student writing, and research suggests that students write better when they know their writing will be read by people other than the teacher. While it is often necessary to assess student writing, it seems unimaginable for the teacher to place a grade at the top of the letter before mailing it. Instead of placing a grade on students' letters, teachers can develop a checklist to use in evaluating students' letters without marking on them.

The third-grade teacher whose students wrote the pen pal letters described earlier developed the checklist presented in Figure 5-8. This checklist identifies specific behaviors and products that are measurable. The checklists are shared with students before they begin to write so they understand what is expected of them and how they will be graded. At an evaluation conference before the letters are mailed, the teacher reviews the checklist with each student. Then the letters are mailed without any evaluative comments or grades written on them, but the completed checklist is placed in students' writing folders. A grading scale can be developed from the checklist. For example, points can be awarded for each checkmark in the *yes* column, or five checkmarks can be required for a grade of A, four checkmarks for a B, and so on.

PEN PAL LETTER CHECKLIST

Name _____

	Yes	No
1. Did you complete the cluster?	☐	☐
2. Did you include questions in your letter?	☐	☐
3. Did you put your letter in the friendly letter form? _____ return address _____ greeting _____ 3 or more paragraphs in the body _____ closing _____ salutation and name	☐	☐
4. Did you write a rough draft of your letter?	☐	☐
5. Did you revise your letter with suggestions from people in your writing group?	☐	☐
6. Did you proofread your letter and correct as many errors as possible?	☐	☐

FIGURE 5-8 *A Checklist for Assessing Students' Pen Pal Letters*

Answering Teachers' Questions About . . . Letter Writing

1. Don't my students need to write practice letters before they write real pen pal letters that we mail?

Writing practice letters is a waste of time because the activity is artificial. When writing just for practice or for a grade, students feel little impetus to do their best work, but when they are writing to an authentic audience—their pen pals—they are careful about their writing because they want to communicate effectively. The instructional strategy for letter writing presented in this chapter provides the opportunity for teachers to introduce or review the friendly letter format during the prewriting stage, to help students revise the content of letters after meeting in writing groups, and for students to identify and correct mechanical or formatting errors during the editing stage. With these activities built into the instructional strategy, students can eliminate most errors before they mail their letters so that writing practice letters is unnecessary.

2. How can I tie letter writing to my literature-based reading program?

Here are three ways you can tie letter writing to literature study. First, students can write letters to you or to classmates about the books they are reading, or they can write postcards to friends and relatives as Mrs. Donnelly's students did. In these letters, they share their reactions to the book, compare the book to others they have read or others by the same author, or offer a recommendation about whether the reader would like the book. My second suggestion is for students to write letters to favorite authors and illustrators. Let students choose who they write to, and be sure to review the guidelines for writing letters to authors and illustrators (see pp. 140–141) before students begin writing. Third, students can assume the role of a character from a favorite book and write a simulated letter from one character to another. Then students can trade letters with classmates and write back and forth.

REFERENCES

Ahlberg, J., & Ahlberg, A. (1986). *The jolly postman; or, Other people's letters.* Boston: Little, Brown.

Boyd, R. (1985). The message board: Language comes alive. In J. M. Newman (Ed.), *Whole language: Theory in use* (pp. 91–98). Portsmouth, NH: Heinemann.

Cleary, B. (1983). *Dear Mr. Henshaw.* New York: Morrow.

Cleary, B. (1985). Dear author, answer this letter now . . . *Instructor, 95,* 22–23, 25.

Crowhurst, M. (1992). Some effects of corresponding with an older audience. *Language Arts, 69,* 268–273.

Dorotik, M., & Betzold, M. R. (1992). Expanding literacy for all. *The Reading Teacher, 45,* 574–578.

Goble, P. (1989). *Iktomi and the berries.* New York: Orchard.

Greenlee, M. E., Hiebert, E. H., Bridge, C. A., & Winograd, P. N. (1986). The effects of different audiences on young writers' letter writing. In

J. A. Niles & R. V. Lalik (Eds.), *Solving problems in literacy: Learners, teachers, and researchers* (pp. 281–289). Rochester, NY: National Reading Conference.

Hoban, L. (1982). *Arthur's pen pal.* New York: Harper and Row.

Karelitz, E. B. (1988). Notewriting: A neglected genre. In T. Newkirk & N. Atwell (Eds.), *Understanding writing* (2nd ed.) (pp. 88–113). Portsmouth, NH: Heinemann.

Lansky, B. *Free stuff for kids.* New York: Simon and Schuster.

MacLachlan, P. (1985). *Sarah, plain and tall.* New York: Harper & Row.

6

Biographical Writing

Overview of Biographical Writing

Purpose Students use biographical writing to chronicle events in their own lives and other people's lives, to reflect on experiences, and to draw generalizations about life.

Audience The audience for personal narratives is often the writers themselves and their classmates and families. Autobiographies and biographies are more sophisticated forms of biographical writing, and these compositions are often shared with wider audiences.

Forms Forms include personal narratives, autobiographies, and biographies.

Topics Topics for personal narratives and autobiographies include events in children's lives, their hobbies, and other interests. Subjects for biographies include family members, community members, well-known historical personalities, and contemporary sports figures, television and film stars, and politicians. Students often read and write biographies in connection with social studies and science theme units.

Approaches Students often write personal narratives during writers' workshop and biographies and autobiographies as projects in literature focus units and in social studies and science theme cycles.

Writing a Class Biography

Mrs. Jordan's first-grade class is studying plants, and as part of the theme cycle, the students want to learn about people who work with plants. They take a field trip to a local plant nursery, interview an agricultural extension agent, and learn about George Washington Carver. Mrs. Jordan reads Aliki's *A Weed Is a Flower: The Life of George Washington Carver* (1988), and after listening to the book read aloud, they get into a circle for a grand conversation to talk about the book.

Mrs. Jordan begins the conversation by asking, "Who would like to begin our conversation about George Washington Carver?" and then the first graders take turns sharing ideas and asking questions. They talk about how Carver was born a slave and was taken away from his mother, how he struggled to learn about plants, and the many uses he found for common plants such as peanuts and sweet potatoes. One child asks why Carver has George Washington's name, another asks if the class can make a meal entirely from peanuts like the botanist did, and another child says that Carver reminds her of Martin Luther King, Jr., whom they had studied earlier in the school year.

Mrs. Jordan seizes this opportunity to review the concept *biography*. She asks students if they know what kind of book *A Weed Is a Flower* is and if they remember other biographies they have read in first grade. One child remembers that a biography "is a story of someone's life," and another child says, "It's a book that tells about the important things that happened in somebody's life." A third child recalls that a biography "tells why a person is remembered today." Mrs. Jordan suggests that the class brainstorm a list of reasons why George Washington Carver is special and remembered today. Then she points out that people like Carver are also a lot like us. They make a second list of the ways that Carver is "just like us." The list includes "he liked peanut butter," "he was black," "he was good," "he went to college and I'm going to college too," and "he wanted people to like him." Each child chooses something from the "special" list or the "just like us" list as the topic for a quickwrite or a quickdraw.

Mrs. Jordan has a set of eight paperback copies of Aliki's book, and children reread the book in small groups with Mrs. Jordan. Several children remember Carver saying, "A weed is a flower growing in the wrong place," and after rereading the book decide to make a mural about it. Other students work together in a group to make a lifeline of Carver's life, noting the important events in his life, from his birth in 1864 to his death at age 79 in 1943. The lifeline is a line marked into ten year intervals on a long sheet of chart paper. Students take turns identifying important events in Carver's life and writing them on the chart. Mrs. Jordan shares other information about the famous botanist and adds some of the information to complete the lifeline. For the year 1890, for instance, one child wrote, "GWC finally earned enough money to go to college in Ames, Iowa." Another group of students marked the locations that Carver traveled to on the large laminated map of the United States that hangs in the classroom, and several others made mobiles about the uses of peanuts. After they finish work, students share their projects with the class.

The class then plans two special whole-class activities. They plan and cook a meal made entirely of vegetables, including peanut butter, and they make a class book about the great botanist. Individually or with a classmate, students choose events from Carver's life to write about. On each page, students write a sentence or two about an event in the botanist's life and add an illustration. Students use the writing process to make their class book the best it can be. They begin by drawing their illustration on "good" paper and writing a rough draft of their text on "draft" paper.

Then the class gets into a circle, arranging themselves so the pages of the book are in sequential order, and students take turns reading their pages. They read through the entire book; then each page is reread and students offer compliments and suggestions about how to communicate more effectively. As students find gaps in their biography, several students volunteer to do additional pages to complete the book. Then students make revisions and meet with the teacher to edit their composi- tions. Finally, students add the text to the illustrations they have already done and the book is compiled. Students line up to sequence the pages, one child makes a cover and title page, and then the book is bound with a plastic spiral. One page from the collaborative biography is presented in Figure 6-1.

Mrs. Jordan includes a blank page at the back of most books for students, par- ents, and other readers to make comments after reading. Students read the book during independent reading, and they take turns taking the book home for parents to read. Here is a sampling of comments on the "Readers' Comments" page:

This book is so good I read it twice!!

The writers and illustrators of this book did a great job!

The children really learned a lot about George Washington Carver.

Cool, dude.

We have enjoyed each of the books this year.

This book was very interesting; we never get too old to learn.

Very, very good book!

Mrs. Jordan teaches thematically, and she ties reading and writing into science and social studies activities. She uses the themes to introduce genres of literature, such as biography, and as jumping off places for writing activities. Mrs. Jordan's stu- dents use informal writing as they brainstorm lists and quickwrite in learning logs, and they use the writing process as they write biographies. Her students used the writing process to write their class biography of George Washington Carver, and be- cause each student or pair of students wrote one page, Mrs. Jordan could model the writing process and complete the book in four days.

*B*iographical writing is writing about people. Elementary students enjoy sharing information about their lives and learning about the lives of well-known person- alities. In this chapter, we focus on three types of biographical writing: personal nar- ratives, autobiographies, and biographies. Personal narratives are accounts of events from writers' own lives, told much like a story. Primary grade students' first writings are typically personal narratives, and older writers continue to write personal narra- tives when they write about and reflect on happenings in their own lives. Autobiogra- phies are more sophisticated, multiple-episode life-stories about the writer, and biographies are other people's life-stories.

FIGURE 6-1 *A Page from a First-Grade Class Biography of George Washington Carver*

In biographical writing, writers combine elements of expository (or informational) writing with narrative (or story) writing. Writers take information from a person's life—dates, places, events, and people—and weave the factual details and sometimes dialogue into an entertaining account that readers can relate to. Through the events they write about, writers portray the person's character or demonstrate why the person is remembered today.

PERSONAL NARRATIVES

Personal narratives are often one of the first types of sustained writing that children do. In this form of biographical writing, students write about themselves and their experiences in the community in which they live. Students in the primary grades as well as older students (and even adults!) become more active, engaged writers as they write about themselves in personal narratives (Steinberg, 1991). One reason that students are so successful in writing personal narratives is that they can draw on what they know best—themselves.

Teachers do not assign topics for personal narratives; instead, students draw from their own lives and experiences and write about things that interest them. A writing might begin as a journal entry about a field trip to the zoo or a birthday party and then be developed and polished through writing process activities. In the writers' workshop approach, students keep a list of possible topics in their writing notebooks. They choose a topic from this list or an event in their life and work through the writing process stages to organize, draft, revise, edit, and publish their writing.

In contrast, very young writers often use an abbreviated writing process. They draw and write their personal narratives directly into a booklet of paper stapled together. Drawing the pictures is their prewriting activity, and writing the words is drafting. They usually omit the revising and editing stages, but they increasingly make changes while they are drafting. In fact, children's desire to go back and make some changes is the best indication that they are becoming aware of their audience and can handle all five stages of the writing process. Whether or not students revise and edit, they publish and share their books, usually with classmates and their families.

Young children's personal narratives are often written with an illustration and a line of text on each page. First-grade Jessica, for example, writes a line of text on each page of her *We Went to the Zoo* book:

▽   Page 1: *We went to the zoo.*
Page 2: *We saw a turtle.*
Page 3: *We saw a bunny and we saw a snake.*
Page 4: *We saw a monkey.*

Jessica wrote this book after a class trip to the zoo, and her experiences are evident in the text and accompanying illustrations.

Young children also write books of lists. Sometimes they write lists of favorite toys, family members, or things they like to do. One example of a book of lists is first-grade Jason's *I Like* book:

▽   Page 1: *I like pizza.*
Page 2: *I like ice cream.*
Page 3: *I like cookies.*
Page 4: *I like salad.*
Page 5: *I like fish.*
Page 6: *But I don't like spinach.*

In both of these personal narratives, the first-grade writers repeated a pattern ("We saw," "I like"), and the pattern structures the text and simplifies the writing task.

Older students and more experienced writers are able to sustain their account without a sentence pattern, as third-grade Sean's account demonstrates:

▽   *When I was three and a half years old, my mother and I had a discussion about cleaning my room. She was a little on the upset side. She told me I couldn't play until I cleaned my room up. She went into the kitchen to cook and left me to clean my room up. About ten minutes later I walked in the kitchen and stood there. My mother asked, "That was fast. Did you already get your room cleaned?" I said, "God told me that I didn't have to clean my room." With a shocked look on my mom's face, she asked again, "What? God will forgive me this day, so get back in your room and get it cleaned up!"*

Sean is a more experienced and more fluent writer than the first graders. He wrote several drafts to develop his account and shared the drafts with classmates, each time revising his writing to extend and elaborate his account in order to communicate more effectively. He also met with the teacher to edit his writing and add conventional spelling, capitalization, and punctuation.

Teachers typically call personal narratives "stories" even though they rarely have the plot and character development of a story. It is a disservice to children to call all writing stories when the writing might be a report, a poem, or a personal narrative because the terminology is confusing and children are less likely to learn to distinguish the various genres or writing forms.

Some picture books written in the first person that tell about realistic life events might be classified as personal narratives. Jane Yolen's *Owl Moon* (1987), an account of a child's walk into the woods on a snowy night to see a great horned owl, is one example, and Cynthia Rylant's *The Relatives Came* (1985), about a time when the relatives came for a visit from Virginia and everyone had a good time, is another. A list of children's books that are written like personal narratives is presented in Figure 6-2. These books might be shared with students as examples of published personal narratives that have the same characteristics as the personal narratives the children write.

FIGURE 6-2 *Books That Are Written Like Personal Narratives*
P = primary grades (K–2); M = middle grades (3–5); U = upper grades (6–8)

Barbour, K. (1987). *Little Nino's pizzeria.* San Diego: Harcourt Brace Jovanovich. (P)

Baylor, B. (1982). *The best town in the world.* New York: Aladdin Books. (M–U)

Brown, R. (1986). *Our cat Flossie.* New York: Dutton. (P)

Bunting, E. (1990). *The wall.* New York: Clarion Books. (M–U)

Giff, P. R. (1980). *Today was a terrible day.* New York: Puffin Books. (See also other books in the same series.) (P–M)

Kellogg, S. (1986). *Best friends.* New York: Dial. (P–M)

Martin, B., Jr., & Archambault, J. (1985). *The ghost-eye tree.* New York: Holt, Rinehart & Winston. (M–U)

Mayer, M. (1968). *There's a nightmare in my closet.* New York: Dial. (P)

Ringold, F. (1991). *Tar beach.* New York: Crown. (P–M)

Rylant, C. (1985). *The relatives came.* New York: Bradbury Press. (M)

Viorst, J. (1971). *The tenth good thing about Barney.* New York: Atheneum. (See other books by the same author.) (M–U)

Waber, B. (1988). *Ira says goodbye.* Boston: Houghton Mifflin. (P–M)

Williams, V. B. (1982). *A chair for my mother.* New York: Mulberry. (See other books in the same series.) (P–M)

Wood, A. (1982). *Quick as a cricket.* London: Child's Play. (P)

Yolen, J. (1987). *Owl moon.* New York: Philomel. (M–U)

Teaching Students to Write Personal Narratives

Students usually write personal narratives during writers' workshop when they are free to choose their own topics for writing and write about topics that are important to them. These are the steps involved in teaching students how to use the writing process to write personal narratives and in sustaining their writing.

Step by Step

1. *Introduce personal narratives.*   Teachers use minilessons to introduce the writing form and teach students how to write personal narratives. In one minilesson, teachers introduce the personal narrative. They explain that students write about events in their own lives and about topics of special interest. They may share examples that students in a previous class have written or books of children's literature (see the list in Figure 6-2) written like personal narratives.

   In another mililesson, teachers help students brainstorm a list of possible writing topics such as a family trip, birth of a baby brother or sister, a pet, a hobby, an accident, a special holiday, a scary experience, or a grandparent's visit. Students keep this list in a writing notebook or a writers' workshop folder and update the list periodically during the year.

   Teachers plan other minilessons about adding details, using dialogue, sequencing events, choosing titles, and writing leads as students indicate the need for additional instruction. These minilessons can be directed toward small groups of students or the whole class.

2. *Use the writing process.*   Students use the writing process to write personal narratives. They begin by making a cluster or drawing a series of pictures to gather and organize their ideas. Then they write a rough draft, meet with classmates in a writing group and revise their drafts based on feedback they receive from classmates. Next they proofread to identify and correct spelling, capitalization, and punctuation errors. Finally, students write the final draft of their composition, add a title page, and compile the pages to make a book. Students move through these activities at their own pace in writers' workshop.

3. *Publish and share the writing.*   Students publish their personal narratives in books. Minilessons might focus on how to make and bind books. Teachers share examples of books other students have made and show various sizes and shapes of books. They also demonstrate how to make book covers, by covering pieces of cardboard with wallpaper, cloth, contact paper, or wrapping paper, and how to compile pages in a book.

   Students also share their books with the class. Often they sit in an author's chair to read their books aloud to a group of classmates. Sharing is an important part of the writing process because it emphasizes that writers write for listeners and readers and that writing is successful when their audience enjoys the book. They might also place their books in the classroom library for classmates to read and reread.

4. *Sustain the writing.*   It is important that students choose topics they care about and want to write about. Otherwise, writers' workshop can seem like an assembly line with children producing book after book without thoughtful work or careful bookmaking. Students get ideas for their writing as they listen to classmates shar-

ing their books and from books of children's literature they are reading. The writing process itself also helps to nurture students' interest in writing because students learn how to develop and refine their compositions.

Young children often use an abbreviated form of the writing process as they write personal narratives. They draw pictures in a booklet as they plan their composition; then they write directly into the book, a sentence or two on each page, using invented spelling. There is little or no revising and editing. After writing, students share their finished books with classmates, families, and friends.

Assessing Students' Personal Narratives

When young children begin writing personal narratives, teachers may want to ask students to keep a list of the books they have written, similar to the list shown in Figure 6-3. This list is an important record that documents students' writing activities because the books themselves are often placed in the class library or taken home to share with family and friends. Students usually keep the list in their writing folders.

Since personal narratives are often the first type of sustained writing that young children do, teachers watch for this accomplishment as a significant development in children's writing development. Teachers should look for the following traits in children's first personal narratives:

▼ There is a common thread through the book.
▼ There is one line of text and an illustration on each page.

Writers' Workshop: List of Books Written

Name _____

Date	Title	Have you shared it?
_____	_____	____
_____	_____	____
_____	_____	____
_____	_____	____
_____	_____	____
_____	_____	____

FIGURE 6-3 *Assessment List for Personal Narratives*

▼ The illustrations and the text are coordinated.
▼ The writer uses the first person.
▼ The book has a title.
▼ The child willingly shares the book with classmates.

As elementary students gain more writing experience and begin working through all five writing process stages, their personal narratives become more developed and polished. Their writings should include many of these qualities:

▼ The account focuses on one event or experience.
▼ Specific people, locations, and objects are named.
▼ Sensory details about the people, locations, and events are included.
▼ Actions are described.
▼ Dialogue or monologue is included.
▼ The events are arranged in an appropriate sequence.
▼ There is suspense or a surprise at the end.
▼ There is comparison or contrast in the account.

These qualities do not develop simultaneously nor does any one personal narrative necessarily incorporate all of them. Think back to the three personal narratives in this section. Each of the accounts includes some of these qualities. Jessica's *We Went to the Zoo* piece, for instance, focuses on a single event, and Jason's *I Like* account has a suprise at the end. Sean's personal narrative is sequential, uses dialogue, and describes actions.

LIFE-STORIES

Autobiographies

An autobiography is the story of a person's life narrated by that person. In writing an autobiography, students relive and document events in their lives, usually in chronological order. They describe memorable events, the ones that are necessary to understand their personalities. A limited number of autobiographies have been written for children, and these life-stories of scientists, entertainers, sports figures, and others provide useful models of the autobiography form. A list of recommended autobiographies for elementary students is presented in Figure 6-4.

Autobiographical writing grows out of children's personal narratives and "All About Me" books that they write in kindergarten and first grade. Children's greatest source of information for writing is their own experiences, and when they write autobiographies, they draw from this wealth of experiences. Two other ways students can share their life stories is by collecting items that represent their lives in life boxes and me quilts.

"All About Me" Books.   Children in kindergarten and first grade often compile "All About Me" books. These first autobiographies usually contain information such as the child's birthday, family members, friends, and favorite activities, with drawings as

FIGURE 6-4 *Recommended Autobiographies for Elementary Students*

Ali, M. (with R. Durham). (1976). *The greatest: Muhammad Ali.* New York: Ballantine. (M–U).

Begley, K. A. (1977). *Deadline.* New York: Putnam. (U)

Bulla, C. R. (1985). *A grain of wheat: A writer begins.* New York: Godine. (U)

Chukosky, K. (1976). *The silver crest: My Russian boyhood* (B. Stillman, Trans.). New York: Holt, Rinehart & Winston. (U)

Collins, M. (1976). *Flying to the moon and other strange places.* New York: Farrar, Straus & Giroux. (M–U)

Dahl, R. (1984). *Boy.* New York: Farrar, Straus & Giroux. (M–U)

de Paola, T. (1989). *The art lesson.* New York: Putnam. (P–M)

Fisher, L. E. (1972). *The death of evening star: Diary of a young New England whaler.* New York: Doubleday. (U)

Fritz, J. (1982). *Homesick: My own story.* New York: Putnam. (M–U)

Gish, L. (1988). *An actor's life for me.* New York: Viking. (U)

Goodall, J. (1988). *My life with the chimpanzees.* New York: Simon and Schuster. (M)

Hamill, D. (with E. Clairmont). (1983). *Dorothy Hamill: On and off the ice.* New York: Knopf. (M)

James, N. (1979). *Alone around the world.* New York: Coward. (U)

Jenner, B. (with R. S. Kiliper). (1980). *The Olympics and me.* New York: Doubleday. (M)

Keller, H. (1980). *The story of my life.* New York: Watermill Press. (M–U)

Maiorano, R. (1980). *Worlds apart: The autobiography of a dancer from Brooklyn.* New York: Coward. (U)

Huynh, Q. N. (1982). *The land I lost: Adventures of a boy in Vietnam.* New York: Harper & Row. (M–U)

North, S. (1963). *Rascal.* New York: Dutton. (M–U)

O'Kelley, M. L. (1983). *From the hills of Georgia: An autobiography in paintings.* Boston: Little, Brown. (P–M–U)

Rudolph, W. (1977). *Wilma. The story of Wilma Rudolph.* New York: New American Library. (U)

Schulz, C. M. (with R. S. Kiliper). (1980). *Charlie Brown, Snoopy and me: And all the other Peanuts characters.* New York: Doubleday. (M–U)

Singer, I. B. (1969). *A day of pleasure: Stories of a boy growing up in Warsaw.* New York: Farrar, Straus & Giroux. (U)

Sullivan, T., & Gill, D. (1975). *If you could see what I hear.* New York: Harper & Row. (U)

well as text used to present the information. Four pages from a first grader's "All About Me" book are presented in Figure 6-5. In these books, the children and the teacher decide on the topic for each page, and after brainstorming possible ideas for the topic, children draw a picture and write about the topic. Children may also need to ask their parents for information about their birth and events during their preschool years. In Figure 6-5, for example, first-grade Jana reports that it was her father who told her she was choosy about the clothes she wore when she was five.

I have 3 best friends. they are very nice to do things with me. My friends names are Randy, Kasey, and Kimberly. I go to Randy's house every morning. Her mom baby sits me.

This is my Grammy's house. I have my own room in it. Sometimes I sleep on the love seat. I like to see papa. Sometimes my papa takes me fishing. I love to go fishing. My Grammy makes me feel special.

I went to Six Flags. I ate eggs before I got on the roller coaster and wen we went down my stomach strted to hurt.

This is me wen I'm, five. I'm, reading a book. My mom comes in and puts out my cloths for me to wear but I didn't, want to wear them. I became very picky about my cloths my dad said.

FIGURE 6-5 *Four Pages from a First Grader's "All About Me" Book*

Life Boxes.   Autobiographies don't have to be written in books. Students can collect four or five small items that represent themselves and events in their lives and place these things in a shoe box, cereal box, or other box. Items such as a baby blanket, a stuffed animal, family photos, postcards from a vacation, pictures of favorite toys or other items cut from magazines, maps showing places the child has visited, a letter from grandma, a mask worn on Halloween, a favorite book, or an award the child has received might be included. Students write a label to explain each item and attach the labels to the things. They also decorate the box and add an appropriate title. They can use a favorite color of paper, drawings of life events, words and pictures cut from magazines, or wallpaper scraps to decorate the box. Students can share the items with classmates orally or use the items in writing an autobiography.

Students can also make a life box after reading a biography. As with autobiographical life boxes, students collect or make three, four, or five items that represent a person's life, add labels to explain the objects, and place them in a decorated box. Life boxes are effective as a first biographical project because students think more critically about the important events in a person's life as they read and plan the items they will use to symbolize the person's life.

Me Quilts.   Me quilts are another autobiography project. Students draw a self-portrait and a series of eight pictures to symbolize special events in their lives. Then they attach the pictures to a large sheet of butcher paper to look like a quilt with the self-portrait in the middle, as shown in Figure 6-6. Students write paragraphs to describe each picture and add these to the quilt and then share them with classmates. They can display their quilts on the classroom wall or present them orally to the class, explaining the pictures and what they represent.

Students can also make biographical quilts with a picture of a well-known person in the center and eight pictures representing special events or objects related to that person's life. Students add paragraphs describing each picture, following the same procedure as with me quilts.

Chapter Books.   Students can write chapter books about important events in their lives. They choose three, four, or five important events to write about and use the writing process to develop and refine their compositions. A second grader's autobiography is presented in Figure 6-7. In this autobiography, you learn about Eddie through six chapters in which he describes himself and his family, his pets, his "favorites," his hobbies, and his vacations to a Texas town.

Biographies

A biography is an account of a person's life written by someone else. Writers try to make this account as accurate and authentic as possible. In researching biographies, they consult a variety of sources of information. The best source of information, of course, is the person himself or herself, and through interviews writers can learn many things about the person. Other primary sources include diaries and letters writ-

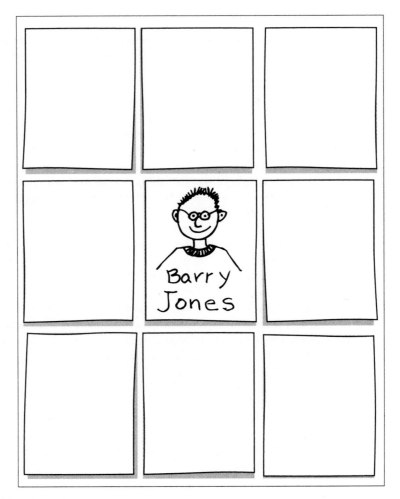

FIGURE 6-6   *Arrangement for a Me Quilt*

ten by the person, photographs, mementos, historical records, and recollections of people who know that person. Secondary sources are books, newspapers, and films about the person written by someone else.

Biographies of well-known people such as explorers, kings, queens, scientists, sports figures, artists, and movie stars, as well as ordinary people who have endured hardship and shown exceptional courage, are available for elementary students to read. A list of recommended biographies is presented in Figure 6-8. Biographers Jean Fritz and Robert Quackenbush have written many biographies for primary- and middle-grade students, some of which are included in the list.

Authors use several different approaches in writing biographies (Fleming & McGinnis, 1985). The most commonly used approach is historical. In this approach,

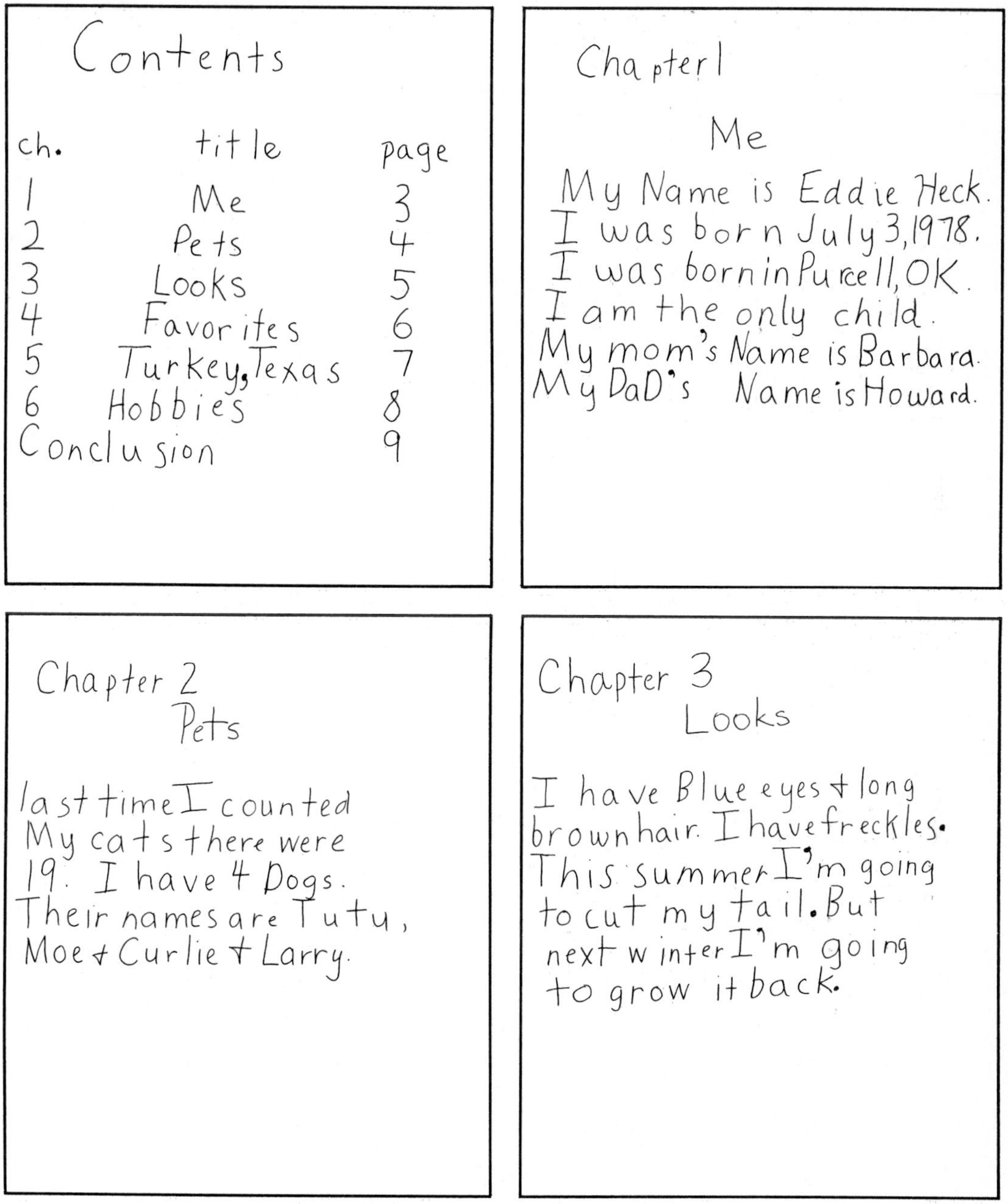
Contents

ch.	title	page
1	Me	3
2	Pets	4
3	Looks	5
4	Favorites	6
5	Turkey, Texas	7
6	Hobbies	8
Conclusion		9

Chapter 1

Me

My Name is Eddie Heck.
I was born July 3, 1978.
I was born in Purcell, OK.
I am the only child.
My mom's Name is Barbara.
My DaD's Name is Howard.

Chapter 2

Pets

last time I counted
My cats there were
19. I have 4 Dogs.
Their names are Tutu,
Moe + Curlie + Larry.

Chapter 3

Looks

I have Blue eyes + long
brown hair. I have freckles.
This summer I'm going
to cut my tail. But
next winter I'm going
to grow it back.

FIGURE 6-7 *A Second Grader's Autobiography:* A Story About Me

Chapter 4
    Favorites
My favorite president
is Georrge Washington.
My favorite pet is a
Dog. My favorite
thing is my Bike.
My favorite toy
is GI. LoE.
My favorite color
is black. My favorite
Game is NINJA.

Chapter 5
        Turkey, Texas
I went to Turkey, Texas
for My first time at
2 ½ yrs. old. I liked
it so much we have gone
ever since. I went to
see BoB Wills and his
Texas Play Boys but
BoB Wills is dead now.

Chapter 6
    Hobbies
My favorite hobbies
are inventing games.
I've invented these
games: NINJA & Goldtar
defender of The
Universe. These are Games
that sometimes I play
by my self and some
times I play with my
friends.

        Conclusion
The day after school
is out I'm going to Dog-
Patch, Arkansas to see
Daisy Mae and Mammy
Yoakum. I may go to
Six Flags this summer.
I may also go to Frontier
City. I will be looking
forward to school
starting.

FIGURE 6-7, *continued*

FIGURE 6-8   *Recommended Biographies for Elementary Students*

Adler, D. A. (1990). *A picture book of Helen Keller.* New York: Holiday House. (See also other books by the same author.) (P–M)

Aliki. (1965). *A weed is a flower: The life of George Washington Carver.* Englewood Cliffs, NJ: Prentice-Hall. (See also other biographies by the same author.) (M)

Anderson, J. (1991). *Christopher Columbus: From vision to voyage.* New York: Dial. (M)

Blassingame, W. (1979). *Thor Heyerdahl: Viking Scientist.* New York: Elsevier/Nelson. (M–U)

Burleigh, R. (1985). *A man named Thoreau.* New York: Atheneum. (U)

Dobrin, A. (1975). *I am a stranger on Earth: The story of Vincent van Gogh.* New York: Warne. (M–U)

Ferris, J. (1988). *Walking the road to freedom: A story about Sojourner Truth.* Minneapolis: Carolrhoda Books. (M)

Freedman, R. (1987). *Lincoln: A photobiography.* New York: Clarion. (M–U)

Fritz, J. (1973). *And then what happened, Paul Revere?* New York: Coward. (See other biographies by the same author.) (P–M)

Giff, P. R. (1987). *Laura Ingalls Wilder.* New York: Viking. (M)

Golenbock, P. (1990). *Teammates.* San Diego: Harcourt Brace Jovanovich. (M)

Greene, C. (1990). *Laura Ingalls Wilder: Author of the Little House books.* Chicago: Childrens Press. (P–M)

Greenfield, E. (1977). *Mary McLeod Bethune.* New York: Crowell. (P–M)

Hamilton, V. (1974). *Paul Robeson: The life and times of a free black man.* New York: Harper & Row. (U)

Jakes, J. (1986). *Susanna of the Alamo: A true story.* New York: Harcourt Brace Jovanovich. (M)

Mitchell, B. (1986). *Click: A story about George Eastman.* Minneapolis: Carolrhoda Books. (M)

Monjo, F. N. (1973). *Me and Willie and Pa: The story of Abraham Lincoln and his son Tad.* New York: Simon & Schuster. (M)

Peterson, H. S. (1967). *Abigail Adams: "Dear partner."* Champaign, IL: Garrard. (M)

Provensen, A., & Provensen, M. (1984). *Leonardo da Vinci.* New York: Viking. (a moveable book) (M–U)

Quackenbush, R. (1981). *Ahoy! Ahoy! are you there? A story of Alexander Graham Bell.* Englewood Cliffs, NJ: Prentice-Hall. (See also other biographies by the same author.) (P–M)

Stanley, D. (1986). *Peter the Great.* New York: Four Winds. (P–M)

Tames, R. (1989). *Anne Frank.* New York: Franklin Watts. (M–U)

Winter, J. (1991). *Diego.* New York: Knopf. (M)

the writer focuses on the dates and events of the person's life and presents them in chronological order. Many biographies that span the person's entire life, such as *Traitor: The Case of Benedict Arnold* (Fritz, 1981) and *A Picture Book of Helen Keller* (Adler, 1990), follow this pattern.

A second approach is the sociological approach. Here the writer describes what life was like during a historical period, providing information about family life, food, clothing, education, economics, transportation, and so on. For instance, in *Worlds*

Apart: The Autobiography of a Dancer from Brooklyn (1980), Robert Maiorano describes his childhood in an impoverished New York City neighborhood and how he escapes it through a career with the Metropolitan Opera Company.

A third approach is psychological; the writer focuses on the conflicts that the person faces. These conflicts may be with oneself, other people, nature, or society. (For more information about conflict, see Chapter 8, "Narrative Writing.") This approach has many elements in common with stories and is most often used in shorter, event or phase biographies. One example is Jean Fritz's single-event biography *And Then What Happened, Paul Revere?* (1973), in which Paul Revere faces conflict with the British army.

Biographies may be categorized as contemporary or historical. Contemporary biographies are written about a living person, especially a person that the writer can interview. In contrast, historical biographies are written about persons who are no longer alive.

When students study someone else's life to prepare for writing a biography, they need to become personally involved in the project (Zarnowski, 1988). There are several ways to engage students in biographical study; that is, to help students walk in the footsteps of the other person. For contemporary biographies, meeting and interviewing the person is the best way. For other biography projects, students read books about the person, view films and videos, dramatize events from the person's life, and write about the persons they are studying. An especially valuable activity is simulated journals in which students assume the persona of the person they are studying and write journal entries just as that person might have. (See Chapter 3 for more information about simulated journals.)

Contemporary Biographies.   Students write biographies about living people they know personally as well as about well-known living personalities, such as the President of the United States or a children's author. Although many primary sources of information are available for researching local people, students may have to depend on secondary sources of information (e.g., books, newspapers, letters) to research well-known and geographically more distant persons. However, it is often possible for students to write letters to well-known persons or, sometimes, to arrange conference telephone calls.

A second-grade class interviewed their principal Mrs. Reno and compiled a biography that became the most popular book in the school. Before the interview, the students brainstormed questions, and each child selected a question to ask. Then Mrs. Reno came to the classroom and answered the children's questions. After the interview, the students compiled a book of their questions and Mrs. Reno's answers. A page from the class collaborative biography is presented in Figure 6-9. You will also notice that the students practiced using quotation marks in their report.

Historical Biographies.   While biographies are based on the facts known about a person's life, some parts of historical biographies are often fictionalized out of necessity. Moreover, dialogue and other details about daily life must often be invented after careful research of the period. In *The Double Life of Pocahontas* by Jean Fritz (1983), for instance, the author had to take what sketchy facts are known about

FIGURE 6-9 *A Page from a Second-Grade Collaborative Biography of the School Principal*

Pocahontas and make some reasonable guesses to fill in missing information. To give one example, historians know that Pocahontas was a young woman when she died in 1617, but they are not sure how old she was when John Smith and the other English settlers arrived in Virginia in 1607. Fritz chose to make her 11 years old when the settlers arrived.

When children write historical biographies, they will have to make some of the same types of reasonable guesses that Jean Fritz did. In the following biography of Daniel Boone, third-grade Charles added details and dialogue to complete his report.

▽   *Daniel Boone was born in 1734 in Omley, Pennsylvania. When Daniel grew up, he hunted a lot. He began his journey to Kentucky to hunt for game.*

Every day, Daniel tried to hunt for game in Kentucky. In the morning, he would catch two or three deer. At night, he wouldn't hunt because all the animals would be hiding. Daniel wouldn't give up hunting for game in Kentucky.

Finally, he decided to travel through Kentucky. Soon Indians took their meat and furs away. Would Daniel and his family survive?

One day when Daniel was walking to his fellow friend's fort, he looked all around. Indians were surrounding him. One Indian called Chief Blackfish said, "Take me to your men. If you do, I will not hurt you or them. If you don't, I will kill you and your friends." Daniel was trapped. When they were walking to the fort, Daniel ran inside. Just then, gunshots were fired. They were at war. Soon the war was over. Daniel's people had won.

Daniel died in 1820 at the age of 85. Daniel Boone is remembered for opening the land of Kentucky for white men to hunt in and fighting for Kentucky.

Teaching Students to Write Life-Stories

Students write life-stories as part of literature focus units and social studies and science theme cycles. During an author unit, students might write a biography of a favorite author, or during a unit focusing on the genre of biography, students read and write biographies of interesting people. Students also write biographies of historical personalities, political figures, and community leaders in connection with social studies themes and biographies of scientists in connection with science themes. Students write autobiographies as part of literature focus units, writers' workshop, and theme cycles on self-awareness, families, and change.

The steps in the teaching strategy are described in the following paragraphs. While the teaching strategy involves similar steps for writing autobiographies and biographies, these two writing forms are different and should be taught separately.

Step by Step

1. *Read to learn about the format and unique conventions.*   Autobiographies and biographies written by others can serve as models for the life stories that students write. The autobiographies listed in Figure 6-4 and the biographies in Figure 6-8 provide examples of both entire-life and single-event life-stories. As students read these books, they can note which events the narrator focuses on, how the narrator presents information and feelings, and what the narrator's viewpoint is. The autobiographies and biographies that students have written in previous years are another source of books for your students to read. While life-stories become prized possessions, some students can often be persuaded to bring their life-stories back the following year to share with your students.

2. *Gather information for the life-story.*   Students gather information about themselves or about the person they will write about in several different ways. For autobiographical writing, students are the best source of information about their life, but they may need to get additional information from parents and other family members. Often parents will share information from baby books and photo albums. Also, older brothers and sisters can share their remembrances. Another strategy students can use to gather information before writing an autobiography is

to collect some objects that symbolize their life and hang them on a "lifeline" clothesline or put them in a life box made from a shoebox (Fleming, 1985). Then students write briefly about each object, explaining what the object is and how it relates to their lives. Students can also decorate the box with words and pictures clipped from magazines to create an autobiographical collage.

For biographical writing, students interview living persons to gather information about their lives. For persons in the community, students can interview the person directly. Telephone interviews and letters are other possibilities for persons who live a distance from the community. For historical biographies, students read books to learn about the person and the time period in which he or she lived. Other sources of information are films, videotapes, and newspaper and magazine articles. Students also need to keep a record of the sources they consult for the bibliography they will include with their biographies.

Students sequence the information they have gathered, either about their life or someone else's, on a lifeline, or timeline. This activity helps students identify and sequence the milestones and other events in the person's life. A lifeline for Benjamin Franklin is presented in Figure 6-10. Students can use the information included on the lifeline to identify topics for the life-story. Three important events in Franklin's life, for example, were writing *Poor Richard's Almanac,* proving that lightning was electricity, and helping to write the Declaration of Independence. These could become the topics that a student writes about in a biography of Franklin.

3. *Organize the information for the life-story.* Students select topics from their lifelines and develop a cluster with each topic as a main idea. They add details from the information they have gathered, and if they do not have four or five details for each topic, they can search for additional information. When students aren't sure if they have enough information, they can cluster the topic using the "5*W*s plus one" questions (who, what, when, where, why, and how) and try to answer the six questions. If they can complete the cluster, students are ready to write, but if they cannot, then they need to gather additional information. The cluster that fourth-grade Brian developed before writing his autobiography is presented in Figure 6-11 with his autobiography. After developing the cluster, students make decisions about the sequence for presenting topics, often in chapters, and add an introduction and conclusion.

4. *Write the life-story using the writing process.* Students use the clusters they developed in the previous step to write their rough drafts. The main ideas become topic sentences, and details are expanded into sentences. After they write the rough draft, students meet in writing groups to get feedback on their writing and then make revisions. Next, they edit their writing and recopy it. They add drawings, photographs, or other memorabilia. For biographies, students also add a bibliography, listing the sources of information they consulted.

Besides making the final copy of their life-stories, students can share what they have learned in other ways. Based on what they have learned through writing a biography, they can dress up as the person and tell about the person's life in first person, or be interviewed by their classmates. For example, Matt could have dressed as Ben Franklin and come to class to be interviewed. Through researching and writing about Ben Franklin's life, he could have become knowledgeable enough to answer questions about Ben's life, his accomplishments, and his role in colonial and revolutionary times.

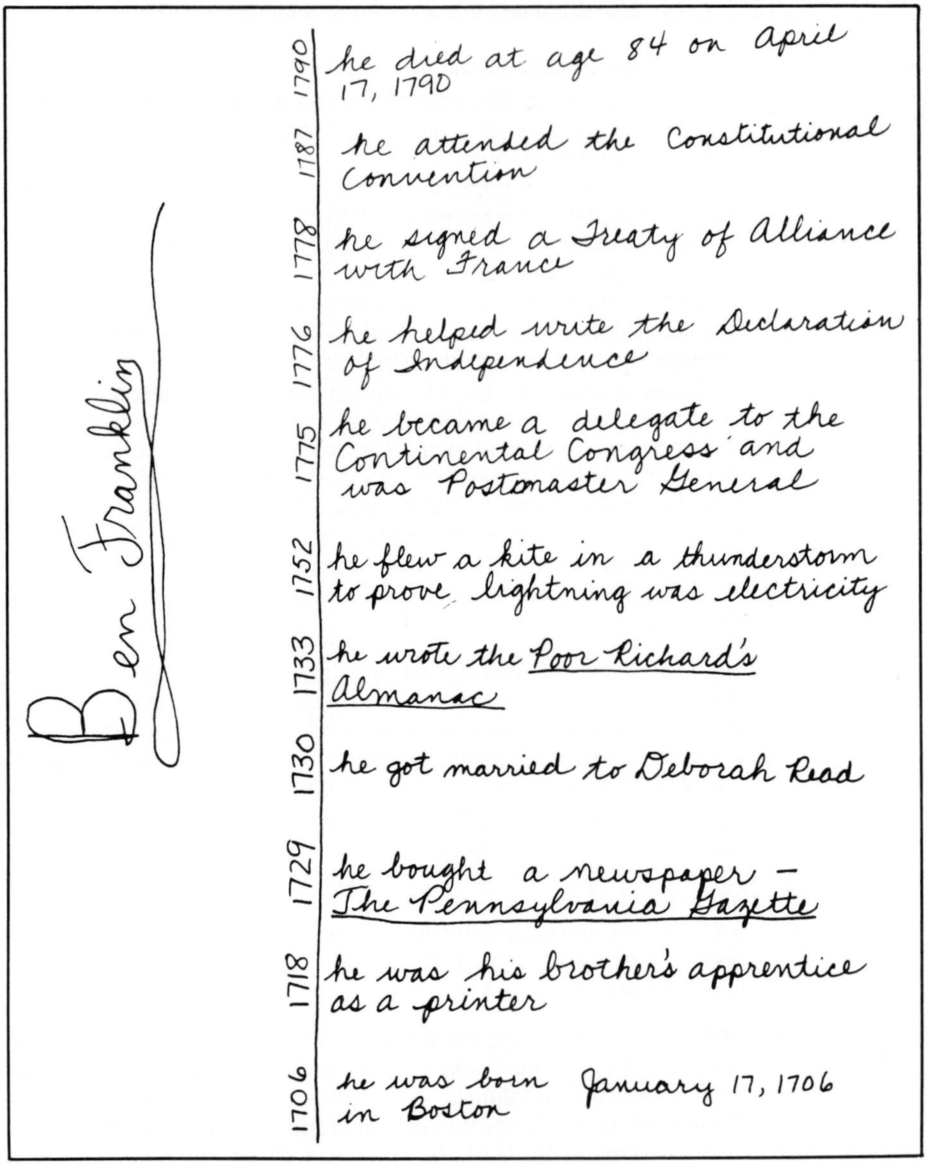

Ben Franklin

1790 — he died at age 84 on April 17, 1790

1187 — he attended the Constitutional Convention

1778 — he signed a Treaty of Alliance with France

1776 — he helped write the Declaration of Independence

1775 — he became a delegate to the Continental Congress and was Postmaster General

1752 — he flew a kite in a thunderstorm to prove lightning was electricity

1733 — he wrote the <u>Poor Richard's Almanac</u>

1730 — he got married to Deborah Read

1729 — he bought a newspaper — <u>The Pennsylvania Gazette</u>

1718 — he was his brother's apprentice as a printer

1706 — he was born January 17, 1706 in Boston

FIGURE 6-10 *A Fourth Grader's Lifeline of Benjamin Franklin*

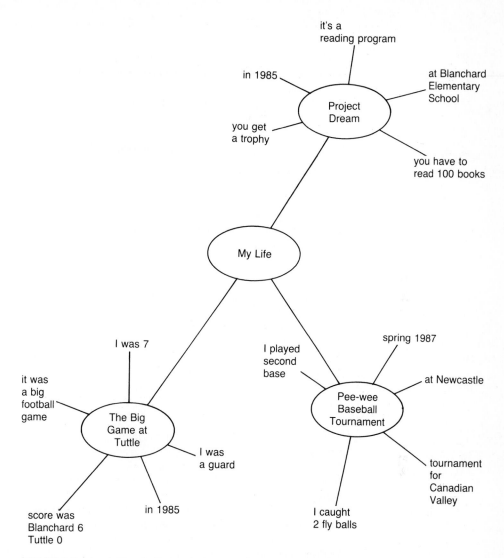

FIGURE 6-11 *A Fourth Grader's Cluster and Autobiography*

Assessing Students' Life-Stories

Students need to know what the requirements are for their autobiography or biography project and how they will be assessed or graded. A checklist approach is recommended. For an autobiography, the checklist might include the following items:

▼ Make a lifeline with at least one important event listed for each year of your life.
▼ Draw a cluster with at least three main-idea topics and at least five details for each topic.

Introduction

I, Brian Spencer, being of sound mind and body, a healthy young boy about 4 ft. 6, with brown eyes and blond hair, do write this autobiography. My nickname is Snake because I am sneaky. At ten years of age, I have managed to survive my 16-year-old brother and my mom and dad!

Chapter 1: The Big Win

There was a big football game between Blanchard and Tuttle in 1985. And Blanchard was ahead. The score was Blanchard six and Tuttle nothing. My position was guard. The guard's position is to block other players. The uniforms are maroon and white. All the round robin games were played at the Blanchard High School field and we won them all. Pretty good for a seven-year-old! HA!

Chapter 2: Round Robin Victory

In the spring of 1987 on a bright sunny Saturday, my pee-wee team and I went to Newcastle to play our big pre-season tournament baseball game. We were all excited and hoping to win. I played second base. I caught two fly balls, but that didn't win the game but I would like to think it did. Anyway we won the round robin tournament for Canadian Valley and I sure was happy!

Chapter 3: Project Dream

In the year 1985 there was a big program called Project Dream. It was a reading program for the elementary students at Blanchard Elementary School. We are supposed to read 100 books a year. At the end of the school year the students that completed their 100 books got a trophy for first place. Anyone that reads a smaller amount of books gets a T-shirt. You could also win other prizes, for example, buttons, posters, and ribbons. I won a T-shirt, a trophy, and ribbons. So encourage your kids to read for Project Dream!

Conclusion

I am in the fourth grade at Blanchard Elementary School. My favorite subject is science. I like science because you get to do a lot of experiments. What I am going to do when I graduate is be a bass guide. A bass guide is to take people to fish.

FIGURE 6-11, *continued*

▼ Write a rough draft with an introduction, three (or more) chapters, and a conclusion.
▼ Meet in a writing group to share your autobiography.
▼ Make at least three changes in your rough draft.
▼ Complete an editing ckecklist with a partner.
▼ Write a final copy with photos or drawings as illustrations.
▼ Add an "All About the Author" page.
▼ Compile your autobiography as a book.
▼ Decorate the cover of your book.

For a biography, the checklist might include the following items:

▼ Learn about the person's life from at least three sources (and no more than one encyclopedia).
▼ Make a lifeline of the person's life with at least 10 important events listed.
▼ Write at least 10 simulated journal entries as the person you are studying.
▼ Make a cluster with at least three main-idea topics and at least five details for each topic.
▼ Write a rough draft with at least three chapters and a bibliography.
▼ Meet in a writing group to share your biography.
▼ Make at least three changes in your rough draft.
▼ Complete an editing checklist with a partner.
▼ Recopy the biography.
▼ Add an "All About the Author" page.

Students keep the checklist in their writing folders, and they check off each item as it is completed. At the end of the project, students submit their entire folders to be assessed or graded. Teachers can award credit for each item on the checklist and tally the points to arrive at a grade. This grade is the process grade because it focuses on the steps involved in the project. Teachers can also read the completed biography and award a second product grade that reflects the quality of the research and writing. Through this approach, students assume a greater responsibility for their own learning, and they can better understand why they received a particular grade.

Answering Teachers' Questions About . . .
Biographical Writing

1. *My second graders are writing personal narratives. In fact, that's all most of them write. How can I get them into writing stories, poems, letters, and other writing forms?*

Choose one of the forms you mentioned and introduce it to your students, perhaps using a class collaboration. Then invite your students to use the form for a genuine writing purpose. For example, your students might become pen pals with students in another school. The first letter might be a class letter, and you can demonstrate how to write a friendly letter as you compose the letter together with your students. Then they can write individual letters to their pen pals several times during the school year. Then continue to introduce other writing forms in connection with literature the students are reading or social studies and science themes.

2. *At which grade levels do you think elementary students should write biographies and autobiographies?*

Primary grade students can write almost all types of writing, including biographical writing. First graders typically write personal narratives, and they can also begin writing collaborative biographies, as Ms. Jordan's first graders did at the beginning of the chapter (see Figure 6-1). Second graders (see Figure 6-7) can write chapter autobiographies, and I'm sure some experienced first-grade writers might also. Most students write personal narratives throughout the elementary grades, but students shouldn't have to write an autobiography or a biography in every grade. I'd recommend that students write a chapter autobiography once or twice during the elementary grades and that they write several biographies in connection with science and social studies themes during the elementary grades.

3. *Can I use stories like Johnny Tremain (Forbes, 1970) and Sarah, Plain and Tall (MacLachlan, 1985) for biographical writing?*

The two books that you mention are stories, not biographies, so they should not be used as examples of biographical writing. Both stories, however, focus on the main character as biographies do, and the main character might even be based on a real person. The line between historical fiction and biography can sometimes be fuzzy, but biographies are written about people who actually lived, and the events described in these books really happened and have been researched, not invented, by the author.

REFERENCES

Adler, D. A. (1990). *A picture book of Helen Keller.* New York: Holiday House.

Aliki. (1988). *A weed is a flower: The life of George Washington Carver.* New York: Simon & Schuster.

Fleming, M. (1985). Writing assignments focusing on autobiographical and biographical topics. In Fleming, M., & McGinnis, J. (Eds.), *Portraits: Biography and autobiography in the secondary school* (pp. 95–97). Urbana, IL: National Council of Teachers of English.

Fleming, M., & McGinnis, J. (Eds.). (1985). *Portraits: Biography and autobiography in the secondary school.* Urbana, IL: National Council of Teachers of English.

Forbes, E. (1970). *Johnny Tremain.* Boston: Houghton Mifflin.

Fritz, J. (1973). *And then what happened, Paul Revere?* New York: Putnam.

Fritz, J. (1981). *Traitor: The case of Benedict Arnold.* New York: Viking.

Fritz, J. (1983). *The double life of Pocahontas.* New York: Putnam.

Harste, J. C., Short, K. G., & Burke, C. (1988). *Creating classrooms for authors: The reading-writing connection.* Portsmouth, NH: Heinemann.

MacLachlan, P. (1985). *Sarah, plain and tall.* New York: Harper & Row.

Maiorano, R. (1980). *Worlds apart: The autobiography of a dancer from Brooklyn.* New York: Coward.

Rylant, C. (1985). *The relatives came.* New York: Bradbury Press.

Steinberg, M. (1991). Personal narratives: Teaching and learning writing from the inside out. In R. Nathan (Ed.), *Writers in the classroom* (pp. 1–13). Norwood, MA: Christopher-Gordon.

Yolen, J. (1987). *Owl moon.* New York: Philomel.

Zarnowski, M. (1988). The middle school student as biographer. *Middle School Journal, 19,* 25–27.

7

Expository Writing

Overview of Expository Writing

Purpose   Students use expository writing to learn and share information.

Audience   Expository writing is often written for a broad, unknown audience. Reports in the format of books can be placed in the school library. Posters, diagrams, and other charts can be displayed in the hallways of the school or in the community.

Forms   The forms include reports, "All About _____" books, ABC books, riddles, posters, diagrams, charts, and cubes. Students can also incorporate information into stories they write.

Topics   Topics relate to science and social studies theme cycles, literature focus units, students' hobbies, and other topics students are knowledgeable about.

Approaches   Sometimes students write books to share information during writers' workshop. They might write "All About _____" books, ABC books, books of riddles, and other reports. More often, however, students use expository writing for projects in social studies and science theme cycles and in literature focus units.

Other   Students organize expository writing using five patterns: description, sequence, comparison, cause and effect, and problem and solution. Cue words are often used to signal these patterns.

Researching Careers

The sixth graders in Ms. Hardy's classroom have taken a computerized test to determine which occupations they are most suited for. On the computer printout, Matt discovers he has aptitude for several different careers, but the one that catches his interest is petrologist. A petrologist? To help Matt and the other students explore careers, Ms. Hardy suggests that they research one of the careers identified by the computer and then compile what they learn in a report.

They begin by brainstorming a list of questions about careers:

▼ How much money can you make in this career?
▼ What kinds of work do you do in this career?
▼ What kind of schooling is needed to prepare for this career?
▼ What are the working conditions?
▼ Would you travel in this career?
▼ What type of person would be happy in this career?

The students decide that the questions about kinds of work and working conditions are the most basic, and they all agree to research these two questions for their reports. They also decide to choose at least two additional questions from the list to investigate.

Next, students draw a cluster with their career as the nucleus word in the middle circle and with four rays, each listing one of the questions to be investigated. Matt chooses these four questions to research: (a) How much money do you make in this career? (b) What kind of work do you do in this career? (c) What kind of schooling is needed for this career? and (d) What are the working conditions in this career? Matt uses library books to find answers to his questions, and he will consult at least three sources which he will list in the bibliography at the end of his report. If he locates a petrologist in his community, he can interview this person as one of his resources. He adds the information he collects to complete his cluster as shown in Figure 7-1.

Ms. Hardy reminds the students that their reports will include an introduction to attract the readers' attention, at least four questions in the body of the report with one paragraph to answer each question, and a brief conclusion. Matt uses the information in his cluster to write a rough draft. First, he writes the four paragraphs for the body of the report. He puts each on a separate sheet of paper after deciding to postpone determining the order of the paragraphs until later. As he adds the information from the cluster to his paragraphs, he checks it off on the cluster. He marks "rough draft" on the top of each page and double-spaces the text so there will be space for revising and editing.

Next, he turns to Eric for advice about writing the introduction and conclusion. Eric also seems unsure about how to proceed. Ms. Hardy notices that a number of students are confused about these two parts, and she invites interested students to meet together for a minilesson. They discuss the purpose of the introduction and conclusion and suggest ways to word these two parts. Students at the minilesson who have already drafted these two parts share their writing. Now Matt returns to his desk and quickly drafts his introduction and conclusion.

The next day Matt rereads his report, adding a word in several places and one additional sentence. He sequences his paragraphs one way and reads it again, but isn't satisfied with the arrangement so he reorders them. Rereading the report, he seems satisfied.

Several days later after most of the students have completed their rough drafts, they meet in writing groups to share their writing. Matt's group calls themselves "The

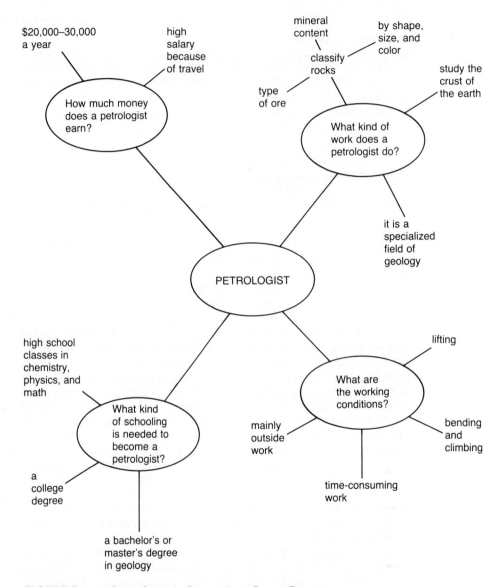

FIGURE 7-1   *A Sixth Grader's Cluster for a Career Report*

Awesome Authors." The four boys in this group pull chairs into a circle, ready to critique each other's writing. Matt reads his report first and receives the following compliments:

> "You had good facts, lots of information about petrologists in your report. It sounds like a pretty interesting career."

> "I like your introduction. It caught my attention."

"You wrote good paragraphs. I could pick out your topic sentences, and I think you stuck to one question in each paragraph."

He asks for suggestions on how to improve his report, and Eric suggests that he list a petrologist's salary by month as well as by year. The boys discuss how to translate a yearly salary of $20,000 to $30,000 to a monthly rate but do not reach a conclusion. Matt asks for other suggestions, and Micha asks for clarification about the type of outside work that petrologists do. Then it is Robert's turn to read his report.

After the writing group, Matt makes the two recommended changes. Then Eric and Matt work together to edit their reports using an editing checklist that they staple on top of their rough drafts. They check for spelling errors, punctuation marks, capital letters at the beginning of sentences and in proper nouns, topic sentences in paragraphs, and correct bibliographic form in the bibliography. After editing, Matt shows his report to Ms. Hardy who reads it quickly, spotting two additional mechanical errors. She also scans the bibliography on the last page, checking that Matt included at least three sources and used the correct bibliographic format. Then she gives Matt the go-ahead to write the final copy of his report. Here is Matt's report:

▽

Petrologists: What Do They Do?

Petrology is an interesting career. If you like the earth and rocks you would probably enjoy this career.

Petrology is the study of rocks and the ground. If you were a petrologist you would classify and determine the rocks you found by their shape, size, and color. You would also classify according to the mineral and types of ore the rock came from. You would study the crust of the earth, and the earth itself. Petrology is a specialized field of geology.

The salary of a petrologist ranges anywhere from $20,000 to $30,000 a year or $2,000 to $3,000 a month. Part of the reason for these wages is because you go to different places a lot and you also travel a lot. You don't stay in the same place very often.

If you want to be a petrologist you will have to go to school about as long as any other career. The most essential classes to take in high school to help you prepare for petrology are chemistry, physics, and math. Petrology also requires at least four years of college. You can either get a bachelor's degree or a master's degree in geology.

The kind of working conditions you will experience in petrology are mainly outside work but some inside work. There is a lot of medium lifting. It also requires a lot of bending and climbing. Being a petrologist is very hard and time-consuming work.

Petrology is a career for people who like studying the ground and the many things it contains.

Bibliography

Fodor, R. V. What Does a Geologist Do? *New York: Dodd, 1977.*

Goldreich, Gloria and Esther. What Can She Be? A Geologist. *New York: Lothrop, Lee & Shepard, 1976.*

no author. Growing Up with Science. *Westport, CT: Suttman, 1984.*

Robinson, H. Alan. "Career Guidance." Collier's Encyclopedia, *vol. 5, pp. 421–444. New York: Macmillan, 1981.*

Matt and his classmates wrote reports for a specific purpose, to learn about a career and to share the information they have learned. They designed their own research questions and pursued the study because of genuine interest. This project might better be called a search, rather than research, project because the students are searching for answers to questions they posed, not just satisfying a teacher's assignment for library research (Macrorie, 1984).

*A*uthors use expository writing to share information with readers. The information might be a description of a career, the steps in building a road, the problems involved in cleaning up the oil spill in Alaska's Prince William Sound, or a comparison of Paul Revere's and Jack Joulett's Revolutionary War rides. Elementary students are interested in learning about the world around them, and informational books help them satisfy their curiosity. Researchers report that even kindergartners enjoy and learn from informational books (Pappas, 1991).

Expository writing forms are also used to write about literature. When students research the setting of a book, for example, the holocaust after reading *Number the Stars* (Lowry, 1989), compare book and film versions of a novel, such as *Tuck Everlasting* (Babbitt, 1975), or investigate a topic related to a story, perhaps owls after reading *Owl Moon* (Yolen, 1987), they are using expository writing. Britton (1970) says this type of writing is intended "to interact with people and things and to make the wheels of the world, for good or ill, go round" (p. 8).

Students learn about expository writing through reading informational books such as *How We Learned the Earth Is Round* (Lauber, 1990) and *Sugaring Time* (Lasky, 1983) and using them as models for their writing (Freeman, 1991). They also learn about expository text structures, the organizational patterns used in informational writing, and find examples of the patterns in informational books. The most common type of expository writing is research reports, and there are many types of reports that elementary students can write. In addition to reports, elementary students compile ABC books, write riddles, and construct posters, diagrams, and other charts to share information.

EXPOSITORY TEXT STRUCTURES

Authors organize different kinds of writing in different ways. When they write to share information, they use expository patterns or text structures. In each pattern, information is organized in a particular way, and words often signal the structure. Five of the most commonly used patterns are description, sequence, comparison, cause and effect, and problem and solution (Meyer & Freedle, 1984; Niles, 1974).

1. *Description.* In this organizational pattern, the writer describes a topic by listing characteristics, features, and examples. Phrases such as *for example* and

characteristics are cue this structure. When students delineate any topic, such as cobras, the planet Jupiter, or Russia, they use description.

2. *Sequence.* The writer lists items or events in numerical or chronological order. Cue words include *first, second, third, next, then,* and *finally.* Directions for completing a math problem, steps in the life cycle of a plant or animal, and events in a biography are often written using the sequence pattern.

3. *Comparison.* The writer explains how two or more things are alike or how they are different. *Different, in contrast, alike, same as,* and *on the other hand* are cue words and phrases that signal this structure. When students compare and contrast book and movie versions of a story, insects with spiders, or life in colonial America with life today, they use this organizational pattern.

4. *Cause and Effect.* The writer explains one or more causes and the resulting effect or effects. *Reasons why, if . . . then, as a result, therefore,* and *because* are words and phrases that cue this structure. Explanations of why the dinosaurs became extinct, the effects of pollution on the environment, or the causes of the American Revolution are written using the cause-and-effect pattern.

5. *Problem and Solution.* In this expository structure, the writer states a problem and provides one or more solutions to the problem. A variation is the question-and-answer format in which the writer poses a question and then answers it. Cue words and phrases include *the problem is, the puzzle is, solve,* and *question . . . answer.* When students write about why money was invented, saving endangered animals, and building dams to stop flooding, they use this structure. Also, students often use the problem and solution pattern in writing advertisements and other persuasive writing. In Figure 7-2, these patterns are summarized.

Diagrams called graphic organizers can be created to help students organize ideas for these organizational patterns (Smith & Tompkins, 1988). Sample diagrams of the graphic organizers are also presented in Figure 7-2.

Reading researchers identified these five patterns by examining content area reading materials to devise ways to help students comprehend those materials more easily. Most of the research on expository text structures has focused on older students' use of these patterns in reading; however, elementary students also use the patterns and cue words in their writing.

A class of second graders examined the five expository text structures and learned that authors use cue words as a "secret code" to signal the structures. Then they read informational books exemplifying each of the expository text structures. After reading, the second graders wrote paragraphs to share what they had learned. Working in small groups, they developed graphic organizers and added main ideas and details from their reading. Then they wrote paragraphs modeling each of the five organizational patterns. These graphic organizers and paragraphs are presented in Figure 7-3. The cue words in each paragraph appear in boldface type.

Pattern	Description	Cue Words	Graphic Organizer	Sample Passage
Description	The author describes a topic by listing characteristics, features, and examples.	for example characteristics are		The Olympic symbol consists of five interlocking rings. The rings represent the five continents—Africa, Asia, Europe, North America, and South America—from which athletes come to compete in the games. The rings are colored black, blue, green, red, and yellow. At least one of these colors is found in the flag of every country sending athletes to compete in the Olympic games.
Sequence	The author lists items or events in numerical or chronological order.	first, second, third next then finally 1. _____ 2. _____ 3. _____ 4. _____ 5. _____		The Olympic games began as athletic festivals to honor the Greek gods. The most important festival was held in the valley of Olympia to honor Zeus, the king of the gods. It was this festival that became the Olympic games in 776 B.C. These games were ended in A.D. 394 by the Roman Emperor who ruled Greece. No Olympic games were held for more than 1,500 years. Then the modern Olympics began in 1896. Almost 300 male athletes competed in the first modern Olympics. In the games held in 1900, female athletes were allowed to compete. The games have continued every four years since 1896 except during World War II, and they will most likely continue for many years to come.
Comparison	The author explains how two or more things are alike and/or how they are different.	different in contrast alike same as on the other hand Alike Different		The modern Olympics is very unlike the ancient Olympic games. Individual events are different. While there were no swimming races in the ancient games, for example, there were chariot races. There were no female contestants and all athletes competed in the nude. Of course, the ancient and modern Olympics are also alike in many ways. Some events, such as the javelin and discus throws, are the same. Some people say that cheating, professionalism, and nationalism in the modern games are a disgrace to the Olympic tradition. But according to the ancient Greek writers, there were many cases of cheating, nationalism, and professionalism in their Olympics, too.

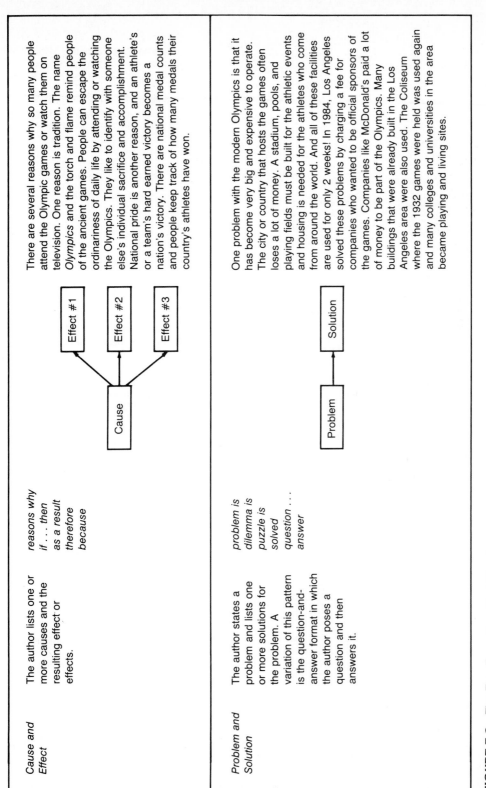

| Cause and Effect | The author lists one or more causes and the resulting effect or effects. | *reasons why* *if . . . then* *as a result* *therefore* *because* | There are several reasons why so many people attend the Olympic games or watch them on television. One reason is tradition. The name *Olympics* and the torch and flame remind people of the ancient games. People can escape the ordinariness of daily life by attending or watching the Olympics. They like to identify with someone else's individual sacrifice and accomplishment. National pride is another reason, and an athlete's or a team's hard earned victory becomes a nation's victory. There are national medal counts and people keep track of how many medals their country's athletes have won. |
| Problem and Solution | The author states a problem and lists one or more solutions for the problem. A variation of this pattern is the question-and-answer format in which the author poses a question and then answers it. | *problem is* *dilemma is* *puzzle is* *solved* *question . . .* *answer* | One problem with the modern Olympics is that it has become very big and expensive to operate. The city or country that hosts the games often loses a lot of money. A stadium, pools, and playing fields must be built for the athletic events and housing is needed for the athletes who come from around the world. And all of these facilities are used for only 2 weeks! In 1984, Los Angeles solved these problems by charging a fee for companies who wanted to be official sponsors of the games. Companies like McDonald's paid a lot of money to be part of the Olympics. Many buildings that were already built in the Los Angeles area were also used. The Coliseum where the 1932 games were held was used again and many colleges and universities in the area became playing and living sites. |

FIGURE 7-2 The Five Expository Text Structures

Adapted from McGee & Richgels, 1985; Smith & Tompkins, 1988.

Description

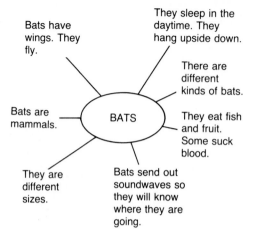

Bats

All bats are mammals. Bats sleep upside down in the daytime. These animals make sounds to know where they are going. Bats find food by sending out soundwaves. They eat fish, blood, insects, rodents, fruits, and nectar. Bats are all different sizes. Some bats have wings that are five feet wide.

Sequence

1. male and female mate
2. female lays eggs
3. eggs hatch
4. a caterpillar eats and grows
5. it sheds its skin several times
6. caterpillar forms a chrysalis
7. butterfly hatches
8. start all over again

The Life of a Monarch Butterfly

A butterfly makes a lot of changes in its life. **First** the male and the female mate. **Next** the female lays eggs. The eggs stick to milkweed leaves for three days. **Then** the eggs hatch into little caterpillars. For five weeks, the caterpillar eats and grows. **After** shedding its skin several times, the caterpillar forms a chrysalis. **After** two weeks, the butterfly hatches out of the chrysalis. **Then** it starts all over again when a butterfly finds a mate.

Comparison

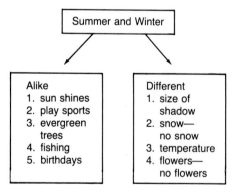

Summer and Winter

Summer and winter are **alike** in a lot of ways. In the winter and the summer the sun shines. You can play sports in both of these seasons. You can have birthdays in the winter and summer. In the winter you can go ice fishing and in the summer you can go fishing. Evergreens stay green in both seasons.

Summer and winter are **different** in a lot of ways. In the winter it snows and in the summer it doesn't. In the winter we have big shadows and in the summer we have little shadows. Summer is hot and winter is cold.

FIGURE 7-3 *Second Graders' Graphic Organizers and Paragraphs Illustrating the Five Expository Text Structures*

Cause and Effect

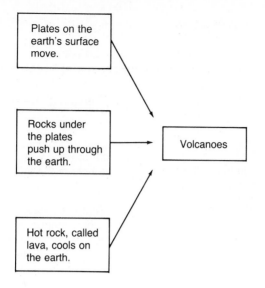

Volcanoes

Do you know what **causes** volcanoes? The plates on the earth's surface rub together and make hot liquid rock underneath the plates. The hot rock pushes up between the plates. Sometimes it makes a big explosion and the lava comes out onto the earth.

Problem and Solution

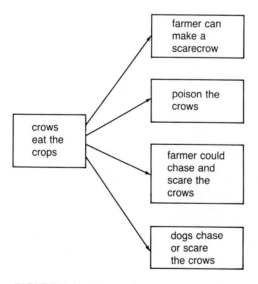

The Problem with Crows

The farmer was having a **problem** with crows eating the crops. One **solution** the farmer tried was to put up a scarecrow. Another idea he had up his sleeve was to poison the crows by spraying the crops with chemicals. The farmer thought about chasing the crows away himself. One more idea the farmer had was to let his dog out to chase the crows.

FIGURE 7-3, continued

187

Teaching Students to Use Expository Text Structures

Students can learn to recognize expository patterns and use them to improve their reading comprehension as well as to organize their writing (Flood, Lapp, & Farnan, 1986; McGee & Richgels, 1985; Piccolo, 1987). Teachers teach students about the five expository text structures through a series of minilessons. The steps in the instructional strategy are

Step
by
Step

1. *Introduce an organizational pattern.*   Explain the pattern and when writers use it, note cue words that signal the pattern, share an example of the pattern, and then describe the graphic organizer for that pattern.

2. *Analyze examples of the pattern in trade books.*   Students locate examples of the expository text structure in informational books, not in stories. A list of informational books illustrating the five expository structures is presented in Figure 7-4. Sometimes the pattern is signaled clearly using titles, topic sentences, and cue words, and sometimes it is not. Students identify cue words when they are used,

FIGURE 7-4   *Informational Books Representing the Expository Text Structures*
P = primary grades (K–2); M = middle grades (3–5); U = upper grades (6–8)

Description

Balestrino, P. (1971). *The skeleton inside you.* New York: Crowell. (P)
Branley, F. M. (1986). *What the moon is like.* New York: Harper & Row. (M)
Hansen, R., & Bell, R. A. (1985). *My first book of space.* New York: Simon & Schuster. (M)
Horvatic, A. (1989). *Simple machines.* New York: Dutton. (M)
Parish, P. (1974). *Dinosaur time.* New York: Harper & Row. (P)

Sequence

Carrick, C. (1978). *Octopus.* New York: Clarion. (M)
Cole, J. (1991). *My puppy is born.* New York: Morrow. (P–M)
Gibbons, G. (1985). *Lights! camera! action!* New York: Crowell. (M)
Jaspersohn, W. (1988). *Ice cream.* New York: Macmillan. (M–U)
Lasky, K. (1983). *Sugaring time.* New York: Macmillan. (M–U)
Macaulay, D. (1977). *Castle.* Boston: Houghton Mifflin. (M–U)
Provensen, A. (1990). *The buck stops here.* New York: HarperCollins. (M–U)

Comparison

Gibbons, G. (1984). *Fire! Fire!* New York: Harper and Row. (P–M)
Lasker, J. (1976). *Merry ever after: The story of two medieval weddings.* New York: Viking. (M–U)
Rowan, J. P. (1985). *Butterflies and moths* (A new true book). Chicago: Children's Press. (M)
Spier, P. (1987). *We the people.* New York: Doubleday. (M–U)

and they talk about why writers may or may not explicitly signal the structure. They also diagram the structure using a graphic organizer.

3. *Write paragraphs using the pattern.* After students analyze examples of the pattern in informational books, they write paragraphs using the pattern. The first writing activity may be a whole-class activity. Later, students write paragraphs in small groups and individually. For prewriting activities, students choose a topic, gather information and organize it using a graphic organizer. Next they write a rough draft of the paragraph, inserting cue words to signal the structure. Then they revise, edit, and write a final copy of the paragraph.

4. *Repeat for each pattern.* Repeat the first three steps for each of the five expository text structures. Once students have learned the organizational patterns, they are ready to use them in their writing.

FIGURE 7-4, *continued*

Cause and Effect

Branley, F. M. (1985). *Flash, crash, rumble, and roll.* New York: Harper & Row. (P–M)
Branley, F. M. (1985). *Volcanoes.* New York: Harper and Row. (P–M)
Branley, F. M. (1986). *What makes day and night?* New York: Harper & Row. (P–M)
Selsam, M. E. (1981). *Where do they go? Insects in winter.* New York: Scholastic. (P–M)
Showers, P. (1985). *What happens to a hamburger?* New York: Harper & Row. (P–M)

Problem and Solution

Cole, J. (1983). *Cars and how they go.* New York: Harper & Row. (P–M)
Horwitz, J. (1984). *Night markets: Bringing food to a city.* New York: Harper & Row. (M–U)
Lauber, P. (1990). *How we learned the Earth is round.* New York: Crowell. (P–M)
Levine, E. (1988). *. . . If you traveled on the underground railroad.* New York: Scholastic. (M–U)
Showers, P. (1980). *No measles, no mumps for me.* New York: Crowell. (P–M)
Simon, S. (1984). *The dinosaur is the biggest animal that ever lived and other wrong ideas you thought were true.* New York: Harper & Row. (P–M)

Combination

Aliki. (1981). *Digging up dinosaurs.* New York: Harper and Row. (M)
de Paola, T. (1978). *The popcorn book.* New York: Holiday House. (P–M)
Podendorf, I. (1982). *Jungles* (A new true book). Chicago: Children's Press. (M)
Sabin, F. (1982). *Amazing world of ants.* Manwah, NJ: Troll. (M)
Simon, S. (1985). *Meet the computer.* New York: Harper & Row. (M–U)
Venutra, P., & Ceserani, G. P. (1985). *In search of Tutankhamun.* Morristown, NJ: Silver Burdett. (U)

5. *Choose the most appropriate pattern to communicate effectively.*   After students learn to use each of the five expository text structures, they need to learn to choose the most appropriate pattern to communicate effectively. Students can experiment to see the appropriateness of various patterns by taking one set of information and writing paragraphs using different organizational patterns. For example, information about igloos might be written as a description, as a comparison with Indian teepees, or as a solution to a housing problem in the arctic region.

Assessing Students' Use of Expository Text Structures.   When students write paragraphs using an expository text structure, they

▼ choose the most appropriate structure
▼ develop a graphic organizer before writing
▼ write a topic sentence that identifies the structure
▼ use cue words to signal the structure

These four components can be used to develop a checklist to assess students' use of expository text structures. Also, teachers may want to monitor students' use of the five structures in research reports and other across-the-curriculum writing.

Knowledge of these organizational patterns is also valuable in writing groups. When students offer compliments, they can mention sequence or the use of cue words to signal the cause-and-effect pattern. Similarly, when offering suggestions for improvement, they can suggest that a classmate try a specific pattern or add cue words.

RESEARCH REPORTS

Too often students are not exposed to research reports until they must write a term paper in high school. Then they become overwhelmed with learning how to take notes on notecards, how to organize and write the paper, and how to compile a bibliography. There is no reason to postpone report writing until students reach high school. Students in the elementary grades can search for answers to questions that interest them and write both class and individual reports (Krogness, 1987; Queenan, 1986). Through early, successful experiences with report writing, students not only learn how to write research reports, but they also gain knowledge in different subject areas.

Contrary to the popular assumption that young children's first writing is narrative, educators have found that kindergartners and first graders write many nonnarrative compositions in which they provide information about familiar topics, such as "Signs of Fall," or directions for familiar activities, such as "How to Feed Your Pet" (Bonin, 1988; Sowers, 1985). Many of these writings might be termed "All About _____ " books, and others are informational pieces that children dictate for the teacher to record. Both activities introduce young children to expository writing.

"All About _____ " Books

In "All About _____ " books, young children write an entire booklet on a single topic. Usually one piece of information and an illustration are presented on each page. First-grade David wrote *The Sea Animals* (presented in Figure 7-5) as a part of a unit on the sea. Notice that David numbered each page of his book, 1 through 4, in the upper right corner of the page. Then he added a cover, and after a minute of confusion he added a zero to the cover so that each page would be numbered. David used invented spelling to spell many words in his report, but the information can be deciphered easily. Also, on page 1, David was experimenting with word boundaries and chose to use a dot to mark the division between words that he recognized as separate words. He considered "The dolphin" and "swim fast" as single units. When he wrote other pages, David's attention changed and he focused on other dimensions of writing.

An "All About _____ " book can be a collaborative production in which each child contributes one page for the book. For example, as a part of the unit on insects, the students in a primary level class for emotionally disturbed children each contrib-

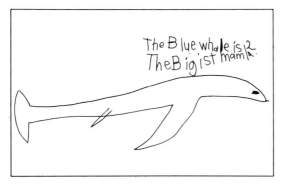

FIGURE 7-5 *A First Grader's "All About _____ " Book*

uted one page to a class book about ladybugs. After collecting some ladybugs to observe in the classroom and reading a book or two about the distinctive insects, the teacher and children brainstormed a list of things they had learned about ladybugs. Then the six children each chose one thing from the list, or another piece of information if they preferred, for their page. They wrote the information on a sheet of paper and added an illustration. Their teacher collected the pages, included a sheet at the end of the book called "How We Learned about Ladybugs," and then added construction paper cover. Here is the group's report:

▽

All About Ladybugs

Page 1: *There are about 600 kinds of ladybugs.*
Page 2: *Ladybugs are supposed to bring you good luck.*
Page 3: *Ladybugs pretend to be dead when frightened.*
Page 4: *Ladybugs like the rain.*
Page 5: *Ladybugs spend the winter in pinecones, cracks, under leaves, and even in houses sleeping and waiting for spring.*
Page 6: *Ladybugs don't bite!*
Page 7: *How We Learned about Ladybugs:*
    1. *We watched three ladybugs that we kept in a jar in our classroom.*
    2. *We read these books:*
       Insects *by Illa Podendorf, 1981.*
       Ladybug, Ladybug, Fly Away Home *by Judy Hawes, 1967.*

Dictated Reports

Young children can dictate reports to their teacher, who serves as scribe. After listening to a guest speaker, viewing a film, or reading several books about a particular topic, kindergartners and first graders can dictate brief reports. A class of kindergartners compiled the book-length report on police officers presented in Figure 7-6. The teacher read two books aloud to the students and Officer Jerry, a police officer, visited the classroom and talked to the students about his job. The students also took a field trip to visit the police station. The teacher took photos of Officer Jerry, his police car, and the police station to illustrate the report. With this background, the students and the teacher together developed a cluster with these main ideas: (a) what police officers do, (b) what equipment police officers have, (c) how police officers travel, (d) where police officers work, and (e) how police officers can be your friends. The students added details and developed each main idea to fill one page of the report. The background of experiences and the clustering activity prepared students to compose their report. After students finished the text of their report, added a bibliography called "How We Learned About Police Officers for Our Report," and inserted the photographs, it was ceremoniously presented to the school library to be enjoyed by all students in the school. The proud authors were the students who borrowed it most frequently because it was "our best book ever"!

FIGURE 7-6   *Kindergartners' Report About Police Officers*

Our Report about Police Officers

Page 1: Police officers help people who are in trouble. They are nice to kids. They are only mean to robbers and bad people. Police officers make people obey the laws. They give tickets to people who drive cars too fast.

Page 2: Men and women can be police officers. They wear blue uniforms like Officer Jerry's. But sometimes police officers wear regular clothes when they work undercover. They wear badges on their uniforms and on their hats. Officer Jerry's badge number is 3407. Police officers have guns, handcuffs, whistles, sticks, and two-way radios. They have to carry all these things.

Page 3: Police officers drive police cars with flashing lights and loud sirens. The cars have radios so the officers can talk to other police officers at the police station. Sometimes they ride on police motorcycles or on police horses or in police helicopters or in police boats.

Page 4: Police officers work at police stations. The jail for the bad people that they catch is right next door. One police officer sits at the radio to talk to the police officers who are driving their cars. The police chief works at the police station, too.

Page 5: Police officers are your friends. They want to help you so you shouldn't be afraid of them. You can ask them if you need some help.

Page 6: How We Learned About Police Officers for Our Report
   1. We read these books:
      Police by Ray Broekel
      What Do They Do? Policemen and Firemen by Carla Greene
   2. We interviewed Officer Jerry.
   3. We visited the police station.

Collaborative Reports

A successful first report-writing experience for middle- and upper-grade students is a class research report. Small groups of students work together to write sections of the work and then compile their sections to form the report. Students benefit from writing a group report first because the group provides a scaffold or support system. Also, by working in groups, the laborious parts of the work are shared.

A group of four fourth graders wrote a collaborative report on hermit crabs. These students sat together at one table and watched the hermit crabs that lived in a terrarium on their table. They cared for these crustaceans for two weeks and made notes of their observations in learning logs. After this period, the students were bursting with questions about the hermit crabs and were eager for answers. They wanted to know what the crabs' real habitat was, what the best habitat was for them in the classroom, how they breathed air, why they lived in borrowed shells, why one pincher was bigger than the other, and so on. Their teacher provided some answers and directed them to books that would provide additional information. As they collected

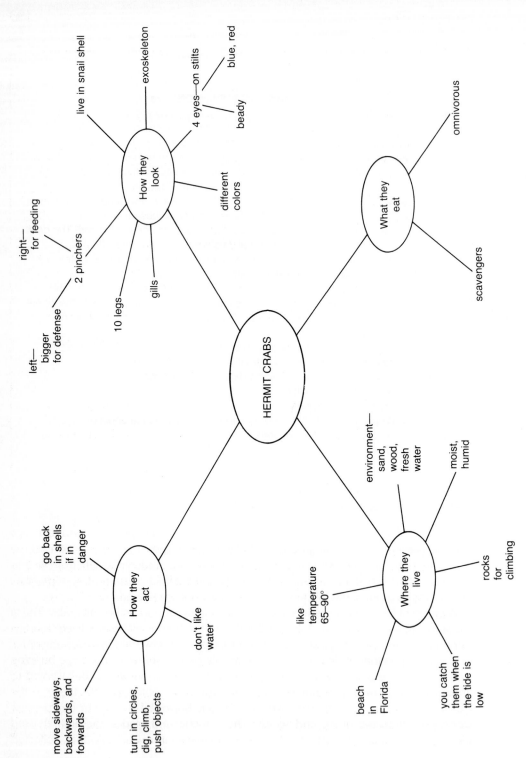

FIGURE 7-7 *Fourth Graders' Cluster and Collaborative Report on Hermit Crabs*

The Encyclopedia About Hermit Crabs

HOW THEY LOOK

Hermit crabs are very much like regular crabs but hermit crabs transfer shells. They have gills. Why? Because they are born in water and when they mature they come to land and kill snails so they can have a shell. They have two beady eyes that look like they are on stilts. Their body is a sight! Their shell looks like a rock. Really it is an exoskeleton which means the skeleton is on the outside. They have two pinchers. The left one is bigger so it is used for defense. The right one is for feeding. They also have ten legs.

WHERE THEY LIVE

Hermit crabs live mostly on beaches in Florida where the weather is 65°–90°. They live in fresh water. They like humid weather and places that have sand, wood, and rocks (for climbing on). The best time to catch hermit crabs is a low tide.

WHAT THEY EAT

Hermit crabs are ominorous scavengers which means they eat just about anything. They even eat leftovers.

HOW THEY ACT

Hermit crabs are very unusual. They go back into their shell if they think there is danger. They are funny because they walk sideways, forwards, and backwards. They can go in circles. They can also get up when they get upside down. And that's how they act.

FIGURE 7-7, *continued*

information, they created a cluster that they taped to their table next to the terrarium. Soon the cluster wasn't an adequate way to report information so they decided to share their knowledge by writing a book which they called *The Encyclopedia About Hermit Crabs.* This book and the cluster used in gathering information for it are presented in Figure 7-7.

The students decided to share the work of writing the book, and they chose four main ideas, one for each student to write. The four main ideas were what hermit crabs look like, how they act, where they live, and what they eat. A different student wrote each section and then returned to the group to share the rough draft. The students gave each other suggestions for revisions. Next they edited their report with the teacher and added an introduction, conclusion, and bibliography. Finally, they recopied their report and added illustrations in a clothbound book that they read to each class in the school before adding it to the school library.

Individual Reports

Toby Fulwiler (1985) recommends that students do authentic research in which they explore topics that interest them or hunt for answers to questions that puzzle them. As students become immersed in theme cycles, questions arise that students want to explore. Students in a fourth-grade class were studying dinosaurs, and they quickly asked more questions than the teacher could answer. She encouraged them to search for answers in the books they had checked out of the school and community public libraries. As they located answers to their questions, the students were eager to share their new knowledge and decided to write reports and publish them as books.

Fourth-grade Dustin's *The World of the Dinosaurs* is presented in Figure 7-8. His report is divided into three chapters, and he also included a table of contents, a bibliography, and an "All About the Author" page at the end. Each chapter focuses on a question he examined. The first chapter, "The Death Star," was written to answer his question about how the dinosaurs became extinct. Dustin wrote the second chapter on the three periods to answer his question about whether or not the dinosaurs all lived at the same time. In the third chapter, Dustin wrote a description of the pterodactyl, an unusual flying lizard that lived when the dinosaurs did. He chose this topic after locating an interesting book about these flying lizards.

TEACHING STUDENTS TO WRITE RESEARCH REPORTS

Students learn how to write research reports through a series of minilessons and several experiences writing class collaboration reports. Through the minilessons, teachers explain how to choose a topic, design research questions, use the writing process to develop and refine the report, and write a bibliography. Then students practice what they have learned as they work with partners or in small groups to write collaborative reports. Through these experiences, students gain both the expertise and confidence to write individual reports.

Students use the writing process as they search for answers to questions about a topic and then compose a report to share what they have learned. Reports are usually written in connection with theme studies, but some students enjoy expository writing or have special interests that they research and write about during writers' workshop. Sometimes theme cycles extend throughout much of the school day, and students read books related to the theme during readers' workshop and write a research report related to the theme during writers' workshop.

Writing Class Collaboration Reports

Students work with partners or in small groups to write collaborative reports in connection with theme studies. Class collaboration reports are a good way for students to learn the steps involved in writing a report and gain experience working through the writing process without the complexities of writing individual reports. The steps are explained in the following paragraphs.

FIGURE 7-8 *A Fourth Grader's Dinosaur Report*

The World of the Dinosaurs

Chapter 1
The Death Star

Over the years, scientists have noticed that almost all stars have a sister star. But what about the sun? Scientists have found out that the sun does have a sister star. It's darker than the sun, and it takes 28 million years to orbit around our solar system. They named it Nemesis after the Greek god of revenge. When Nemesis reaches its closest point to the sun, it makes the asteroid belt go beserk! Asteroids and comets were flying everywhere! The earth was a disaster! Scientists have studied and found out that if a comet or an asteroid hit the earth it would be like dropping an atomic bomb (or a thousand billion tons of dynamite) on the earth. Whenever that happens, almost everything on the face of the earth is destroyed. The next time Nemesis reaches its closest point to the sun will be in about fifteen million years.

Chapter 2
The Three Periods: Triassic, Jurassic, and Cretaceous

There were three periods when the dinosaurs came, and then they were just wiped off the face of the earth. It may have been the Death Star. Whatever the reason, nobody knows. The three periods were the Triassic, Jurassic, and the Cretaceous.

Most of the smaller animals like Orniholestes and Hysilophodon came in the Triassic Period. They were mostly plant eaters.

Most of the flying dinosaurs like Pteradactyl and Pteranadon came in the Jurassic Period. A number of the big plant eaters like Brontosaurus and Brachiosaurus also came in that period. A lot of sea reptiles came in that time, too.

The bigger dinosaurs like Tyrannosaurus Rex and Trachodon came in the Cretaceous Period. Most of these were meat eaters.

Chapter 3
Pterodactyl: The Flying Lizard

The Pterodactyl is a flying lizard that lived millions of years ago when the dinosaurs lived. Pterodactyl means "flying lizard." It was huge animal. It had skin stretched between the hind limb and a long digit of the forelimb. It didn't have any feathers. Some had a wingspan of 20 feet. Some paleontologists think Pterodactyl slept like a bat, upside down, because of the shape of its wings. It had a long beak and very sharp teeth. When it would hunt for food, it would fly close to the water and look for fish. When it saw one, it would dive in and get it. It also had sharp claws that helped it grab things. The Pterodactyl had a strange looking tail. It was long with a ball shape at the end. Some people say it really looked like a flying lizard.

*Step
by
Step*

1. *Choose a topic.*   The first step in writing class collaboration research reports is to choose a topic that students are studying or want to study. Almost any topic in social studies, science, or current events that can be subdivided into 4 to 10 parts works well for class reports. Possible general topics include oceans, dinosaurs, the solar system, the human body, continents, life in the Middle Ages, and transportation.

    From these general topics, students choose specific topics that small groups or pairs of students research. For example, for a report on the continents, students choose which continent they will research, or for a report on the solar system they choose which planet to research. For other theme cycles, such as dinosaurs or the Middle Ages, students may not be able to identify the specific research topic until they have learned more and designed some research questions.

2. *Design research questions.*   As students study the topic, research questions emerge. They brainstorm a list of questions on a chart posted in the classroom and add to the list as other questions arise. In a report on the human body, for example, small groups of students studying each organ may decide to research the same three, four, or five questions, such as these: "What does the organ look like?" "What job does the organ do?" "Where is the organ located in the human body?" Interestingly, elementary students who research the human body often want to include a question on whether or not a person can live without the organ. This interest may stem from news reports about organ transplants.

    Students studying a period of history such as the Middle Ages might brainstorm the following questions about life in that era: "What did the people wear?" "What did they eat?" "What were their communities like?" "What kind of entertainment did people enjoy?" "What occupations did they have?" "How did people protect themselves?" "What kinds of transportation did people use?" Each small group selects one of these questions as the specific topic for its report and develops questions related to the topic.

    To rehearse the process before students research and write their section of the report, the teacher and students may work through the procedure using one of the research questions the students did not choose. As a class, students gather information, organize it, and then write the section of the report using the drafting, revising, and editing stages of the writing process.

3. *Gather and organize information.*   Students work in small groups or in pairs to search for answers to their research questions. These questions provide the structure for data collection because students are seeking answers to specific questions, not just randomly writing information. Students can use clusters or data charts (McKenzie, 1979) to record the information they gather. An example of a cluster and data chart for the report on the human body is presented in Figure 7-9. The research questions are the same for each data collection instrument. On a cluster, students add details to each main-idea ray, and on data charts they record information from the first source in the first row under the appropriate questions, from the second source in the second row, and so on. These two instruments are effective because they organize data collection question by question and limit the amount of information that can be gathered from any source. For both clusters and data charts, students list their sources of information on the back of the sheet of paper.

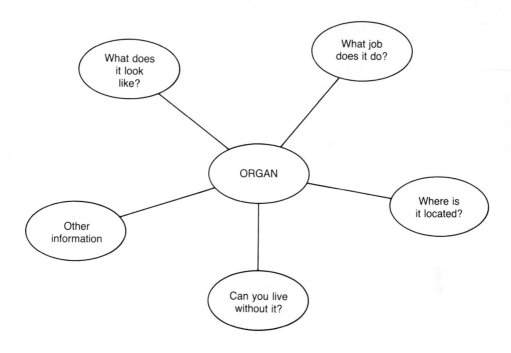

DATA CHART

Researcher _____   Organ _____

Source	What does the organ look like?	What job does the organ do?	Where is the organ located?	Can you live without the organ?	Other information
1					
2					
3					

FIGURE 7-9   *A Cluster and a Data Chart for Research on a Part of the Human Body*

Students gather information from a variety of reference materials, including trade books, textbooks, encyclopedias, magazines, films, videotapes, filmstrips, field trips, interviews, demonstrations, and observations. Teachers often require that students consult two or three different sources and that no more than one source be an encyclopedia.

Too often report writing has been equated with copying facts out of an encyclopedia. Elementary students are not too young to understand what plagiarism is and why it is wrong. Even primary grade students realize that they should not "borrow" items belonging to classmates and pretend the items are theirs. Similarly, students should not borrow someone else's words, especially without giving credit in the composition. The format of clusters and data charts makes it easier for students to take notes without plagiarizing.

After students gather information, they read over it to check that they have answered their research questions fully and delete any unnecessary or redundant information. Next, they consider how they will organize and sequence the information in their rough drafts. Some students tentatively number the research questions in the order they plan to use them in their composition. They also identify a piece of information that is especially interesting to use as the lead-in to their section.

4. *Draft the sections of the report.*   With this preparation, students draft their sections using the information from the cluster or data chart and organizing the information according to one of the expository text structures. They skip every other line to allow space for revising and editing on the rough draft. Because students are working in pairs or small groups, one student can be the scribe to write the draft while the other students in the group dictate the sentences. Next, they share their draft with students from other small groups and revise it on the basis of feedback they receive. Last, students proofread and correct mechanical errors.

5. *Compile the sections.*   Students bring their completed sections for the research report and compile them. As a class, they write the introduction, conclusion, and bibliography and add them to the report. A list of the authors of each section should also be added at the end. After all the parts are compiled, the entire report is read aloud so that students can catch any inconsistencies or redundant passages.   .

6. *Publish the report.*   The last step in writing a class collaboration research report is to publish it. A final copy with all of the parts of the report in the correct sequence is made. If the report has been written on a word processor, it is easy to print out the final copy. Otherwise, the report can be typed or recopied by hand. Copies are made for each student, and special bound copies can be constructed for the class or school library.

Writing Individual Reports

Writing an individual report is similar to writing a collaborative report. Students design research questions, gather information to answer the questions, and then report what they have learned. Writing individually makes two significant changes necessary. Students must narrow their topics and then assume the entire responsibility for writing the report. These are the steps in writing individual research reports:

Step by Step

1. *Choose and narrow a topic.* Students choose topics for research reports from content area units, hobbies, or other interests. After choosing a general topic, such as cats or the human body, they need to narrow their topic so that it is manageable. The broad topic of cats might be narrowed to pet cats or tigers and the human body to one organ or organ system.

2. *Design research questions.* Students design research questions by brainstorming a list of questions that they want to find answers to in a learning log. Then they review their list, combine some questions, delete others, and finally arrive at four to six questions that are worthy of answering. As they begin their search, new questions may be added and others deleted if they reach a dead end.

3. *Gather and organize information.* As in collaborative reports, students use clusters or data charts to gather and organize information. For upper-grade students, data charts with their rectangular spaces for writing information serve as a transition between clusters and notecards.

4. *Draft the report.* Students write a rough draft using the information they have gathered in the previous step. Each research question can become a paragraph, a section, or a chapter in the report. As they draft each section of the report, students organize their writing using an appropriate text structure.

5. *Revise and edit the report.* Students meet in writing groups to share their rough drafts, and they make revisions based on the feedback they receive from their classmates. After they make the needed revisions, students use an editing checklist to proofread their reports and identify and correct mechanical errors.

6. *Publish the report.* Students recopy their reports in books and add bibliographic information. Research reports can also be published in several other ways. For example, students can produce filmstrip or video presentations, create a series of illustrated charts or dioramas, or they can dramatize the information presented in the report.

Assessing Students' Research Reports

Students need to know what the requirements are for the research project and how they will be assessed or graded. Many teachers develop a checklist with the requirements for the project and distribute this to students before they begin working. In this way, students know what is expected of them and they assume responsibility for completing each step of the assignment. For an individual research report, the checklist might include these observable behaviors and products:

▼ Choose a narrow topic.
▼ Identify four or five research questions.
▼ Use a cluster to gather information to answer the questions.
▼ Write a rough draft with a section (or chapter) to answer each question.

▼ Meet in writing groups to share your report.
▼ Make at least three changes in your rough draft.
▼ Complete an editing checklist with a partner.
▼ Add a bibliography.
▼ Write the final copy of the report.
▼ Share the report with someone.

This checklist can be made simpler or more complex depending on the age and experiences of the students.

Students staple the checklist to the inside cover of the folder in which they keep all the work for the project. As each requirement is completed, they check it off. In this way, students monitor their own work and learn that writing is a process, not just a final product.

When the project is completed, students submit their entire folders to the teacher to be assessed. All of the requirements listed on the checklist are considered in determining the student's grade. If the checklist has 10 requirements, each requirement might be worth 10 points, and the grading can be done objectively on an 100-point scale. Thus, if the student's project is complete with all required materials, the student scores 100 or a grade of A. Points can be subtracted for work that is sloppy or incomplete. If additional grades are necessary, each item on the checklist can be graded separately. If a quality assessment of the final copy of the research report is needed, then a second grade can be awarded.

It is more important that students understand how to conduct research to find answers to questions that puzzle them than it is to be successful on one particular report-writing project. McGinley and Madigan (1990) recommend that students reflect on the research process they used and write about that process in order to appreciate that the research process is a powerful learning tool. Students can write about each step in the research and writing process in their learning logs or write a reflective analysis of their work after they complete a research project.

OTHER WAYS TO SHARE INFORMATION

Research reports are the conventional way to share information through writing, but there are many other ways students can share information. Through riddles, ABC books, and many other forms, students can apply expository text structures.

ABC Books

Students can use the letters of the alphabet to organize the information they want to share in an ABC or alphabet book. Alphabet books such as *Ashanti to Zulu: African Traditions* (Musgrove, 1976) about African cultures, *Eight Hands Round: A Patchwork Alphabet* (Paul, 1991) about quilting, and *Illuminations* (Hunt, 1989) about medieval life can be used as models. Students begin by brainstorming information related to the topic being studied and identify a word or fact for each letter of the alphabet. Then students work individually, in pairs, or in small groups to compose pages for the ABC book. The format for the pages is similar to the one used in alphabet books by professional authors. Students write the letter in one corner of the page, draw an illustration, and write a sentence or paragraph to describe the word or fact. The text usually begins " _____ is for _____ ," and then a sentence or paragraph description follows.

A second-grade class chose to organize their report on insects as an alphabet book. The *G* page is presented in Figure 7-10. These students used the writing process to draft, revise, edit, and publish their pages.

Riddles

Students can compose riddles to share information they have discovered. Riddles use a question-and-answer format and incorporate two or three facts, or clues, in the question part. Sometimes the answer is written upside down on the page, on the back of the page with the question, or on the next page of a book. The writing process is important for creating riddles, and during the revising stage, students make sure

FIGURE 7-10 *One Page from a Second-Grade ABC Book on Insects*

they have included essential descriptive information and that the information is correct.

Small groups of students or the whole class can compose books of riddles related to social studies or science themes. During a study of life in the desert, first graders wrote these riddles as part of a class book:

▽   *I live in underground cities of tunnels.*
I get my name from my barking cry.
I eat grass and other plants.
What am I?
(a prairie dog)

I fly in wide circles above the earth.
I sometimes am called a buzzard.
What am I?
(a vulture)

Posters, Diagrams, and Charts

Students can make posters, diagrams, and charts to learn and share information. They might make murals, design clusters, draw Venn diagrams, make graphs, draw maps, and do many other types of projects. In these projects, students combine drawing and writing to apply the expository text structures. Here are some examples:

▼ *Description.* As part of a study of medieval life, seventh-grade students draw diagrams and label the parts of a castle or fortress. Third-grade students make a cluster with information about Jupiter or another planet in the solar system.
▼ *Sequence.* After reading *The Very Hungry Caterpillar* (Carle, 1969), first graders draw circle diagrams to illustrate the life cycle of a butterfly.
▼ *Compare and Contrast.* Fourth-grade students make a Venn diagram (two interlocking circles, one labeled "Then" and the other "Now") to compare and contrast pioneer life with life today. Kindergartners make posters to illustrate each of the four seasons.
▼ *Cause and Effect.* As a part of a drug abuse program, sixth graders make posters to point out the effects of smoking, drugs, and drinking.
▼ *Problem and Solution.* During a theme cycle on ecology, eighth-grade students work in small groups to brainstorm a chart of ecological problems and ways to solve them. Third graders make posters showing ways to save energy as part of a science theme on natural resources.

Cubes

A cube has six sides, and in this expository writing activity, students explore a topic from six dimensions or sides by doing the following:

1. *Describe it.* Describe its colors, shapes, and sizes.
2. *Compare it.* What is it similar to or different from?
3. *Associate it.* What does it make you think of?

4. *Analyze it.* Tell how it is made or what it is composed of.
5. *Apply it.* What can you do with it? How is it used?
6. *Argue for or against it.* Take a stand and list reasons supporting it.

Almost any topic can be examined from these six dimensions, from earthquakes to the California gold rush, from eagles to microcomputers, from the Great Wall of China to ancient Egypt. Figure 7-11 presents a sixth-grade class's cube on junk food that was written as part of a theme on nutrition.

FIGURE 7-11 *A Sixth-Grade Collaborative Cube on Junk Food*
Source: Tompkins & Camp, 1988, p. 213.

Junk Food

1. Describe it.
Junk food is delicious! Some junk food is made of chocolate, like chocolate ice cream and brownies. Some junk food is salty, like potato chips and pretzels. Other junk food is usually sweet or sugary, like sugar cookies, sweet rolls, or soft drinks. Junk food packages are colorful and often show you what's inside to get your attention. Most of the packages are made of paper or plastic, and they make crinkly sounds.

2. Compare it.
Junk food tastes better than nutritious food, but nutritious food is better for you. Nutritious food is less sweet and salty. Parents would rather you eat nutritious food than junk food because nutritious food keeps you healthy, but kids would rather eat junk food because it tastes better and is more fun to eat.

3. Associate it.
Most often you eat junk food at get-togethers with friends. At parties, junk food such as chips and dip and soft drinks are served. At movies, you can buy popcorn, candy, nachos, and many other kinds of junk food. Other places where people get together and eat junk food are skating rinks, sporting events, and concerts.

4. Analyze it.
Junk food is not good to eat because of all the oils, sugar, salt, and calories. Most of them have artificial colorings and flavorings. Many junk foods are low in vitamins and protein, but they have a high percentage of fats.

5. Apply it.
The most important thing you can do with junk food is to eat it. Some other uses are popcorn decorations at Christmas time, Halloween treats, and Easter candy. You can sell it to raise money for charities, clubs, and schools. Last year we sold junk food to raise money for the Statue of Liberty.

6. Argue for or against it.
We're for junk food because it tastes good. Even though it's not good for you, people like it and buy it. If there were no more junk food, a lot of people would be unemployed, such as dentists. Bakeries, convenience stores, fast food restaurants, grocery stores, and ice cream parlors would lose a lot of business if people didn't buy junk food. The Declaration of Independence guarantees our rights and freedoms, and Thomas Jefferson might have said, "Life, Liberty, and the Pursuit of Junk Food." We believe that he who wants something pleasing shall have it!

Students often work together in small groups to do a cube. Students divide into six groups, and each group examines the topic from one dimension. Together, they develop a paragraph or two to explore their dimension. Students brainstorm ideas, use the ideas to develop a paragraph or two, revise, and edit. Then one student in the group writes the final copy. All six groups share their writing with the class. The final copies can be taped to a large square box and displayed in the classroom.

Other Genre

Students can choose other ways of presenting the information they have gathered (Wilde, 1988). For example, they can present the information in a story, letter, or poem format rather than as a report. Seventh-grade Chris has woven the information he learned about eagles' mating habits into this report which is written in a narrative format:

$\triangledown$

Lord Eagle

One morning Lord Eagle woke up. Lady Eagle was still asleep. Lord Eagle flew out of their four foot deep nest. Then he flew to a perch in their tree. Lord Eagle stands three feet tall and with a wing span of eight feet. Lord Eagle flew to a perch in a tree beside a nearby river and waited for a careless fish to swim near the surface. When one did, Lord Eagle swooped down and dipped his talons just below the surface of the river, grabbing the fish! He flew to the ground. With his sharp curved beak, he tore strips of the fish off and swallowed it.

Once Lady Eagle has had her breakfast, the Lord and Lady fly through the sky. Today is different. It is about time for Lord Eagle to fertilize the eggs. Eagles usually lay two eggs at a time. This is the second year Lord and Lady Eagle have flown together. Eagles stay together until one dies.

Lord and Lady Eagle soar in the sky, going upward until just small dots in the sky are seen from earth. Since this is their mating period, they lock claws and close their wings. They plummet earthward, tumbling. Falling a couple of hundred feet. Then opening their wings and releasing each other's claws, they soar upward again. This is repeated.

It is time to add to the nest. Lord Eagle found a good tree branch still attached to the tree. He flies up and swoops down. With his strong wings and claws, he tears the branch off. Then he adds it to the nest.

The day is over for the eagles so they settle into the nest.

Answering Teachers' Questions About...
Expository Writing

1. *You must be kidding. My second graders can't write research reports. They still need to learn basic reading and writing skills.*

The writing samples in this chapter show that second graders *can* write research reports. The question you seem to be asking is why should second graders write reports. Writing collaborative and individual research reports is not frivolous! Children learn basic reading and writing skills as they develop research questions, read to find answers, and then write a report to share what they have learned. What is more basic than having students read to find answers to research questions? They apply decoding and comprehension skills as they read, searching for answers to their questions. What is more basic than having students share their findings through writing? They use the writing process to write their reports. Report writing is authentic and meaningful, the kind of activity that promotes basic reading and writing skills.

2. *When do I teach outlining?*

Outlining is a sticking point for many writers. Because the format of an outline seems so formidable, students often write it *after* the report. I recommend that outlining not be taught to elementary students because it is unnecessary. Instead, have students use clusters and data charts to organize their writing. These forms are more effective and flexible than outlining. If you do teach outlining, have students make a cluster first and then transfer the information from the cluster to the outline. Each main idea item from the cluster be-

comes a main idea in the outline and is marked with a Roman numeral. The details are listed under the main ideas and are marked with uppercase letters. If additional details have been added, they are marked with lowercase letters and written under the particular detail. For example, the "How they act" section of the cluster on hermit crabs presented in Figure 7-7 can be rewritten this way as an outline:

A. How They Act
   1. Move sideways, backwards, and forwards
   2. Turn in circles, dig, climb, push objects
   3. Go back in shells if in danger
   4. Don't like water

3. *Why do you insist that students, even first graders, should add a bibliography to their reports?*

Students should give credit to the sources they used in their reports. Adding a bibliography lends credibility to the report and helps assure the reader that the information is accurate. Adding a bibliography to a report is not a complicated matter even though some junior and senior high school students who have never written a report before seem overwhelmed when asked to write a bibliography—a word they often confuse with biography. In contrast, elementary students accept the responsibility easily when it has been a natural part of report writing since kindergarten. Young children simply add a page at the end of their reports to tell everyone who reads it how they became experts about the subject and found answers to their research questions. It is sufficient if kindergartners and first graders list only the name and author of the book. Students at each grade level gradually add more information so that upper grade students include author, title, city of publication, publisher, and copyright date for the books they reference.

Another benefit is that middle graders begin to note that the authors of the informational books they read have references, too, and they become more critical readers when they look for evidence of the accuracy of information they are reading.

REFERENCES

Babbitt, N. (1975). *Tuck everlasting.* New York: Farrar, Straus & Giroux.

Bonin, S. (1988). Beyond storyland: Young writers can tell it other ways. In T. Newkirk & N. Atwell (Eds.), *Understanding writing* (2nd ed.). (pp. 47–51). Portsmouth, NH: Heinemann.

Britton, J. (1970). *Language and learning.* New York: Penguin Books.

Carle, E. (1969). *The very hungry caterpillar.* New York: Philomel.

Flood, J., Lapp, D., & Farnan, N. (1986). A reading-writing procedure that teaches expository paragraph structure. *The Reading Teacher, 39,* 556–562.

Freeman, E. B. (1991). Informational books: Models for student report writing. *Language Arts, 68,* 470–473.

Fulwiler, T. (1985). Research writing. In M. Schwartz (Ed.), *Writing for many roles* (pp. 207–230). Upper Montclair, NJ: Boynton/Cook.

Hunt, J. (1989). *Illuminations.* New York: Bradbury Press.

Krogness, M. M. (1987). Folklore: A matter of the heart and the heart of the matter. *Language Arts, 64,* 808–818.

Lasky, K. (1983). *Sugaring time.* New York: Macmillan.

Lauber, P. (1990). *How we learned the earth is round.* New York: Crowell.

Lowry, L. (1989). *Number the stars.* Boston: Houghton Mifflin.

McGee, L. M., & Richgels, D. J. (1985). Teaching expository text structure to elementary students. *The Reading Teacher, 38,* 739–748.

McGinley, W., & Madigan, D. (1990). The research "story": A forum for integrating reading, writing, and learning. *Language Arts, 67,* 474–483.

Macrorie, K. (1984). *Searching writing: A context book.* Upper Montclair, NJ: Boynton/Cook.

McKenzie, G. R. (1979). Data charts: A crutch for helping pupils organize reports. *Language Arts, 56,* 784–788.

Meyer, B. J., & Freedle, R. O. (1984). Effects of discourse type on recall. *American Educational Research Journal, 21,* 121–143.

Musgrove, M. (1976). *Ashanti to Zulu: African traditions.* New York: Dial.

Neeld, E. C. (1986). *Writing.* Glenview, IL: Scott Foresman.

Niles, O. S. (1974). Organization perceived. In H. L. Herber (Ed.), *Perspectives in reading: Developing study skills in secondary schools* (pp. 57–76). Newark, DE: International Reading Association.

Pappas, C. C. (1991). Fostering full access to literacy by including information books. *Language Arts, 68,* 449–462.

Paul, A. W. (1991). *Eight hands round: A patchwork alphabet.* New York: HarperCollins.

Piccolo, J. A. (1987). Expository text structures: Teaching and learning strategies. *The Reading Teacher, 40,* 838–847.

Queenan, M. (1986). Finding grain in the marble. *Language Arts, 63,* 666–673.

Smith, P. L., & Tompkins, G. E. (1988). Structured notetaking: A new strategy for content area readers. *The Journal of Reading, 32,* 46–53.

Sowers, S. (1985). The story and the 'all about' book. In J. Hansen, T. Newkirk, & D. Graves (Eds.), *Breaking ground: Teachers relate reading and writing in the elementary school* (pp. 73–82). Portsmouth, NH: Heinemann.

Tompkins, G. E., & Camp, D. E. (1988). Rx for writer's block. *Childhood Education, 64,* 209–214.

Wilde, J. (1988). The written report: Old wine in new bottles. In T. Newkirk & N. Atwell (Eds.), *Understanding writing* (2nd ed.). (pp. 179–190). Portsmouth, NH: Heinemann.

Yolen, J. (1987). *Owl moon.* New York: Philomel.

8

Narrative Writing

Overview of Narrative Writing

Purpose   Students use narrative writing to create stories that entertain. They retell familiar stories, write sequels and new episodes for favorite characters, and compose original stories.

Audience   Students write stories for classmates, their families, and other well-known and trusted audiences. They also publish their stories as books that are placed in the class library or school library.

Forms   Forms include stories that are often bound into books, class collaboration stories, and scripts for puppet shows and readers' theater.

Topics   Students retell familiar stories, tell stories from other viewpoints, and create original stories and sequels for favorite stories.

Approaches Students write stories during writers' workshop and also as part of theme studies. In a literature focus unit, students retell a story from another viewpoint or write a sequel for a familiar story. In a theme cycle, students might write stories incorporating concepts they have learned.

Other   A story or narrative is an account of an event or a series of events, either fictitious or true, that entertains readers. A fully developed story involves a conflict which is introduced in the beginning, becomes more complicated in the middle, and is resolved at the end.

Retelling and Writing Stories

"Clever trick number 4!" cries LaWanda. "That mean ol' crocodile is pretending to be a picnic bench."

"Don't worry, Trunky is going to warn the kids," replies Ashton. The children in Ms. Dillen's first-grade classroom are listening to their teacher reread a favorite story, Roald Dahl's *The Enormous Crocodile* (1978) as part of a focus unit on the book. They eagerly listen to the enormous crocodile's four clever (but unsuccessful) attempts to catch a fat and juicy child to eat for supper, and they join in as Ms. Dillen reads, predicting the failure of the crocodile's tricks again and again. While many adults find the story repulsive, these first graders love it.

Recognizing the students' interest in this story, Ms. Dillen decides to use the story to introduce her first graders to the most basic components of plot. She explains that stories have three parts: a beginning, a middle, and an end. She and the children retell the beginning, middle, and end of *The Enormous Crocodile*. Next, she draws a cluster on the chalkboard with the title of the story in a circle and three rays marked "Beginning," "Middle" and "End." The children identify the events that belong in each story part and complete the story cluster as shown in Figure 8-1.

The following day, Ms. Dillen asks if the children want to write their own version of the story in a big book (a large book made out of sheets of posterboard that the class can read together). They shout and clap their enthusiasm. Ms. Dillen begins by reviewing the story with the children, using the story cluster to organize the retelling. The children decide to write a six-page book, with one page for the beginning, one page for each of the four tricks, and one page for the end. (Later a title page will be added.) Next, she divides the chalkboard into six columns and asks the students to dictate the story. She records their dictation on the chalkboard, page by page. Then the children reread their story and suggest several changes. Ms. Dillen, using proofreader's marks, incorporates the changes agreed upon by the class. After a final reading, the children draw and write the big book. Some children draw illustrations on large sheets of posterboard, and other children write the text, above or below the illustrations on each page. Another illustrator and writer create the title page. Then the pages are compiled and bound. Here is their completed story:

▽
The Enormous Crocodile

Page 1: *The enormous crocodile wanted to eat the children in Ms. Dillen's class.*

Page 2: *The enormous crocodile made himself look like a coconut tree. The trick didn't work.*

Page 3: *The crocodile tried another trick. He made himself into a seesaw. But Muggle-Wump warned the children.*

Page 4: *The crocodile turned himself into a merry-go-round. The Roly-Poly Bird warned the kids. Clever trick three didn't work!*

Page 5: *The crocodile was a picnic bench. Trunky warned the children. Clever trick four did not work either.*

Page 6: *Trunky spun the enormous crocodile around and around. He threw him up into the sun.*

The children personalized the story by having the enormous crocodile want to eat the children in their class rather than the children in the nearby town, as Roald Dahl wrote in his version of the story, and they used the repetition of clever tricks to recall the story events.

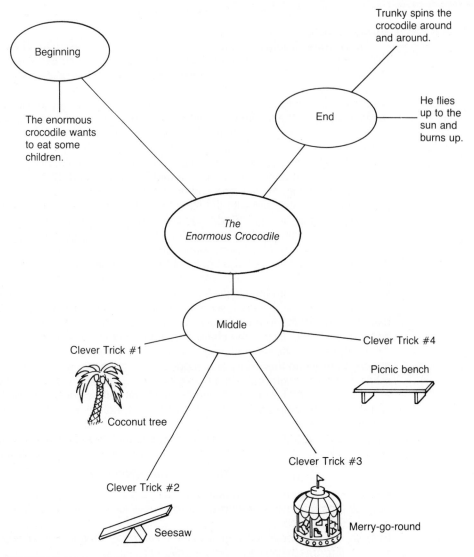

FIGURE 8-1   Story Cluster for The Enormous Crocodile

Several days later, the children participate in other response projects. Some children make finger puppets to use in retelling the story. They draw pictures of the characters, cut them out, and tape the pictures to strips of paper that they fit around their fingers. As soon as the puppets are made, students break into small groups to tell the story to each other. Others write retellings of the story, with one page for the beginning, four pages for the middle, and one page for the end. Then they add a cover and staple their completed booklets together. Barry's retelling is presented in Figure 8-2.

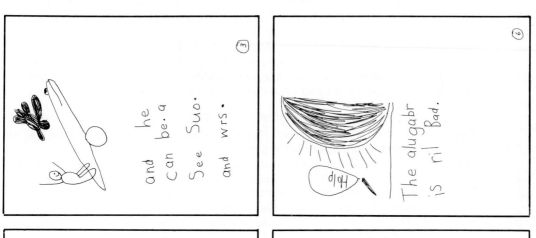
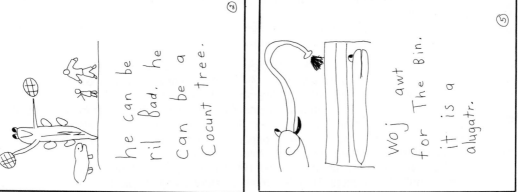
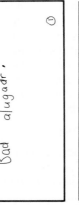

FIGURE 8-2 A First Grader's Retelling of The Enormous Crocodile

Next, Ms. Dillen suggests that they write another class story using clever tricks. They brainstorm a list of clever tricks and discuss possible plots. The class decides to write a story about six hungry rabbits who use clever tricks to fool a fox so they can eat the vegetables in the garden. They decide on three clever tricks and develop a story cluster with a beginning, middle, and end. With this preparation, they dictate the story to Ms. Dillen, who records it on the chalkboard. They refine their story and then Ms. Dillen makes copies for each child. Here is their story:

▽

The Hungry Rabbits

Page 1: *Once there were six rabbits. They wanted carrots and lettuce. But the fox chased the rabbits out of the garden.*

Page 2: *The rabbits think of clever tricks. They tell the fox there's a deer in the forest so the fox will chase the deer instead of them. But the trick didn't work.*

Page 3: *The rabbits dig a hole trying to get to the garden but they didn't dig far enough. They were only by the fence.*

Page 4: *Then the rabbits ran to the briar patch and jumped over it. The fox tried to jump over it but landed in it. "Ouch, ouch," cried the fox. He couldn't get out.*

Page 5: *So the rabbits jumped real high over the briars and got the carrots and lettuce. And they lived happily ever after.*

As the children are finishing their class story, many are already talking about clever trick stories they want to write. Ms. Dillen provides the guidelines. Like their class story, children's individual stories should have a beginning, three (or more) clever tricks in the middle, and an ending. Children pile up five, six or more pages of paper on their desks and begin to work. Some begin illustrating their stories, some begin writing, and others mark their papers with the words *beginning, middle-1, middle-2, middle-3,* and *end* before writing or drawing.

Eddie has his story already in mind. He quickly sets to work drawing a picture in the top half of each page. Then he writes his story, using the pictures he has drawn, much as an adult uses an outline. As he writes, using a combination of invented and standard spelling, Eddie becomes more and more animated. As soon as he finishes writing, he gets construction paper for a cover and staples his storybook together. He goes over to Barry's desk to share his story with his best friend. "Hey, Bar', listen to this. You're gonna love it," he says. And Barry does. Other children crowd around to read Eddie's story, and soon Ms. Dillen moves this group of children over to the author's chair to share their stories. They clap as each story is read and offer compliments about the first-grade authors' use of clever clues and surprise endings.

This is Eddie's story, written in standard spelling:

▽

The Dog

Page 1: *The little dog is very, very hungry and he sees a little rabbit. He chases the rabbit but he ran too fast.*

Page 2: *Clever trick no. 1. The dog jumped on the rabbit's tail but the trick didn't work.*

Page 3: *Clever trick no. 2. He hid under the bushes and jumped out of the bush but he missed the rabbits and they ran away.*

Page 4: *Clever trick no. 3. The dog dressed up into a carrot and the rabbit walked by the dog and the dog ate him.*

Page 5: *That's the end.*

Eddie's story is well-developed. He established a conflict between the hungry dog and the rabbit in the beginning; in the middle he presented three attempts to catch the rabbit; and with the third attempt, the dog is successful. While the ending is not as elaborated as it might be, it follows the style often used in folktales (e.g., "Snip, snap snout, this tale's told out!") and in television cartoon shows (e.g., "That's all folks!").

*T*he first graders in Ms. Dillen's class are learning about stories by listening to stories read aloud, examining how authors organize their stories, and by writing stories themselves. Distinguished British educator Harold Rosen (1986) pleads for elementary teachers to provide more opportunities, or "generous space," for story-telling—both oral and written—to teach children about narrative discourse, its meaning, voice, and seduction. In this chapter, we examine children's concept of story, discuss five elements of story structure and suggest strategies for teaching students to write stories.

CHILDREN'S CONCEPT OF STORY

Even before they enter school, young children have a rudimentary awareness of what makes a story; that is, they have a concept of story or story schema. Children's concept of story includes some understanding of the elements of story structure, such as character, plot, and setting, as well as the conventions that authors use in stories. This knowledge is usually intuitive; that is, children are not conscious of what they know. Golden (1984) describes children's concept of story as part of their cognitive structure: "a mental representation of story structure, essentially an outline of the basic story elements and their organization" (p. 578).

Researchers have documented that children's concept of story begins in the pre-school years, and that children as young as 2-1/2 years of age have a rudimentary sense of story (Applebee, 1978, 1980; Pitcher & Prelinger, 1963). Children acquire this concept of story gradually, through listening to stories read to them, later by reading stories themselves, and by telling and writing stories. Not surprisingly, older children have a better understanding of story structure and conventions than younger children do. Similarly, the stories that older children tell and write are increasingly more complex; the plot structures are more tightly organized, and the characters are more fully developed. Yet Applebee (1980) found that by the time children begin kindergarten they have already developed a concept of what a story is, and these expectations guide them as they respond to stories and tell their own stories. For example, he found that kindergartners could use three story markers: the convention "Once upon a time . . ." to begin a story, the past tense for telling a story, and formal endings such as "The End" or "they lived happily ever after."

Most of the research examining students' understanding of story structure and conventions has been applied to reading. Concept of story plays an important role in students' ability to comprehend and recall information from the stories they read (Mandler & Johnson, 1977; Rumelhart, 1975; Stein & Glenn, 1979). However, children's concept of story is just as important in writing (Golden, 1984). Just as they draw on their concept of story in reading stories, students use this knowledge in writing stories.

Five different types of activities can help elementary students develop and refine their concept of story, preparing them to better understand the stories they read and create the stories they write. These activities are reading stories, talking about stories, retelling stories, examining the structure of stories, and writing stories. It is important that students read and respond to high-quality literature. In a recent study, Dressel (1990) found that students who read and discussed higher-quality stories wrote stories of greater literary quality than did students who read low-quality stories.

Reading Stories

Reading stories aloud and providing opportunities for children to read stories themselves is the most basic way to help children develop a concept of story. Reading to young children helps them internalize the structure of stories and to assimilate the sophisticated language structures that authors use (Purcell-Gates, 1988). Reading aloud is also essential for elementary students even though many teachers mistakenly feel that after children have learned to read they no longer need to be read to. Reading aloud provides the opportunity to share with children literature that they might otherwise miss. After the shared reading experience, the teacher and students can talk about the story together.

Primary grade students often beg to have a familiar book reread. While it is important to share a wide variety of books with children, researchers have found that children benefit in specific ways from repeated readings. Through these repetitions, students gain control over the parts of a story and synthesize the story parts into a whole. The quality of children's responses to a repeated story also changes (Beaver, 1982).

Martinez and Roser (1985) examined young children's responses to stories and found that as stories become increasingly familiar, students' responses indicate a greater depth of understanding. They found that children talked almost twice as much about familiar books as about unfamiliar books that had been read only once or twice. The form and focus of children's talk changed, too. While children tended to ask questions about unfamiliar stories, they made comments about familiar stories. With unfamiliar stories, children's talk focused on characters; the focus changed to details and word meanings when children talked about familiar stories. Martinez and Roser also found that children's comments after repeated readings were more probing and more specific, suggesting that they had greater insights into the story.

Talking About Stories

In a survey of nursery schools and kindergartens, Morrow (1982) found that teachers typically neither preceded nor followed the stories they read aloud with questions or discussions. The few times that teachers asked questions about stories, they usually asked for factual details. They rarely asked questions that emphasized structural elements of a story, such as setting, theme, or plot or questions that elicited interpretive and critical thinking. Morrow concluded that the story-reading events showed little or no evidence that teachers provided children with organizational strategies for understanding the stories.

Students need opportunities to talk about the stories they have read and listened to read aloud. Eeds and Wells (1989) suggest that instead of "gentle inquisitions," teachers and students have "grand conversations" about literature (p. 4). Grand conversations can be held in small groups or as a class. Students sit in a circle, and to start the conversation the teacher asks, "What do you think?" During this first part of the conversation, students share their reactions, comments, and questions. They talk informally, without raising hands and waiting to be called on by the teacher; instead, students build on classmates' comments. Teachers participate in the discussion to learn rather than to judge. There are no "correct" or "right" comments to make, and through the discussion the group becomes a community of learners and create a shared, social response.

During the second part of the conversation, the teacher directs the conversation. Stephanie McConaughy (1980) recommends that teachers ask questions about the plot, theme, and characters, and that these questions be tailored to students' developmental level. Questions to primary grade students, for example, might focus on story events while questions to older students might deal with theme, characters, and the motivations behind the characters' actions.

Retelling Stories

Retelling a story provides an opportunity for interaction between teller and listener, for active engagement with literature, and for the transfer of meaning from author/teller to reader/listener. Students also make the language of the stories part of their own language (Hade, 1988).

Too often, retelling stories has been seen by many teachers as a time-consuming frill; however, studies by Lesley Morrow (1984, 1985a, 1985b, 1986) have documented the educational value of this activity.

In a series of three studies conducted with kindergarten students, Morrow examined the effect of retelling activities on students' understanding of stories. In the first study, one group of kindergartners retold a story that had been read to them while another group drew pictures of the story. According to the results of a comprehension test that included both questions about story structure and "traditional" questions, students who participated in the retelling activity scored higher than students who drew pictures. Next, Morrow compared the value of "simple" retelling with guided retelling over an extended time period. Kindergartners in one group retold well-structured stories and were guided in their retellings by teachers who focused on the stories' structural framework, while students in the other group retold the stories without any prompts from the teacher. She found that students who retold stories with guidance understood the stories better according to a comprehension test that included both "traditional" and story-structure questions. Also, the children who retold stories with guidance used more structural elements and used them in a proper sequence during the retelling activities. In the third study, Morrow examined the effect of guided story retellings in preparing kindergarteners to tell original stories. One group of students retold stories that had been read to them, and the other group of students drew pictures about the stories. Morrow found that students who participated in retelling activities created more complex stories that included more information about setting and plot. She also found that the students who retold stories used more sophisticated language in their original stories. The results of these three studies suggest that, through retelling stories, children learn about story structure, understand stories better, and grow in their language ability.

Examining the Structure of Stories

Stories are organized in predictable ways, and children who are aware of these organizational arrangements use this knowledge to know what to expect in a story (Gordon & Braun, 1982; McConaughy, 1980). Researchers have developed several different approaches for analyzing the structure of stories. Cognitive psychologists, for instance, have developed a story grammar that includes the following elements: a setting, an initiating event, an internal response, a goal, an attempt, an outcome, a consequence, and a reaction (Mandler & Johnson, 1977). In contrast, rhetoricians describe the structure of stories using the elements of plot, setting, character, theme, and point of view. This chapter focuses on how these five elements are used in teaching students how authors organize their stories. This choice was made because the literary elements provide a general structure rather than a prescriptive formula for children's story writing, and they seem to better describe the more complex stories that children read and write.

Because research has demonstrated that knowledge of story structure improves students' understanding and production of stories, many educators recommend that teachers explicitly teach the structure of stories. Several strategies for teaching students about the structure of stories have been recommended (Fitzgerald & Spiegel, 1983; Gordon & Braun, 1982; Spiegel & Fitzgerald, 1986; Tompkins & McGee, 1989). The common features of these strategies are

1. An element of story structure (or story part) is presented, often using a chart to summarize important information.
2. Students read stories exemplifying this element.
3. Students discuss how the element was used in the stories they read.
4. Students participate in a variety of activities to reinforce their understanding of the element, including drawing diagrams of the story, comparing story versions, and retelling the story.
5. Students write stories incorporating the element being studied.

These activities involve both direct instruction about the elements of story structure and the integration of reading, writing, and oral language activities.

Writing Stories

Writing is a valuable way of learning (Emig, 1977), and by writing stories children apply their expanding knowledge of stories, including the structural elements as well as creative story ideas. For example, second-grade Micah wrote the following story about a snake with a problem.

▽
The Snake and His Blocked Door

Page 1: *Once there was a long snake. He had a problem. His front door is blocked by a piece of thick wood.*

Page 2: *He tried to push it off but he was too small.*

Page 3: *So he went to the king, Bill Boa Constrictor.*

Page 4: *He said, "This is the work of humans. I think you should dig a new door. I can't dig. I am too young."*
"Yes," said the Boa.

Page 5: *So he got home and night came. So he burrowed in a hole for the night.*

Page 6: *The snake got up. He went to the Snake Store and got some breakfast.*

Page 7: *After breakfast he went home and tried to think how to get in.*

Page 8: *So he went to the king.*

Page 9: *He said, "King, I am locked out. Could I spend the night here?"*
"Of course!"

Page 10: *That night he had a dream about the most wonderful things.*

Page 11: *The next day he went home and remembered about his back door!*

In his story, Micah sets up a problem to solve, and he heightens interest in the story as readers learn about how the snake struggles to solve the problem. First, he tries to push the block of wood away, but the snake is too small. Next, he asks his king for help, and the king suggests that he dig a new door. Third, after spending a miserable night burrowed in a hole and thinking hard and long (but unsuccessfully), he asks to stay with the king. Finally, after a wonderful dream he remembers about his back door! Micah cleverly combines what he has learned about the structure of stories with a creative story idea.

ELEMENTS OF STORY STRUCTURE

Stories have unique elements of structure that distinguish them from other forms of writing. In fact, the structure of stories is quite complex as authors manipulate character, plot, setting, and other elements to produce an interesting story. Five elements of story structure—plot, setting, character, theme, and point of view—will be discussed in this section, with familiar and award-winning trade books used to illustrate each element.

Plot

Plot is the sequence of events involving characters in conflict situations in the beginning, middle, and end of a story. The plot is based on the goals of one or more characters (Lukens, 1991). The main character (or characters) wants to achieve a certain goal, and other characters try to prevent the main character from being successful. The story is put into motion as the main character attempts to overcome obstacles to reach a goal or solve a problem.

Beginning-Middle-End.   The most basic aspect of plot is the division of the main events of a story into three parts: the beginning, middle, and end. (With upper-grade students the terms often used are introduction, development or complication, and resolution.) In *Where the Wild Things Are* (Sendak, 1963), for instance, the three story parts can be picked out easily. As the story begins, Max plays a mischievous wolf and is sent to his room for misbehaving. In the middle, Max magically travels to the land of the wild things to become their king. Then Max feels lonely and returns home to find his supper waiting and still hot—the end of the story. A cluster for *Where the Wild Things Are* is presented in Figure 8-3.

Authors include specific types of information in each part of the story. In the beginning, they introduce the characters, describe the setting, and present a problem. The author uses the characters, setting, and events to develop the plot and sustain the theme through the story. In the middle, authors introduce conflict. They create roadblocks for the characters that keep them from solving their problems. How the characters deal with these obstacles adds suspense, which keeps readers interested. In the end, readers learn whether or not the characters' struggles are successful.

Almost any story can be divided into these three parts. Stories that have an easily identifiable beginning, middle, and end are listed in Figure 8-4.

Conflict.   Conflict is the tension or opposition between forces in the plot, and it is usually the element that entices readers to continue reading the story. Conflict usually takes one of four forms (Lukens, 1991):

1. Conflict between a character and nature
2. Conflict between a character and society
3. Conflict between characters
4. Conflict within a character

Conflict between a character and nature is represented in stories in which severe weather plays an important role, as in Jean Craighead George's *Julie of the Wolves* (1972), and in stories set in isolated geographic locations, such as Scott O'Dell's *Island of the Blue Dolphins* (1960) in which the Indian girl Karana struggles to survive alone on a Pacific island. In some stories, a character's activities and beliefs are different from those held by other members of the society, and these differences cause conflict. One example of this type of conflict is Elizabeth Speare's *The Witch of Blackbird Pond* (1958) in which Kit Tyler is accused of being a witch because she continues in a New England Puritan community activities that were acceptable in the Caribbean community where she grew up. Conflict between characters is commonly used in children's literature. In Judy Blume's *Tales of a Fourth Grade Nothing* (1972), for instance, the never-ending conflict between Peter and his little brother Fudge is what makes the story interesting. The fourth type of conflict is conflict within a character, and stories such as Bernard Waber's *Ira Sleeps Over* (1972) and Betsy

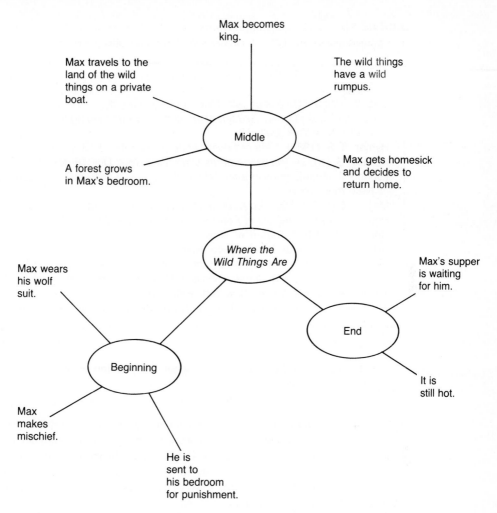

FIGURE 8-3 *A Beginning-Middle-End Cluster for* Where the Wild Things Are

Byars's *The Summer of the Swans* (1970) are examples. In *Ira Sleeps Over,* 6-year-old Ira must decide whether to take his teddy bear with him when he goes next door to spend the night with a friend. In *The Summer of the Swans,* Sara feels guilty when her mentally retarded brother wanders off and is lost. A list of stories representing the four types of conflict is presented in Figure 8-5.

Plot Development. Authors develop plot through the introduction, development, and resolution of the conflict. Plot development can be broken down into four steps:

1. A problem that introduces conflict is presented in the beginning of a story.
2. Characters face roadblocks as they attempt to solve the problem in the middle of the story.

FIGURE 8-4   *Stories Illustrating Beginning–Middle–End*
P = primary grades (K–2); M = middle grades (3–5); U = upper grades (6–8)

Andersen, H. C. (1979). *The ugly duckling.* New York: Harcourt Brace Jovanovich. (P–M)

Gag, W. (1956). *Millions of cats.* New York: Coward. (P)

Gallo, D. R. (Ed.) (1984). *Sixteen short stories by outstanding writers for young adults.* New York: Dell. (U)

Hyman, T. S. (1983). *Little red riding hood.* New York: Holiday House. (P)

Kellogg, S. (1973). *The island of the skog.* New York: Dial. (P–M)

London, J. (1960). *To build a fire: The call of the wild and other selected stories.* New York: Signet. (U)

Mayer, M. (1987). *The pied piper of Hamelin.* New York: Macmillan. (M)

Potter, B. (1902). *The tale of Peter Rabbit.* New York: Warne. (P)

Rogasky, B. (1982). *Rapunzel.* New York: Holiday House. (M–U)

Schulevitz, U. (1978). *The treasure.* New York: Farrar. (M)

Sendak, M. (1963). *Where the wild things are.* New York: Harper and Row. (P)

Van Allsburg, C. (1981). *Jumanji.* Boston: Houghton Mifflin. (M)

Yorinks, A. (1986). *Hey, Al.* New York: Farrar. (P)

Zemach, H., & Zemach, M. (1973). *Duffy and the devil.* New York: Farrar. (P–M)

---

3. The high point in the action occurs when the problem is about to be solved. This high point separates the middle and end of the story.
4. The problem is solved and the roadblocks are overcome at the end of the story.

The problem is introduced at the beginning of the story, and the main character (or characters) is faced with trying to solve it. This problem determines the conflict. In *The Pied Piper of Hamelin* (Mayer, 1987), the problem is that the town of Hamelin is infested with rats, and conflict develops between the townspeople and the Pied Piper who has been hired to rid the town of the rats. This conflict can be characterized as a conflict between characters.

Once the problem has been introduced, the author throws roadblocks in the way of an easy solution. As one roadblock is removed, another emerges to thwart the main character. Postponing the solution by introducing roadblocks is the core of plot development. Stories may contain any number of roadblocks, but many children's stories contain three, four, or five roadblocks.

In *The Pied Piper of Hamelin,* the first conflict comes when the townspeople demand that the mayor get rid of the rats. The mayor promises to do something, but he doesn't know what to do. Next, the piper visits the mayor and offers to rid the town of the rats. The mayor promises to pay the piper 1,000 pieces of silver. Third, the piper gets rid of the rats. He plays a mesmerizing tune on his pipe, and the rats follow him out of town and are drowned in a nearby river. Fourth, it appears that the problem is solved, but the mayor belittles the piper's accomplishment and refuses to pay the agreed-upon reward. When the mayor refuses, the piper threatens terrible consequences if he is not paid.

FIGURE 8-5   *Stories Illustrating the Four Types of Conflict*

Conflict Between a Character and Nature

Ardizzone, E. (1971). *Little Tim and the brave sea captain.* New York: Scholastic. (P)

George, J. C. (1972). *Julie of the wolves.* New York: Harper & Row. (M–U)

O'Dell, S. (1960). *Island of the blue dolphins.* Boston: Houghton Mifflin. (M–U)

Sperry, A. (1968). *Call it courage.* New York: Macmillan. (U)

Conflict Between a Character and Society

Hickman, J. (1978). *Zoar blue.* New York: Macmillan. (U)

Kellogg, S. (1973). *The island of the skog.* New York: Dial. (P–M)

O'Brien, R. C. (1971). *Mrs. Frisby and the rats of NIMH.* New York: Atheneum. (M)

Speare, E. G. (1958). *The witch of Blackbird Pond.* Boston: Houghton Mifflin. (M–U)

Conflict Between Characters

Blume, J. (1972). *Tales of a fourth grade nothing.* New York: Dutton. (M)

Hoban, R. (1970). *A bargain for Frances.* New York: Scholastic. (P)

Raskin, E. (1978). *The westing game.* New York: Dutton. (U)

Zelinsky, P. O. (1986). *Rumpelstiltskin.* New York: Dutton. (P–M)

Conflict Within a Character

Byars, B. (1970). *The summer of the swans.* New York: Viking. (M)

Fritz, J. (1958). *The cabin faced west.* New York: Coward-McCann. (M)

Taylor, T. (1969). *The cay.* New York: Doubleday. (U)

Waber, B. (1972). *Ira sleeps over.* Boston: Houghton Mifflin. (P)

The high point of the action is when the solution of the problem hangs in the balance. Tension is high, and readers continue reading to learn whether or not the main characters will solve the problem. In *The Pied Piper of Hamelin,* readers experience some relief because the town of Hamelin has been saved, but tension exists because of the disagreement between the mayor and the piper. The piper plays his pipe again, this time enticing all the children to follow him out of Hamelin. They follow him to a nearby mountain, which they enter through a magic door. The mayor and other townspeople are left with their money but without their children.

At the end of the story, the problem is solved. Only one little lame boy whom the piper cures returns to tell the story and remind everyone that "a promise is a promise" and "the piper must be paid."

The plot of a story can be diagrammed or charted. A basic plot diagram, shaped somewhat like a mountain, is presented in Figure 8-6, showing the four steps of plot development—introduction of the problem, roadblocks, high point in the action, and solution of the problem. Information about any story's plot can be added to this diagram. As an example, a plot diagram of *The Pied Piper of Hamelin* is presented in Figure 8-7.

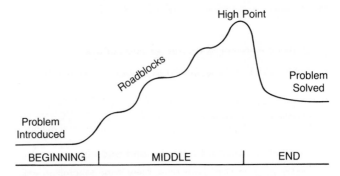

FIGURE 8-6 *A Basic Plot Diagram*

Setting

In some stories the setting, called a backdrop setting, is barely sketched. The setting in many folktales, for example, is relatively unimportant and may simply use the convention, "Once upon a time . . ." to set the stage. In other stories, however, the setting is elaborated and integral to the story's effectiveness. These settings are called integral settings (Lukens, 1991). Whether or not the setting is important to plot and character development determines how much attention writers give to describing the setting. Some stories could take place anywhere, and the setting requires little description; in others, however, the setting must be specific, and authors must take care to ensure the authenticity of the historical period or geographic location in which the story is set.

Of the elements of story structure, setting is the one many people feel most comfortable with. Often they think that setting is simply where the story takes place. Certainly location is an important dimension of setting, but there are three other dimensions as well: weather, time, and time period.

Location.   Location is a very important dimension of setting in many stories. The Boston Commons in *Make Way for Ducklings* (McCloskey, 1969), the Alaskan North Slope in *Julie of the Wolves* (George, 1972), and New York City's Metropolitan Museum of Art in *From the Mixed-up Files of Mrs. Basil E. Frankweiler* (Konigsburg, 1983) are integral to these stories' plots. The settings are artfully described by the authors and add something unique to the story. In contrast, many stories take place in everyday settings that do not contribute to the story's effectiveness.

Weather.   Weather is a second dimension of setting and, like location, is crucial in some stories. For example, a rainstorm is essential to the plot development in both *Bridge to Terabithia* (Paterson, 1977) and *Sam, Bangs, and Moonshine* (Ness, 1966). At other times, the author may not even mention the weather because it does not have an impact on the story. Many stories take place on warm, sunny days. Think about the impact weather could have on a story; for example, what might have happened if a snow storm had prevented Little Red Riding Hood from reaching her grandmother's house?

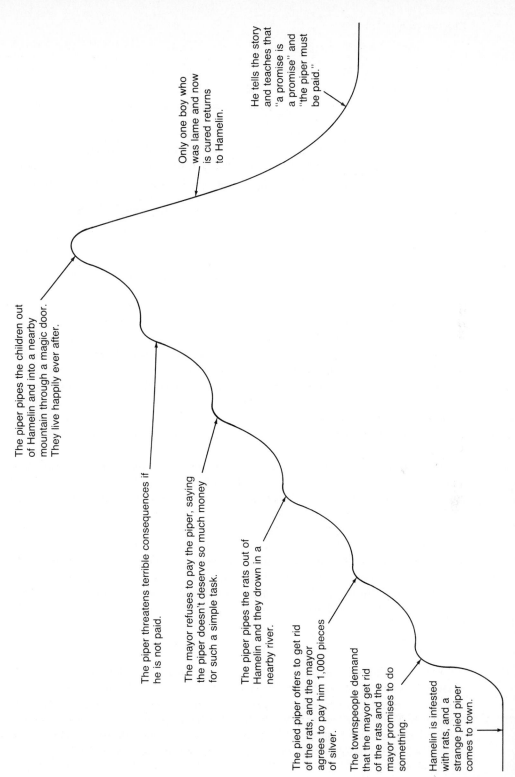

The piper pipes the children out of Hamelin and into a nearby mountain through a magic door. They live happily ever after.

Only one boy who was lame and now is cured returns to Hamelin.

He tells the story and teaches that "a promise is a promise" and "the piper must be paid."

The piper threatens terrible consequences if he is not paid.

The mayor refuses to pay the piper, saying the piper doesn't deserve so much money for such a simple task.

The piper pipes the rats out of Hamelin and they drown in a nearby river.

The pied piper offers to get rid of the rats, and the mayor agrees to pay him 1,000 pieces of silver.

The townspeople demand that the mayor get rid of the rats and the mayor promises to do something.

Hamelin is infested with rats, and a strange pied piper comes to town.

FIGURE 8-7 *Plot diagram for* The Pied Piper of Hamelin

Time.   The third dimension, time, includes both time of day and the passage of time within a story. The time of day is not significant in many children's stories, except for Halloween or ghost stories, which typically take place after dark. In stories that take place at night, such as the folktale *The Teeny-Tiny Woman* (Galdone, 1984), time is a more important dimension than in stories that take place during the day because events that happen at night seem more scary than those that happen during the day.

Many short stories span a brief period of time, often less than a day, and sometimes less than an hour. In Chris Van Allsburg's *Jumanji* (1981), for instance, Peter and Judy's bizarre adventure in which their house is overtaken by an exotic jungle lasts only the several hours their parents are at the opera. Other stories, such as *The Ugly Duckling* (Andersen, 1979), span a time period long enough for the main character to grow to maturity.

Time Period.   The fourth dimension of setting is the time period in which a story is set. The time period is important in stories that are set in the past or in the future. If *The Witch of Blackbird Pond* (Speare, 1958) and *Beyond the Divide* (Lasky, 1983) were set in different eras, for example, they would lose much of their impact. Today, few people would believe that Kit Tyler is a witch, and travel across the United States would not be nearly so difficult today with modern conveniences. Other stories, such as *A Wrinkle in Time* (L'Engle, 1962), take place in the future where events occur that are not possible today. A list of stories with integral settings is presented in Figure 8-8. These stories illustrate the four dimensions of setting—location, weather, time, and time period.

Even though settings are often taken for granted in stories, an integral setting exerts a great deal of influence on the story. Watson (1991) recommends that teachers help students to recognize the importance of setting as a literary element and the connections between setting and plot, character, and other elements. For example, in *Number the Stars* (Lowry, 1989), a story of two friends, a Christian child and a Jewish child, set in Denmark during World War II, the setting is integral to the development of the story. The time period influences the plot development because readers anticipate that the Nazis will try to relocate the Jewish girl and her family and that the Christian girl and her family will try to protect or rescue the Jewish family. Readers also have expectations about the characters. The Christian girl and the Jewish girl may have different physical features, but it is likely that both will be called upon to perform courageous actions.

Character

Characters are the people or personified animals who are involved in the story. Often character is the most important element of story structure because the experience the author creates for readers is centered around a character or group of characters. Usually, one fully rounded and two or three supporting characters are introduced and developed in a story. Fully developed main characters have all the characteristics of real people. A list of fully developed main characters in children's stories is presented in Figure 8-9.

FIGURE 8-8   *Stories with Integral Settings*

Andersen, H. C. (1979). *The ugly duckling.* New York: Harcourt Brace Jovanovich. (P–M)

Babbitt, N. (1975). *Tuck everlasting.* New York: Farrar, Straus & Giroux. (M–U)

Cauley, L. B. (1984). *The town mouse and the country mouse.* New York: Putnam. (P–M)

Fritz, J. (1982). *Homesick: My own story.* New York: Putnam. (M–U)

Galdone, P. (1984). *The teeny-tiny woman.* New York: Clarion. (P)

George, J. C. (1972). *Julie of the wolves.* New York: Harper & Row. (M–U)

Hodges, Margaret. (1984). *Saint George and the dragon.* Boston: Little, Brown. (M–U)

Konigsburg, E. L. (1983). *From the mixed-up files of Mrs. Basil E. Frankweiler.* New York: Atheneum. (M)

Lasky, K. (1983). *Beyond the divide.* New York: Macmillan. (M–U)

L'Engle, M. (1962). *A wrinkle in time.* New York: Farrar, Straus & Giroux. (U)

McCloskey, R. (1969). *Make way for ducklings.* New York: Viking. (P)

Ness, E. (1966). *Sam, Bangs and moonshine.* New York: Holt. (P)

Paterson, K. (1977). *Bridge to Terabithia.* New York: Crowell. (M–U)

Speare, E. (1958). *The witch of Blackbird Pond.* Boston: Houghton Mifflin. (M–U)

Van Allsburg, C. (1981). *Jumanji.* Boston: Houghton Mifflin. (P–M)

White, E. B. (1952). *Charlotte's web.* New York: Harper & Row. (M)

Wilder, L. I. (1971). *The long winter.* New York: Harper & Row. (M)

The supporting characters may be individualized, but they will be portrayed much less vividly than the main character. The extent to which the supporting characters are developed depends on the author's purpose and the needs of the story. In *Queenie Peavy* (Burch, 1966), for instance, Queenie is the main character, and we get to know her as a real person. She pretends that she is tough, as she does when the other children taunt her because her father is in the chain gang, but actually Queenie is a sensitive girl who wants a family to care for her. In contrast, Robert Burch tells us very little about the supporting characters in the story: Queenie's parents, her neighbors, her classmates, and her teachers. This story focuses on Queenie and how this lonely 13-year-old copes with times that have "turned off hard" in the 1930s.

Authors must determine how to develop and present characters to involve readers in the experiences they are writing about. They develop characters in four ways: (a) appearance, (b) action, (c) dialogue, and (d) monologue.

Appearance.   Authors describe how their characters look as the story develops; however, they generally provide some physical description when characters are introduced. Readers learn about characters by the description of their facial features, body shapes, habits of dress, mannerisms, and gestures. For example, Roald Dahl vividly describes James's two wicked aunts in *James and the Giant Peach* (1961):

Aunt Sponge was enormously fat and very short. She had small piggy eyes, a sunken mouth, and one of those white flabby faces that looked exactly as though it had been boiled.

FIGURE 8-9   *Fully Developed Characters in Children's Literature*

Character	Story
Queenie	Burch, R. (1966). *Queenie Peavy.* New York: Viking. (U)
Leigh	Cleary, B. (1983). *Dear Mr. Henshaw.* New York: Morrow. (M)
Harriet	Fitzhugh, L. (1964). *Harriet the spy.* New York: Harper & Row. (M)
Sam	George, J. C. (1959). *My side of the mountain.* New York: Dutton. (U)
Frances	Hoban, R. (1976). *Best friends for Frances.* New York: Harper & Row. (P)
Anastasia	Lowry, L. (1979). *Anastasia Krupnik.* Boston: Houghton Mifflin. (M)
Karana	O'Dell, S. (1960). *Island of the blue dolphins.* Boston: Houghton Mifflin. (M–U)
Gilly	Paterson, K. (1978). *The great Gilly Hopkins.* New York: Crowell. (M–U)
Peter	Potter, B. (1902). *The tale of Peter Rabbit.* New York: Warne. (P)
Matt	Speare, E. (1983). *The sign of the beaver.* Boston: Houghton Mifflin. (M–U)
Mafatu	Sperry, A. (1968). *Call it courage.* New York: Macmillan. (U)
Cassie	Taylor, M. (1976). *Roll of thunder, hear my cry.* New York: Dial. (U)

She was like a great white soggy overboiled cabbage. Aunt Spiker, on the other hand, was lean and tall and bony, and she wore steel-rimmed spectacles that fixed onto the end of her nose with a clip. She had a screeching voice and long wet narrow lips, and whenever she got angry or excited, little flecks of spit would come shooting out of her mouth as she talked. (p. 7)

Dahl's descriptions bring these two despicable characters vividly to life. He has carefully chosen the specific details to influence readers to appreciate James's dismay at having to live with these two aunts.

Action.   What a character does is the best way of knowing about that character. In Betsy Byars's story about three unwanted children, *The Pinballs* (1977), 15-year-old Carlie is described as being "as hard to crack as a coconut" (p. 4), and her dialogue is harsh and sarcastic; however, Carlie's actions belie these other ways of knowing about her. She demonstrates through her actions that she cares about her two fellow pinballs and the foster family who cares for them. For example, she gets Harvey a puppy as a birthday present and sneaks it into the hospital.

Dialogue.   Another important technique that authors use to develop their characters is dialogue. What characters say is important, but so is the way they speak. The level of formality of the language that characters use is usually determined by the social situation. A character might speak less formally with a friend than with respected elders or characters in positions of authority. The geographic location of the story and the socioeconomic status of the characters also determine the way the characters speak. For example, in *Roll of Thunder, Hear My Cry* (Taylor, 1976), Cassie and her family speak Black English, and in *Ida Early Comes over the Mountain* (Burch, 1980), Ida's speech is characteristic of rural Georgia, and she says, "Howdy-do?" and "Yes, sir-ee." Even in animal stories such as *Rabbit Hill* (Lawson, 1972), dialect is important. Uncle Analdas from Danbury speaks a rural dialect in contrast to the "proper" standard English spoken by the animals on the hill.

Monologue.   Authors also provide insight into their characters by revealing the characters' thoughts. In *Anastasia Krupnik* (Lowry, 1979), for example, Lois Lowry shares 10-year-old Anastasia's thinking with the reader. Anastasia has enjoyed being an only child, and she is very upset that her mother is pregnant. To deal with Anastasia's feelings of sibling rivalry, her parents suggest that she choose a name for the new baby, and Anastasia agrees. Through monologue readers learn why Anastasia has agreed to choose the name: She will pick the most awful name she can think of for the baby. Lowry also has Anastasia keep a journal in which she lists things she likes and hates, another reflection of her thinking.

Theme

Theme is the underlying meaning of a story and embodies general truths about society or human nature. According to Lehr (1991), the theme "steps back from the literal interpretation" to state the more general truths (p. 2). The theme usually deals with the characters' emotions and values.

Themes can be stated explicitly or implicitly (Lukens, 1991). Explicit themes are stated openly and clearly in the story, while implicit themes are implied through the characters' actions, dialogue, and monologue as they strive to resolve their problems. Friendship, responsibility, courage, and kindness to others are common topics around which authors build themes in children's literature.

In *Charlotte's Web* (1952), E. B. White builds a theme around the topic of friendship. Wilbur, who is grateful for Charlotte's encouragement and protection, remarks that "friendship is one of the most satisfying things in the world" (cited in Lukens, 1991, p. 102). Wilbur's statement is an example of an explicitly stated theme. Friendship is also central to *Bridge to Terabithia* (Paterson, 1977), but it is implied through Jess and Leslie's enduring friendship rather than explicitly stated in the text.

During the elementary grades, children develop and refine their understanding of theme. Kindergartners have a very rudimentary sense of theme, and through a wide exposure to literature and many opportunities to discuss books, students grow in their ability to construct themes and talk about them (Au, 1992). Even so, students in the middle and upper grades often think about theme differently than adults do (Lehr, 1991). Older children and adults become more sensitive to the structure of stories, develop a greater ability to generalize the events of the story, increasingly understand the characters' motivations and the subtleties of the plot, and expand their own worldviews and ability to interpret literature.

A list of stories with thought-provoking themes is presented in Figure 8-10. Many stories have more than one theme, and as students talk about stories, they may head toward a different theme than the one the teacher had in mind. Teachers can gain new insights about themes from their students (Au, 1992).

Point of View

People see other people and the world from different points of view. Listening to several people recount an event they have witnessed proves the impact of the viewpoint. The focus of the narrator determines to a great extent readers' understanding of the story—the characters, the events—and whether or not readers will believe what they are being told. The student author must decide who will tell the story and follow that viewpoint consistently. Four points of view are first-person viewpoint, omniscient viewpoint, limited omniscient viewpoint, and objective viewpoint (Lukens, 1991). A list of stories written from each point of view is presented in Figure 8-11.

First-Person Viewpoint.   Authors use the first-person viewpoint when they tell the story through the eyes of one character using the first-person pronoun *I*. This point of view is used so the reader can live the story as the narrator tells it. The narrator, usually the main character, speaks as an eyewitness and a participant in the events. For example, in *The Slave Dancer* (Fox, 1973), Jessie tells the story of his kidnapping and frightful voyage on a slave ship, and in *Alexander and the Terrible, Horrible, No Good, Very Bad Day* (Viorst, 1977), Alexander tells about a day when everything

FIGURE 8-10   *Stories with Thought-Provoking Themes*

Andersen, H. C. (1965). *The nightingale.* New York: Harper & Row. (M–U)
Cooney, B. (1958). *Chanticleer and the fox.* New York: Crowell. (P–M)
Galdone, P. (1968). *Henny Penny.* New York: Clarion. (P)
Greene, B. (1973). *Summer of my German soldier.* New York: Dial. (U)
Lawson, R. (1972). *Rabbit Hill.* New York: Viking. (M)
L'Engle, M. (1962). *A wrinkle in time.* New York: Farrar, Straus & Giroux. (U)
Lewis, C. S. (1981). *The lion, the witch and the wardrobe.* New York: Macmillan. (M–U)
Mayer, M. (1987). *The pied piper of Hamelin.* New York: Macmillan. (M)
Neville, E. (1963). *It's like this cat.* New York: Harper & Row. (U)
Piper, W. (1954). *The little engine that could.* New York: Platt & Munk. (P)
Steig, W. (1982). *Doctor De Soto.* New York: Farrar, Straus & Giroux. (P)
Westcott, N. B. (1984). *The emperor's new clothes.* Boston: Little, Brown. (P–M)
White, E. B. (1952). *Charlotte's web.* New York: Harper & Row. (M)
Yep, L. (1977). *Child of the owl.* New York: Harper & Row. (M–U)
Yorinks, A. (1986). *Hey, Al.* New York: Farrar, Straus & Giroux. (P)

FIGURE 8-11   *Stories Illustrating the Four Viewpoints*

First-person Viewpoint

Greene, B. (1974). *Philip Hall likes me. I reckon maybe.* New York: Dial. (M–U)
Howe, D., & Howe, J. (1979). *Bunnicula.* New York: Atheneum. (M)
MacLachlan, P. (1985). *Sarah, plain and tall.* New York: Harper & Row. (M)
Viorst, J. (1977). *Alexander and the terrible, horrible, no good, very bad day.* New York: Atheneum. (P)

Omniscient Viewpoint

Babbitt, N. (1975). *Tuck everlasting.* New York: Farrar, Straus & Giroux. (M–U)
Grahame, K. (1961). *The wind in the willows.* New York: Scribner. (M)
Lewis, C. S. (1981). *The lion, the witch and the wardrobe.* New York: Macmillan. (M–U)
Steig, William. (1982). *Doctor De Soto.* New York: Farrar, Straus & Giroux. (P)

Limited Omniscient Viewpoint

Burch, R. (1966). *Queenie Peavy.* New York: Dell. (U)
Cleary, B. (1981). *Ramona Quimby, age 8.* New York: Random House. (M)
Lionni, L. (1969). *Alexander and the wind-up mouse.* New York: Pantheon. (P)
Lowry, L. (1979). *Anastasia Krupnik.* Boston: Houghton Mifflin. (M)

Objective Viewpoint

Brown, M. (1954). *Cinderella.* New York: Scribner. (P)
Lobel, A. (1972). *Frog and toad together.* New York: Harper & Row. (P)
Wells, R. (1973). *Benjamin and Tulip.* New York: Dial. (P)
Zemach, M. (1983). *The little red hen.* New York: Farrar, Straus & Giroux. (P)

---

seemed to go wrong for him. One limitation to this viewpoint is that the narrator must remain an eyewitness.

Omniscient Viewpoint.   Here the author is godlike, seeing all and knowing all. The author tells the readers about the thought processes of each character without worrying about how the information is obtained. William Steig's *Doctor De Soto* (1982), a story about a mouse dentist who outwits a fox with a toothache, is an example of a story written from the omniscient viewpoint. Steig lets readers know that the fox is thinking about eating the dentist as soon as his toothache is cured and that the mouse dentist is aware of the fox's thoughts and plans a clever trick.

Limited Omniscient Viewpoint.   Authors use this point of view to overhear the thoughts of one of the characters without being all-knowing and all-seeing. The story is told in third person, and the author concentrates on the thoughts, feelings, and significant past experiences of the main character or another important character. Robert Burch uses the limited omniscient viewpoint in *Queenie Peavy* (1966), and

Queenie is the character Burch concentrates on, showing why she has a chip on her shoulder and how she overcomes it.

Objective Viewpoint.   Authors use the objective viewpoint as though they were making a film of the story and can learn only from what is visible and audible and what others say about the characters and situations. Readers are eyewitnesses to the story and are confined to the immediate scene. A limitation is that the author cannot probe very deeply into characters. Stories such as *Cinderella* (Brown, 1954) and *The Little Red Hen* (Zemach, 1983) are examples of stories told from the objective viewpoint. In these stories, authors focus on recounting the events of the story rather than developing the personalities of the characters.

These five elements are the building blocks of stories. With this structure, authors, both children and adults, can let their creativity flow and combine ideas with structure to craft a good story.

TEACHING STUDENTS TO WRITE STORIES

Children develop their concept of story through listening to stories read aloud and telling stories during the preschool years. With this introduction to narratives, elementary students are ready to learn more about how stories are organized and how authors use the elements of story structure to create stories. Students use this knowledge to compose the stories they write as well as to comprehend stories they read.

The teaching strategy presented in this section builds on students' concept of story by examining the elements of story structure—plot, setting, character, theme, and point of view—in connection with a reading or literature program and then having students apply these elements in writing stories. Rather than a collection of cookbooklike activities, this strategy is a holistic approach in which students read, talk, think, and write stories. The reader-writer connection is crucial. As readers, students consider how the author used a particular structure and consider its impact; then, as writers, they experiment with the structure in the stories they write and consider the impact on their classmates who read the stories.

Preparing to Teach

Step by Step

1. *Learn about the element.*   Review the information about the element of story structure presented in this chapter and in other reference books, such as Rebecca Lukens's *A Critical Handbook of Children's Literature* (1991).

2. *Collect stories illustrating the element.*   Collect as many stories illustrating the element as possible. Folktales, other short stories, and novels can be used as examples. It is helpful to collect multiple copies of books that students will read independently. Stories can also be tape-recorded for students to listen to in a listening center. Also identify stories in basal reading textbooks that illustrate specific elements of story structure. Lists of stories that illustrate specific elements can be found in earlier sections in this chapter.

3. *Analyze the element in stories.* Read the stories to learn how authors use the element in constructing their stories. Take notes on how authors use the element in particular stories to aid in teaching.

4. *Develop charts.* Develop one or more charts to present the information to students. The charts should define the element and list characteristics of the element. Develop and laminate the charts; then add children's words in grease pencil. In this way, the charts can be personalized for each group of students.

Teaching an Element of Story Structure

Teachers introduce their students to an element of story structure using the stories they collected and the instructional materials they developed. Students read stories and analyze how authors use the element in the story. Next, they participate in exploration activities, such as retelling stories and drawing clusters, in which they investigate how authors used the element in particular stories. With this background of experiences, students write collaborative and individual stories applying what they have learned about the element. The basic teaching steps are described below:

Step by Step

1. *Introduce the element.* Introduce the element of story structure and develop charts to define the element and/or list the characteristics of the element. Figure 8-12 presents sample charts that can be developed for each element of story structure. Leave space on the charts for students to add information about the element in their own words. Next, read several stories illustrating the element to students or have students read the stories themselves. After reading, discuss the story to probe students' awareness of how the author used the element in constructing the story.

2. *Analyze the element in stories.* Have students read or listen to one or more stories read aloud that illustrate the element. After reading, students analyze how the author used the element in each story. They should tie their analyses to the definition and the characteristics of the element presented in the first step. Students can also make their own copies of the chart to put in their writer's notebooks.

3. *Participate in exploration activities.* Students participate in exploration activities in which they investigate how authors use the element in particular stories. Possible activities include retelling stories orally, with drawings, and in writing; dramatizing stories with puppets and with informal drama; and drawing clusters to graphically display the structure of stories. These exploration activities are described in the next section.

4. *Review the element.* Review the characteristics of the element being studied using the charts introduced earlier. Ask students to restate the definition and characteristics of the element in their own words, using one book they have read to illustrate the characteristics.

5. *Write a class collaboration story.* Have students apply what they have learned about the element of story structure by writing a class (or group) collaboration

Chart 1	Chart 2	Chart 3
Stories	**Beginnings of Stories**	**Middles of Stories**
Stories have three parts:	Writers put these things in the beginning of a story.	Writers put these things in the middle of a story.
1. A beginning	1.	1.
2. A middle	2.	2.
3. An end	3.	3.
		4.
		5.

Chart 4	Chart 5
Ends of Stories	**Conflict**
Writers put these things in the end of a story.	Conflict is the problem that characters face in the story. There are four kinds of conflict:
1.	1. Conflict between a character and nature
2.	2. Conflict between a character and society
3.	3. Conflict between characters
	4. Conflict within a character

FIGURE 8-12   *Charts for the Elements of Story Structure*

236

Chart 6

Plot

Plot is the sequence of events in a story. It has four parts:

1. A problem: The problem introduces conflict at the beginning of the story.

2. Roadblocks: Characters face roadblocks as they try to solve the problem in the middle of the story.

3. The High Point: The high point in the action occurs when the problem is about to be solved. It separates the middle and the end.

4. The Solution: The problem is solved and the road-blocks are overcome at the end of the story.

Chart 7

Setting

The setting is where and when the story takes place.

1. Location: Stories can take place anywhere.

2. Weather: Stories take place in different kinds of weather.

3. Time of Day: Stories take place during the day or at night.

4. Time Period: Stories take place in the past, at the current time, or in the future.

Chart 8

Characters

Writers develop characters in four ways:

1. Appearance: How characters look

2. Action: What characters do

3. Dialogue: What characters say

4. Monologue: What characters think

Chart 9

Theme

Theme is the underlying meaning of a story.

1. Explicit themes are stated clearly in the story.

2. Implicit themes are suggested by the characters, action and monologue

Chart 10

Point of View

Writers tell the story according to one of four viewpoints:

1. First-Person Viewpoint: The writer tells the story through the eyes of one character using "I."

2. Omniscient Viewpoint: The writer sees all and knows all about each character.

3. Limited Omniscient Viewpoint: The writer focuses on one character and tells that character's thoughts and feelings.

4. Objective Viewpoint: The writer focuses on the events of the story without telling what the characters are thinking and feeling.

FIGURE 8-12, *continued*

story. A collaborative story provides students with a rehearsal before they write stories independently. Review the element of story structure and refer to the appropriate chart as the story is being written. Encourage students to offer ideas for the story and explain how to incorporate the element into the story. Follow the writing process stages by writing a rough draft on the chalkboard, chart paper, or overhead transparency. Then have students revise the story, working both to improve the content as well as to check that the element of story structure being studied has been incorporated in the story. Next, edit the story and make a final copy to be shared with all class members. Two collaborative stories written by a class of transitional students (students who have completed kindergarten but need additional experiences before first grade) are presented in Figure 8-13. The second story became necessary when students couldn't agree on the ending for the first story. As a compromise, the teacher promised the students who wanted a different ending that they could write a sequel.

6. *Write individual stories.* Students write individual stories incorporating the element being studied and other elements of story structure that they have already learned. Students use the process approach to writing. The activities involved in the preceding five steps of this instructional strategy constitute the prewriting stage. In this step, students complete the remaining stages of the writing process. First, they write rough drafts of their stories and meet in writing groups to share their writing. Writing-group members focus their comments on both the content of the story and how effectively the writer has used the element of story structure being studied. Next, they revise using the feedback they receive. After editing their stories and correcting as many mechanical errors as possible, students recopy the stories and share them with an appropriate audience.

Exploration Activities. Students investigate how authors use plot, character, setting, theme, and point of view through exploration activities. As they retell and dramatize stories, compare versions of stories, and write new versions, students are elaborating their concepts of story and gaining the experience necessary to write well-developed stories. Ten useful exploration activities are described below.

1. *Class Collaboration Retelling of Stories.* Choose a favorite story that students have read or listened to several times and have each student draw or write a retelling of a page or short part of the story. Then collect each child's contribution and compile them to make a class book. Younger students can draw pictures and dictate their retellings, which the teacher prints in large type. Then these pictures and text can be attached to sheets of posterboard to make a big book that students can read together.

2. *Retelling and Telling Stories.* Students retell familiar stories to small groups of classmates using simple hand or finger puppets or with pictures on a flannel board. Similarly, students can create their own stories to tell. A gingerbread boy might become a gingerbread bunny that runs away with a basket of Easter eggs, or Max might make a second trip to visit the wild things.

3. *Retelling Stories with Pictures.* Students retell a favorite story by drawing a series of pictures and compiling them to make a wordless picture book. Young chil-

STORY 1: BILLY AND THE LEPRECHAUN

Once upon a time there was a little leprechaun named Fred. He had a miserable life because nobody would believe that he had a pot of gold. Also, Fred was always being teased because he was the smallest leprechaun. Fred did have a pot of gold that was hidden underground in a tunnel under a mushroom. This mushroom was Fred's home.

One afternoon a little boy named Billy was walking in the meadow. Suddenly, he heard the grass moving. Billy was startled by the noise, but he was brave and went over to see what it was. He found a little man that he recognized as a leprechaun.

Billy grabbed the leprechaun by the seat of his britches and said, "What is your name and where is your gold?"

"My name is Fred and my gold is hidden."

"Well, I won't let you go until you give me your gold," said Billy.

Then Fred said, "I will not give you my gold!"

"Well," said Billy, "You are not obeying fairy law and I will tell the fairies on you."

"So what, I don't care," said Fred.

So Billy thought to himself, "I will tease Fred and make him angry so he will accidently tell me where his gold is hidden."

So Billy said, "You are so little you haven't been alive long enough to earn some gold."

Fred said, "Yes, I have."

"No you haven't."

"Yes I have," said Fred.

"Then prove it," said Billy.

Fred said, "All right, I'll prove it. Just follow me."

In the mushroom was a trap door that led to a big tunnel. This tunnel was big enough for Billy and the leprechaun. It was dark and spooky in the tunnel with bats flying everywhere. They kept on sliding and crawling until they saw the sparkling gold.

Billy said, "There is so much gold. It is too heavy to carry all by myself. I will have to go get a wagon to carry it."

"Then, I'll stay here and guard it," said Fred.

"What if you are tricking me?" said Billy.

"Oh no, I wouldn't be tricking you."

"Then, I'll go get the wagon," said Billy.

Fred watched as Billy started to walk all the way back to town. As soon as Billy was out of sight, Fred went to get some more real mushrooms that looked just like his home. He stuck them all around the meadow and then went back to his tunnel.

Hours later, Billy came back and he saw all the mushrooms around the meadow. He knew it would take too long to find the right one so he gave up and went home. Fred the leprechaun lived happily ever after after counting his gold.

FIGURE 8-13 Class Collaboration Story

STORY 2: BILLY'S REVENGE

It was Wednesday. Billy and his friends were thinking about how they could get Fred the leprechaun's gold. Billy had told his friends how he had met the leprechaun in the meadow under a mushroom and been tricked by him.

His friends believed him because they all knew that leprechauns were tricky. So they decided to help Billy get the gold back from Fred. Billy told them that if they helped him, they would split up all the gold. They knew that they would have to trick Fred and fight dirty to get the gold.

This was the plan. They decided that Billy's friend Spike who was little, fat, and wrinkly, would dress like a leprechaun and pretend to be Fred's long lost brother. They put a fake mustache and beard on him and then bought green clothes and a hat from the costume store for him to wear.

Billy, Spike, and all the other boys and girls rode down to the meadow on a wagon pulled by horses. There they saw only one mushroom. Fred had taken all the other mushrooms away because he didn't think that Billy would be back.

The boys and girls hid in the trees while Spike went to knock on the door. Fred the leprechaun opened the door and said, "Who are you?"

Spike said, "I am your long lost brother and I live in New Mexico. I have traveled a long way. Can I lie down somewhere?"

"Yes, you can brother," said Fred.

Spike lay down and began to talk to Fred.

Spike asked, "Fred, how much gold have you made during all these years?"

"Trillions and trillions and billions and millions and I used to hide it in the tunnel under my mushroom until this little pest named Billy came along and tried to steal it. Now I hide it inside the apple tree on the left side of my house," said Fred.

All this time, Billy and his friends were listening at the door that Fred had forgotten to close. As soon as they heard where the gold was hidden, they went to the apple tree on the left, took the chain saw that they had brought, and chopped down the tree. Fred never heard any noise outside because Spike liked rock and roll music and had turned the radio on full blast.

As the tree fell down, the gold flew out. All the girls and boys put the gold into the wagon and they rode home. In the meantime, Spike danced by the window and he saw his friends signal him to leave. As Spike saw the signal, he danced right out the door and ran as fast as he could to Billy's house. Fred didn't see him leave because he was dancing the other way.

Finally, Fred turned and noticed that Spike was gone. In a flash, he rushed out to check on his gold and he found that it was missing. All of it was gone except 20 pieces. Then Fred noticed a sign. The sign said:

Dear Fred,

I like you Fred, but you were so mean to me that I wanted to take revenge. I left you 20 pieces of gold. That should be enough and I know that you can make more.

Love,
Billy, Spike, and Friends

Fred felt a little bit better and started on a hunt to find more gold.

This time Billy lived happily ever after counting his half of the gold.

FIGURE 8-13, continued

dren can make a booklet by folding one sheet of drawing paper in quarters like a
greeting card. Then they write the title of the book on the front; on the three remaining
pages, they draw illustrations to represent the beginning, middle, and end of the story.
A sample four-sided booklet is presented in Figure 8-14. Older students can produce
a film of a favorite story by drawing a series of pictures on a long sheet of butcher
paper and scrolling the pictures on a screen made out of a cardboard box. Students
can also draw pictures to retell a story on a filmstrip. (Filmstrip kits with blank film
and colored pens are available from school supply stores.)

   4.   *Retelling Stories in Writing.*   Students write retellings of favorite stories in
their own words. Predictable books, stories that use repetition, are often the easiest
to retell. Students do not copy the text out of a book; rather, they retell a story that
they know well. Sixth-grade Ilya wrote the following retelling of *Little Red Riding
Hood.* Notice that her sentences are written in alphabetical order. The first sentence
begins with A, the second with B, the third with C, and so on.

FIGURE 8-14   *A Four-Sided Booklet Retelling* The Tale of Peter Rabbit

▽   **Little Red Riding Hood**

*"Another plain day," said Little Red Riding Hood. "Boy, oh boy, oh boy," she won-
dered. "Could I do something fun today?"*

*"Dear," called her mother to Little Red Riding Hood. "Eat your breakfast and
then take these goodies to grandma's house."*

*"Fine, I'll do it. Great," said Little Red Riding Hood. "My first time I get to go
through the forest."*

"Hold it," said a wolf in the forest. "I want to look in that basket of yours."

*"Just stay out of there, you wolf. Keep your hands off me! Let go of me, you
wolf." Mighty and brave, she slapped the wolf. Not knowing what to do, she ran
down the path to grandma's house.*

*Open minded, the wolf ran to grandma's house. Putting his hands through the
window, he climbed in and swallowed grandma. Quietly he jumped in her bed.*

*Running to grandma's house, still scared from the wolf, Little Red Riding Hood
knocked on grandma's door. Silently the wolf came to meet her. Too late for Red
Riding Hood to run, she panicked and yelled. Unaware she was. Very loudly her yell
traveled through the forest. Wondering what it was, a woodsman heard it and came
to grandma's house and killed the wolf. X-raying the body of the wolf, he saw
grandma.*

*"Your help sure has paid off," said Little Red Riding Hood after the woodsman
saved her. Zooming from grandma's house came Little Red Riding Hood, to tell her
mom what had just happened.*

After writing, students can point out how they used the element of story structure
being studied in their retelling. They can point out the conflict situation, the point of
view, repeated words, or the beginning, middle, and end parts. This activity is a good
confidence-builder for students who can't seem to continue a story to its conclusion.
By using a story they are familiar with, they are more successful.

5. *Dramatizing Stories.*   Students dramatize favorite stories or use puppets to
retell a story. These dramatizations should be informal; fancy props are unnecessary
and students should not memorize or read dialogue.

6. *Drawing Story Clusters and Other Diagrams.*   Students draw beginning-
middle-end story clusters, repetition clusters, and plot diagrams for stories they have
read.

7. *Comparing Versions of Stories.*   Students compare different versions of folktales such as *The Hare and the Tortoise* and *The Gingerbread Boy.* A list of various
picture book versions of familiar folktales is presented in Figure 8-15. Students can
compare the beginning, middle, and end of each version. In one version of *The Hare
and the Tortoise,* for example, the beginning is much longer as the author describes
the elaborate plans for the race, while in other versions the beginning is brief. Students can also compare the events in each story. The characters that the Gingerbread
Boy runs past vary in different versions, and in one version of *Cinderella* the heroine
attends the ball twice.

8. *Creating Character Clusters.*   Students complete a character cluster for a
fully developed main character as shown in Figure 8-16. This character cluster de-

FIGURE 8-15   *Different Versions of Familiar Folktales*

The Hare and the Tortoise

Castle, C. (1985). *The hare and the tortoise.* New York: Dutton.
Galdone, P. (1962). *The hare and the tortoise.* New York: McGraw-Hill.
Stevens, J. (1984). *The tortoise and the hare.* New York: Holiday House.
Wildsmith, B. (1966). *The hare and the tortoise.* Oxford: Oxford University Press.

Jack and the Beanstalk

Cauley, L. B. (1983). *Jack and the beanstalk.* New York: Putnam.
De Regniers, B. S. (1985). *Jack and the beanstalk.* New York: Atheneum.
Haley, G. (1986). *Jack and the bean tree.* New York: Crown.
Howe, J. (1989). *Jack and the beanstalk.* Boston: Little, Brown.
Johnson, D. W. (1976). *Jack and the beanstalk.* Boston: Little, Brown.
Kellogg, S. (1991). *Jack and the beanstalk.* New York: Morrow.
Still, J. (1977). *Jack and the wonder beans.* New York: Putnam.

Cinderella

Brown, M. (1954). *Cinderella.* New York: Scribner.
Climo, S. (1989). *The Egyptian cinderella.* New York: Crowell.
Climo, S. (1993). *The Korean cinderella.* New York: HarperCollins.
Cole, B. (1987). *Prince Cinders.* New York: Putnam.
Cole, B. (1986). *Princess Smartypants.* New York: Putnam.
Ehrlich, A. (1985). *Cinderella.* New York: Dial.
Galdone, P. (1978). *Cinderella.* New York: McGraw-Hill.
Grimm, J. C. K. (1981). *Cinderella.* New York: Greenwillow.
Hook, W. H. (1987). *Moss gown.* New York: Clarion.
Huck, C. (1989). *Princess Furball.* New York: Greenwillow.
Karlin, B. (1989). *Cinderella.* Boston: Little, Brown.
Perrault, C. (1972). *Cinderella.* New York: Penguin.
Shorto, R. (1990). *Cinderella/Cinderella: The untold story.* New York: Birch Lane Press.
Steptoe, J. (1987). *Mufaro's beautiful daughters: An African tale.* New York: Lothrop.

The Gingerbread Boy

Asbjornsen, P. C., & Moe, J. (1980). *The runaway pancake.* New York: Larousse.
Brown, M. (1972). *The bun: A tale from Russia.* New York: Harcourt Brace Jovanovich.
Cauley, L. B. (1988). *The pancake boy: An old Norwegian folk tale.* New York: Putnam.
Galdone, P. (1975). *The gingerbread boy.* New York: Seabury.
Jacobs, J. (n.d.). *Johnny-cake.* New York: Putnam.
Jarrell, R. (1964). *The gingerbread rabbit.* New York: Collier.
Lobel, A. (1978). *The pancake.* New York: Greenwillow.
Oppenheim, J. (1986). *You can't catch me!* Boston: Houghton Mifflin.
Sawyer, R. (1953). *Journey cake, ho!* New York: Viking.

FIGURE 8-15, *continued*

Little Red Riding Hood

Emberly, M. (1990). *Ruby.* Boston: Little, Brown.
Galdone, P. (1974). *Little red riding hood.* New York: McGraw-Hill.
Grimm, J. (1983). *Little red cap.* New York: Morrow.
Goodall, J. (1988). *Little red riding hood.* New York: Macmillan.
Hyman, T. S. (1983). *Little red riding hood.* New York: Holiday House.
Marshall, J. (1987). *Little red riding hood.* New York: Dial.
Rowland, D. (1991). *Little red riding hood/The wolf's tale.* New York: Birch Lane
    Press.
Young, E. (1989). *Lon Po Po: A red-riding hood story from China.* New York: Philo-
    mel.

---

scribes Rumpelstiltskin from Paul O. Zelinsky's retelling of the Grimms' folktale of the same name (1986). Rumpelstiltskin, the name of the character, is the nucleus word for the cluster, and the four ways authors develop characters—appearance, action, dialogue, and monologue—are the main ideas for the rays. Details about the character are added to each main idea, as the cluster illustrates.

9. *Writing Dialogue.* Students choose an excerpt from a favorite story and create a script with dialogue. Then students read the script to classmates as a readers' theater presentation. Also, students can draw comic strips for an excerpt from a story and add dialogue. Students might try varying the register of the language, from informal to very formal, from standard to nonstandard English, to appreciate the power of language.

10. *Retelling Stories from Different Points of View.* Students experiment with point of view to understand how the author's viewpoint can slant a story. To demonstrate how point of view changes according to the viewpoint of the person telling the story, read Judy Blume's *The Pain and the Great One* (1974) to students. In this book, the same brief story is told twice, first from the viewpoint of "the great one," an 8-year-old sister, and then from the viewpoint of "the pain," the 6-year-old brother. Even children in the primary grades are struck by how different the two versions are and how the narrator filters the information.

Another way to demonstrate the impact of different viewpoints is for students to retell or rewrite a familiar story, such as *Little Red Riding Hood* (Galdone, 1974), from different points of view—through the eyes of Little Red Riding Hood, her sick, old grandmother, the hungry wolf, or the woodsman.

As they shift the point of view, students learn that they can change some aspects of a story but not others. To help them appreciate how these changes affect a story, have them take a story such as C. S. Lewis's *The Lion, the Witch and the Wardrobe* (1981), which is told from the omniscient viewpoint, and retell short episodes from

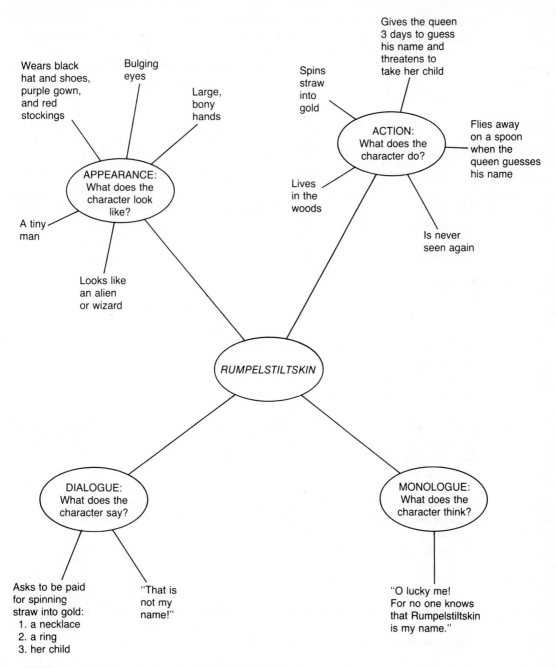

Wears black
hat and shoes,
purple gown,
and red
stockings

Bulging
eyes

Large,
bony
hands

Gives the queen
3 days to guess
his name and
threatens to
take her child

Spins
straw
into
gold

Flies away
on a spoon
when the
queen guesses
his name

APPEARANCE:
What does the
character look
like?

ACTION:
What does the
character do?

A tiny
man

Lives
in the
woods

Is never
seen again

Looks like
an alien
or wizard

RUMPELSTILTSKIN

DIALOGUE:
What does the
character say?

MONOLOGUE:
What does the
character think?

Asks to be paid
for spinning
straw into gold:
1. a necklace
2. a ring
3. her child

"That is
not my
name!"

"O lucky me!
For no one knows
that Rumpelstiltskin
is my name."

FIGURE 8-16 *A Character Cluster for* Rumpelstiltskin

the viewpoints of each character as well as from the four basic viewpoints. The omniscient viewpoint is a good one to start with because in this viewpoint the readers learn all. As students shift to other points of view, they must decide what to leave out according to the new perspective. They must decide whether to tell the story in first or third person and what kinds of information about the characters they are permitted to share.

Assessing Stories that Students Write

Assessing the stories that students write through this approach involves far more than simply judging the quality of the finished stories. Any assessment should also take into account students' activities and learning as they study the element of story structure as well as the activities students engage in as they write and refine their stories. These four components should be considered in assessing students' stories: (a) students' study of the element of story structure, (b) their knowledge about and application of the element in writing, (c) their use of the writing process, and (d) the quality of the finished stories.

The first component is students' participation in the study of the element of story structure. Assess students' participation in these ways:

▼ Did the student read stories illustrating the element?
▼ Did the student participate in discussions analyzing how the element was used in particular stories?
▼ Did the student participate in one or more application activities?

The second component is students' knowledge of the element of story structure and their application of the element in the stories they write. Determining whether students learned about the element and applied what they have learned in their stories is crucial in assessing students' stories. Consider the following points:

▼ Can the student define or identify the characteristics of the element?
▼ Can the student explain how the element being studied was used in a particular story?
▼ Did the student apply the element in the story he or she has written?

Use of the process approach to write their stories is another component of evaluation. Learning about the element is a prewriting activity, and after they learn about the element, students draft, revise, edit, and share their stories as they do with other types of writing. Assess students' use of the writing process by observing them as they write and asking these questions:

▼ Did the student write a rough draft?
▼ Did the student participate in a writing group?
▼ Did the student revise the story according to feedback received from the writing group?

▼ Did the student proofread the story and correct as many mechanical errors as possible?

▼ Did the student share the story?

The fourth component is the quality of the story. Quality is difficult to measure, but it is often described as creativeness or inventiveness. In addition, a second aspect of quality is organization. Students who write high-quality, interesting stories use the elements of story structure to their advantage. Ask these questions to assess the quality of children's stories.

▼ Is the story interesting?

▼ Is the story well organized?

These four components and the questions listed under each can be used in assessing students' stories. Assessing or grading students' stories is more than simply evaluating the quality of the finished product, and any assessment should reflect all components of students' involvement with stories. For more information about assessing students' writing, see Chapter 12.

Answering Teachers' Questions About . . .
Narrative Writing

1. *It sounds as if this approach is very time-consuming, and I don't have any time to spend on teaching writing. What can I do?*

Your concern is a common one. Many teachers feel frustrated as they try to squeeze writing instruction into an already full school day. One way to make time to teach students about the elements of story structure and have them write stories is to incorporate the activities discussed in this chapter into the reading program. Stories in basal reading texts illustrate many of the elements of story structure, and they can be supplemented with class sets of some of the stories suggested in this chapter, stories that you read aloud to the entire class, and library books that students read independently. As students read the stories in the basal readers or in trade books, focus the discussion on the elements of story

structure rather than on other questions provided in teacher manuals. If you teach creatively, you can use a combination of basal readers and trade books to teach students about stories.

2. *I told my sixth graders about plot and then they wrote stories. I was very disappointed with their stories. They weren't very good.*

It sounds as if you explained plot to the students rather than helped the students analyze stories to see how authors use plot in their stories. It is important to follow the instructional strategy laid out in this chapter and allow time for students to examine and experiment with plot before they write stories. It isn't enough to explain an element of story structure to students. Did students write a class collaboration story before they wrote individual stories?

Writing a collaborative story is an important step because it gives you an opportunity to see if the students understand the element and how to apply it in their stories.

3. *Is there a sequence I should follow in teaching the elements of story structure, or can I teach them all together?*

Each element of story structure should be taught separately, and it is best to teach the elements in the order presented in this chapter. Plot (and the concept of beginning-middle-end in particular) is the most basic element of story structure. Even older children need to understand this basic organizational pattern before examining the other elements. If students haven't been taught about plot, setting, character, theme, and point of view, they need to study each element and write stories incorporating each.

4. *What should I do when Wilson can't write an individual story?*

I'd recommend that you work with Wilson to find out *why* he can't write a story. First, check his understanding of the elements of story structure. Can he explain the element of story structure and give examples? If not, he is not prepared to write a story incorporating that element and should be involved in additional activities to examine the element. Second, check Wilson's ability to retell a story he has read that incorporates the element. Can he retell a story orally? If not, read a short story to him or have him read one himself and retell it to you. If he can retell a story successfully, you might want to have Wilson retell a story in writing instead of writing an original story. Third, check to see if he has an idea for his story. If he doesn't, talk to him about possible story ideas, encourage him to write a sequel to a story he has read, or, if all else fails, suggest that he retell a favorite story. It is important for Wilson to write something so he can overcome his writer's block.

REFERENCES

Andersen, H. C. (1979). *The ugly duckling.* New York: Harcourt Brace Jovanovich.

Applebee, A. N. (1978). *The child's concept of story: Ages 2 to 17.* Chicago: University of Chicago Press.

Applebee, A. N. (1980). Children's narratives: New directions. *The Reading Teacher, 34,* 137–142.

Au, K. H. (1992). Constructing the theme of a story. *Language Arts, 69,* 106–111.

Beaver, J. M. (1982). "Say it! Over and over." *Language Arts, 59,* 143–148.

Blume, J. (1972). *Tales of a fourth grade nothing.* New York: Dutton.

Blume, J. (1974). *The pain and the great one.* New York: Bradbury.

Brown, M. (1954). *Cinderella.* New York: Scribner.

Burch, R. (1966). *Queenie Peavy.* New York: Viking.

Burch, R. (1980). *Ida Early comes over the mountain.* New York: Viking.

Byars, B. (1970). *The summer of the swans.* New York: Viking.

Byars, B. (1977). *The pinballs.* New York: Harper.

Dahl, R. (1961). *James and the giant peach.* New York: Knopf.

Dahl, R. (1978). *The enormous crocodile.* New York: Knopf.

Dressel, J. H. (1990). The effects of listening to and discussing different qualities of children's literature on the narrative writing of fifth graders.

Research in the Teaching of English, 24, 397–414.

Eeds, M. & Wells, D. (1989). Grand conversations: An exploration of meaning construction in literature study groups. *Research in the Teaching of English, 23,* 4–29.

Emig, J. (1977). Writing as a mode of learning. *College Composition and Communication, 28,* 122–128.

Fitzgerald, J., & Spiegel, D. L. (1983). Enhancing children's reading comprehension through instruction in narrative structure. *Journal of Reading Behavior, 15,* 1–17.

Fox, P. (1973). *The slave dancer.* New York: Bradbury.

Galdone, P. (1974). *Little Red Riding Hood.* New York: Seabury.

Galdone, P. (1984). *The teeny-tiny woman.* New York: Clarion.

George, J. C. (1972). *Julie of the wolves.* New York: Harper & Row.

Golden, J. M. (1984). Children's concept of story in reading and writing. *The Reading Teacher, 37,* 578–584.

Gordon, C. J., & Braun, C. (1982). Story schemata: Metatextual aid to reading and writing. In J. A. Niles & L. A. Harris (Eds.), *New inquiries in reading: Research and instruction.* Rochester, NY: National Reading Conference.

Hade, D. D. (1988). Children, stories, and narrative transformations. *Research in the Teaching of English, 22,* 310–325.

Konigsburg, E. L. (1983). *From the mixed up files of Mrs. Basil E. Frankweiler.* New York: Atheneum.

Lasky, K. (1983). *Beyond the divide.* New York: Macmillan.

Lawson, R. (1972). *Rabbit Hill.* New York: Penguin.

Lehr, S. S. (1991). *The child's developing sense of theme: Responses to literature.* New York: Teachers College Press.

L'Engle, M. (1962). *A wrinkle in time.* New York: Farrar, Straus & Giroux.

Lewis, C. S. (1981). *The lion, the witch and the wardrobe.* New York: Macmillan.

Lowry, L. (1979). *Anastasia Krupnik.* Boston: Houghton Mifflin.

Lowry, L. (1989). *Number the stars.* Boston: Houghton Mifflin.

Lukens, R. J. (1991). *A critical handbook of children's literature* (4th ed.). Glenview, IL: Scott, Foresman.

Mandler, J. M., & Johnson, N. S. (1977). Remembrance of things parsed: Story structure and recall. *Cognitive Psychology, 9,* 111–115.

Martinez, M. & Roser, N. (1985). Read it again: The value of repeated readings during storytime. *The Reading Teacher, 38,* 782–786.

Mayer, M. (1987). *The Pied Piper of Hamelin.* New York: Macmillan.

McCloskey, R. (1969). *Make way for ducklings.* New York: Viking.

McConaughy, S. H. (1980). Using story structure in the classroom. *Language Arts, 57,* 157–165.

Morrow, L. M. (1982). Relationships between literature programs, library corner designs and children's use of literature. *Journal of Educational Research, 75,* 339–344.

Morrow, L. M. (1984). Effects of story retelling on young children's comprehension and sense of story structure. In J. A. Niles and L. A. Harris (Eds.), *Changing perspectives on research in reading/language processing and instruction* (pp. 96–100). Rochester, NY: National Reading Conference.

Morrow, L. M. (1985a). Reading and retelling stories: Strategies for emergent readers. *The Reading Teacher, 38,* 870–875.

Morrow, L. M. (1985b). Retelling stories: A strategy for improving young children's comprehension, concept of story structure, and oral language complexity. *Elementary School Journal, 85,* 647–661.

Morrow, L. M. (1986). Effects of structural guidance in story retellings on children's dictation of original stories. *Journal of Reading Behavior, 18,* 135–152.

Ness, E. (1966). *Sam, Bangs and moonshine.* New York: Holt.

O'Dell, S. (1960). *Island of the blue dolphins.* Boston: Houghton Mifflin.

Paterson, K. (1977). *Bridge to Terabithia.* New York: Crowell.

Pitcher, E. G., & Prelinger, E. (1963). *Children tell stories: An analysis of fantasy.* New York: International Universities Press.

Potter, B. (1902). *The tale of Peter Rabbit.* New York: Warne.

Purcell-Gates, V. (1988). Lexical and syntactic knowledge of written narrative held by well-read-to kindergartners and second graders. *Research in the Teaching of English, 22,* 128–160.

Rosen, H. (1986). The importance of story. *Language Arts, 63,* 226–237.

Rumelhart, D. (1975). Notes on a schema for stories. In D. G. Bobrow (Ed.), *Representation and understanding: Studies in cognitive science.* New York: Academic Press.

Sendak, M. (1963). *Where the wild things are.* New York: Harper & Row.

Speare, E. G. (1958). *The witch of Blackbird Pond.* Boston: Houghton Mifflin.

Spiegel, D. L. & Fitzgerald, J. (1986). Improving reading comprehension through instruction about story parts. *The Reading Teacher, 39,* 676–682.

Steig, W. (1982). *Doctor De Soto.* New York: Farrar, Straus & Giroux.

Stein, N. L., & Glenn, C. G. (1979). An analysis of story comprehension in elementary school children. In R. O. Freedle (Ed.), *New directions in discourse processing.* Norwood, NJ: Ablex.

Taylor, M. C. (1976). *Roll of thunder, hear my cry.* New York: Dial.

Tompkins, G. E., & McGee, L. M. (1989). In K. D. Muth (Ed.), *Children's comprehension of narrative and expository text: Research into practice (pp. 59–78).* Newark, DE: International Reading Association.

Tompkins, G. E., & Webeler, M. B. (1983). What will happen next? Using predictable books with young children. *The Reading Teacher, 36,* 498–502.

Van Allsburg, C. (1981). *Jumanji.* Boston: Houghton Mifflin.

Viorst, J. (1977). *Alexander and the terrible, horrible, no good, very bad day.* New York: Atheneum.

Waber, B. (1972). *Ira sleeps over.* Boston: Houghton Mifflin.

Watson, J. J. (1991). An integral setting tells more than when and where. *The Reading Teacher, 44,* 638–646.

White, E. B. (1952). *Charlotte's web.* New York: Harper & Row.

Zelinsky, P. O. (1986). *Rumpelstiltskin.* New York: Dutton.

Zemach, M. (1983). *The little red hen.* New York: Farrar, Straus & Giroux.

9

Poetry Writing

Overview of Poetry Writing

Purpose   Students write poetry to play with words, create images, explore feelings, and entertain.

Audience   Poems are usually shared orally so that the audience can appreciate the word-play, rhythm, and other poetic devices. Often students share their poems and other wordplays with classmates by reading them aloud or preparing an anthology.

Forms   Forms include formula poems, free-form poems, syllable- and word-count poems, rhymed verse forms, and poems modeled on other poems.

Topics   Students draw topics from personal experiences and poems they have read. Students often write about pets and special interests such as dinosaurs.

Approaches   Students learn about wordplay, poetic forms, and poetic devices through mini-lessons during readers' and writers' workshop and literature focus units. They write poems during writers' workshop and as responses to literature and projects during theme studies.

Other   Most children are inclined toward poetry, but when they equate poetry with rhymed verse, the poems they compose are stilted and artificial. As elementary students learn about poetic forms and devices, they can write poetry successfully because of their spontaneity and playfulness with words.

Reading and Writing Poetry

Miss Clark's sixth-grade class is reading and writing poetry during a four-week genre unit. During the first week, students focus on Jack Prelutsky and his poems. They read poems during readers' workshop and write responses to them. Through minilessons they learn about the poet and his poems. Then they apply what they have learned as they write poems during writers' workshop. The daily schedule is as follows:

8:45–9:30	Readers' Workshop
	Students read poems independently and write responses in poetry logs.
9:30–9:45	Sharing
	Students share poems they have read, and the class uses choral reading to reread favorite Prelutsky poems copied onto chart paper.
9:45–10:10	Minilesson
	Miss Clark teaches reading and writing minilessons about Prelutsky and his poems, poetic forms, and poetic devices.
10:10–10:45	Writers' Workshop
	Students write poems using the writing process, some of which are modeled on Prelutsky's poems.
10:45–11:00	Sharing
	Students read poems they have written to the class.

During readers' workshop, students read self-selected books from a text set (or collection) of poetry books written by Jack Prelutsky that are displayed in a special poetry box in the classroom library. Figure 9-1 presents a list of the books in Miss

FIGURE 9-1   *Text Set of Poetry Books Written by Jack Prelutsky*

Circus. (1974). New York: Macmillan.
It's Christmas. (1981). New York: Greenwillow.
It's Halloween. (1977). New York: Greenwillow.
It's snowing! It's snowing! (1984). New York: Greenwillow.
It's Thanksgiving. (1982). New York: Greenwillow.
It's Valentine's Day. (1983). New York: Greenwillow.
My parents think I'm sleeping. (1985). New York: Greenwillow.
Nightmares: Poems to trouble your sleep. (1976). New York: Greenwillow.
Rainy rainy Saturday. (1980). New York: Greenwillow.
Ride a purple pelican. (1986). New York: Greenwillow.
Rolling Harvey down the hill. (1980). New York: Greenwillow.
Something big has been here. (1990). New York: Greenwillow.
The baby uggs are hatching. (1982). New York: Mulberry.
The headless horseman rides tonight. (1980). New York: Greenwillow.
The new kid on the block. (1984). New York: Greenwillow.
The snopp on the sidewalk and other poems. (1977). New York: Greenwillow.
Toucans two and other poems. New York: Macmillan.
Tyrannosaurus was a beast. (1988). New York: Greenwillow.
Zoo doings. (1983). New York: Greenwillow.

Clark's text set. She has several copies of each of the books available for students to read. After independent reading time, students gather together to share some of the poems they have read. Three favorite poems are "The New Kid on the Block," "Mean Maxine," and "Louder Than a Clap of Thunder!" all from Prelutsky's *The New Kid on the Block* (1984). Students have copied these poems on large chart paper, and the class rereads the poems as a choral reading or sings them to familiar tunes such as "Yankee Doodle" almost every day.

Each day students write in a poetry log about the poems they are reading during readers' workshop. In these entries, students write about poems they like, record observations about Prelutsky as a poet, list poetic devices that Prelutsky uses, and comment on relationships between the poems and their own lives. Here is one student's response to "Louder Than a Clap of Thunder!" from *The New Kid on the Block:*

▽   *I love this poem. It's fun to read because you can sort of yell and it's the truth for my dad. He snores real loud, real, real loud. And I think Jack Prelutsky was smart to use comparisons. He keeps you guessing until the last line that it is all about snoring. I think that's why the title is just the first line of the poem because if he called it "My Father's Snoring" it would give away the surprise. It's not a very good title. Sort of boring. I would call it "Can You Beat This?" I'm going to write a poem like this but change it to* softer than *and write about how soft my cat is when she tiptoes across my bed. Or when she curls up in my lap.*

Miss Clark teaches a minilesson each day, and she uses Prelutsky's poems as examples for the concepts she is teaching. On Monday, her minilesson focuses on the poet and his life. Because rhyme is an important device in Prelutsky's poems, she makes this her topic for the minilesson on Tuesday. Miss Clark shares several poems with different rhyme schemes, and students examine the arrangements. They also talk about repetition and imagery as alternatives to rhyme.

On Wednesday, Miss Clark reads "The Baby Uggs Are Hatching" (Prelutsky, 1982) and teaches a minilesson on inventing words. She suggests that students might want to create creatures like the uggs, invent names for them, and write their own verses following the format of the poem during writers' workshop. On Thursday, she teaches a minilesson on alliteration after sharing several poems from Prelutsky's *The Headless Horseman Rides Tonight* (1980). Many of the students especially enjoy these spooky poems, and Prelutsky uses alliteration effectively in the poems to evoke a frightening mood.

In the fifth minilesson on Friday, Miss Clark explains how to write color poems after reading "What Happens to the Colors?" in *My Parents Think I'm Sleeping* (1985) and sharing other color poems from *Hailstones and Halibut Bones* (O'Neill, 1961). Later during writers' workshop, students try their hand at writing color poems in which they begin each line or stanza with the name of the color. Here is one student's poem about gray:

▽   *Gray is smoke, billowing*
                       from a burning house,
                       Or clouds in a stormy sky,
                       Gray is my Grandma's hair
                       permed at the beauty salon,

Or rocks on a mountainside.
Gray is an elephant's hide
wrinkled and covered with dust,
Or me when I'm feeling down.

During writers' workshop students write their own poems. They experiment with the poetic forms that Miss Clark teaches and other forms that they have learned previously. They draft their poems, meet together in writing groups to revise their poems, edit them with Miss Clark, and then write the final copy in the second half of their poetry logs.

One day during writers' workshop, the students work together as a class to write a new version of Prelutsky's poem "I'm Thankful" (1984). They follow Prelutsky's format, even the "except" arrangement of the last line. Here is an excerpt from the class poem:

▽

I'm Thankful

I'm thankful for my telephone
It hardly ever rings.
I'm thankful for my cat.
She scratched me in the face.
I'm thankful for my basketball.
It broke my mother's vase.
I'm thankful for my bicycle.
I ran into a car.
I'm thankful for my skateboard.
I fell and scraped my knees.
I'm thankful for so many things
Except, of course, for peas!

Students also prepare a reading-writing project at the end of the week. Miss Clark and the class brainstorm a list of more than 20 possible projects, and students work individually or in small groups on self-selected projects. Some students write letters to Jack Prelutsky, and some make a collection of favorite Prelutsky poems. One group of students videotapes a choral reading of several Prelutsky poems to share with the class. Others write their own poems and compile them in an anthology or turn a Prelutsky poem into a picture book with one stanza illustrated on each page.

C hildren are natural poets. Through their observations of children, the Opies (1959) have verified that children have a natural affinity for songs, verses, and rhymes. Babies and preschoolers respond positively when their parents or other caregivers repeat Mother Goose rhymes, read A. A. Milne's Winnie-the-Pooh stories, and sing songs to them. Elementary students continue this interest in poetry as they create jump-rope rhymes and other ditties on the playground.

Miss Clark's students affirm this interest in poetry. They were enthusiastically involved in reading and writing poetry and thought of themselves as poets. Jack Prelutsky and other poets who write for children have created many collections of poems that spark students' interest in poetry. These poets write about topics, such as poltergeists, parents, and dinosaurs, that appeal to children. When students know how to write poems and use poetic devices, they can create vivid word pictures, powerful images, and emotional expressions. The teacher's role is to teach these concepts through minilessons and to provide opportunities for students to read and write poetry during readers' and writers' workshop, literature focus units, and social studies and science theme cycles.

In this chapter, the focus is on teaching students how to write poetry. The first section focuses on wordplay and explores the power of words and phrases. Through these activities, students learn ways to use language to create strong images and word pictures. In the second section, five types of poems—formula poems, free-form poems, syllable- and word-count poems, rhymed verse poems, and model poems—are described, and sample poems written by elementary students are presented. The strategy for teaching children to write these five types of poems is presented in the third section, and the chapter concludes with information about poetic devices, such as alliteration and onomatopoeia, that students incorporate in the poems they write.

WORDPLAY

Students play with words as they put words together in unusual ways, invent new words, learn that words can have many meanings, and experiment with the sound of words. These experiences are necessary for students to appreciate what a powerful tool words are for creating images, communicating ideas, and reflecting on life. Five types of wordplay activities are discussed in this section: (a) learning the meaning of words, through words with more than one meaning, homophones, and idioms, (b) creating new words, through compounding, adding affixes, coining, inventing trademarks and acronyms, clipping, and composing "sniglets," (c) laughing with language, using jokes and riddles, (d) creating word pictures, using words, pictures, and sentences, and (e) playing with rhyme to create special sound effects. A list of wordplay books is presented in Figure 9-2. These books demonstrate how people experiment, laugh, and create pictures with language.

Learning the Meaning of Words

The meaning of words is crucial in wordplay. Many riddles, for instance, depend on words with multiple meanings. A familiar riddle asks, "How are children and fish alike?" and the answer is "Both are in school." The word *school* is ambiguous, and understanding this riddle requires knowledge of the second meaning of *school*—a group of fish or aquatic animals traveling together. While young children often assume a one-to-one relationship between words and their meanings, elementary students, as they gain more experience with language, learn that words have multiple

FIGURE 9-2   *Wordplay Books*

P = primary grades (K–2); M = middle grades (3–5); U = upper grades (6–8)

Adler, D. A. (1987). *Remember Betsy Floss and other colonial American riddles.* New York: Holiday House. (M–U)

Bancheck, L. (1976). *Snake in, snake out.* New York: Crowell. (M)

Barrett, J. (1983). *A snake is totally tail.* New York: Atheneum. (P–M)

Bayer, J. (1984). *A my name is Alice.* New York: Dial. (P–M)

Brown, M. (1983). *What do you call a dumb bunny? And other rabbit riddles, games, jokes, and cartoons.* Boston: Little, Brown. (P–M)

Burns, M. (1981). *The hink pink book.* Boston: Little, Brown.

Cox, J. A. (1980). *Put your foot in your mouth and other silly sayings.* New York: Random House. (P–M)

Degen, B. (1983). *Jamberry.* New York: Harper & Row. (P)

Elting, M. & Folsom, M. (1980). *Q is for duck: An alphabet guessing game.* New York: Clarion. (P–M)

Esbensen, B. J. (1986). *Words with wrinkled knees.* New York: Crowell. (M–U)

Folsom, M., & Folsom, M. (1985). *Easy as pie: A guessing game of sayings.* New York: Clarion. (P–M)

Funk, C. E. (1948). *A hog on ice and other curious expressions.* New York: Harper & Row. (U)

Gounaud, K. J. (1981). *A very mice joke book.* Boston: Houghton Mifflin. (M)

Gwynne, F. (1970). *The king who rained.* New York: Dutton. (M–U)

Gwynne, F. (1976). *A chocolate moose for dinner.* New York: Dutton. (M–U)

Gwynne, F. (1980). *The sixteen hand horse.* New York: Prentice-Hall. (M–U)

Gwynne, F. (1988). *A little pigeon toad.* New York: Simon & Schuster. (M–U)

Hall, R. & Friends. *Sniglets for kids.* Yellow Springs, OH: Antioch. (M–U)

Hanson, J. (1972). *Homographs: Bow and bow and other words that look the same but sound as different as sow and sow.* Minneapolis: Lerner. (M)

Hanson, J. (1973). *Homographic homophones. Fly and fly and other words that look and sound the same but are as different in meaning as bat and bat.* Minneapolis: Lerner. (M)

Houget, S. R. (1983). *I unpacked my grandmother's trunk: A picture book game.* New York: Dutton. (P–M)

Hunt, B. K. (1975). *Your ant is a which: Fun with homophones.* New York: Harcourt Brace Jovanovich. (P–M)

Juster, N. (1982), *Otter nonsense.* New York: Philomel. (P–M)

Kellogg, S. (1987). *Aster Aardvark's alphabet adventures.* New York: Morrow. (P–M)

Maestro, G. (1984). *What's a frank Frank? Tasty homograph riddles.* New York: Clarion. (P–M)

Maestro, G. (1986). *What's mite might?* New York: Clarion. (M)

Most, B. (1980). *There's an ant in Anthony.* New York: Morrow. (P–M)

Most, B. (1991). *A dinosaur named after me.* San Diego: Harcourt Brace Jovanovich. (P–M)

Most, B. (1992). *Zoodles.* San Diego: Harcourt Brace Jovanovich. (P–M)

Perl, L. (1988). *Don't sing before breakfast, don't sing in the moonlight.* New York: Random House. (M–U)

FIGURE 9-2, *continued*

Schwartz, A. (1973). *Tomfoolery: Trickery and foolery with words.* Philadelphia: Lippincott. (M–U)

Schwartz, A. (1982). *The cat's elbow and other secret languages.* New York: Farrar, Straus & Giroux. (M–U)

Steig, W. (1968). *C D B!* New York: Simon & Schuster. (M–U)

Steig, W. (1984). *C D C?* New York: Farrar, Straus & Giroux. (M–U)

Sterne, N. (1979). *Tyrannosaurus wrecks: A book of dinosaur riddles.* New York: Crowell. (M)

Tallon, R. (1979). *Zoophabets.* New York: Scholastic. (P–M)

Terban, M. (1982). *Eight ate: A feast of homonym riddles.* New York: Clarion. (P–M)

Terban, M. (1983). *In a pickle and other funny idioms.* New York: Clarion. (M)

Terban, M. (1985). *Too hot to hoot: Funny palindrome riddles.* New York: Clarion. (M–U)

Terban, M. (1987). *Mad as a wet hen! and other funny idioms.* New York: Clarion Books. (M)

Terban, M. (1988). *Guppies in tuxedos: Funny eponyms.* New York: Clarion. (M–U)

Terban, M. (1988). *The dove dove: Funny homograph riddles.* New York: Clarion. (M–U)

Terban, M. (1989). *Superdupers! Really funny real words.* New York: Clarion. (M–U)

Terban, M. (1990). *Punching the clock: Funny action idioms.* New York: Clarion. (M)

Terban, M. (1991). *Hey, hay! A wagonful of funny homonym riddles.* New York: Clarion. (M–U)

Tobias, H. & Baskin, L. (1972). *Hosie's alphabet.* New York: Viking. (M–U)

Van Allsburg, C. (1987). *The z was zapped.* Boston: Houghton Mifflin. (M)

Zalben, J. B. (1977). *Lewis Carroll's jabberwocky.* New York: Warne. (M–U)

meanings, that the sound of certain words called homophones doesn't predict meaning, and that some words have both literal and figurative meanings. This ability to understand and appreciate multiple meanings makes wordplay possible for children.

Words with Multiple Meanings.   One of the concepts that students learn about words during the elementary grades is that words have more than one meaning. The word *bank,* for example, has at least 12 different meanings:

1. a piled-up mass of snow or clouds
2. the slope of land beside a lake or river
3. the slope of a road on a turn
4. the lateral tilting of an airplane in a turn
5. to cover a fire with ashes for slow burning
6. a business establishment that receives and lends money
7. a container in which money is saved
8. a supply for use in emergencies (e.g., blood bank)

9. a place of storage (e.g., computer's memory bank)
10. to count on
11. similar things arranged in a row (e.g., a bank of elevators)
12. to arrange things in a row

Why do some words have many different meanings? The meanings of *bank* in this example come from three different sources. The first 5 meanings come from an Old Norse (or Viking) word, and all deal with something slanted or making a slanted motion. Meanings 6 through 10 come from the Italian word *banca,* which originally meant a money changer's table. These meanings deal with financial banking except meaning 10, "to count on," which requires a bit more thought. We use the saying "to bank on" figuratively to mean "to depend on," but it began more literally, from the actual counting of money on a table. Meanings 11 and 12 come from the Old French word *banc,* meaning "a bench." Words acquire multiple meanings as society becomes more complex and finer shades of meaning become necessary. For example, meanings 8 and 9 of bank, "an emergency supply" and "a storage place," are fairly new. As with many words with multiple meanings, it is a linguistic accident that three original words from three languages with their related meanings came to be spelled the same way.

Words assume additional meanings when an affix is added or they are compounded (used together with another word). Consider the word *night,* and the variety of words and phrases that incorporate *night* such as *night blindness, nightcap, nightclub, night crawler, nightfall, nightgown, nightingale, nightlife, nightly, nightmare, night owl, night school, nightstick,* and *nighttime.* Students can compile a list of such words or make a booklet illustrating the words. Figure 9-3 presents a list of more than 100 *down* words that a sixth-grade class compiled.

Homophones. *Homophones* are words that sound alike but are spelled differently, such as *fairy* and *ferry.* In most cases, these homophones happen by chance; they develop from entirely different root words and even from words in two different languages (Tompkins & Yaden, 1986). Other homophones, such as *flower* and *flour,* and *flea* and *flee,* are related etymologically; the first word in each pair is derived from the second. Homophones are confusing because the two words sound alike and their spellings sometimes differ only by a letter or two.

Primary grade students often notice homophones in books they are reading and ask questions about them. This interest often cues teachers to explain homophones in a minilesson or to plan a series of minilessons and other activities that focus on these sound-alike words. Teachers often share homophone riddle books, including *Your Ant Is a Which* (Hunt, 1976), *Eight Ate: A Feast of Homonym Riddles* (Terban, 1982), and *Hey, Hay: A Wagonful of Funny Homonym Riddles* (Terban, 1991), and then students often make their own homophone books in which they draw pictures to illustrate pairs of homophones and use confusing word pairs in sentences. A page comparing *night* and *knight* from a second grader's homophone book is presented in Figure 9-4. On this page, the student has drawn pictures of the two homophones and used both words in a sentence.

FIGURE 9-3   A Sixth-Grade Class Collaboration List of Down Words

downtown	climb down	reach down	downward
touchdown	down payment	write down	hunt down
get down	sit down	settle down	knock down
chow down	throw down	down it	breakdown
shake down	cut down	goose down	sundown
squat down	downhill	hop down	fall down
showdown	low down	hands down	tear down
lie down	slow down	downfall	turn down
quiet down	down right	close down	push down
shut down	beam down	run down	downstairs
shot down	downy	pin down	look down
cool down	downer	come down	inside down
crackdown	downslope	slam down	zip down
countdown	kickdown	slap down	pour down
pass down	stare down	hoe down	down pour
pass me down	boggy down	lock down	tape down
burn down	put down	water down	downgrade
downbeat	wrestle down	downturn	downstream
down to earth	flop down	stuff down	mow down
shimmey down	hung down	downcast	downhearted
downtrodden	chase down	hurl down	beat down

Idioms.   Idioms are figurative sayings such as "It's raining cats and dogs" or "I'm all ears." They are sometimes confusing for children, especially children who are learning English as a second language, because the phrases have both literal and figurative meanings. Children must move beyond the literal meaning of the individual words in order to understand the idiom.

Teachers can introduce idioms by sharing books such as Fred Gwynne's *The King Who Rained* (1970), *A Chocolate Moose for Dinner* (1976), *The Sixteen Hand Horse* (1980), and *A Little Pigeon Toad* (1988). These picture books present literal interpretations of well-known idiomatic sayings, and students enjoy trying to guess the figurative meaning. Together the class talks about what a speaker means when he or she says "I'm all ears" and what the words themselves suggest—that a person is covered with ears. The teacher introduces the term *figurative meaning* for what the words mean and *literal meaning* for what the words say.

After students become familiar with idioms, they can compile a list of them on a chart to hang in the classroom. Students often incorporate idioms into their journal entries and even choose idioms to explain in their journals. One fourth grader wrote this about the saying "I have a frog in my throat":

▽ *I remember that my Gramps used to always say, "I have a frog in my throat." I know it sounds silly, but I used to think he really did and I would ask him to let me look in*

FIGURE 9-4 *A Page from a Second Grader's Homophone Book*

his throat to see it. That always made him laugh but one time he let me. He opened his mouth and I looked and looked but I couldn't see any frog. I thought it was hiding under his tongue. I was a little kid then so that was why I was thinking the literal meaning.

Students also design posters to illustrate the literal meaning of favorite idiomatic phrases. A fourth grader's poster illustrating the literal meaning of "Hold your horses" is presented in Figure 9-5. After students share their idiom posters with classmates, they add explanations to their posters. This information was added to the poster shown in Figure 9-5:

▽ *"Hold your horses" is an all-American saying. At first it was just literal and it meant that people should hold their horses so that they didn't run away. That was when people rode on horseback or in buggies and wagons. It was part of the best of the American West! But now people don't hold horses much any more but they still say, "Hold your horses!" Now it is figurative and it means "Do not get too excited!" or "Hey, you calm down!"*

Students often become curious about how and why idioms developed, and teachers can share *Put Your Foot in Your Mouth and Other Silly Sayings* (Cox, 1980),

FIGURE 9-5   *A Fourth Grader's Idiom Poster*

Marvin Terban's *In a Pickle and Other Funny Idioms* (1983), *Mad as a Wet Hen! and Other Funy Idioms* (1987), and *Punching the Clock: Funny Action Idioms* (1990). These books provide easy-to-read and understandable information about the origins of many familiar idioms.

"Thumbs up" and "thumbs down," for example, originated in ancient Rome. Spectators at gladiator contests voted with their thumbs on whether the losers of the fights should live or die. "Cut off your nose to spite your face" is another old idiom that has been traced to King Henry IV of France who in 1593 considered making war on his own citizens until his advisers changed his mind. Other idioms are American. "Left holding the bag" comes from a trick country boys played on city boys in the 1800s, "too big for your britches" refers to the hand-me-down pants American boys wore a hundred years ago, and "like greased lightning" is an American expression for something that is very fast. Pioneers greased wagon wheels to make them go faster, so what could be faster than greased lightning? Teachers can also consult Charles Funk's *A Hog on Ice and Other Curious Expressions* (1948), though it is too difficult for most students to read on their own.

Creating New Words[1]

New words continually appear in English, many created to describe new inventions and scientific projects. Some of the newest words come from computer science. They are created in a variety of ways, including compounding, adding affixes, coining, and clipping.

Compounding.   *Compounding* means combining two existing words to create a new word. *Friendship* and *childhood* are two examples of words that were compounded by the Anglo-Saxons more than a thousand years ago. More recently created compounds include *body language* and *software.* Compound words usually progress through three stages. They begin as separate words (e.g., *ice cream*), later are hyphenated (e.g., *baby-sit*), and finally are written as one word (e.g., *splashdown*). There are many exceptions to this rule, such as the compound words *post office* and *high school,* which have remained separate words. Other compound words use Greek and Latin elements. Scientific terms, such as *stethoscope* and *television,* were developed this way.

Adding Affixes.   Vocabulary is created by adding prefixes and suffixes to existing words. For example, *pre-,* a Latin prefix meaning "before" or "in front of" occurs in words such as *precinct, prehistoric, preview, premonition,* and *preschool.* Prefixes and suffixes used in English words come from English, Latin, and Greek. Children in the upper elementary grades typically study prefixes and suffixes, and as part of their wordplay students can create new words using affixes. The students in one fifth-grade class coined the word *precess* for the recess before school. They used the word this way: "Do we have outside precess today?"

Coining.   Creative people have always coined new words. Lewis Carroll, author of *Alice in Wonderland* and *Through the Looking Glass,* is perhaps the best-known inventor of words. He called his new words *portmanteau words,* borrowing from the British word for a suitcase that opens into two halves because his new words were created by blending two words into one. The well-known example *chortle,* a blend of *snort* and *chuckle,* is from the poem "Jabberwocky." Jan Breskin Zalben's beautifully illustrated picturebook version of *Jabberwocky* (1977) is very popular with elementary students. Other examples of blended words include *brunch* (*breakfast* + *lunch*), *electrocute* (*electric* + *execute*), *guesstimate* (*guess* + *estimate*), and *smog* (*smoke* + *fog*).

Authors frequently create new words in the stories they write, and students should be alert to the possibility of finding a created word as they read or as they listen to stories read aloud. Adrienne Adams used *woggle* in *A Woggle of Witches* (1971), and Elinor Horwitz described the night as *bimulous* in *When the Sky Is Like Lace* (1975).

---

[1]   Adapted from Tompkins & Yaden, 1986.

A group of first graders created an ABC book in which they created and described mythical creatures beginning with each letter of the alphabet. Figure 9-6 presents the D page from the book, introducing a new plant-eater named the *Dandelionsaurus*. Taking words and word parts and combining them in new ways is fun for children, who don't feel restricted to using words that have been already created.

Trademarks and Acronyms.   Two other types of coined words are trademarks and acronyms. Examples of well-known trademarks, or brand names, include *Kleenex, Coca-Cola, Xerox,* and *nylon*. Nylon, for instance, was invented by scientists working in New York and London, and they named their product by combining *ny,* the abbreviation for New York, with *lon,* the first three letters of London. *Acronyms,* words formed by combining the initial letters of several words, include *radar, laser,* and *scuba. Scuba* was formed by combining the initial letters of the term *self-contained underwater breathing apparatus.*

Clipping.   Clipping is a process of shortening existing words. For instance, *zoo* is the shortened form of *zoological park,* and *pants* comes from *pantaloons.* Most clipped words are only one syllable long and are used in informal conversation. For example, children may shorten a favorite teacher's name from Mrs. Edison to Mrs. E.

Students create words to add pizzazz to their writing, and some terms created to fill a particular need may become part of the everyday jargon in your classroom. For example, a group of third graders clipped two words to create the word *crocket* (*croc* + *ket*), to describe the crocodile who became a rocket at the end of Roald Dahl's *The Enormous Crocodile* (1978).

Sniglets.   A "sniglet" is a word that isn't in the dictionary, but should be. Once example of a sniglet is *beavo,* a pencil covered with teeth marks (Hall, 1985). This type of word play was created by Rich Hall on HBO's "Not Necessarily the News," and several books of sniglets have been published, including one especially for children, *Sniglets for Kids* (Hall, 1985). Elementary students enjoy reading these books and creating their own words. To create a sniglet, they use compounding, adding affixes, coining, and clipping. The sniglet *tappee,* created by a fifth grader, is presented in Figure 9-7. In this word, the student used the Latin suffix *-ee,* meaning "one who."

Laughing with Language

As children learn that words have the power to amuse, they enjoy reading, telling, and writing riddles and jokes. Linda Gibson Geller (1985) has researched children's humorous language and identified two stages of riddle play that elementary students move through. Primary grade children experiment with the riddle form and its content, while middle- and upper-grade students explore the paradoxical constructions in riddles. Riddles are written in a question-and-answer format, but at first young children may only ask questions or ask questions and offer unrelated answers. With more experience, students provide both questions and related answers, and their answers may be either descriptive or nonsensical. An example of the descriptive answer to the

Dandelionsaurus

He weighs 400000 pounds. And he likes to eat dandelions. He is very very strong. And he is the bigget plant eater on earth and the stronget to.

The end.

FIGURE 9-6 *A Coined Word from a First Grader's ABC Book of Mythical Creatures*

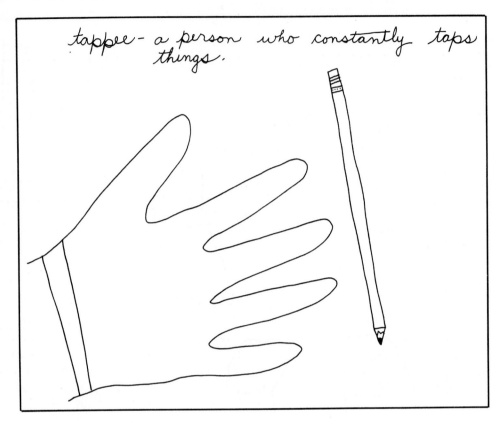

FIGURE 9-7 A Fifth Grader's Sniglet

question "Why did the turtle go out of his shell?" is "because he was getting too big for it." An example of a nonsensical answer involving an invented word for the riddle "Why did the cat want to catch a snake?" is "because he wanted to turn into a rattle-cat" (Geller, 1981, p. 672). Many primary grade students' riddles seem foolish by adult standards, but this wordplay is an important precursor to creating true riddles.

Riddles depend on manipulating words with multiple meanings or similar sounds and on using metaphors. The Opies (1959) identified five riddle strategies used by elementary students:

1. Using multiple referents for a noun: "What has an eye but cannot see? (a needle)."
2. Combining literal and figurative interpretations for a single phrase: "Why did the clockmaker throw the clock out the window? (because he wanted to see time fly)."
3. Shifting word boundaries to suggest another meaning: "Why did the cookie cry? (because its mother was a wafer so long)."
4. Separating a word into syllables to suggest another meaning: "When is a door not a door? (when it's a jar)."
5. Creating a metaphor: "What are polka dots on your face? (pimples)."

Children begin riddle play by telling familiar riddles and reading riddles written by others. Several excellent books of riddles to share with elementary students are Noelle Sterne's *Tyrannosaurus Wrecks: A Book of Dinosaur Riddles* (1979), *What Do You Call a Dumb Bunny? And Other Rabbit Riddles, Games, Jokes, and Cartoons* by Marc Brown (1983), and Marvin Terban's *Eight Ate: A Feast of Homonym Riddles* (1982). Soon children are composing their own riddles by adapting riddles they have read and creating new ones. Others take jokes and turn them into riddles. An excellent book for helping children write riddles is *Fiddle with a Riddle: Write Your Own Riddles* by Joanne E. Bernstein (1979).

Larissa, a third grader, wrote this riddle using two meanings for *Milky Way:* "Why did the astronaut go to the Milky Way? (because he wanted a Milky Way Bar)." Terry, a fifth grader, wrote this riddle using the homophones *hair* and *hare:* "What is gray and jumpy and on your head? (a gray hare)." The riddles children write may have a visual component. A sixth grader created the humorous cartoon presented in Figure 9-8 based on two meanings of *sidekick.*

Creating Word Pictures

In the primary grades, children learn to write words in horizontal lines from left to right and top to bottom across a sheet of paper just as the lines in a book are printed. However, they enjoy breaking this pattern and creating pictures out of the words themselves. These literal, or concrete, word pictures can be single-word pictures or a string of words or a sentence arranged in a picture. Four types of concrete word pictures are described below, and examples are presented in Figure 9-9.

Using Words to Draw a Picture. Children use words instead of lines to draw a picture representing *lamb, rabbit,* and *television* in Figure 9-9. In these word pictures, the children first drew the picture using lines and then placed a second sheet of paper over the drawing and replaced all or most of the lines with repeated words.

Writing a Word to Illustrate Its Meaning. Students can write descriptive words such as *falling, bite,* and *disappear* so that the arrangement, size, and intensity of the letters in the word illustrate the meaning. The words *explode* and *nervous* are written pictorially in Figure 9-9. Students might also write the names of objects and animals, such as *bird* and *cacti,* so that features of the thing being named are illustrated in the name.

Writing Sentences to Create Word Pictures. Students can compose a descriptive phrase, sentence, or paragraph and write it in the shape of an object. A heart, pizza, and ice cream cone are represented in Figure 9-9. An asterisk indicates where to start reading each word picture.

Representing Words and Sayings in Pictures. In a more sophisticated form of word pictures, students can illustrate or represent a word or idiom with a picture. In

FIGURE 9-8   *A Sixth Grader's Wordplay Cartoon*

Figure 9-9, the word *heartbroken* is represented with a heart splitting in two, and the saying "face the music" is represented by a face with musical notes depicting its features.

Playing with Rhyme

Through their experience with Dr. Seuss stories, finger plays, and nursery rhymes, kindergartners and first graders enjoy creating rhymes. Unfortunately many children equate rhyme with poetry, and often their dependence on rhyme thwarts their attempts to write poetry. Nonetheless, rhyme is a special kind of wordplay and one that children enjoy. A small group of first graders created their own version of *Oh, A-Hunting We Will Go* (Langstaff, 1974). After reading the book, they identified the refrain (lines 1, 2, and 5) and added their own rhyming couplets:

▽

Oh, a hunting we will go,
a-hunting we will go.
We'll catch a little bear
and curl his hair,
and never let him go.

Oh, a-hunting we will go,
a-hunting we will go.
We'll catch a little snake
and hit him with a rake,
and never let him go.

Oh, a-hunting we will go,
a-hunting we will go.
We'll catch a little bunny
and fill her full of honey,
and never let her go.

Oh, a-hunting we will go,
a-hunting we will go.
We'll catch a little mole
and put him in a hole,
and never let him go.

Oh, a-hunting we will go,
a-hunting we will go.
We'll catch a little bug
and give him a big hug
and never let him go.

Oh, we'll put them in a ring
and listen to them sing
and then we'll let them go.

Using Words to Draw a Picture

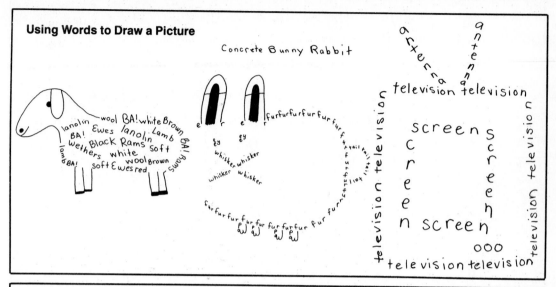

Writing a Word to Illustrate Its Meaning

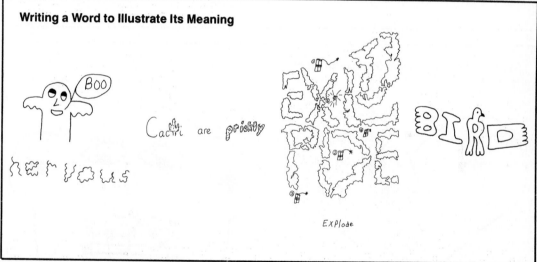

FIGURE 9-9   *Examples of Students' Word Pictures*

The first graders wrote this collaboration with the teacher taking dictation on a large sheet of paper. After the rough draft was written, students reread it, checking the rhymes and changing a word here or there. Then each student chose one stanza to copy and illustrate. The pages were collected and compiled to make a book. Children shared the book with their classmates, with each student reading his or her own page.

Hink-Pinks. "Hink-pinks" are short rhyming riddles or expressions that describe something. Hink-pinks are composed of two one-syllable rhyming words. Hinky-

Writing Sentences to Create Word Pictures

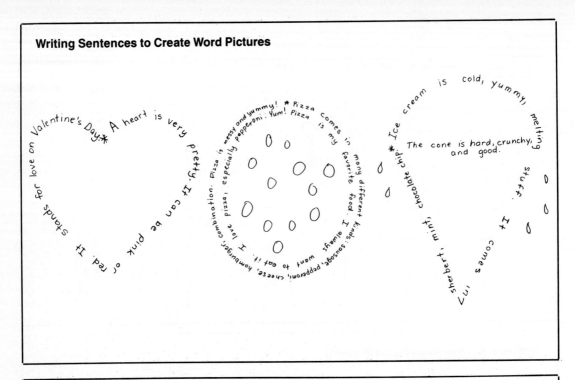

Representing Words and Sayings in Pictures

heart broken

face the music

FIGURE 9-9, continued

pinkies have two two-syllable words, and hinkity-pinkities have two three-syllable words (Geller, 1981). Two books of hink-pinks are *Play Day: A Book of Terse Verse* (McMillan, 1991), which is geared for primary students, and *The Hink Pink Book* (Burns, 1981), which appeals to middle- and upper-grade students. Here are two examples of hink-pinks written by upper-grade students:

▽
        Gas station   *What do you call an astronaut?*
            Car   *A sky guy.*
            Bar

POETIC FORMS

On St. Patrick's Day, Mrs. Garner hangs a large sheet of green paper on the wall and asks her second graders to help write a poem about the color green. The children eagerly suggest things that are green: caterpillars, apples, grasshoppers, frogs, leprechauns, alligators, aliens, and so on. Then Mrs. Garner explains that the list can become a poem, and while the children look skeptical, she chooses one of the items in the brainstormed list and writes: "Green is aliens from outer space." Quickly Naomi suggests another line: "Green is the paper you're writing on for St. Patrick's Day." Other children grasp the pattern and suggest additional lines for the poem. Mrs. Garner reads the poem in a dramatic voice, lengthening some words, softening others, but she ends the list abruptly. Spontaneously, Antoine adds: "And that's what is green!" The children clap their hands as Mrs. Garner adds the line to complete their green poem:

▽
Too Much Green

Green is aliens from outer space.
Green is the paper you're writing on for St. Patrick's Day.
Green is a caterpillar climbing up the trunk of a tree.
Green is an inchworm measuring.
Green is a green hairdo.
Green is a fierce alligator.
Green is a shiny apple.
Green is Kool-aid that you drink.
Green is a leaping grasshopper.
Green is a hopping frog.
Green is the grass that a leprechaun steps on.
And that's what is green!

Elementary students can successfully write poetry using poetic formulas. They can write formula poems by beginning each line with particular words (as in color poems), counting syllables for haiku, or creating word pictures in concrete poems. Because such poems are written quickly and guidelines are provided, children can use the writing process to revise, edit, and share their writing without a time-consuming process of making changes, correcting errors, and recopying. Poetry also allows students more freedom in how they use the mechanics of writing such as punctuation, capitalization, and page arrangement.

Many types of poetry that children write do not use rhyme. Rhyme is the sticking point for many would-be poets. In searching for a rhyming word, children often create inane verse such as

▽

> *I see a funny little goat*
> *Wearing a blue sailor's coat*
> *Sitting in an old motorboat.*

This is not to suggest that children should not be allowed to write rhyming poetry, but rhyme should never be imposed as a criterion for acceptable poetry. Children will use rhyme when it fits naturally into their writing. As children write poetry during the elementary grades, they are searching for their own voices, and they need freedom to do that. Freed from the pressure to create rhyming poetry or other constraints, children create sensitive word pictures, vivid images, and unique comparisons in their poems, as the poems presented throughout this chapter illustrate.

Five types of poetic forms are presented in this section: formula poems, free-form poems, syllable- and word-count poems, rhymed poems, and model poems. Elementary students' poems illustrate each poetic form, and additional examples are presented in the appendix at the end of the book. The additional examples are included to provide model poems written by students in the primary, middle, and upper grades to use when teaching these poetic forms. The poems written by kindergarteners and first graders may seem little more than lists of sentences compared to the more sophisticated poems written by older students. The range of poems, however, effectively shows how elementary and middle school students grow in their ability to write poetry through these writing activities.

Formula Poems

Poetic formulas may seem like recipes to be followed rigidly, but that is not how they are intended. Rather, they provide a scaffold or skeleton for students' poems. After collecting words, images, and comparisons through brainstorming, clustering, quick-writing, or another prewriting strategy, students craft their poems, choosing words and arranging them to create a message. Meaning is always most important; form follows the search for meaning. Children "dig for poems" (Valentine, 1986) by investigating words, ideas, poetic forms, rhyme, rhythm, and conventions. Poet Kenneth Koch (1970) worked with students in the elementary grades and developed some simple formulas that make it easy for nearly every child to become a successful poet. Some of these forms may seem more like sentences than poems, but the line between poetry and prose is blurry, and these beginning poetry experiences help direct children toward poetic expression. Koch suggests a structure in which children begin every line the same way or insert a particular kind of word in every line. This structure involves the use of repetition, a stylistic device that can be much more effective for young poets than rhyme.

Such poetic formulas provide a structure that is easy and fun for students to follow. Many teachers are at first skeptical about the effectiveness of formula poems. However, after they introduce their students to them, they often report that these poetry-writing activities are among the most successful writing experiences their students have ever participated in.

"I Wish . . ." Poems. Children begin each line of their poems with the words "I wish" and then complete the line with a wish (Koch, 1970). In this second-grade class collaboration, children simply listed their wishes:

▽

Our Wishes

I wish I had all the money in the world.
I wish I was a star fallen down from Mars.
I wish I were a butterfly.
I wish I were a teddy bear.
I wish I had a cat.
I wish I were a pink rose.
I wish it wouldn't rain today.
I wish I didn't have to wash a dish.
I wish I had a flying carpet.
I wish I could go to Disney World.
I wish school was out.
I wish I could go outside and play.

After this first experience, students choose one of their wishes and expand on the idea in several more lines. Seven-year-old Brandi chose her wish, "I wish I were a teddy bear," and wrote:

▽

I Wish

I wish I were a teddy bear
Who sat on a beautiful bed
Who got a hug every night
By a little girl or boy.
Maybe tonight I'll get my wish
And wake up on a little girl's bed
And then I'll be as happy as can be.

Color Poems. Students begin each line of their poems with a color. The same color may be repeated in each line, or a different color may be used (Koch, 1970). For example, second-grade Cheyenne describes yellow in this color poem:

▽

Yellow

Yellow is bright,
Yellow is light.
Yellow glows in the dark,
Yellow likes to lark.
Yellow is an autumn tree,
Yellow is giving to you and me.

In her poem, Cheyenne uses rhyming words effectively, and in searching for a rhyming word for *dark,* she creates a particularly powerful line, "Yellow likes to lark." Older students, like seventh-grade Nancy in the following poem, expand each of their ideas into a stanza:

▽

Black

Black is a deep hole
sitting in the ground
waiting for animals
that live inside.

Black is a beautiful horse
standing on a high hill
with the wind
swirling its mane.

Black is a winter night sky
without stars
to keep it
company.

Black is a panther
creeping around a jungle
searching for
its prey.

Mary O'Neill's book of color poems, *Hailstones and Halibut Bones: Adventures in Color* (1961), may also be shared with students; however, O'Neill uses rhyme as an important poetic device, and it is important to emphasize that students' poems need not rhyme.

Writing color poems can be coordinated with teaching young children to read and write the color words. Instead of having kindergartners and first graders read color words on worksheets and then color pictures with the designated colors, students can create color poems in booklets of paper stapled together. They write and illustrate one line of the poem on each page.

Five-Senses Poems.   Children write about a topic by describing it with each of the five senses. These poems are usually five lines long, with one line for each sense, as the following poem written by a seventh grader demonstrates:

▽

Winter

Winter smells like chimney smoke.
Winter tastes like ice.
Winter looks like heaven.
Winter feels like a deep freeze.
Winter sounds like a howling wolf.

Sometimes students add an additional line at the beginning or end of a poem, as sixth-grade Amy did in this Valentine's Day poem:

▽

Valentine's Day

Smells like chocolate candy
Looks like a flower garden

Tastes like sugar
Feels like silk
Sounds like a symphony orchestra
Too bad it comes only once a year!

It is often helpful to have students develop a five-senses cluster to collect ideas for each sense. From the cluster, students select the most vivid or strongest idea for each sense to use in a line of the poem.

"If I Were . . ." Poems.   Children write about how they would feel and what they would do if they were something else—a Tyrannosaurus Rex, a hamburger, or sunshine (Koch, 1970). They begin each poem with "If I were" and tell what it would be like to be that thing. For example, 8-year-old Jeff writes about what he would do if he were a giant:

▽

If I were a giant
I would drink up the seas
And I would touch the sun.
I would eat the world
And stick my head in space.

Students use personification in composing "If I were . . ." poems, explore ideas and feelings, and consider the world from a different vantage point.

"I Used to . . . /But Now . . ." Poems.   In these contrast poems, students begin the first line (and every odd-numbered line) with "I used to" and the second line (and every even-numbered line) with "But now" (Koch, 1970). Using this formula, students can explore ways in which they have changed as well as how things in the world change. Eighth-grade Sondra writes from the point of view of a piece of gold ore:

▽

I used to be a hunk of gold sitting in
A mine having no worries
Or responsibilities.
Now I'm a wedding band bonding
Two people together, with all
The worries in the world.

A third-grade teacher adapted this formula for her social studies class, and her students wrote a class collaboration poem using the pattern "I used to think . . ./But now I know . . ." and information they had learned during a unit on the Plains Indians. Here is their poem:

▽

But Now I Know about the Plains Indians

I used to think that Indians always wore beads,
but now I know they didn't until the white men came.
I used to think that Indians used pouches to carry their babies,
but now I know that they used cradle boards, too.
I used to think that Indians didn't paint their teepees,
but now I know that they did.

I used to think that one chief ruled all the tribes,
but now I know that there are different chiefs for each tribe.
I used to think that Indians had guns,
but now I know that Indians didn't before the white men came.
I used to think that Indians burned wood,
but now I know they burned buffalo chips.
I used to think that Indians caught their horses,
but now I know they got them from the Spaniards.

Lie Poems.   Children write a poem in which nothing is true or with a lie in each line (Koch, 1970). It is important to explain that these "lies" are imaginary or make-believe statements, such as "I live on Pluto," rather than real lies. A group of fifth graders collaborated on this lie poem:

▽

I am an owl who sleeps during the night
and is awake all day.
My favorite food is fuzzy caterpillar knees
and I eat a gallon of them every day.
My home is in a cabin
at the top of Mt. Everest.
I get younger as I get older
and when I'm 50, I'll be a owlet.
I can fly across the Atlantic Ocean
in five minutes or maybe less.
I talk a secret language
that only kids and owls understand.

Lie poems are more appropriate for older students who understand the difference between the lies they aren't supposed to tell and the imaginary lies in these poems.

"_____ Is . . ." Poems.   In description or definition poems, students describe what something is or what something or someone means to them. To begin, the teacher or students identify a topic, filling in the blank with a word such as *anger, a friend, liberty,* or *fear.* Then students start each line in the same way and describe or define the thing they have chosen. Ryan, a sixth grader, wrote the following poem in which he described fear:

▽

Fear is not knowing what's around the next corner.
Fear is strange noises scratching on my window at night.
Fear is a cold hand touching you in an old, dusty hallway.
Fear is being in a jet that's losing altitude at 50,000 feet.
Fear is the earth blowing up.

Ryan evoked strong, concrete images of fear in his poem, and students often write very powerful poems using this formula when they move beyond "Happiness is . . ." and "Love is. . . ."

Preposition Poems.   Students begin each line of preposition poems with a preposition, and a delightful poetic rewording of lines often results. A fourth grader wrote this preposition poem about a race with a friend:

▽

We Ran Forever

About noon one day
Along came my friend
To say, "Want to go for a run?"
Below the stairs my mom said, "Go!"
Without waiting, I flew out the door,
Down the steps,
Across the lawn, and
Past the world we ran, forever.

It is helpful for children to brainstorm a list of prepositions to refer to when they write preposition poems. As they write, students may find that they need to drop the formula for a line or two to give the content of their poems top priority, or they may mistakenly begin a line with an infinitive verb (e.g., "to say") rather than a preposition, as in "We Ran Forever." The forms presented in this section provide a structure or skeleton for students' writing that should be adapted as needed.

Free-Form Poems

In free-form poems, children put words and phrases together to express a thought or tell a story without concern for rhyme, repetition, or other patterns. The number of words on a line and use of punctuation vary. In the following poem, eighth-grade Bobby poignantly describes his topic using only 15 well-chosen words:

▽

Loneliness

A lifetime
Of broken dreams
And promises
Lost love
Hurt
My heart
Cries
In silence

In contrast, Don, a sixth grader, writes a humorous free-form poem about misplaced homework:

▽

Excuse for Not Having Homework

Oh no, my English homework
Cannot be found—
Nor my science book.
Did my dog eat it?
Or maybe I dropped my mitt on it.
Possibly, Martians took it away,
Or it fell deep down in the hay.
Maybe it's lost or shut in the door.
Oh no, I broke my rule—
I forgot and left it at school!

Students can use several methods for writing free-form poems. First, they can select words and phrases from brainstormed lists and clusters they have written and compile them to create a free-form poem. As an alternative, they write a paragraph and then "unwrite" to create the poem by deleting unnecessary words. The remaining words are arranged to look like a poem. Eighth-grade Craig wrote his poem this way:

▽

A Step Back in Time

It is late evening
On a river bank.
The sky has clouds
That seem to be moving
Towards the moon.
The only light is my lantern,
Which gives enough glare to see
A few feet in front of me.
Several sounds are heard
In the distance: an owl
Hooting in the trees,
A deer crossing the river.
Life overflows around me
Like many different colored bugs.
The wind is chilly,
Making the large pines dance.
The sand is damp.
It's like the beginning of time,
Before man existed,
Just animals and plants.

Concrete Poems.   Students create concrete poems by arranging words pictorially on a page or by combining art and writing. Words, phrases, and sentences can be written in the shape of an object, or word pictures can be inserted within poems that are written left to right and top to bottom on a sheet of paper. These concrete poems are extensions of the word pictures discussed in the section "Wordplay." Three examples of concrete poems are presented in Figure 9-10. In the "Washington Monument" poem, fourth graders brainstormed a list of facts about the monument and then combined their ideas to form the sentence that was written in the shape of the Washington, DC, landmark. In the "Key" and "Lightbulb" poems, seventh graders used the same approach to create their concrete poems. Several books of concrete poems that will give students ideas for their poems include *Concrete Is Not Always Hard* (Pilon, 1972), *Seeing Things* (Froman, 1974), and *Walking Talking Words* (Sherman, 1980).

Found Poems.   Students create poems by culling words from other sources, such as newspaper articles, songs, and stories. Seventh-grade Eric found this poem in an article about racecar driver Richard Petty:

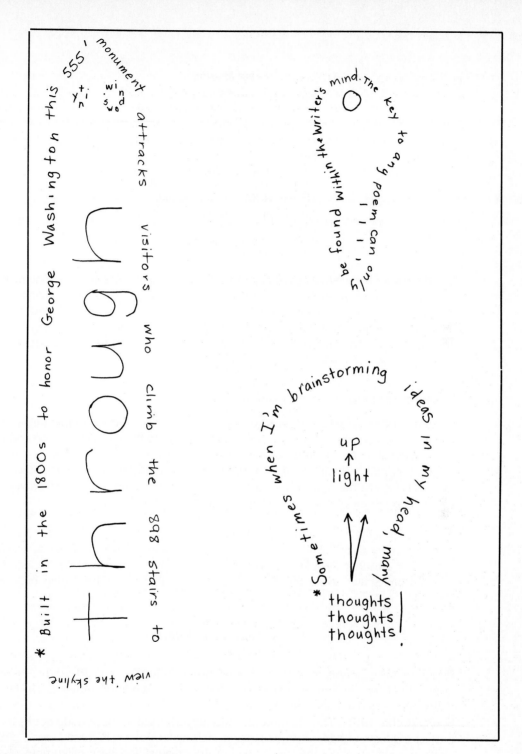

FIGURE 9-10 *Students' Concrete Poems*

▽

Fast Moving

Moving down the track,
faster than fast, is Richard Petty
seven-time winner of
the crowned jewel
Daytona 500.
At 210 mph—dangerous—
pushing his engine to the limit.
Other NASCARs running fast
but Richard Petty takes the lead
at last.
Running across the line
with good time.

Eric developed his poem by circling powerful words and phrases in the 33-line newspaper article and then writing the words in a poetic arrangement. After reading over the draft, he deleted two words and added three other words not included in the newspaper article that were needed for transitions in the poem. By writing found poems, students have the opportunity to manipulate words and sentence structures they don't write themselves.

Syllable- and Word-Count Poems

Haiku and other syllable- and word-count poems provide a structure that helps students succeed in writing; however, the need to adhere to the formula in these poems may restrict students' freedom of expression. In other words, the structure of these poems may both help and hinder students. The exact syllable counts force students to search for just the right words to express their ideas and feelings and provide a valuable opportunity for students to use a thesaurus and dictionary.

Haiku.   The best known syllable-counting poem is *haiku* (high-KOO), a Japanese poetic form consisting of 17 syllables arranged in 3 lines of 5–7–5. Haiku deals with nature and presents a single clear image. It is a concise form, much like a telegram. Ten-year-old Shawn wrote this haiku about the feeling of mud swishing between his toes:

▽

The mud feels slimy
As it splashes through my toes
Making them vanish.

Books of haiku poems to share with students include *My Own Rhythm: An Approach to Haiku* (Atwood, 1973), *Haiku: The Mood of the Earth* (Atwood, 1971), *In a Spring Garden* (Lewis, 1965), *Cricket Songs* (Behn, 1964), and *More Cricket Songs* (Behn, 1971). The photographs and artwork used in these trade books may provide students with ideas for illustrating their haiku poems. Richard Lewis (1968, 1970) has written about the lives of two of the greatest Japanese haiku poets, Issa and Basho. He provides biographical information as well as a collection of poems in these books.

Tanka. *Tanka* (TANK-ah) is a Japanese verse form containing 31 syllables arranged in 5 lines of 5–7–5–7–7. This form is very similar to haiku except that two additional lines of 7 syllables each are added to the haiku form. Quenton, age 14, wrote this tanka about spring that was published in his middle school anthology:

▽

Trees are budding out;
Grass is sprouting everywhere
Birds chirping again,
They are signs of happiness
Spring is coming once again.

Students may "unwrite" parts of their poems if the lines are too long by deleting one or more words. For example, in the spring poem, if the fourth line had been too long, Quenton could have shortened it to "Signs of happiness."

Cinquains. A *cinquain* (SIN-cane) is a 5-line poem containing 22 syllables in a 2–4–6–8–2 syllable pattern. Cinquains usually describe something, but they may also tell a story. Encourage students to search for words and phrases that are precise, vivid, and sensual. Have students ask themselves what their subject looks like, smells like, sounds like, and tastes like and record their ideas using a five-senses cluster. The formula is

Line 1: a one-word subject with two syllables

Line 2: four syllables describing the subject

Line 3: six syllables showing action

Line 4: eight syllables expressing a feeling or observation about the subject

Line 5: two syllables describing and renaming the subject

This cinquain poem was written by sixth-grade Kevin:

▽

Wrestling
skinny, fat
coaching, arguing, pinning
trying hard to win
tournament

If you compare Kevin's poem to the cinquain formula, you'll notice that some lines are short a syllable or two. Kevin bent some of the guidelines in choosing words to create a powerful image of wrestling. The message of the poem is always more important than adhering to the formula.

An alternative cinquain form contains five lines but does not follow the syllable count. Instead, each line contains a specified number of words rather than syllables. Thus, the first line contains a one-word title, the second line has two words that describe the title, the third line has three words that express action, the fourth line has four words that express feelings, and the fifth line contains a two-word synonym for the title.

Diamantes.   Iris Tiedt (1970) invented the *diamante* (dee-ah-MAHN-tay), a seven-line contrast poem written in the shape of a diamond. In this poetic form, students apply their knowledge of opposites and parts of speech. The formula is

Line 1: one noun as the subject

Line 2: two adjectives describing the subject

Line 3: three participles (ending in *-ing*) telling about the subject

Line 4: four nouns (the first two related to the subject and the second two related to the opposite)

Line 5: three participles telling about the opposite

Line 6: two adjectives describing the opposite

Line 7: one noun that is the opposite of the subject

When the poem is written, it is arranged in a diamond shape. Sixth-grade Shelley wrote the following diamente about heaven and hell:

HEAVEN

happy, love

laughing, hunting, everlasting

pearly gates, Zion, Satan, netherworld

burning, blazing, yelling

pain, fire

HELL

Notice that Shelley created a contrast between heaven, the subject represented by the noun in the first line, and hell, the opposite in the last line. Creating the contrast gives students the opportunity to play with words and extend their understanding of opposites. The third word *Satan* in the fourth line marks the transition from heaven to hell.

Rhymed Verse Poems

Several rhymed verse forms such as limericks and clerihews can be used effectively with middle- and upper-grade students. In using these forms, it is important that teachers try to ensure that the rhyme schemes do not restrict students' creative and imaginative expressions.

Limericks.   The *limerick* is a form of light verse that uses both rhyme and rhythm. The poem consists of five lines. The first, second, and fifth lines rhyme, while the third and fourth lines rhyme with each other and are shorter than the other three lines. The rhyme scheme is a–a–b–b–a. Often the last line contains a funny or surprise ending as shown in the following limerick written by eighth-grade Angela:

There once was a frog named Pete

Who did nothing but sit and eat.

He examined each fly

With so careful an eye

And then said, "You're dead meat."

Writing limericks can be a challenging assignment for many upper-grade students, but middle-grade students can also be successful with this poetic form, especially when they work together and write a class collaboration. This class collaboration limerick was written by fourth graders:

▽

Leprechaun

There once was a lucky leprechaun
That rode on a big, fat fawn.
He ate a cat,
And got so fat,
To lose some weight he had to mow the lawn.

Limericks are believed to have originated in the city of Limerick, Ireland, and were first popularized over a century ago by Edward Lear (1812–1888). Poet X. J. Kennedy (1982) describes limericks as the most popular type of poem in the English language today. Introduce students to limericks by reading aloud some of Lear's verses so that students can appreciate the rhythm (stressed and unstressed syllables) of the verse. One fine edition of Lear's limericks is *How Pleasant to Know Mr. Lear!* (Livingston, 1982). Another book of limericks that students will enjoy is *They've Discovered a Head in the Box of Bread and Other Laughable Limericks* (Brewton & Blackburn, 1978). Arnold Lobel has also written a book of unique pig limericks, *Pigericks* (1983). After sharing Lobel's pigericks, students will want to write "birdericks" or "fishericks."

Clerihews.   A *clerihew* (KLER-i-hyoo) is a four-line rhymed verse that describes a person. The form is named for Edmund Clerihew Bentley (1875–1956), a British detective writer who invented it. The formula is

Line 1: the person's name

Line 2: rhymes with the first line

Lines 3 and 4: rhyme with each other

Clerihews can be written about anyone—historical figures, characters in stories, and even the students themselves. The following clerihew was written by an eighth-grader named Johnny about another John:

▽

John Wayne
Is in the Cowboy Hall of fame.
In movies he shot his gun the best,
And that's how he won the west.

Model Poems

Students can write poems that are modeled on poems composed by adult poets. Kenneth Koch suggests this approach in *Rose, Where Did You Get That Red* (1973). According to this approach, students read a poem and then write their own poems using the same theme expressed in the model poem.

Apologies. Using William Carlos Williams's poem "This is Just to Say" as the model poem, children write a poem in which they apologize for something they are secretly glad they did (Koch, 1973). Middle- and upper-grade students are very familiar with offering apologies, and they enjoy writing humorous apologies to inanimate things. For example, fifth-grade Clay wrote an apology to his eraser:

▽

> Dear Eraser,
> This is just to say
> I'm so sorry
> for
> biting you off
> my pencil
> and
> eating you
> and
> putting you
> in
> my digestive
> system.
> Forgive me!
> Forgive me
> p-l-e-e-e-a-s-e-e-e.

Apology poems don't have to be humorous; they may be sensitive, genuine apologies as in this poem written by seventh-grade Angela:

▽

> **Open Up**
> I didn't
> open my
> immature eyes
> to see
> the pain
> within you
> a death
> had caused.
> Forgive me,
> I misunderstood
> your anguished
> broken heart.

Invitations. Students write poems in which they invite someone to a magical, beautiful place full of sounds and colors and where all kinds of marvelous things happen. The model poem is William Shakespeare's "Come unto These Yellow Sands" (Koch, 1973). The guidelines for writing an invitation poem are that it must be an invitation to a magical place and include sound or color words. The following invitation poem written by seventh-grade Nikki follows these two guidelines:

▽
The Golden Shore

Come unto the golden shore
Where days are filled with laughter,
And nights filled with whispering winds.
Where sunflowers and sun
Are filled with love.
Come take my hand
As we walk into the sun.

Prayers from the Ark. Students write a poem or prayer from the viewpoint of an animal, following the model poems in Carmen Bernos de Gasztold's *Prayers from the Ark* (1965). Gasztold, a French nun during World War II, wrote poems in which she assumed the persona of the animals on Noah's ark as they prayed to God, questioning their existence and thanking Him for His mercies. Children can write similar poems in which they assume the persona of an animal. Second-grade Candice assumes the persona of the Easter Bunny for her prayer:

▽
Dear Lord,
I am the bunny.
Why did you make me so fluffy?
I thank you for keeping the carrots
sweet and orange so I can be strong.
Thank you for making me the Easter Bunny.
Oh, I almost forgot, bless you
for last month's big crop of carrots.

If I Were in Charge of the World. Students write poems in which they describe what they would do if they were in charge of the world. Judith Viorst's poem, "If I Were in Charge of the World" (1981) is the model for this poetic form. Children are eager to share ideas about how they would change the world, as this fourth-grade collaborative poem illustrates:

▽
If I Were In Charge of the World

If I were in charge of the world
School would be for one month,
Movies and videogames would be free, and
Foods would be McCalorieless at McDonalds.
Poor people would have a home,
Bubble gum would cost a penny, and
Kids would have cars to drive.
Parents wouldn't argue,
Christmas would be in July and December, and
We would never have bedtimes.
A kid would be president,
I'd meet my long lost cousin, and
Candybars would be vegetables.
I would own the mall,
People would have as much money as they wanted, and
There would be no drugs.

TEACHING STUDENTS TO WRITE POEMS

Students learn to write poems through minilessons about wordplay, poetic forms, and poetic devices, through reading poems, and through writing poems. They refine their concept of poetry as they learn about the genre, just as Miss Clark's sixth graders did in the vignette at the beginning of the chapter.

Students write poems in connection with a focus unit on poetry, in response to literature they have read, and in writers' workshop. Students also write poetry in connection with social studies and science theme cycles. They might, for example, write an "If I Were in Charge of the World" poem from Paul Revere's point of view or from the viewpoint of a favorite book character. Students might also write five-senses poems in connection with a theme cycle on the four seasons or "If I were . . ." poems or concrete poems about animals as part of a theme on animals.

Introducing Students to Poetry

Many children have misconceptions about what poetry is and how to write it. Too often they think poetry must rhyme or they are unsure about what it should look like on a page. Children need to have a concept of poetry before beginning to write poems. One way to expand students' knowledge of poetry is to share a variety of poems written by children and adults. Choose from poems included in this chapter as well as poems written by well-known poets who write for children, such as Karla Kuskin (1975, 1980), David McCord (1962, 1967, 1977), Jack Prelutsky (1976, 1977, 1983), and Shel Silverstein (1974, 1981). Include poems that do not rhyme and concrete poems with creative arrangements on the page.

Another way to introduce poetry is to read excerpts from the first chapter of Lois Lowry's *Anastasia Krupnik* (1979). In this book, 10-year-old Anastasia, the main character of the story, is excited about fourth grade when her teacher, Mrs. Westvessel, announces that the class will write poems. Anastasia works at home for eight nights to write a poem. Lowry does an excellent job of describing how writers search long and hard for words to express their meaning and the delight that comes when writers realize their poems are finished. On the appointed day, Anastasia and her classmates bring their poems to class to read aloud. One student reads his four-line rhymed verse aloud:

> I have a dog whose name is Spot.
> He likes to eat and drink a lot.
> When I put water in his dish,
> He laps it up just like a fish. (p. 10)

Anastasia is not impressed. She knows that the child who wrote the poem has a dog named Sputnik, not Spot! But Mrs. Westvessel gives it an A and hangs it on the bulletin board. Soon it is Anastasia's turn. She is nervous because her poem is very different. She reads her poem about tiny creatures that move about in tidepools at night:

> hush hush the sea-soft night is aswim
>   with winklesquirm creatures
>   listen(!)
> to them move smooth in the moistly dark
> here in the whisperwarm wet. (pp. 11–12)

In this free-form poem without rhyme or capital letters, Anastasia has created a marvelous word-picture with invented words such as *whisperwarm* and *wrinklesquirm.* Regrettably, Mrs. Westvessel has an antiquated view that poems should be about serious subjects only, be composed with rhyming sentences, and use conventional capitalization and punctuation. Mrs. Westvessel doesn't understand Anastasia's poem and gives Anastasia an F because she didn't follow directions.

While this episode from the book presents a depressing picture of elementary teachers and their lack of knowledge about poetry, it is a dramatic introduction to what poetry is and what it is not. After reading excerpts from this first chapter of *Anastasia Krupnik,* develop a chart with your students comparing what poetry is in Mrs. Westvessel's class and what poetry is in your class. A class of upper-grade students developed the chart in Figure 9-11. Expanding children's understanding of poetry is a crucial first step because, although most children have some knowledge about poetry, many of their notions are more like Mrs. Westvessel's than like Anastasia's.

Teaching Students to Write Poems Following a Poetic Form

After being introduced to an enlightened view of poetry, children are ready to write poetry. Beginning with formula poems (e.g., "I wish . . ." poems and color poems) will probably make the writing easier for young children or for students who have had little or no experiences with poetry. The steps for writing any type of poetry are as follows:

Step by Step

1. *Explain the poetic form.*   The teacher describes the poetic form and explains what is included in each line or stanza. Displaying a chart that describes the form or having students write a brief description of the poetic form in their writers' notebooks will help them remember it.

2. *Share examples written by children.*   The teacher reads poems adhering to the poetic form that have been written by children. Poems included in this chapter may be shared, as well as additional poems written by your students. Point out how the writer of each poem used the form. Poems written by adults may also be shared.

3. *Review the poetic form.*   After explaining the poetic form and sharing poems, review the form with students and read one or two more poems that follow the form. Have students explain how the poems fit the form or have them quickwrite about the poetic form to check their understanding. In the following quickwrite, Eric, a seventh grader, writes about his assignment to write a concrete poem:

   I don't know what I'm going to do about my concrete poem but I'm sure I will come up with something sooner or later. I have to write a poem in the shape of

FIGURE 9-11   *Guidelines for Writing Poems*

Rules About Writing Poetry

Mrs. Westvessel's Rules	Our Rules
1. Poems must rhyme.	1. Poems do not have to rhyme.
2. The first letter in each line must be capitalized.	2. The first letter in each line does not have to be capitalized.
3. Each line must start at the left margin.	3. Poems can take different shapes and be anywhere on a page.
4. Poems must have a certain rhythm.	4. You hear the writer's voice in a poem—with or without rhythm.
5. Poems should be written about serious things.	5. Poems can be about anything— serious or silly things.
6. Poems should be punctuated like other types of writing.	6. Poems can be punctuated in different ways or not be punctuated at all.
7. Poems are failures if they don't follow these rules.	7. There are no real rules for poems, and no poem is a failure.

---

some object. Maybe I'll do one on a shape of a horse. Hey, that sounds good to me. I think I'll do that. Oh wait, how about a car? Ya, even better. All right, this quickwriting stuff really works. Know what? I have nothing to say so I hope my five minutes are about up cause my arm is getting tired of writing. I'm lost for words.

4. *Write class collaboration poems.*   Have children write a class collaboration poem before writing individual poems. Students can each contribute a line for a class collaboration "I wish . . ." poem or a couplet for an "I used to . . . /But now . . ." poem. For other types of poems, such as apology or concrete poems, students can work together by suggesting ideas and words for the poem. They dictate the poem to the teacher who records it on the chalkboard or on chart paper. Older students can work in small groups to create their poems. Through writing a class collaboration poem, students review the form and gather ideas that they might later use in writing their own poems. The teacher should compliment students when they use wordplay or poetic devices. As always, encourage students to be creative with language. Students also need to know how to arrange the poem on the page, how to use capital letters and punctuation marks, and why it may be necessary to delete unnecessary words.

Children in a fourth-fifth-grade remedial reading class composed the class collaboration poem "If I Were a Tornado" presented in Figure 9-12. The class began by clustering ideas about tornadoes, and then students used the words in the cluster in dictating a rough draft of the poem. After reading the draft aloud, one child commented that the poem looked "too full of words" and counted 52 words in the poem. The children decided to "unwrite" some of the unnecessary words

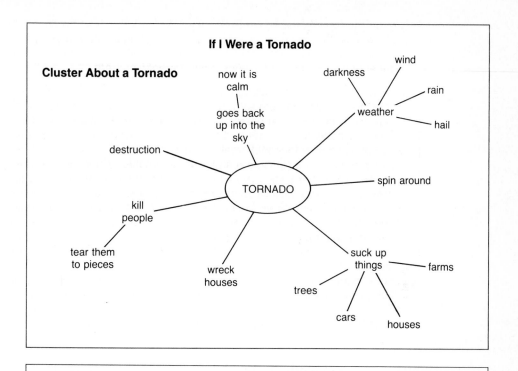

If I Were a Tornado

Cluster About a Tornado

TORNADO

- now it is calm — goes back up into the sky
- darkness
- wind
- weather — rain
- weather — hail
- spin around
- destruction
- kill people — tear them to pieces
- wreck houses
- suck up things — farms
- suck up things — trees
- suck up things — cars
- suck up things — houses

Rough Draft

If I were a tornado,
I'd bring darkness, wind, rain and hail
I'd spin around fl-rr-sss
I'd suck things like houses and cars up
   into me
I'd wreck up houses
I'd kill people—tear them to pieces
And then I'd go back up into the sky
Leaving behind destruction
And everything calm.

Final Draft

If I were a tornado,
I'd bring darkness, wind, rain
Spin around fl-rr-sss
Suck houses up into the sky
Drop the wrecked houses
Kill people—tear them to pieces
Then go back up into the sky
Leaving behind death and destruction.

FIGURE 9-12 Steps in Writing a Class Collaboration Poem

(e.g., the repetitious "I'd" at the beginning of four lines) and reduced the number of words in the poem to 39. After making the changes and reading the revised poem aloud, the children declared the poem finished. It was then copied on a sheet of paper, and copies were made for each student.

5. *Write individual poems using the writing process.*   The four steps listed above constitute prewriting, and with this background of experiences students are prepared to write their own poems following the poetic form they have been taught. Students prewrite to gather and organize ideas, write rough drafts, meet in writing groups to receive feedback, make revisions based on this feedback, and then edit their poems with a classmate and with the teacher. Students then share their poems in any of a variety of ways. Often students keep their poems in a poetry notebook. Other possibilities include making filmstrips and oral presentations.

   Too often teachers will simply explain several poetic forms and then allow students to choose any form they like and write poems. This approach ignores the teaching component; it's back to the "assign and do" syndrome. Instead, students need to learn and experiment with each poetic form. After these preliminary experiences, they can apply what they have learned and write poems adhering to any of the poetic forms they have studied. Class collaborations are a crucial component because they provide a practice run for children who are not sure what to do. The 5 minutes it takes to write a class collaboration poem may make the difference between success and failure for many would-be poets.

Assessing Students' Poems

A variety of poetic formulas have been presented in this chapter. These formulas allow students to experiment with different ways to express their thoughts. Although children should experiment with a variety of forms during the elementary grades, they should not be tested on their knowledge of particular forms. Knowing that a haiku is a Japanese form composed of 17 syllables arranged in 3 lines will not make a child a poet. Instead, information about the forms should be available in the classroom.

   Assessing the quality of students' poems is especially difficult because poems are creative combinations of wordplay, poetic form, and poetic devices. Instead of trying to give a grade for quality, student writing may be assessed on these three criteria:

▼ Has the student written the poem following the formula presented in class?
▼ Has the student used the process approach in writing, revising, and editing the poem?
▼ Has the student used wordplay or a poetic device in the poem?

Teachers might also ask students to assess their own progress in writing poems. Students should keep copies of the poems they write in their writing folders or poetry booklets so they can review and assess their work. If a grade for quality is absolutely necessary, students should be permitted to choose several of the poems in their writing folders to be evaluated.

POETIC DEVICES

Seventh-grade Joe rereads the final copy of his poem "Eagle" before turning it in to the class literary magazine:

Eagle

*Eagle, is it the color
you see from the sky,
or is it the movement
that catches your eye?*

*Eagle, at what moment do you know
as you dive from the sky,
precisely when something will die?*

*Eagle, do you have fear
while you dive and peal,
or might your nerves be made of steel?*

*Eagle, what are your thoughts,
as your claws and beak
prepare the main course?*

*Eagle, do you know,
as you perch majestically on the tree,
that you represent our country's liberty?*

It's one of the best poems he has ever written, and with a slight smile on his lips, he turns it in. Returning to his desk, he thumps a classmate from his writing group on the arm and gives the thumbs-up sign.

His writing group had suggested that Joe begin each stanza with the word "Eagle" and end each stanza with a question mark. Those ideas strengthened his writing.

Good poets choose words carefully. They create strong images when they use unexpected comparisons, repeat sounds within a line or stanza, imitate sounds, repeat words and phrases, and choose rhyming words. These techniques are called *poetic devices.* Many children notice these devices when they read poems, and they need to be aware of these devices before they can use them in their writing. Knowledge of the appropriate terminology—comparison, alliteration, onomatopoeia, repetition, and rhyme—is also helpful in writing discussion groups, when students compliment classmates on their use of a device or suggest that they try a particular device.

Comparison

One way to describe something is to compare it to something else. Students can compare images, feelings, and actions to other things using two types of comparison—similes and metaphors. A *simile* is an explicit comparison of one thing to another by stating that one thing is like something else. Similes are signaled by the use of *like* or *as.* In contrast, a metaphor compares two things by implying that one thing *is* something else, without using *like* or *as*. Being able to differentiate between the two terms is less important than using comparisons to make writing more vivid. For example, children might compare anger to a thunderstorm. Using a simile, they might say, "Anger is like a thunderstorm, screaming with thunder-feelings and lightning-words." Or, as a metaphor, they might say, "Anger is a volcano, erupting with poisonous words and hot-lava actions."

There are many stale comparisons, such as "high as a kite" and "soft as a feather." Students begin by learning traditional comparisons and idioms, and then invent fresh, unexpected comparisons. Sixth-grade Amanda uses a combination of expected and unexpected comparisons in the following poem:

▽

People

People are like birds
who are constantly getting their feathers ruffled.
People are like alligators
who find pleasure in evil cleverness.
People are like bees
who are always busy.
People are like penguins
who want to have fun.
People are like platypuses—
*   unexplainable!*

Alliteration

Alliteration is the repetition of the same initial consonant sound in consecutive words or in words in close proximity. Repeating the same initial sound makes poetry fun to read, and children enjoy reading and reciting alliterative books such as Jane Bayer's *A My Name is Alice* (1984) and Chris Van Allsburg's *The Z Was Zapped* (1987). After reading one of these books, children can create their own versions. A fourth-grade class created their own version of Van Allsburg's book which they called "The Z was Zipped." Students divided into pairs, and each pair composed two pages for the class book. On the front of the sheet of paper, students illustrated their letter, and on the back they wrote a sentence to describe their illustration, following Van Allsburg's pattern. Four pages from the book are presented in Figure 9-13. The alliterative sentences for each page are presented below, but before reading the sentences, examine the illustrations and try to guess what the children wrote.

     The D got dunked by the duck.

The Y was yachting on the Yangtze.

The T was totally terrified.

The O was occupied oddly by the ox.

Tongue twisters are an exaggerated form of alliteration in which every word (or almost every word) in the twister begins with the same letter. Dr. Seuss's *Oh Say Can You Say?* (1979) is an easy-to-read collection of tongue twisters for primary

FIGURE 9-13 *An Excerpt from a Fourth-Grade Class Book* The Z was Zipped

grade students. Alvin Schwartz's *A Twister of Twists, a Tangler of Tongues* (1972) and Steven Kellogg's *Aster Aardvark's Alphabet Adventures* (1987) are two good books of tongue twisters for middle- and upper-grade students.

Practice with tongue twisters and alliterative books increases children's awareness of the repetition of words with the same initial sounds in the poems they read and write. Few students consciously think about adding alliteration to a poem they are writing, but they get high praise in writing groups when classmates note alliteration and compliment the writer on it.

Onomatopoeia

Onomatopoeia is a device in which poets use sound words to make their writing more sensory and more vivid. These sound words, such as *crash, slurp, varoom,* and *me-e-e-ow,* sound like their meanings. Students can compile a list of sound words found in stories and poems they read. The list can be displayed on a classroom chart or entered in their writer's journals to be referred to when students write their own poems.

Peter Spier has compiled two books of sound words. *Gobble Growl Grunt* (1971) is about animal sounds, and *Crash! Bang! Boom!* (1972) is about the sounds people and machines make. Students can use these books in selecting sound words to use in their writing. Comic strips are another good source of sound words. Children collect frames from comic strips with sound words and add them to a classroom chart. Collecting these words naturally leads to a discussion of the spelling of sound words, one area of spelling in which children have a great deal of freedom. Sounds can be stretched out by repeating letters in words, such as g-r-r-r.

In *Wishes, Lies and Dreams* (1970) Kenneth Koch recommends having children write noise poems in which they include a noise or sound word in each line. These first poems may sound contrived (e.g., "A dog barks bow-wow"), but through these experiences children learn to use onomatopoeia. This poem, written by seventh-grade Brian, illustrates onomatopoeia:

▽

Greyhound

Fast and slick
Out of the dogbox—
ZOOM, ZOOM, ZOOM
Burst into the air
Then they smoothly touch the ground.

Repetition of Words

Repetition of words and phrases is another device that writers of stories and poems can use effectively to structure their writing and add interest. Edgar Allen Poe's effective use of the fearful word *nevermore* in "The Raven" is one poetic example, as is the gingerbread boy's boastful refrain in *The Gingerbread Boy.*

An easy way to introduce repetition of words in poetry is through a class collaboration poem. In this collaborative poem, a first grader's comment "Gee, it's fun wishing!" is repeated after every three wishes:

Wishing Time

I wish I could go to the moon.
I wish I had a pony.
I wish I was a professional baseball player
Gee, it's fun wishing!

I wish I had a million dollars.
I wish I could go to Disneyland.
I wish I could be a movie star.
Gee, it's fun wishing!

I wish I owned a toy store.
I wish I was the smartest kid in the world.
I wish I could never stop wishing.
Gee, it's fun wishing!

This repetition adds structure and enjoyment. As students read the poem aloud, the teacher reads each stanza and the students chant the refrain. In the following poem, a fifth grader writes about a piece of chocolate, using the refrain "Here it comes" to heighten anticipation and to structure the poem:

Chocolate

I drool.
Here it comes.
The golden brown covering never looked
so scrumptious, so tempting, so addicting.
Here it comes.
I don't know anything that's going on around me.
All I can concentrate on is chocolate.
Here it comes.
I can feel the sweet, rich, thick chocolate
on the roof of my mouth. A-a-a-ah-h!
And the chocolate is gone.

One way to suggest an improvement in a child's poem is to suggest that the child repeat a particularly effective phrase throughout the poem.

Rhyme

It is unfortunate that rhyme has been considered almost synonymous with poetry. While rhyme is an important part of many types of poetry, it can dominate the poetry of many young children. When rhyme comes naturally, it adds a delightful quality to children's writing, but when it *equals* poetry, it gets in the way of wordplay and vivid images. In the following Halloween poem, a fifth grader describes a witch's brew using rhyming words and an invented magical word, *allakaboo:*

▽

> *Bats, spiders, and lizards, too*
> *Rats, snakes—Allakaboo!*
> *Eggs and spiderwebs, a-choo*
> *Wings of a bug—Allakaboo—*
> *a witch's brew!*

Answering Teachers' Questions About . . . Poetry Writing

1. Isn't it true that children either have poetic ability or they don't?

Perhaps it is true that great poets are born, not made, but every child can write poems and enjoy the experience. Children benefit from experiences with poems; they develop a sensitivity to language and learn to play with words and evoke fresh images with words. The poetic forms presented in this chapter have been field-tested with students in kindergarten through eighth grade, and both teachers and students find these poetry-writing activities to be valuable learning experiences.

2. My students think that poems must rhyme. How can I convince them that poems don't have to rhyme?

Many children think that poems must rhyme. Reading the excerpt from Lowry's *Anastasia Krupnik* (1979) and developing a list of poetry rules for your class like the one described in Figure 9-11 will introduce the concept that poems are more than strings of rhyming words. Teaching students about concrete poems, haiku, and other forms that don't use rhyme will help them understand that they have options other than rhyming in poetry. Also read aloud to students some poetry that does not rhyme.

3. My students' poems look more like paragraphs that poems. What can I do?

Have students examine the poems written in books to see how they are arranged on the page. Also, write class poems and discuss with students the various options that poets have for arranging their poems on the page. To demonstrate some of the options, have small groups of students each design a different arrangement for a class collaboration poem. If you have access to a word processor, have students type their poems on the computer and arrange the poem in various ways. For example:

> Words
> written
> up
> and
> down
> and
> centered
> SMACK
> in the middle
> of
> the
> page—
> That's a poem
> to me!

If the poems also sound like a paragraph, some "unwriting" might be necessary in which children delete unnecessary and repetitive function words. For example, this paragraph was unwritten to create the poem printed on the previous page:

> In a poem you can write words up and down on a page. They are centered right in the middle of the page. They are fun to write. That's what a poem is to me.

4. *How can I teach poetry when I've never liked it or been any good at writing poetry myself?*

Teachers often ask this question, and I tell them that this is a new way of writing poetry. The emphasis has changed from rhyming verse to wordplay and expressing feelings and word pictures. Children's enthusiasm for this type of poetry is contagious; even the most skeptical teacher quickly becomes a convert.

REFERENCES

Adams, A. (1971). *A woggle of witches.* New York: Scribner.

Atwood, S. (1971). *Haiku: The mood of the Earth.* New York: Scribner.

Atwood, S. (1973). *My own rhythm: An approach to haiku.* New York: Scribner.

Bayer, J. (1984). *A my name is Alice.* New York: Dial.

Behn, H. (1964). *Cricket songs.* New York: Harcourt Brace Jovanovich.

Behn, H. (1971). *More cricket songs.* New York: Harcourt Brace Jovanovich.

Bernstein, J. E. (1979). *Fiddle with a riddle: Write your own riddles.* New York: Dutton.

Brewton, J. E., & Blackburn, L. A. (1978). *They've discovered a head in the box of bread and other laughable limericks.* New York: Crowell.

Brown, M. (1983). *What do you call a dumb bunny? And other rabbit riddles, games, jokes, and cartoons.* Boston: Little, Brown.

Burns, M. (1981). *The hink pink book.* Boston: Little, Brown.

Cox, J. A. (1980). *Put your foot in your mouth and other silly sayings.* New York: Random House.

Dahl, R. (1978). *The enormous crocodile.* New York: Knopf.

de Grasztold, C. B. (1965). *Prayers from the ark.* New York: Penguin Books.

Froman, R. (1974). *Seeing things: A book of poems.* New York: Crowell.

Funk, C. E. (1984). *A hog on ice and other curious expressions.* New York: Harper & Row.

Geller, L. G. (1981). Riddling: A playful way to explore language. *Language Arts, 58,* pp. 669–674.

Geller, L. G. (1985). *Word play and language learning for children.* Urbana, IL: National Council of Teachers of English.

Gwynne, F. (1970). *The king who rained.* New York: Windmill Books.

Gwynne, F. (1976). *A chocolate moose for dinner.* New York: Windmill Books.

Gwynne, F. (1980). *The sixteen hand horse.* New York: Prentice-Hall.

Gwynne, F. (1988). *A little pigeon toad.* New York: Simon & Schuster.

Hall, R., & Friends. (1985). *Sniglets for kids.* Yellow Springs, OH: Antioch.

Horwitz, E. L. (1975). *When the sky is like lace.* Philadelphia: Lippincott.

Hunt, B. K. (1976). *Your ant is a which.* New York: Harcourt Brace Jovanovich.

Kellogg, S. (1987). *Aster Aardvark's alphabet adventures.* New York: Morrow.

Kennedy, X. J., & Kennedy, D. M. (1982). *Knock at a star: A child's introduction to poetry.* Boston: Little, Brown.

Koch, K. (1970). *Wishes, lies, and dreams.* New York: Vintage.

Koch, K. (1973). *Rose, where did you get that red.* New York: Vintage.

Kuskin, K. (1980). *Dogs and dragons, trees and dreams.* New York: Harper & Row.

Kuskin, K. (1975). *Near the window tree.* New York: Harper & Row.

Langstaff, J. (1974). *Oh, a-hunting we will go.* New York: Atheneum.

Lewis, R. (Ed.) (1965). *In a spring garden.* New York: Dial.

Lewis, R. (1968). *Of this world: A poet's life in poetry.* New York: Dial.

Lewis, R. (1970). *The way of silence: The prose and poetry of Basho.* New York: Dial.

Livingston, M. C. (Ed.) (1982). *How pleasant to know Mr. Lear!* New York: Holiday House.

Lobel, A. (1983). *Pigericks: A book of pig limericks.* New York: Harper & Row.

Lowry, L. (1979). *Anastasia Krupnik.* Boston: Houghton Mifflin.

McCord, D. (1962). *Take sky.* Boston: Little, Brown.

McCord, D. (1967). *Everytime I climb a tree.* Boston: Little, Brown.

McCord, D. (1977). *One at a time: Collected poems for the young.* Boston: Little, Brown.

McMillan, B. (1991). *Play day: A book of terse verse.* New York: Holiday House.

O'Neill M. (1961). *Hailstones and halibut bones: Adventures in color.* Garden City, NJ: Doubleday.

Opie, I., & Opie, P. (1959). *The lore and language of school children.* Oxford: Oxford University Press.

Pilon, B. (1972). *Concrete is not always hard.* Middletown, CT; Xerox Educational Publications.

Prelutsky, J. (1976). *Nightmares: Poems to trouble your sleep.* New York: Greenwillow.

Prelutsky, J. (1977). *The snoop on the sidewalk and other poems.* New York: Greenwillow.

Prelutsky, J. (1980). *The headless horseman rides tonight: More poems to trouble your sleep.* New York: Greenwillow.

Prelutsky, J. (1982). *The baby uggs are hatching.* New York: Mulberry.

Prelutsky, J. (1983). *The Random House book of poetry for children.* New York: Random House.

Prelutsky, J. (1984). *The new kid on the block.* New York: Greenwillow.

Prelutsky, J. (1985). *My parents think I'm sleeping.* New York: Greenwillow.

Schwartz, A. (1972). *A twister of twists, a tangler of tongues.* New York: Harper & Row.

Seuss, Dr. (1979). *Oh say can you say?* New York: Random House.

Sherman, I. (1980). *Walking talking words.* New York: Harcourt Brace Jovanovich.

Silverstein, S. (1974). *Where the sidewalk ends.* New York: Harper & Row.

Silverstein, S. (1981). *The light in the attic.* New York: Harper & Row.

Spier, P. (1971). *Gobble growl grunt.* New York: Doubleday.

Spier, P. (1972). *Crash! Bang! Boom!* New York: Doubleday.

Sterne, N. (1979). *Tyrannosaurus wrecks: A book of dinosaur riddles.* New York: Crowell.

Terban, M. (1982). *Eight ate: A feast of homonym riddles.* New York: Clarion.

Terban, M. (1983). *In a pickle and other funny idioms.* New York: Clarion.

Terban, M. (1987). *Mad as a wet hen! and other funny idioms.* New York: Clarion.

Terban, M. (1990). *Punching the clock: Funny action idioms.* New York: Clarion.

Terban, M. (1991). *Hey, hay: A wagonful of funny homonym riddles.* New York: Clarion.

Tiedt, I. (1970). Exploring poetry patterns. *Elementary English, 45,* 1082–1084.

Tompkins, G. E., & Yaden, D. B., Jr. (1986). *Answering students' questions about words.* Urbana, IL: ERIC Clearinghouse on Reading and Communication Skills and National Council of Teachers of English.

Valentine, S. L. (1986). Beginning poets dig for poems. *Language Arts, 63,* 246–252.

Van Allsburg, C. (1987). *The Z was zapped.* Boston: Houghton Mifflin.

Viorst, J. (1981). *If I were in charge of the world and other worries.* New York: Atheneum.

Zalben, J. B. (1977). *Lewis Carroll's Jabberwocky.* New York: Warne.

Zolotow, C. (1980). *Say it!* New York: Harper & Row.

10

Persuasive Writing

Overview of Persuasive Writing

Purpose Students use persuasive writing to argue logically with reasons, to present another viewpoint, to sway opinions, to convince someone to their way of thinking.

Audience The audience may be known or unknown. When students write a state legislator, the audience is known, but when they write to the editor of a newspaper, the audience is unknown. It is crucial that writers have a clear sense of audience and that they adapt their writing and the reasoning they use to their audience.

Forms Forms include essays, letters, letters to the editor, advertisements, and commercials.

Topics Students write about personal, community, and national issues. They write book reviews, make book and film comparisons, and create advertisements and commercials for products and services.

Approaches Students often use persuasive writing in connection with literature focus units and theme studies.

Other Teachers have assumed that only older students could write persuasively, but even students in the primary grades can present an argument and substantiate it with reasons.

Writing Mother's Day Cards

It is a week before Mother's Day, and a group of first graders in Mrs. Carson's classroom are meeting to talk about the Mother's Day cards they want to make. Earlier that morning at the whole-class meeting that Mrs. Carson uses to begin each writing workshop session, Mrs. Carson had mentioned Mother's Day and encouraged the children to think about making Mother's Day cards or some other writing for their mothers. Now Mrs. Carson is meeting with a group to talk about their Mother's Day projects.

Five children are in the writing group: Maria, Bobby, Elizabeth, Teri, and John. John is a leader in the group, and as soon as Mrs. Carson asks the children what ideas they have for Mother's Day projects, he explains, "I want to make a card to tell my mom that she's the best mom in the world. I know she is and I want to tell her." Mrs. Carson follows his lead. "John, what does she do that makes you think she is the best mom?" John thinks for a minute and then begins to list her attributes: "My mom cooks me the best meals . . . she taught me to read when I was a little kid . . . you know, she takes care of me. . . ." Teri, Bobby and the other children in the writing group join in the discussion, talking about their moms and what makes them special.

Four of the five students in the group decide to write letters to their moms telling why they are the best moms in the world. The fifth child chooses to write a poem instead, and she gets to work on her project. Mrs. Carson continues to meet with the other four students to talk about persuasive writing. Mrs. Carson says, "I think you are telling me that you want to convince your mom and everyone else who reads your Mother's Day card that your mom is the best. You will want to have lots of reasons or examples to make your point. John told us several reasons why his mom is the best. Can you think of some reasons why your mom is the best, too?"

The students share ideas, and then Mrs. Carson reviews the writing process and the steps they will follow in writing their letters. She asks them to draw a cluster and include at least three reasons why their moms are the best, and she remains with the group while they get started. Then she moves off to another writing group.

Over the next two days, these four students write rough drafts of their cards. They all begin their cards by saying that their moms are the best and then incorporate the reasons and examples from their clusters into their writing. This group of four first graders is a very supportive group. (As they write, they share their drafts with each other and get compliments and feedback on their writing. They also get ideas from each other. One child writes "I love you 100 times" on her rough draft, and soon others are writing "I love you 10,000 times" and another "I love you 1,000,000 times." Students aren't sure how to write such large numbers, so when Mrs. Carson checks on the group, she takes a moment to explain how to write large numbers.

On Wednesday, Mrs. Carson meets with the writing group about revising their cards. As each child reads his or her card, Mrs. Carson and group members offer compliments and make suggestions for improvement. Mrs. Carson notices that John is the only student to have an ending for his card. Taking a moment to talk about writing, she reminds the group that many kinds of writing have a beginning, middle, and end. She uses a sandwich model made of two pieces of light-brown sponge cut into the shape of slices of bread, slices of meat and cheese cut from felt, rubber pickles, and mesh lettuce. She reminds them, "The beginning is the statement that your moms are the best," and she points to the top slice of bread. "The middle is where your reasons and examples go," and she points to the meat, cheese, and other ingredients. Then she points to the bottom slice of bread and asks, "Do your cards have an end?" John announces that his did, and he reads it aloud: "See I told you

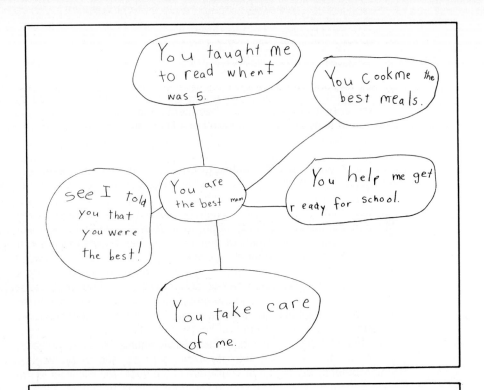

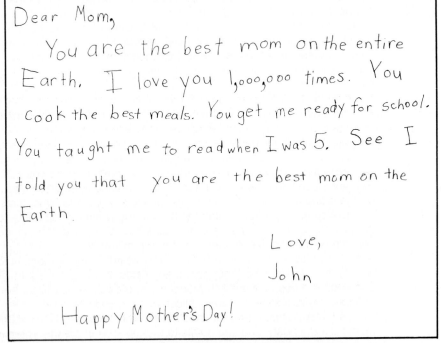

FIGURE 10-1   A First Grader's Cluster and Mother's Day Message

that you are the best mom on the Earth." No one else had an ending, so Mrs. Carson and John help the students write endings, such as "And that's why you are the bestest" and "Thank you for loving me so much."

After students make their revisions, Mrs. Carson meets with the writing group again to help them edit their writing. The three editing skills that she focuses on are spelling, capitalization, and punctuation. For some writing assignments, Mrs. Carson focuses on adding punctuation marks or capital letters and encourages children to keep their invented spelling; however, this is an important writing project, and the children want their cards to be as adultlike as possible. Mrs. Carson reads over each paper and points out corrections. She explains some of the changes, and for others she simply says, "Adults usually put a comma here, so is it OK if I add it?"

After editing, students copy their letters on "good paper" and glue the paper to the construction-paper cards they have decorated. On Thursday and Friday afternoons, the class meets together to share their cards before they take them home. Mrs. Carson always makes time for students to share their writing to help students develop a sense of authorship and feel that they are members of a community of writers.

John's cluster and Mother's Day message are presented in Figure 10-1. Notice that this message written by a first grader includes the same three parts that older students who write more complex persuasive essays and letters use: a beginning, in which the position is stated, the middle, which provides at least three supporting reasons, and the end, in which the position is restated.

P arents have little doubt that children are effective persuaders as they argue to stay up beyond their bedtimes or plead to keep as a pet the stray puppy they have found. John's letter to his mother shows that primary grade students can write persuasively, even though researchers have found that children's persuasive writing abilities develop more slowly than their abilities in any other genre (Applebee, Langer, & Mullis, 1986; Hidi & Hildyard, 1983).

A sense of audience and the ability to tailor writing to fit the audience is perhaps most important in persuasive writing because the writer can judge how effective the persuasion is by readers' reactions. While an audience's enjoyment of a story or poem or the information learned from a research report can be hard to gauge, the effect of persuasion on others is not. Researchers examining audience adaptation (Crowhurst & Piché, 1979; Kroll, 1978; Rubin & Piché, 1979) have found that upper-grade students were unable to decenter their writing and focus on the needs of their audience. More recently, Barry Kroll (1984) found that sixth graders could adapt to their audience in writing persuasive letters. He concluded that when students have a clear purpose and plausible reason for writing, they can adapt their writing to meet the needs of their readers.

Persuasive arguments can be written as essays or as letters. Students write essays arguing against the use of drugs or book reports to recommend a book they have read. In these essays, students present a point of view and then defend the position by citing several supporting reasons or examples. Students also write letters to legislators or letters to the editor of the local newspaper to express their opinions about community, state, or national issues and to try to persuade others to support their viewpoint. Persuasive writing can take the form of advertisements. Through print advertisements on posters and scripted video commercials, students use both persuasion and propaganda to influence people to "buy" ideas, products, and services.

PERSUASION AND PROPAGANDA

To persuade is to win someone over to your viewpoint or cause. Persuasion involves a reasoned or logical appeal in contrast to propaganda, which has a more sinister connotation. Propaganda can be deceptive, hyped, emotion-laden, or one-sided. While the purpose of both is to influence, there are ethical differences.

Three Ways to Persuade

People can be persuaded in three basic ways. The first appeal a writer can make is based on reason. People seek to make logical generalizations and draw cause-and-effect conclusions, whether from absolute facts or from strong possibilities. For example, people can be persuaded to practice more healthful living if told about the results of medical research. It is, of course, necessary to distinguish between reasonable and unreasonable appeals. For example, urging people to stand on their head every day for 30 minutes based on the claim that it will increase their intelligence is an unreasonable appeal.

A second way to persuade is through an appeal to character. Other people are important to us, and we can be persuaded by what another person recommends if we trust that person. Trust comes from personal knowledge of the person or the reputation of the person who is trying to persuade: Does the persuader have the expertise or personal experience necessary to endorse a product or a cause? For example, can we believe what scientists say about the dangers of nuclear energy? Can we believe what a sports personality says about the effectiveness of a particular sports shoe?

The third way people can be persuaded is by an appeal to their emotions. Emotional appeals can be as strong as intellectual appeals because people have a strong concern for their well-being and the rights of others. We support or reject arguments according to our strong feelings about what is ethical and socially responsible. At the same time, fear and the need for peer acceptance are strong feelings that also influence our opinions and beliefs.

Any of the three appeals can be used to try to persuade another person. For example, when a child tries to persuade her parents that her bedtime should be delayed by 30 minutes, she might argue that neighbors allow their children to stay up later; this is an appeal to character. If the argument focuses on the amount of sleep that a 10-year-old needs, it is an appeal to reason. When the child finally announces that she has the earliest bedtime of anyone in her fourth-grade class and it makes her feel like a baby, the appeal is to the emotions.

These same three types of appeal are used in in-school persuasion. When trying to persuade classmates to read a particular book in a "book-selling" poster project, for example, students might argue that the book should be read because it is short and interesting (reason), because it is hilarious and you'll laugh (emotion), or because it is the most popular book in the second grade and everyone else is reading it (character).

Propaganda

The word *propaganda* suggests something shady or underhanded. While propaganda, like persuasion, is designed to influence people's beliefs and actions, propagandists may use underhanded techniques to distort, conceal, and exaggerate the facts. Two of these techniques are deceptive language and propaganda devices.

People seeking to influence us often use words that evoke a variety of responses. For example, they claim something is "improved," "more natural," or "50% better." Such loaded words are deceptive because they have positive connotations but may have no basis in fact. For example, when a product is advertised as 50% better, consumers need to ask, "50% better than what?" That question is rarely answered in advertisements.

Doublespeak is another type of deceptive language. It is language that is evasive, euphemistic, confusing, and self-contradictory. For example, janitors may be called "maintenance engineers," and repeats of television shows are termed "encore telecasts." William Lutz (1984) cites a number of kinds of doublespeak including euphemisms and inflated language, which elementary students can easily understand. Other kinds of doublespeak, such as jargon specific to particular groups, overwhelming an audience with words, and language that pretends to communicate but does not, are more appropriate for teaching older students about propaganda.

Euphemisms are words or phrases, such as "passed away," that are used to avoid a harsh or distasteful reality. They are often used out of concern for someone's feelings rather than to deceive. Inflated language includes words designed to make the ordinary seem extraordinary. For example, car mechanics become "automotive internists," and used cars become "pre-owned." Examples of deceptive language are listed in Figure 10-2. Children need to learn that people sometimes use words that only pretend to communicate; at other times they use words to intentionally misrepresent. For instance, a wallet advertised as genuine imitation leather is a vinyl wallet, and a faux diamond ring is made of glass. (The word *faux* is French for *false*.) Children need to be able to interpret this deceptive language and to avoid using it themselves.

Advertisers use propaganda devices, such as testimonials, bandwagon effect, and rewards, to sell their products. Nine devices that elementary students can identify are listed in Figure 10-3. Students can locate examples of each propaganda device in advertisements and discuss the effects the device has on them. They can also investigate how the same devices are used in advertisements directed at youngsters, teenagers, and adults. For instance, while a snack food advertisement with a sticker or toy in the package will appeal to a youngster, an appliance advertisement with a

FIGURE 10-2   *Examples of Deceptive Language*
Source: Lutz, n.d.

Loaded Words	Doublespeak
best buy	bathroom tissue (toilet paper)
better than	civil disorder (riot)
carefree	correctional facility (jail, prison)
discount	dentures (false teeth)
easier	disadvantaged (poor)
extra strong	encore telecast (re-run)
fortified	funeral director (undertaker)
fresh	genuine imitation leather (vinyl)
guaranteed	inner city (slum, ghetto)
improved	inoperative statement or misspeak (lie)
longer lasting	memorial park (cemetery)
lowest	mobile home (house trailer)
maximum	nervous wetness (sweat)
more natural	occasional irregularity (constipation)
more powerful	passed away (died)
new/newer	people expressways (sidewalks)
plus	personal preservation flotation device (life preserver)
stronger	pre-owned or experienced (used)
ultra	pupil station (student's desk)
virtually	senior citizen (old person)
	terminal living (dying)
	urban transportation specialist (cab driver, bus driver)

factory rebate will appeal to an adult. The propaganda device for both ads is the same: a reward! These devices can be used to sell ideas as well as products. Public service announcements about quitting smoking or wearing seat belts as well as political advertisements, endorsements, and speeches use these same devices.

When students locate advertisements and commercials that they believe are misleading or deceptive, they can write letters of complaint to the following watchdog agencies:

Action for Children's Television
46 Austin Street
Newtonville, MA 02160

Children's Advertising Review Unit
Council of Better Business Bureaus
845 Third Avenue
New York, NY 10022

Federal Trade Commission
Pennsylvania Avenue at
  Sixth Street NW
Washington, DC 20580

Zillions Ad Complaints
256 Washington Street
Mt. Vernon, NY 10553

In their letters, students should carefully describe the advertisement and explain what bothers them about it. They should also tell where they saw the advertisement (name of magazine and issue) or where they saw or heard the commercial (date, time, and channel).

1. Glittering Generality

Generalities such as "motherhood," "justice," and "The American Way" are used to enhance the quality of a product or the character of a political figure. Propagandists select a generality so attractive that listeners do not challenge the speaker's real point. If a candidate for public office happens to be a mother, for example, the speaker may say, "Our civilization could not survive without mothers." The generalization is true, of course, and listeners may—if they are not careful—accept the candidate without asking these questions: Is she a mother? Is she a good mother? Does being a mother have anything to do with being a good candidate?

2. Testimonial

To convince people to purchase a product, an advertiser associates it with a popular personality such as an athlete or film star. For example, "Bozo Cereal must be good because Joe Footballstar eats it every morning." Similarly, film stars endorse candidates for political office and telethons to raise money for medical research and other causes. Consider these questions: Is the person familiar with the product being advertised? Does the person offering the testimonial have the expertise necessary to judge the quality of the product, event, or candidate?

3. Transfer

In this device, which is similar to the testimonial technique, the persuader tries to transfer the authority and prestige of some person or object to another person or object that will then be accepted. Good examples are found regularly in advertising: A film star is shown using Super Soap, and viewers are supposed to believe that they too may have healthy, youthful skin if they use the same soap. Likewise, politicians like to be seen with famous athletes or entertainers in hopes that the luster of the stars will rub off on them. This technique is also known as guilt or glory by association. Questions to determine the effect of this device are the same as for the testimonial technique.

4. Name-calling

Here advertisers try to pin a bad label on something they want listeners to dislike so that it will automatically be rejected or condemned. In a discussion of health insurance, for example, an opponent may call the sponsor of a bill a socialist. Whether or not the sponsor is a socialist does not matter to the name-caller; the purpose is to have any unpleasant associations of the term rub off on the victim. Listeners should ask themselves whether or not the label has any effect on the product.

5. Plain Folks

Assuming that most listeners favor common, ordinary people (rather than elitish, stuffed shirts), many politicians like to assume the appearance of common folk. One candidate, who really went to Harvard and wore $400 suits, campaigned in clothes from J.C. Penney's and spoke backcountry dialect. "Look at me, folks," the candidate wanted to say, "I'm just a regular country boy like you; I wouldn't sell you a bill of goods!" To determine the effect of this device, listeners should ask these questions: Is the person really the type of person he or she is portraying? Does the person really share the ideas of the people with whom he or she professes to identify?

6. Card Stacking

In presenting complex issues, the unscrupulous persuader often chooses only those items that favor one side of an issue. Any unfavorable facts are suppressed. To consider the argument objectively, listeners must seek additional information about other viewpoints.

7. Bandwagon

This technique appeals to many people's need to be a part of a group. Advertisers claim that everyone is using this product and you should, too. For example, "more physicians recommend this pill than any other." (Notice that the advertisement doesn't specify what "any other" is.) Questions to consider include the following: Does everyone really use this product? What is it better than? Why should I jump on the bandwagon?

8. Snob Appeal

In contrast to the plain folks device, persuaders use snob appeal to try to appeal to the people who want to become part of an elite or exclusive group. Advertisements for expensive clothes, cosmetics, and gourmet foods often use this technique. Listeners should consider these questions in evaluating commercials and advertisements using this device: Is the product of high quality or does it have an expensive nametag? Is the product of higher quality than other non-snobbish brands?

9. Rewards

Increasingly, advertisers offer rewards for buying their products. For many years, snack food and cereal products offered toys and other gimmicks in their product packages. More often, adults are being lured by this device, too. Free gifts, rebates from manufacturers, low-cost financing, and other rewards are being offered for the purchase of expensive items such as appliances and automobiles. Listeners should consider the value of these rewards and whether they increase the cost of the product.

FIGURE 10-3 Propaganda Devices
Techniques 1–6 adapted from Devine, 1982, pp. 39–40.

TYPES OF PERSUASIVE WRITING

Persuasion is a part of everyday life. Children and adults frequently try to convince others to do or believe a certain thing. Andrew Wilkinson and his colleagues (1980) investigated the ability of children (ages 7–13) to write persuasively. They found that children at all ages could state an opinion, and, not surprisingly, as they grew older they were better able to provide a logical justification for their opinions. Younger children were very egocentric in their reasoning and often failed to consider others' viewpoints. Furthermore, they found that children age 10 and older often wrote self-contradictory essays. In these essays, students started with a definite position, but through writing a justification for that position they concluded with a position that was opposite of the one made in the beginning. However, it should be noted that these students wrote single draft compositions and did not participate in writing groups to critique and revise their writing.

Topics for persuasive writing come from at-home and in-school activities as well as from content area study. At home, children might try to persuade their parents to let them go to bed later, play on a football team, go to a slumber party, buy new clothes or shoes, join the Boy or Girl Scouts, increase their allowance, buy a new toy, or have a pet. At school, children might try to persuade their teachers to let them have less homework, have outside recess in cold weather, change lunchroom rules, or sponsor a student council election. In the subjects they study, students can use writing to persuade others to stop smoking, avoid drugs, save the world from the destruction of a nuclear war, stop polluting our environment, endorse particular political candidates, read a certain book, see a certain movie, or support community, state, or national issues.

Organization of an Argument

An argument has a beginning, middle, and end, much like a story does. In the beginning, writers state their position, argument, or opinion clearly. In the middle, the opinion is developed. Writers select and present three or more reasons or pieces of evidence to support their position. These reasons may appeal to logic, character, or emotions. Writers sequence the evidence in a logical order and use concrete examples whenever possible. They often use cue words such as *first, second,* and *third* to alert readers to the organization. In the end, writers lead their readers to draw the conclusion that they intend using one or more of these techniques: giving a personal statement, making a prediction, or summarizing the major points. The organization of an argument is illustrated schematically in Figure 10-4.

Marion Crowhurst (1991) has identified several problems in students' persuasive writing that this organizational scheme can help to ameliorate. First, students' persuasive compositions are typically shorter than the stories and reports that they write. In these shorter compositions, students neither develop their arguments nor provide reasons to support their arguments. Second, their persuasive essays show poor organization, because students are unfamiliar with how an argument should be structured. Third, students' writing style is often inappropriate. Their language is informal,

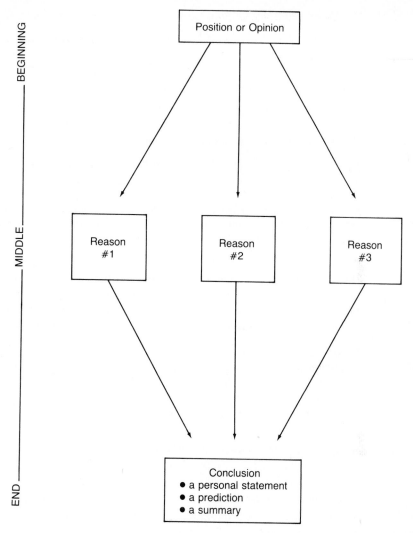

FIGURE 10-4 *Organizational Scheme of an Argument*

and they use words such as *also* to tie arguments together rather than the more sophisticated stylistic devices, such as *if . . . then* statements, typically used in persuasive writing. When students talk their way through the organizational scheme as a prewriting activity and listen to classmates discuss their plans, students develop more sophisticated writing styles and tighter arguments.

While the organization of an argument typically involves a statement, the development of three (or more) reasons, and a conclusion, this scheme is not equivalent to a traditional five-paragraph theme. Persuasive writing requires a much more highly elaborated schema than the simplistic, formulaic five-paragraph theme (Crowhurst,

1991). In persuasive writing, students devise ways to introduce an argument, present supporting reasons, draw conclusions, and convince the reader to accept the writer's viewpoint.

Persuasive Essays

Students write persuasive essays in which they argue on topics they have strong beliefs and opinions about. For example, sixth-grade Michael wrote the following essay about drinking soft drinks during class:

▽ *I think we, the students of Deer Creek School, should be allowed to drink refreshments during class. One reason is that it seems to speed the passing of the day. Secondly, I feel it is unfair and rude for teachers to drink coffee and soft drinks in front of the students. Finally, I think if the students were not worried about making trips to the water fountain, they would concentrate more on school work. Being allowed to drink refreshments would be a wonderful addition to the school day.*

Michael's essay is well organized with a well-articulated beginning, middle, and end. He begins by clearly stating his position in the first sentence. Next, he lists three reasons and cues readers to the reasons using the words *one reason, secondly,* and *finally.* In the last sentence, Michael concludes the argument by making a prediction.

On another topic, girls' right to play any sport, sixth-grade Amy writes:

▽ *I think there should be more sports for girls. Girls are capable of playing sports such as soccer and football. Some girls dislike basketball, but they want to participate in other sports. If girls could participate in other sports, they could learn to coordinate as a team. Everyone needs exercise and alternative activities would keep all females physically fit. Girls should have the chance to participate and excel in other sports.*

Amy's essay also follows the three-part organizational structure, but she does not direct attention to her reasons using cue words as Michael did. She begins with a clear statement of her position, and at the end she uses a summary or generalization to conclude her appeal.

Persuasive Letters

Students can also write persuasive letters. As with other types of letters, these letters are written to real audiences and are mailed. As part of a unit on drugs, students in a fifth-grade class each chose a family member or a friend to write a persuasive letter to. Some children wrote to parents or grandparents, arguing that they should stop smoking; others wrote to siblings or friends, urging them not to take drugs or not to mix drinking and driving. Fifth-grade Tom wrote this letter to his friend Mike:

▽ *Dear Mike,*

I think drugs are very bad. They hurt people a lot and they can cost money. Mike, I know you're 15 and you don't think drugs can hurt you, but you can get addicted to drugs just the same as everybody else.

You can get hurt taking drugs, Mike. Some of the possible consequences are that you may get hurt dealing drugs, you may get AIDS by sharing infected needles or the pressure may become so great you just commit suicide. You might hurt others, too. You could rob a bank, hurt people in an auto accident, or just get violent and hurt someone. Michael, you might lose a friend and get into fights, be unpopular, or just be sad.

Drugs are out and it's the truth. More people are saying no to drugs. It isn't worth it, so be smart, not stupid, and don't get into trouble. Don't waste your time, and it costs lots of money to do drugs and you will be depressed a lot.

Many people say drugs are only as bad as cigarettes. That is not so. See Mike, you could go from $1 a day on cigarettes to $100 a day on heroin. Money and health problems arise from drugs. Each year, 200,000 are hurt by drugs and 25,000 people die from drug-related accidents. Half a million people are arrested for drugs each year.

So, doing drugs is wrong. This evidence is that you should not take any kind of drugs, Mike. I hope you make the right decision.

Your friend,
Tom

In his letter, Tom uses appeals to reason, character, and emotion. He uses statistics and cause-and-effect arguments in his rational appeal to Michael to not use drugs. He says in his appeal to character that people who take drugs are stupid, and he evokes the universal fear of contracting AIDS in his appeal to emotion. Tom tells Michael that he might die or hurt other people if he takes drugs.

Persuasive letters can also be sent to newspapers. A letter sent to the editor of a local newspaper is presented in Figure 10-5. In this letter, seventh-grade Becky argues that the adult admission prices that teens pay at movies are unfair considering that they are not allowed to see adult movies.

In Theme Studies

As part of a theme cycle on the American Revolution, a class of fifth graders wrote persuasive essays. The teacher asked students to think about whether or not the American Revolution was a good or necessary thing. Did they favor the patriot or loyalist position? The students brainstormed a list of reasons in support of the Revolution and a list of reasons in opposition. Then students picked one side or the other and wrote an essay articulating their position. They began by stating their position, provided at least three reasons to support their view, and then concluded the essay. Fifth-grade Marshall wrote:

▽ *I am in favor of the American Revolution and here are three of my reasons. First, after the colonists won the war, they could believe in God how they wanted. Next, if we didn't win the war, we would probably be British and not American. Third, after the war, the colonists could speak their mind without being tortured or killed. That is why I am for the American Revolution.*

FIGURE 10-5   *A Seventh Grader's Letter to the Editor*
Source: *The Norman* (Okla.) *Transcript,* Sunday, February 28, 1988

Editor, The Transcript:
   I am a student at Longfellow Middle School. I am writing to express my feelings on the price teenagers pay to get into the movie theater. In most movie theaters at the age of 13, they consider you an adult, so you have to pay full price. But you pay the adult price to see a children's movie. They say we aren't old enough to see these movies, yet they consider us adult enough to pay the adult price. Why is this? I strongly urge the movie theaters to think this through and change the price, so if you are an adult you pay the adult price to see an adult movie and if you are a child you pay to see a children's movie. I am not saying that at the age of 13 you should be able to see "R" rated movies, but I'm saying don't make us pay for them. Let us pay for what we see.

REBECCA PIERCE
Norman

Tim took the opposing point of view and wrote:

▽   *I'm against the American Revolution. I think it was a bad war and unnecessary for several reasons. The first reason is that the colonists were already pretty much free, and they didn't need to have a war. The second reason is that there was way too much suffering, fighting, and loss of life. The last reason was that it was a tremendous loss of lots of money. These are three reasons why I'm against the Revolutionary War.*

TEACHING STUDENTS TO WRITE PERSUASIVELY

Students are introduced to persuasive writing through a series of minilessons in which they investigate persuasive techniques. Then students apply what they have learned to write persuasive essays and letters as part of literature focus units and social studies and science theme cycles. The minilessons are important because research has shown that students' persuasive writing can be improved through instruction (Crowhurst, 1991). The steps in the teaching strategy are as follows:

Step by Step

1. *Examine how persuasion is used in everyday life.*   Talk with students about the points of view and positions people take on various issues. Also, share a children's book such as *Molly's Pilgrim* (Cohen, 1983), *Oliver Button Is a Sissy* (de Paola, 1979), or *William's Doll* (Zolotow, 1972) in which the authors try to persuade readers to their viewpoint. Crowhurst's (1991) research suggests interrelationships between reading and writing, and she recommends using literature as a

model for persuasive writing. In *Molly's Pilgrim,* for example, Barbara Cohen argues that there are modern-day Pilgrims like Molly's mother who emigrated from Russia and came to America for religious freedom. Read one or more of these books and discuss the argument with students.

After reading and discussing the story, teachers and students work together to develop an argument organizer similar to the one presented in Figure 10-4 to map out the persuasion used in the story. Then the class writes a collaborative summary of the argument. A class of fourth graders created a scheme after reading and discussing *Molly's Pilgrim* and then wrote a class collaboration summary which is presented in Figure 10-6.

2. *Identify a topic and develop a list of reasons to support the position.* Students identify a topic for their essays and as a prewriting activity create a scheme to plan their essay, as shown in Figure 10-4. Through this activity, students gather and organize their ideas before beginning to write. Fifth-grade Lance wrote a letter to his Uncle Bobby to try to persuade him to stop smoking. His organizational scheme and letter are presented in Figure 10-7.

Betty Jane Wagner (1986) found that middle- and upper-grade students wrote significantly better persuasive letters after role-playing. In particular, Wagner reported that students who had participated in informal drama tailored their persuasion to their audience more effectively than students who did not. Role-playing before writing the rough draft may help students to write better persuasive essays.

3. *Write the rough draft.* Students write rough drafts of their essays using the scheme developed during prewriting. As with other types of rough drafts, students label their papers as rough drafts and write on every other line to leave space for revision.

4. *Revise and edit the essay.* After writing their rough drafts, students revise and edit them. Before meeting in a writing group, students may first revise their own papers, reviewing to make sure they have developed the beginning, middle, and end of their essays. Students can use a "Writer's Revision Checklist," as shown in Figure 10-8, to revise their essays. After completing the checklist, they make any needed changes before sharing their compositions in writing groups.

When students share their compositions in writing groups, they may ask their classmates to complete a "Reader's Revision Checklist," as shown in Figure 10-9. After classmates complete this form, writers compare their own responses with those of their classmates. If readers' comments differ significantly from the writer's, then students should conclude that they are not communicating effectively and that additional revision is necessary. Discussing these revision checklists can be the major activity of the writing group, or group members may offer compliments, have the writer ask clarifying questions, and then offer suggestions for improvement.

Lance and his writing group members completed the revision checklists illustrated in Figures 10-8 and 10-9, and their responses were very similar, suggesting to Lance that his readers were understanding his argument. Then Lance received compliments from writing-group members about the number and quality of pieces of evidence he used in the essay. Lance asked his writing-group members if he needed to resequence his pieces of evidence, and his classmates responded that the order was fine. Finally, his classmates suggested that he elaborate on the

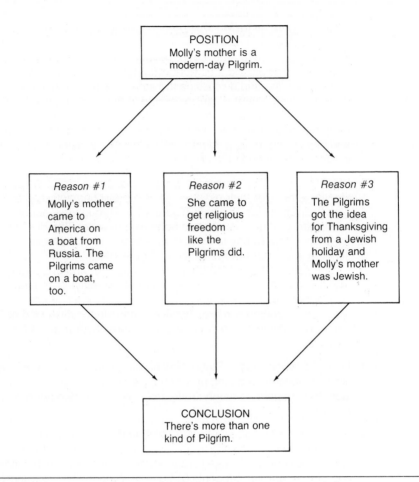

POSITION
Molly's mother is a
modern-day Pilgrim.

Reason #1

Molly's mother
came to
America on
a boat from
Russia. The
Pilgrims came
on a boat,
too.

Reason #2

She came to
get religious
freedom
like the
Pilgrims did.

Reason #3

The Pilgrims
got the idea
for Thanksgiving
from a Jewish
holiday and
Molly's mother
was Jewish.

CONCLUSION
There's more than one
kind of Pilgrim.

Summary

Molly's mother is a Pilgrim, but she's not a Pilgrim from the first Thanksgiving in 1621. She's a modern-day Pilgrim. Here are three reasons why we believe this. First, Molly's mother came to America on a boat from Russia and the first Pilgrims came on a boat, too. It was named the Mayflower. Second, Molly's mother came to America for religious freedom. She was Jewish and in Russia, people weren't nice to Jews. The first Pilgrims came to America for religious freedom, too, because they couldn't worship God like they wanted in England. Third, the Pilgrims got the idea for Thanksgiving from a Jewish holiday called Tabernacles and Molly's mother was Jewish so it was her holiday, too. There's more than one kind of Pilgrim and even though Molly's mother wasn't a Pilgrim in 1621, she is one now.

FIGURE 10-6 *An Organizational Scheme and Summary of* Molly's Pilgrim

second and fourth pieces of evidence, and he decided to expand the second argument about emphysema.

Then students proofread their essays, hunting for mechanical errors, and later they correct these errors. Lance and a classmate proofread his paper and located some of his spelling, capitalization, and punctuation errors. Then Lance met with his teacher for a final proofreading. After most of the errors had been corrected, Lance recopied his letter to Uncle Bobby.

5. *Share the writing.* As with other types of writing, persuasive writing should be shared with a real audience. Compositions may be shared by being read aloud or displayed on posters, greeting cards, or a bulletin board. They can also be published in the school newspaper. Letters should be sent to the person to whom they are addressed, or letters to the editor can be published in school and local newspapers.

Assessing Students' Persuasive Writing

The process that students use to plan and write persuasive compositions is at least as important as the quality of their arguments, and a process approach to assessment is recommended. The assessment instrument should include the steps that students move through as they develop their compositions, such as the following:

▼ Students create a plan for their writing using a scheme or cluster.
▼ Students write a rough draft.
▼ Students complete a "Writer's Revision Checklist."
▼ Students meet in writing groups to share their rough drafts.
▼ Students have classmates complete a "Reader's Revision Checklist."
▼ Students compare the revision checklists.
▼ Students make one or two revisions based on the revision checklists and suggestions made in writing groups.
▼ Students proofread their compositions and correct as many mechanical errors as possible.
▼ Students make a final copy of their compositions.
▼ Students share their compositions with an appropriate audience.

A checklist can be developed from these steps and be used in assessing students' compositions. This checklist should be created and distributed to students before beginning the project so they can keep track of their progress.

When an assessment of the quality of students' writings is necessary, the three items included in the revision checklists (see Figures 10-8 and 10-9) may be used as criteria. It is important that the criteria that students use in revising their compositions are the same ones that teachers use in judging the quality of their compositions.

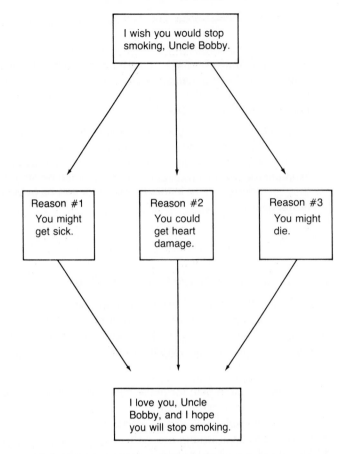

FIGURE 10-7   *A Fifth Grader's Scheme and Final Copy of His Persuasive Letter*

ADVERTISEMENTS

Children are exposed to advertising as they watch television, view billboard posters, and read magazines. Because so many advertisements are directed at children, it is essential that they learn to judge their claims critically. For example, do the sports shoes being advertised actually help you to run faster? Will a certain breakfast cereal make you a better football player? Will a certain toy make you more popular?

Children need to learn how to be critical consumers of advertisements (Rudasill, 1986; Tutolo, 1981). Advertisers use appeals to reason, character, and emotion, just as writers of other types of persuasive language do, to promote products, ideas, and services. However, advertisers may also use propaganda as they attempt to influence our beliefs and actions.

Two types of advertisements that elementary students can examine and compose are print advertisements and commercials. Students read print advertisements in magazines, as posters on bulletin boards, and as billboards. They view commercials on television and listen to them on radio.

Final Copy

Dear Uncle Bobby,

Please listen to me. I wish you would stop smoking. If you don't stop smoking, you will get sick and you might die. You could get heart damage and that means you might die. I don't want you to die.

There is a disease called emphysema. If you smoke long enough, you will get it. Then if you try to walk a mile, it would seem like you walked fifty miles. Emphysema is a deadly disease.

When I hang around you and you smoke it is hurting my health as well as yours. You're polluting the air in your own house. That means you are hurting your own family.

I think smoking can kill you. If I get to be president, I will take them cigarettes and burn them. I think smoking is down right ridiculous.

If you stop smoking now, your heart will probably slow down and your lungs will be healthy again. Your whole body will shape up.

I love you Uncle Bobby and I hope you will think about what I said and stop smoking.

Love,
Lance

FIGURE 10-7, *continued*

Print Advertisements

As a part of a unit on drugs, a class of sixth graders designed posters to display in their community to warn youngsters about the dangers of drugs. In the poster presented in Figure 10-10 Steve used a logical cause-and-effect appeal to warn of the dangers of driving under the influence of alcohol or drugs. The loaded words are *gamble* and *the odds are,* and card stacking is the propaganda device used in this ad.

Students can also design lost-and-found advertisements. After reading Mercer Mayer's *Liverwurst Is Missing* (1981), fourth-grade Kyle designed the poster illustrated in Figure 10-11 to help locate Liverwurst, the baby rhinosterwurst who is missing from the circus. In the story, Liverwurst is finally found and saved from a terrible fate: becoming the world's first rhino-burger. Kyle's poster provides the important, logical-appeal information and picture typically found on lost-and-found posters and promises a reward. Liverwurst's tears in the picture add an emotional appeal.

Commercials

A small group of fifth graders created a commercial for a dating service they created called "Dream Date." In their commercial, students used testimonials and rewards as the propaganda devices. The students portrayed young women who met their hus-

Name _____   Yes   No

1. At the beginning, did you state your position or opinion   ☐   ☐
   clearly?

   Write your position here:

   _____

   _____

   _____

2. In the middle, did you present three pieces of evidence   ☐   ☐
   to support your position?

   Write your pieces of evidence here:

   1. _____

   2. _____

   3. _____

3. At the end, did you lead your readers to the conclusion?   ☐   ☐

   How did you lead them?
   ☐ Gave a personal statement.
   ☐ Made a prediction.
   ☐ Summarized the three main points.

FIGURE 10-8   *Writer's Revision Checklist for Persuasive Writing*

bands through the service and were living happily ever after. The rewards were a honeymoon for one young woman and becoming pregnant for another.

The storyboard for the "Dream Date" commercial is presented in Figure 10-12. This storyboard was developed from the script and includes camera directions in the left column, a sketch of the scene in the middle column, and the script in the right column. After completing the storyboard, students rehearse the commercial, add music and sound effects, and then present the skit. Students enjoy having their commercial videotaped so they can view it themselves.

TEACHING STUDENTS TO WRITE ADVERTISEMENTS

Students learn to write advertisements through a series of minilessons in which they investigate persuasive appeals and propaganda techniques. Then students apply what they have learned to create print advertisements or television commercials for an idea or for a product or service they have created. These writing projects can be connected to literature focus units and social studies and science theme cycles. The steps in the teaching strategy are as follows:

Name _____ Yes No

1. At the beginning, did the writer state his/her position or   ☐   ☐
   opinion clearly?

   Write the position here:

   _____

   _____

   _____

2. In the middle, did the writer present three pieces of   ☐   ☐
   evidence to support the position?

   Write the pieces of evidence here:

   1. _____

   2. _____

   3. _____

3. At the end, did the lead you to the conclusion?   ☐   ☐

   How did he/she lead you?
   ☐ Gave a personal statement.
   ☐ Made a prediction.
   ☐ Summarized the three main points.

FIGURE 10-9   *Reader's Revision Checklist for Persuasive Writing*

*Step
by
Step*

1. *Examine advertisements.*   Students look for different types of advertisements
   from television, radio, billboards, newspapers, magazines, and even T-shirts. They
   collect copies of these advertisements to examine, including television commercials that have been videotaped. Working in small groups, students examine the
   advertisements and use the following questions to detect propaganda:

   ▼ What is the speaker's purpose?
   ▼ What are the speaker's credentials?
   ▼ Is there evidence of bias?
   ▼ Does the speaker use persuasive language?
   ▼ Does the speaker make sweeping generalizations or unsupported inferences?
   ▼ Do opinions predominate the talk?
   ▼ Does the speaker use any propaganda devices?
   ▼ Do I accept the message? (Devine, 1982, pp. 41–42)

Students examine advertisements and then decide how the writer is trying to persuade them to support the idea, use the service, or purchase the product. They
can also compare the amount of text to the amount of picture space. Appeals
based on logic typically allocate more space to text than appeals based on character or emotions.

FIGURE 10-10   *A Sixth Grader's Advertisement About Drugs*

2. *Create a product or service to advertise.*   Working in small groups or individually, students create a product or service to advertise. Possible products include breakfast cereals, toys, beauty and diet products, and sports equipment. Students might create homework services and house-sitting services. They can also choose community or environmental issues to advertise.

3. *Design the advertisement.*   Students design a print advertisement on a poster using art and text to present the message or write a script for a commercial. As they create their rough drafts of the advertisement, students use specific types of persuasive language and propaganda devices to sell their idea, product, or service. They choose the type or types of persuasion that are most effective for the audience they want to reach.

4. *Use the writing process to refine and polish the advertisement.*   Students complete the writing process by meeting in writing groups to refine their advertisements. Writing-group members focus their compliments on the use of persuasive language and propaganda devices in the advertisement. Their suggestions should deal with the most effective ways to sell the idea, product, or service. Writers should also be prepared to tell writing-group members which propaganda techniques they used and why. Students should take special care to edit print advertisements before making the final copy. For commercials, less attention is placed on editing because students will present the commercial as a skit. Instead, students will develop a storyboard in which they coordinate camera and stage directions with the script (see Figure 10-12).

FIGURE 10-11   *A Fourth Grader's Lost-and-Found Poster*

FIGURE 10-12 *Fifth Graders' "Dream Date" Commercial*

5. *Present the advertisement.* Students share their advertisements with an appropriate audience. The ads students develop can be shared with classmates and with students in other classes. They can display poster advertisements related to community and environmental issues around the community. Students can also share commercials through live presentations and videotaped presentations with classmates and students in other classes.

6. *Critique the use of persuasion and propaganda.* As a last step, students assess their advertisements. In their critiques, they list the persuasive techniques and propaganda devices used in their print ads, and for commercials they explain the techniques they used in the production.

Assessing Students' Advertisements

Teachers assess students' advertisements according to the process that students use in creating the ads. Students should be able to identify and explain why they used particular persuasive techniques and propaganda devices. The steps in the process are subdivided into specific activities, and a checklist for assessing students' advertisements is presented in Figure 10-13. Two columns are included on the right side

Checklist for Assessing Students' Advertisements	Student's Check	Teacher's Check
Name _____		
1. Student examines advertisements and detects propaganda.	☐	☐
2. Student creates a product or service to advertise.	☐	☐
3. Student designs a print advertisement on a chart, using art and text to present the message.	☐	☐
4. Student meets in a writing group to share the advertisement.	☐	☐
5. Student revises the ad and makes at least one change.	☐	☐
6. Student and a partner edit the advertisement.	☐	☐
7. Student meets with the teacher for a final editing.	☐	☐
8. Student prepares a final copy of the advertisement.	☐	☐
9. Student shares the advertisement with an appropriate audience.	☐	☐
10. Student critiques the use of persuasion and propaganda in the advertisement.	☐	☐

FIGURE 10-13 A Checklist for Assessing Students' Advertisements

of the checklist, one for students to track their progress and one for the teacher to use. As with other types of process assessment checklists, students should receive a copy of the checklist *before* beginning the advertisement project. In this way, students understand how they will be assessed and can monitor their own progress. The checklist can be easily adapted for commercials.

Answering Teachers' Questions About...
Persuasive Writing

1. *You must be kidding. My primary graders can't write persuasively.*

Even kindergartners and first graders use persuasion in their everyday talk. With guidance and encouragement, they can use the same kinds of persuasion in their writing. The Mother's Day letters that Mrs. Carson's first graders wrote (see Figure 10-1) are a good example of the kind of persuasive writing primary grade students can do.

2. *I'm confused. What's the difference between persuasion and propaganda?*

That's a good question. People use both persuasion and propaganda to influence someone to do or believe something. In both, people use appeals to reason, character, and feelings. The difference is that propagandists may use deceptive language and propaganda devices that distort, conceal, or exaggerate. The line between persuasion and propaganda is thin. Because it is so easy to cross back and forth between the two, children must learn to detect propaganda in order not to be swayed by it. One of the best ways for children to learn this is through writing persuasive essays and advertisements themselves.

3. *Writing advertisements seems awfully time-consuming.*

Yes, it does take time to teach students about persuasive language and propaganda devices. It also takes time for students to invent products or services and write ads or commercials. However, these activities teach students so much about oral and written language and consumer issues that I believe it is worth the time. As students are examining ads, they use critical thinking skills and learn to be more careful consumers as well as to read and write.

4. *Can I tie persuasive writing to content areas?*

Yes, students can write persuasively about topics they are learning in science and social studies. For example they can argue about historical events and even about contributions of various historical figures. They can investigate current issues about quotas for immigrants, English as the official language of the United States, or the rights of Native Americans. They can clarify positions on scientific concepts and consider topical issues such as nuclear energy, acid rain, pollution, and conservation efforts.

REFERENCES

Applebee, A. N., Langer, J. A., & Mullis, I. V. (1986). *The writing report card: Writing achievement in American Schools.* Princeton, NJ: Educational Testing Service.

Cohen, B. (1983). *Molly's pilgrim.* New York: Lothrop, Lee & Shepard.

Crowhurst, M. (1991). Interrelationships between reading and writing persuasive discourse. *Research in the teaching of English, 25,* 314–338.

Crowhurst, M., & Piché, G. L. (1979). Audience and mode of discourse effects on syntactic complexity in writing at two grade levels. *Research in the Teaching of English, 13,* 101–109.

de Paola, T. (1979). *Oliver Button is a Sissy.* New York: Harcourt Brace Jovanovich.

Devine, T. G. (1982). *Listening skills schoolwide: Activities and programs.* Urbana, IL: ERIC Clearinghouse on Reading and Communication Skills and the National Council of Teachers of English.

Hidi, S., & Hildyard, A. (1983). The comparison of oral and written productions in two discourse modes. *Discourse Processes, 6,* 91–105.

Kroll, B. M. (1978). Cognitive egocentrism and the problem of audience awareness in written discourse. *Research in the Teaching of English, 12,* 269–281.

Kroll, B. M. (1984). Audience adaption in children's persuasive letters. *Written Communication, 1,* 407–427.

Lutz, W. (1984). Notes toward a description of doublespeak. *Quarterly Review of Doublespeak, 10,* 1–2.

Lutz, W. (n.d.). *Some examples of doublespeak.* Unpublished manuscript. National Council of Teachers of English Committee on Public Doublespeak.

Mayer, M. (1981). *Liverwurst is missing.* New York: Four Winds Press.

Rubin, D. L., & Piché, G. L. (1979). Development in syntactic and strategic aspects of audience adaption skills in written persuasive communication. *Research in the Teaching of English, 13,* 293–316.

Rudasill, L. (1986). Advertising gimmicks: Teaching critical thinking. In J. Golub (Ed.), *Activities to promote critical thinking* (pp. 127–129). Urbana, IL: National Council of Teachers of English.

Tutolo, D. (1981). Critical listening/reading of advertisements. *Language Arts, 58,* 679–683.

Wagner, B. J. (1986). The effects of role-playing on written persuasion: An age and channel comparison of fourth and eighth graders. Unpublished doctoral dissertation, University of Illinois at Chicago. (University Microfilms No. 8705196).

Wilkinson, A., Barnsley, G., Hanna, P., & Swan, M. (1980). *Assessing language development.* Oxford: Oxford University Press.

Zolotow, C. (1972). *William's doll.* New York: Harper & Row.

11

Writers' Tools

Learning to Proofread

Fourth-grade Stephanie pulls her chair over to Danielle's desk, and they trade rough drafts of their pen pal letters. A copy of Stephanie's letter with the spelling errors corrected appears in Figure 11-1. Each girl reads through the draft, checking for spelling errors. They point at each word with a green pen and pronounce the word softly, using pronunciation as an aid to spelling whenever they can. Danielle circles the word *anser* on Stephanie's letter because she thinks it might be misspelled. She mumbles that it just doesn't look right. Then they continue reading.

When they finish reading their two-page letters, each girl has circled 5 to 10 words. They share their findings with each other, agree or disagree about misspellings, write known correct spellings above circled spelling words. Then they ask Katrina, who happens to walk by Danielle's desk, for advice about spelling several remaining words. She can't help with these words, but she does note one other spell-

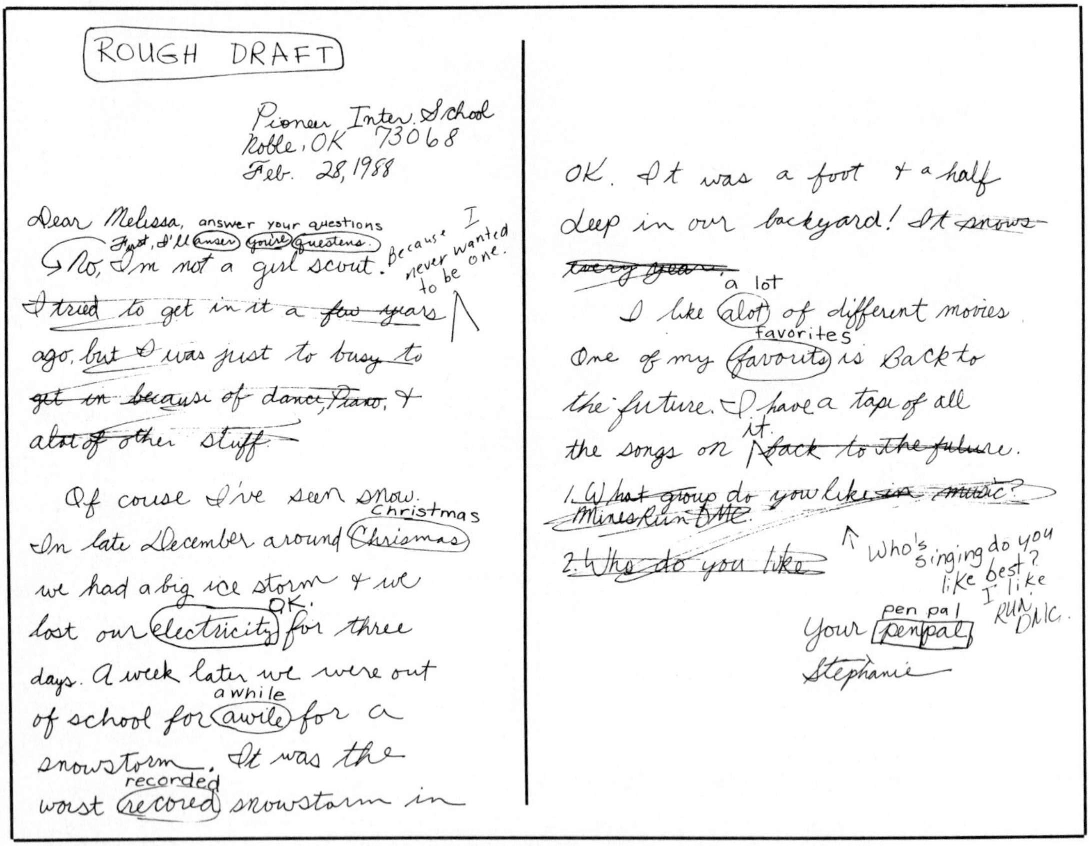

FIGURE 11-1   The Rough Draft of a Fourth Grader's Pen Pal Letter

	Author	Editor
1. I have circled misspelled words.	☐	☐
2. I have checked for these spelling monsters:	☐	☐

    ☐ friend
    ☐ school
    ☐ their-there-they're
    ☐ a lot

| 3. I have checked that proper nouns and adjectives begin with capital letters. | ☐ | ☐ |

    Pioneer *Intermediate* S*chool*
    American flag

| 4. I have added commas to separate items in a series. | ☐ | ☐ |
| 5. I have checked for the friendly letter format: | ☐ | ☐ |

    ☐ return address
    ☐ date
    ☐ greeting
    ☐ closing

Signatures: _____   _____
         Author   Editor

FIGURE 11-2 *An Editing Checklist for a Pen Pal Letter*

ing error she sees on Danielle's paper. Finally they resort to the dictionary to locate the correct spelling for *colet* (*collect*), *awile* (*awhile*), *Chrismas* (*Christmas*), *achemet* (*achievement*), and *favorit* (*favorite*), words that neither girl is sure how to spell. Then they add a checkmark to the spelling box in the editor's column on their editing checklists.

This editing checklist has a second spelling requirement. A copy of the editing checklist is in Figure 11-2. The girls are to reread the pen pal letters checking specifically for the following words that their teacher, Mrs. Jacks, has noticed were used and frequently misspelled in their previous pen pal letters. Her students check specifically for these words and correct them if they are misspelled. The words are: *friend, school, their-there-they're,* and *a lot.* They find *a lot* spelled as one word in Stephanie's letter, and they make the correction. None of these words are misspelled in Danielle's letter.

Tomorrow the girls will finish checking for punctuation, capitalization, and friendly letter format errors, which are the remaining three categories included on their editing checklists. For today, the rough drafts are returned to their writing folders.

S tudents should understand that spelling is merely a tool for writers, a tool that allows writers to communicate effectively and efficiently with readers. Donald Graves (1983) explains:

> Spelling is for writing. Children may achieve high scores on phonic inventories, or weekly spelling tests. But the ultimate test is what the child does under "game" conditions, within the process of moving toward meaning. (pp. 193–194)

This chapter focuses on four writers' tools: spelling, grammar, handwriting, and microcomputers. Like spelling words correctly, using good grammar and legible handwriting is a courtesy to readers, and writers must attend to these features of their writing in the revising, editing, and sharing stages of the writing process. They are important when the writing will be made public; they are of far less concern when the writing is private, for the writer alone.

In contrast to the other writers' tools, microcomputers are mechanical tools. As microcomputers become familiar tools in elementary classrooms, children will find that writing, revising, and editing are simplified through word processing software. Each writing tool is discussed separately, and suggestions are offered about teaching the use of the tool in conjunction with writing activities.

SPELLING

The alphabetic principle suggests that there should be a one-to-one correspondence between graphemes (the letters) and phonemes (the sounds) such that each letter consistently represents one sound. English does not have this correspondence. Twenty-six letters, used singly or in combination, represent approximately 44 phonemes. Moreover, three letters—*c, q,* and *x*—are superfluous because they do not represent unique phonemes. The letter *c,* for instance, can be used either to represent /k/ as in *cat* or /s/ as in *decide.* The letter *c* can also be combined with *h* to represent the digraph /ch/. To further complicate the situation, there are more than 500 spellings (and perhaps as many as 2,000) to represent these 44 phonemes. For example, the long *e,* according to Ernest Horn (1957), is spelled 14 ways in English words! This situation is known as a "lack of fit." A list of common spelling options for long *e* and other phonemes is presented in Figure 11-3.

The reasons for this lack of fit can be found by examining events in the history of the English language. Approximately 75% of English words have been borrowed from other languages, and many of these words, especially the more recently acquired words (e.g., *cul-de-sac,* which was borrowed from French in the early 1700s and literally means "bottom of a sack"), have retained their native spellings. The spellings of other words have been tinkered with by linguists. More than 400 years ago, for instance, in an effort to relate the word *island* to its supposed French or Latin origin, the unnecessary and unpronounced *s* was added. However, *island* (spelled *ilond* in the Middle Ages) is a native English word, and the current spelling sends a false message about the word's etymology.

The controversy about whether English is a phonetic language has been waged for years, and will not likely be settled soon. Yet, the fact remains that spelling is a problem for many children. Because of the lack of fit between phonemes and graphemes, it is unlikely that children will learn to spell simply by sounding out words, even though that is the strategy that they are often advised to use by well-meaning teachers and parents. Instead, it is necessary to examine how children actually learn to spell and how their spelling development relates to writing.

Invented Spelling

Charles Read (1971, 1975, 1986) studied preschoolers' efforts to spell words and found that they used their knowledge of the alphabet and the English spelling system to invent spellings for words. These children used letter names to spell words, such as *U* (*you*), *ME* (*me*), and *R* (*are*), and they used consonant sounds rather consistently: *GRL* (*girl*), *TIGR* (*tiger*), and *NIT* (*night*). The preschoolers used several unusual but phonetically based spelling patterns to represent affricates. They spelled *tr* with *chr* (e.g., *CHRIBLES* for *troubles*), spelled *dr* with *jr* (e.g., *JRAGIN* for *dragon*) and substituted *d* for *t* (e.g., *PREDE* for *pretty*). Words with long vowels were spelled using letter names: *MI* (*my*), *LADE* (*lady*), and *FEL* (*feel*). The children used several ingenious strategies to spell words with short vowels. These 3-, 4-, and 5-year-olds rather consistently selected letters to represent short vowels on the basis of place of articulation in the mouth. Short *i* was represented with *e* as in *FES* (*fish*), short *e* with *a* as in *LAFFT* (*left*), and short *o* with *i* as in *CLIK* (*clock*). Although these spellings may seem odd to adults, they are based on phonetic relationships. The children often omitted nasals within words (e.g., *ED* for *end*) and substituted *-eg* or *-ig* for *-ing* (e.g., *CUMIG* for *coming* and *GOWEG* for *going*). Also they often ignored the vowel in unaccented syllables as illustrated in *AFTR* (*after*) and *MUTHR* (*mother*).

These children developed strategies for their spellings based on their knowledge of phonology, their knowledge of letter names, their judgments of phonetic similarities and differences, and their ability to abstract phonetic information from letter names. Read suggested that from among the many components in the phonological system, children abstract out certain phonetic details and preserve other phonetic details in their invented spellings.

Based on Charles Read's seminal work, other researchers began to systematically study the development of young children's spelling abilities. Henderson and his colleagues (Beers & Henderson, 1977; Gentry, 1978, 1981; Templeton, 1979; Zutell, 1979) have studied the manner in which children proceed developmentally from invented spelling to correct spelling.

Researchers have found that not all children do invent spellings in exactly the same way or at the same speed, but they do develop spelling strategies in roughly the same sequence (Henderson, 1980a). The five stages that children move through as they become conventional spellers are (a) precommunicative spelling, (b) semiphonetic spelling, (c) phonetic spelling, (d) transitional spelling, and (e) conventional spelling (Gentry, 1978, 1981, 1982a, 1982b). The characteristics of each of the five stages of invented spelling are summarized in Figure 11-4.

FIGURE 11-3   *Common Spelling Options for Phonemes*

Source: "Common Spelling Options" by E. Horn, 1957, *Elementary School Journal, 57,* pp. 426–428. Copyright 1957 by The University of Chicago Press. Reprinted by permission.

Sound	Spellings	Examples	Sound	Spellings	Examples
ā	a-e	date	l	l	last
	a	angel		ll	allow
	ai	aid		le	automobile
	ay	day	m	m	man
ch	ch	church		me	come
	t(u)	picture		mm	comment
	tch	watch	n	n	no
	ti	question		ne	done
ē	ea	each	ng	ng	thing
	ee	feel		n	bank, anger
	e	evil	ō	o	go
	e-e	these		o-e	note
	ea-e	breathe		ow	own
ĕ	e	end		oa	load
	ea	head	ô	o	office
f	f	feel		a	all
	ff	sheriff		au	author
	ph	photograph		aw	saw
j	ge	strange	oi	oi	oil
	g	general		oy	boy
	j	job	o͞o	oo	book
	dge	bridge		u	put
k	c	call		ou	could
	k	keep		o	woman
	x	expect, luxury			
	ck	black			
	qu	quite, bouquet			

Stage 1: Precommunicative Spelling.   In this stage, children string scribbles, letters, and letterlike forms together, but they do not associate the marks they make with any specific phonemes. Precommunicative spelling represents children's natural, early expression of the alphabet and other concepts about writing. They may write from left to right, right to left, top to bottom, or randomly across the page. Some precommunicative spellers have a large repertoire of letter forms to use in writing, while others repeat a small number of letters over and over. Children may use both upper- and lowercase letters, but they show a distinct preference for uppercase letters. At this stage, children have not discovered the alphabetic principle—that graphemes represent phonemes in words. This stage is typical of preschoolers, ages 3 through 5.

FIGURE 11-3, *continued*

Sound	Spellings	Examples	Sound	Spellings	Examples
$\overline{oo}$	u	cruel	y	u	union
	oo	noon		u-e	use
	u-e	rule		y	yes
	o-e	lose		i	onion
	ue	blue		ue	value
	o	to		ew	few
	ou	group	z	s	present
ou	ou	out		se	applause
	ow	cow		ze	gauze
s	s	sick	syllabic *l*	le	able
	ce	office		al	animal
	c	city		el	cancel
	ss	class		il	civil
	se	else	syllabic *n*	en	written
	x(ks)	box		on	lesson
sh	ti	attention		an	important
	sh	she		in	cousin
	ci	ancient		contractions	didn't
	ssi	admission		ain	certain
t	t	teacher	stressed	er	her
	te	definite	syllabic *r*	ur	church
	ed	furnished		ir	first
	tt	attend		or	world
ŭ	u	ugly		ear	heard
	o	company		our	courage
	ou	country	unstressed	er	better
ū	u	union	syllabic *r*	or	favor
	u-e	use		ure	picture
	ue	value		ar	dollar
	ew	few			

Stage 2: Semiphonetic Spelling. At this stage, children begin to represent some phonemes in words with the correct graphemes, indicating that they are acquiring a rudimentary understanding of the alphabetic principle, that a link exists between letters and sounds. The spellings are very abbreviated, often using only one, two, or three letters to represent an entire word. Examples of stage 2 spelling include: *ET* (*eat*), *KLZ* (*closed*), and *LF* (*laugh*). As these examples illustrate, semiphonetic spellers use a letter-name strategy to determine which letters to use in spelling a word, and their spellings represent some sound features of words while ignoring other equally important features. Semiphonetic spellers include 5- and 6-year-old children.

FIGURE 11-4   *Characteristics of the Invented Spelling Stages*
Adapted from Gentry, 1982a, pp. 192–200.

Stage 1: Precommunicative Spelling

Uses scribbles, letterlike forms, letters, and sometimes numbers to represent a message.

Writes from left to right, right to left, top to bottom, or randomly on the page.

Shows no understanding of phoneme-grapheme correspondence.

Repeats a few letters again and again or uses most of the letters of the alphabet.

Mixes upper- and lowercase letters but shows a preference for uppercase letters.

Stage 2: Semiphonetic Spelling

Becomes aware of the alphabetic principle that letters are used to represent sounds.

Uses abbreviated one-, two-, or three-letter spellings to represent an entire word.

Uses letter-name strategy to spell words.

Stage 3: Phonetic Spelling

Represents all essential sound features of a word in spelling.

Develops particular spellings for long and short vowels, plural and past tense markers, and other aspects of spelling.

Chooses letters on the basis of sound without regard for English letter sequences or other conventions.

Stage 3: Phonetic Spelling.   In this stage, children's understanding of the alphabetic principle is further refined. They continue to use letter names to represent sounds, but they also use consonant and short vowel sounds. Examples of stage 3 spelling include: *LIV* (*live*), *DRAS* (*dress*), and *PEKT* (*peeked*). As these examples show, children choose letter on the basis of sound alone without considering acceptable English letter sequences (e.g., using *-T* rather than *-ed* as a past tense marker in *peeked*) or other spelling conventions. These spellings do not resemble English words, and although children's spelling in this stage does not look like adult spelling, it usually can be deciphered. The major achievement of this stage is that for the first time children represent all essential sound features in the words being spelled. Henderson (1980b) explains that words are "bewilderingly homographic" at this stage because children spell on the basis of sound alone. For example, *bat, bet,* and *bait* might all be spelled *BAT* at this stage (Read, 1971). Phonetic spellers are typically 6-year-old children.

Stage 4: Transitional Spelling.   Transitional spellers come close to the conventional spellings of English words. They spell many words correctly, but words with

FIGURE 11-4, *continued*

Stage 4: Transitional Spelling

Adheres to basic conventions of English orthography.

Begins to use morphological and visual information in addition to phonetic information.

May include all appropriate letters in a word but reverse some of them.

Uses alternate spellings for the same sound in different words, but only partially understands the conditions governing their use.

Spells many words correctly.

Stage 5: Conventional Spelling

Applies the basic rules of the English orthographic system.

Extends knowledge of word structure including the spelling of affixes, contractions, compound words, and homonyms.

Demonstrates growing accuracy in using silent consonants and doubling consonants before adding suffixes.

Recognizes when a word doesn't "look right" and can consider alternate spellings for the same sound.

Learns irregular spelling patterns.

Learns consonant and vowel alternations and other morphological structures.

Spells most words correctly.

---

irregular spellings continue to be misspelled. Examples of stage four spelling include *HUOSE* (*house*), *TRUBAL* (*trouble*), *EAGEL* (*eagle*), and *AFTERNEWN* (*afternoon*). This stage is characterized by children's increased ability to represent the features of English orthography. They have internalized information about spelling patterns and the underlying rules of English spelling. First, they include a vowel in every syllable as the *trouble* and *eagle* spellings show. Next, they demonstrate knowledge of vowel patterns even though they might make a faulty decision about which marker to use. For example, *toad* is often spelled *TODE* when children choose the wrong vowel marker or *TAOD* when the two vowels are reversed. Also, transitional spellers use common letter patterns in their spelling, such as *YOUNIGHTED* for *united* and *HIGHCKED* for *hiked*. In this stage, children use conventional alternatives for representing sounds, and, although they continue to misspell words according to adult standards, transitional spelling is closer to adult spelling. It resembles English orthography and can easily be read. As the preceding examples show, children stop relying entirely on phonological information and begin to use visual clues and morphological (word parts) information as well. Morphological information includes knowledge about plurals, possessives, past tense, and compounding. Transitional spellers generally include 7- and 8-year-old children.

Stage 5: Conventional Spelling.   As the name implies, children spell many, many words conventionally at this stage, but not all words. Children have mastered the basic principles of English orthography, and this achievement indicates their preparation for formal spelling instruction (Gentry, 1981, 1982a). Children typically reach this stage and are ready for formal spelling instruction at age 8 or 9. During the next four or five years, they learn to control homonyms (e.g., *road/rode*), contractions, consonant doubling and adding affixes (e.g., *runing/running*), and vowel and consonant alternations (e.g., *nation/national*). They also learn to spell most common irregularly spelled words and become familiar with spelling alternatives, or different ways to spell the same sound.

Researchers are continuing to study children's spelling development beyond age 8. Much of the research has focused on the relationship between reading and spelling (Anderson, 1985). Researchers examined the spelling strategies that poor readers in fourth through sixth grade used and found that these students were likely to use a sounding-out strategy. Good readers used a variety of spelling strategies, including using visual information, knowledge about root words and affixes, and analogy to known words, in spelling (Barron, 1980; Marsh, Friedman, Desberg, & Welsh, 1980). Uta Firth (1980) concluded that older students who are good readers and spellers make spelling errors that are characteristic of the transitional stage, while students who are poor readers and spellers make spelling errors that are characteristic of the semiphonetic and phonetic stages. With further research, it seems reasonable that several additional stages will be identified to more accurately describe children's spelling development through eighth grade.

Children's movement through these stages depends on immersion in a written language environment with daily opportunities to read and write. Also, teachers should deemphasize conventional spelling during this period and be tolerant of children's invented spelling, even celebrating students' nonstandard spellings. By analyzing spelling errors, teachers can determine when children have reached the fifth stage and are ready for formal spelling instruction.

Analyzing Children's Spelling Errors

Teachers can analyze the spelling errors in children's compositions by classifying the errors according to the five stages of spelling development. This analysis will provide information about the student's current level of spelling development and the kinds of spelling errors that child makes. Also, knowing the stage of a student's spelling development will suggest an appropriate type of spelling instruction. Children who are not yet at the stage of conventional spelling—that is, students who do not spell approximately 90% of spelling words correctly and whose errors are not mostly at the transitional level—do not benefit from formal spelling instruction. Early instruction interferes with spelling development because children move from phonetic spelling to memorizing spelling words without learning visual and morphological strategies.

A composition written by Marc, a first grader, is presented in Figure 11-5. Note that he reverses *b* and *s* and these two reversals make his writing more difficult to decipher. Here's a translation of Marc's composition:

To bay a porezun at
home kob uz anb seb
that a bome wuz in
or skuwl anb mab
uz go at zid anb
mak be uz wat a haf
uf a awr anb it mad
uz wazt or time on
lorenee ing. the enb.

FIGURE 11-5 *A First Grader's Composition Using Invented Spelling*

▽ *Today a person at home called us and said that a bomb was in our school and made us go outside and made us wait a half of an hour and it made us waste our time on learning. The end.*

Marc was writing about a traumatic event, and it was appropriate that he used invented spelling in his composition. Primary grade students need to feel free to write using invented spelling, and correct spelling needs to be added only if the composition will "go public" or if for some specific reason "adult" spelling is needed. Differentiating between "child" and "adult" spelling prematurely interferes with children's natural spelling development and makes children dependent on adults to supply correct spelling.

The words in students' writing can be categorized using a chart, as illustrated in Figure 11-6, to gauge students' stage of spelling development and to anticipate upcoming changes in their spelling strategies. On the chart, write the stages of spelling development across the top and list each word in the student's composition under one of the categories, ignoring proper nouns, capitalization errors, and poorly formed or reversed letters. Because a quick review of Marc's writing revealed no precommunicative spellings, this category was not included in the analysis.

Perhaps the most interesting thing about Marc's writing is that he spelled 56% of the words correctly. Only one word *kod* (*called*) is categorized as semiphonetic, and

FIGURE 11-6   *An Analysis of a First Grader's Invented Spelling*

	Semiphonetic	Phonetic	Transitional	Conventional
	kod	sed	poresun	today
		wus	bome	a
		or	skuwl	at
		mad	makde	home
		at sid	loreneeing	us
		wat		and
		haf		that
		uf		a
		awr		in
		mad		and
		wast		us
		or		go
				and
				us
				a
				a
				and
				it
				us
				time
				on
				the
				end
Total Words	1	12	5	23
Percent	3	29	12	56

it was classified this way because the spelling is very abbreviated, with only the first and last sounds represented. The 12 words that were categorized as phonetic are words in which it appears his spelling represents only the sounds heard. Unpronounced letters, such as the final *e* in *made* and the *i* in *wait,* are not represented in the spelling. Marc pronounces *our* as though it were a homophone for *or,* so *or* is a reasonable phonetic spelling. Homophone errors are phonological because the child focuses on sound, not meaning.

The words categorized as transitional illustrate the use of some type of spelling strategy other than sound. In *BOME* (*bomb*), for example, Marc applies the final *e* rule which he recently learned even though it isn't appropriate in this word. In time he will learn to spell the word with an unpronounced *b* and that this *b* is needed because the word *bomb* is a newer, shortened form of *bombard* in which the *b* in the middle of the word is pronounced. The *b* remains in *bomb* to show the etymology of the word. The word *MAKDE* is especially interesting. Marc pronounced the word *maked,* and the *DE* is a reversal of letters, a common characteristic of transitional spelling. Transitional spellers often spell *girl* as *gril* and *friend* as *freind.* That *made,* not *maked,* is the past tense of *make* is a grammatical error and unimportant in determining the stage of spelling development. *LORENEEING* (*learning*) is categorized as transitional because Marc added long vowel markers (an *e* after *lor* and *ee* after *n*). Since the spelling is based on his pronunciation of *learning,* the long vowel markers and the correct spelling of the suffix *-ing* signal a transitional spelling. Categorizing spelling errors in a child's composition and computing the percentage of errors in each category is a useful tool for diagnosing the child's level of spelling development and readiness for spelling instruction. From the spelling in Marc's composition, he might be classified as a phonetic speller who is moving toward the transitional stage. Marc's composition in Figure 11-5 was written in January of his first-grade year, and he is making expected progress in spelling. During the next few months, he will begin to notice that his spelling doesn't look right (e.g., *SED* for *said, UF* for *of*) and will note visual features of words. He will apply the vowel rules he is learning more effectively, particularly the final *e* (*MAD* will become *made, SID* will become *side,* and *WAST* will become *waste*).

Marc is not ready for formal spelling instruction in which he memorizes the correct spelling of words because he has not yet internalized the visual and morphological spelling strategies of the transitional stage. Also, Marc will probably self-correct the two letter reversals through daily writing experiences and as long as he is not placed under great pressure to form the letters correctly.

Teaching Spelling Using Writing Errors

Spelling is a writer's tool, and it is best learned through writing. Students who write daily and are encouraged in kindergarten and first grade to use invented spellings will move naturally toward correct spelling. As they begin to write, children guess at how words are spelled using their knowledge of letter names and sounds. Clarke (1988) found that first graders who used invented spelling as they wrote were better spellers than other students who were encouraged to spell words correctly as they wrote. Through reading and writing, they gradually recognize that the words they are reading and writing are spelled the same way each time. When students recognize that words have consistent spellings, they are ready to be helped in a direct way. Teachers begin to point out the conventions of the spelling system, but children continue to develop their basic knowledge about English orthography through writing, not through weekly spelling tests.

Many teachers are questioning whether formal spelling instruction is necessary in holistic classrooms where students read and write every day. Teachers report that their students learn to spell more quickly without the interruption of weekly spelling tests. Moreover, students do not always learn to spell words through the weekly study-test format. Many of us remember memorizing a list of spelling words only to forget them the day after taking the test. Instead of giving lists of spelling words and weekly tests, these teachers are teaching minilessons about spelling strategies and skills, showing students how to proofread to identify spelling errors in their compositions, and helping each student focus attention on commonly misspelled words.

Formal spelling instruction, if it is used, should begin when children reach the conventional stage of spelling development, not at a particular grade level. Some students may be ready in second grade and others not until the third or fourth grade, or even later. Guidelines for teaching spelling from students' writing follow.

Choosing Spelling Words.   Once children move from transitional spelling to conventional spelling, they are ready for formal spelling instruction. Children's spelling words should come from their writing because these are the words that they want and need to be able to spell. A master list of these words can be compiled from several sources. Teachers can keep a list of words that have been misspelled in students' rough drafts, words that students ask how to spell, and words related to literature focus units and theme studies. Also, students can suggest words that they want to learn to spell.

Taking a Pretest to Identify Spelling Words.   Students take a pretest in which they attempt to spell the words on the master list. Then from their misspelled words, they identify approximately 10 words to learn that week. Children take responsibility for accurately evaluating their own pretests, identifying the words they will study, and then making two lists of these identified words, one for themselves and one for the teacher to keep on file. Students who do not miss many words on the pretest can select other words to learn or not participate in spelling activities that week.

Practice Activities.   Students don't need a wide variety of fill-in-the-blank or put-your-spelling-words-in-sentences activities to learn to spell words. Instead, they use a simple approach to practicing words that takes only about 5 minutes a day. Time saved by this approach can be devoted to more meaningful reading and writing activities. These are the steps in the strategy:

1. Look at the word and say it.
2. Read each letter in the word.
3. Close your eyes and spell the word to yourself.
4. Look at the word. Did you spell it correctly?
5. Copy the word from your list.
6. Cover the word and write it again.
7. Look at the word. Did you write it correctly?
8. If you made any mistakes, repeat the steps. (Cook, Esposito, Gabrielson, & Turner, 1984, p. 1)

This is the only type of practice activity that is necessary. No busy-work activities are needed, such as writing spelling words in sentences or identifying the opposites or rhyming partners of the spelling words.

Final Test.   After several days of practice, students take a final test in which words are dictated and spelled. Students should not write the word in dictated sentences because this is a spelling test, not a secretary's dictation test. The teacher can read the entire spelling list and students write only the words they studied, or students can divide into pairs and test each other using the copy of their spelling words given to the teacher previously. If the teacher reads the entire spelling list aloud, students need to prepare in advance by identifying the numbers of their personal spelling words so that they will spell their own words rather than the entire list. Any words that the students misspell should become a part of their spelling list for the following week.

The Spelling-Writing Connection

Elementary students make spelling errors in their writing because of the English orthographic system. Sometimes these errors need to be corrected; sometimes they do not. When children are writing informally in journals, as in a prewriting activity, or writing their rough drafts, invented spellings and other spelling errors should be ignored. Similarly, young children's invented spellings should not be corrected. However, when students want to make their compositions public, conventional spelling is a courtesy to readers. Through a process approach to writing, students who are planning to make their compositions public, as Stephanie and Danielle will with their pen pal letters, use the editing stage of the writing process to identify and correct misspelled words.

In addition to dealing with spelling errors in the editing stage of the writing process, there are three other components in the spelling-writing connection: learning to use a dictionary, keeping spelling logs, and developing a spelling conscience.

Learning to Use a Dictionary. While it is relatively easy to find a known word in the dictionary, it is much harder to locate an unfamiliar word, and students need to learn what to do when they do not know how to spell a word. They should consider spelling options and predict possible spellings for unknown words and then check their predicted spellings by consulting a dictionary. This strategy involves six steps:

1. Identify root words and affixes.
2. Consider related words (e.g., *medicine/medical*).
3. Determine the sounds in the word.
4. Generate a list of spelling options for each sound.
5. Select the most likely alternative.
6. Consult a dictionary to check the correct spelling.

The fourth step is undoubtedly the most difficult one in the strategy. Using both their knowledge of phonology and morphology, students develop a list of possible spellings. For some words, phoneme-grapheme relationships may rate primary consideration in generating spelling options, while for others root words and affixes or related words may be more important in determining how the word is spelled.

Keeping a Spelling Log. One strategy for helping upper-grade students deal with their spelling errors is a spelling log (VanDeWeghe, 1982). Students keep a personal spelling notebook in which they list their misspellings and the correct spellings. They also consider why the spelling confuses them and design a mnemonic device to remember the correct spelling of the word. A sample spelling log is presented in Figure 11-7.

This strategy is important because researchers have found that words rarely have only one possible misspelling. Instead, many words have a number of trouble spots, and what is a trouble spot for one student may not be for another. Therefore, students must analyze their own spelling errors and design their own mnemonic devices. While this is a strategy that many good spellers use intuitively, formalizing the strategy will help less strongly motivated students.

Developing a Spelling Conscience.   Spelling involves more than just learning to spell specific words, whether they are drawn from children's writing or from words listed in spelling textbooks. Robert Hillerich (1977) believes that students need to develop a spelling conscience, or a positive attitude toward spelling and a concern for using standard spelling. He lists two dimensions of a spelling conscience: understanding that standard spelling is a courtesy to readers and developing the ability to proofread to spot and correct misspellings.

Students in the middle and upper grades need to learn that it is unrealistic to expect readers to decipher numerous misspelled words as they read a piece of writing. This first dimension, understanding that standard spelling is a courtesy to readers, develops as students write frequently and for varied audiences. By writing for a variety of audiences, students acquire a concept of audience and realize that there are readers to read their writing. As students move from writing for themselves to writing that communicates, they internalize this concept. Teachers help students to recognize the purpose of standard spelling by providing meaningful writing activities directed to a variety of genuine audiences.

FIGURE 11-7 *An Upper Grade Student's Spelling Log*
Source: VanDeWeghe, 1982, p. 102.

My Spelling Log			
Correct Spelling	My Misspelling	Why the Word Confuses Me	Helps to Remember the Correct Spelling
demonstrate	demenstrate	I use *e* instead of *o*.	A demo is used to demonstrate.
coarse	course	I get it mixed up with course as a class.	*a* = coarse is hard.
meant	ment	I spell it like I think it sounds.	It's the past of *mean*.

The second dimension, proofreading for spelling errors, is an essential part of the writing process. As discussed in Chapter 1, proofreading is part of the editing stage, and it should be introduced in kindergarten and first grade rather than postponing it until the middle grades. Young children and their teachers can proofread class collaboration stories together, and students can be encouraged to read over their own compositions and make necessary changes as soon as they begin writing. With this beginning, students will accept proofreading as a natural part of both spelling and writing, and together with their growing awareness of audience, students will appreciate the importance of proofreading to correct misspellings and other mechanical errors.

GRAMMAR AND USAGE

▽   *Me and him brung them two little kittens home.*

Nothing don't scare that monster.

George Washington who was the first president.

Then my mom and dad done got divorced.

He cry but he say, "I ain't hurt."

Elvis Presley was a real good singer.

These sentences were extracted from elementary students' rough drafts. Each sentence contains one or more errors; some would be categorized as grammar errors and others as usage errors. Grammar is the description of the structure of a language, and it involves principles of word and sentence formation. In contrast, usage refers to using the appropriate word in a sentence. It is the socially preferred way of using language within a dialect. Fraser and Hodson (1978) explain the distinction between grammar and usage this way: "Grammar is the rationale of language; usage is its etiquette" (p. 52).

Dealing with Grammar and Usage Errors

Teaching grammar will not help students correct usage errors. In fact, teaching either grammar or usage to elementary students will probably not eliminate these errors in their speech or writing because the concepts are abstract. Educators have recommended for many years that this type of instruction be postponed at least until junior high school when students are more likely to be able to think abstractly (Fraser & Hodson, 1978; Haley-James, 1981).

Children learn English grammar intuitively as they learn to speak. They have almost completed learning the process by the time they enter kindergarten. The purpose of grammar instruction, then, is to make this intuitive knowledge about the English language explicit and to provide labels for sentence types, parts of sentences, and words within sentences. Children speak the dialect that their parents and community members speak. This dialect, whether standard or nonstandard, is informal and differs to some degree from the written standard English that students will read and write in elementary school (Pooley, 1974).

Because children's knowledge of grammar and usage depends on language spoken in their homes and neighborhoods, some primary grade students do not recognize any difference between *me* and *him* and *he* and *I*. When this error is brought to these children's attention, they do not understand because semantically, the two versions are identical. Moreover, *me* and *him* sounds right to these students because they hear this construction at home. When other corrections are pointed out to middle- and upper-grade students, they repeat the correct form, shake their heads, and say that it doesn't sound right. *Real* sounds better to some students than *really* because it is more familiar to them. An explanation that adverbs, not adjectives, modify adjectives is not useful either, even if students have had grammar instruction. Too often the correction of usage errors is a repudiation of the language spoken in children's homes. Correction should include an explanation that written language requires a more formal language dialect or register.

A better way to correct grammar and usage errors is to use a problem-solving approach during the editing stage of the writing process. Locating and correcting errors in students' writing is not as threatening as correcting their talk because it is not as personal. During editing, students are error-hunting, trying to make their papers "optimally readable" (Smith, 1982). They recognize that it is a courtesy to readers to make their papers as correct as possible. Classmates note errors and correct each other, and teachers point out other errors. Sometimes teachers explain the correction (e.g., the past tense of *bring* is *brought,* not *brung*), and at other times they simply mark the correction, saying, "When we write, we usually write it this way." Also, some errors should be ignored, especially young children's errors. Correcting too many errors will only teach students that their language is inferior or inadequate. Guidelines for correcting students' grammar and usage errors are summarized in Figure 11-8.

Sentence-Building Activities

Students experiment with grammatical structures as they revise their writing. As students manipulate sentences by adding, deleting, substituting, and moving words within a sentence, they become more aware of the structure of sentences (Hutson, 1980). Three types of sentence-building activities that children can participate in using sentences taken from their compositions are sentence slotting, sentence expansion and sentence combining. Through sentence slotting activities, students experiment with the functions of words and phrases in a sentence. Students learn about the effect of adding modifiers through sentence expansion activities, and in sentence combining, they combine short, choppy sentences to build more complex sentences.

Sentence Slotting.   Students learn how words and phrases function in sentences when they brainstorm a list of alternatives for an ineffective word. One way to use the activity is to give students a sentence with a slot or blank, for example, "A horse _____

FIGURE 11-8   *Guidelines for Correcting Students' Grammar and Usage Errors in Compositions*

1. Use a problem-solving approach to correct grammar and usage errors.
2. Correct errors in the editing stage of the writing process.
3. Consider the function, audience, and form of the composition when determining whether to correct errors or which errors to correct.
4. Let student know that correcting grammatical and usage errors is a courtesy to readers.
5. Keep explanations for the corrections brief.
6. Sometimes simply make the change and say that "in writing it is written this way."
7. Don't ask students if the correction makes the writing "sound better."
8. Use sentence-building activities to rid the composition of lackluster and repetitious words and short, choppy sentences.
9. Ignore some errors, especially in young children's writing.
10. Respect the language of children's home and community, and introduce standard written English as "book language."

across the field." Students brainstorm words or phrases that can be used to complete the sentence. The purpose of this activity is to demonstrate the function of words in sentences.

For example, in a writing group, students are sharing dinosaur reports, and a classmate may suggest that a vivid verb is needed to replace *ate* in the sentence "The Tyrannosaurus Rex ate plant eaters." Another classmate may recognize that a writer has begun each sentence about Tyrannosaurus Rex with *he.* The writer agrees that the problem exists and asks for help in thinking of alternatives. Writing-group members suggest the following:

▽   _____ *was a meat eater.*

(He)

It

Tyrannosaurus Rex

The dinosaur

This ancient reptile

The thunder-lizard

This carnivore

The king of the dinosaurs

The writer can replace *he* with some of these alternatives to make the paragraph about Tyrannosaurus Rex more interesting.

Sentence Expansion.   Students take basic sentences, such as "Brontosaurus walked" or "Pteranodon flew," and expand them by adding descriptive words, comparisons, and other modifiers. The "5 Ws plus one" strategy helps students focus on expanding particular aspects of the sentence. For example:

Basic sentence:	A Pteranodon flies.
What kind?	huge
Where?	past a tar pit where a Tyrannosaurus Rex is stuck
Why?	to see why the terrible lizard is howling
How?	with its leathery wings outstretched
Expanded sentence:	A huge Pteranodon flies with its leathery wings outstretched past a tar pit where a Tyrannosaurus Rex is stuck to see why the terrible lizard is howling.

Depending on the questions asked and the answers given, many other expanded sentences are possible from the same basic sentence. Students enjoy working in small groups to expand the same basic sentence and then comparing the expanded versions each group produces. Instead of using the "5 Ws plus one" to expand sentences, upper-grade students can supply a specific part of speech for each expansion.

This strategy can also be used in revision. For example, Nikki wrote this sentence in a chapter of her report about dinosaur nests: "Dinosaur moms lay eggs in nests." Writing-group members asked Nikki to tell more about the eggs and the nests. They asked these questions and Nikki jotted down these answers:

Where do they build nests?	in sandy and rocky places covered with sand to hide the eggs
What do they look like?	big and kind of flat
How big are they?	big enough for five or six large eggs
Does the dinosaur mom stay with the nest like ducks do?	some do and some don't

Later Nikki wrote this revision in which she added the information her classmates asked about:

▽ *Dinosaur moms lay eggs in nests they build in sandy and rocky places. They lay five or six large eggs in the big nests. Next they cover the nests with sand to hide the eggs from other dinosaurs that like to eat eggs. Some dinosaur moms stay with the nests like ducks do and some don't.*

Sentence Combining.   Sentence combining is a strategy in which two or more short sentences are combined. They can be joined or embedded in a variety of ways. For example, the two sentences "Triceratops was a plant eater" and "Triceratops had three horns on its head" can be combined in several ways:

Triceratops was a plant eater and had three horns on its head.

Triceratops, a plant eater, had three horns on its head.

Triceratops, with three horns on its head, was a plant eater.

In the first combined sentence, the two short sentences were joined with *and* to make a compound sentence; in the second and third combined sentences, the short sentences were embedded.

Sentence combining was the focus of a study by Mellon (1969). His work suggested that sentence-combining activities might be a profitable way to increase the rate of students' syntactic development. Work by Hunt and O'Donnell (1970) and by O'Hare (1973) showed that students could improve their writing when sentence-combining exercises were taught. As a result of these studies, many teachers have introduced sentence-combining activities to their students.

In writing groups, students often suggest sentence combining for descriptive paragraphs that are essentially lists of characteristics. For example, Brady shared this description of Tyrannosaurus Rex with his classmates:

▽ *He is called the king. He was a meat eater or carnivore. He was as tall as a telephone pole. He walked on two legs. He was 50 feet long. His teeth were six inches long. He was a terrible lizard.*

As soon as he read this paragraph aloud, Brady realized he had used *he* too often and prepared to make some changes. Writing-group members mentioned that his sentences seemed short and choppy and suggested he could combine some of them. They suggested combining the tall and long sentences, the king and terrible lizard sentences, and the meat eater and teeth sentences. The children worked with Brady to help him draft the new sentences. Here is his revision:

▽ *Tyrannosaurus Rex was called the king of the dinosaurs. He was a meat eater or carnivore with six-inch long teeth. This dinosaur was as tall as a telephone pole and he was 50 feet long. He walked on two legs. He was a really, really terrible lizard.*

Sentence-combining activities give students opportunities to manipulate sentence structures; however, the activities are rather artificial unless they come from children's own writing or are connected with writing assignments (Lawlor, 1983; Strong, 1986). Weaver (1979) cautions that "sentence combining activities are only an adjunct to the writing program and should never be used as a substitute for actual writing" (pp. 83–84).

The Grammar and Usage–Writing Connection

Conventional wisdom is that knowledge about grammar and usage should improve students' writing, but research since the beginning of this century has not confirmed this assumption. Based on their review of research studies conducted before 1963, Braddock, Lloyd-Jones, and Schoer (1963) concluded:

> The teaching of formal grammar has a negligible or, because it usually displaces some instruction and practice in actual composition, even a harmful effect on the improvement of writing. (pp. 37–38)

Since that time, other studies have reached the same conclusion (Elley, Barham, Lamb, and Wyllie, 1976).

While there is much controversy about the value of teaching grammar to elementary students, grammar is part of the elementary language arts curriculum and will undoubtedly remain so for some time to come. Given this fact, it is only reasonable to suggest that grammar should be taught in the most beneficial manner possible. Some researchers suggest that integrating grammar study with writing may produce the best results (Noyce & Christie, 1983). Also, Peter Elbow (1973) and Shirley Haley-James (1981) view grammar as a tool for writers and recommend integrating grammar instruction with the revising and editing stages of the writing process.

HANDWRITING

Like spelling and grammar, handwriting is a functional tool for writers. Donald Graves (1983) explains:

> Children win prizes for fine script, parents and teachers nod approval for a crisp, well-crafted page, a good impression is made on a job application blank . . . all important elements, but they pale next to the *substance* they carry. (p. 171)

It is important to distinguish between writing and handwriting. Writing is the content of a composition, while handwriting is the formation of alphabetic symbols on paper.

The Goal of Handwriting

Too often, teachers insist that students demonstrate their best handwriting every time they pick up a pencil or a pen. This requirement is very unrealistic; certainly there are times when handwriting is important, but sometimes speed or other considerations outweigh neatness. Even though a few students take great pleasure in flawless handwriting skills, most students feel that excessive attention to handwriting is boring and unnecessary. Instead, the goal should be for students to develop and use legible handwriting to communicate effectively through writing.

Students need to develop a legible and fluent style of handwriting to fully participate in all writing activities. Legibility means that the writing can be easily and quickly read. Fluency means the writing can be easily and quickly written. When students are writing for public display, legibility is more important than when they are doing private writing, but fluency is always important. Whether students are writing for themselves or others, they need to be able to write quickly and easily.

The best way to help students develop fluency and legibility is to use handwriting for genuine and functional public writing activities. A letter sent to a favorite author that is returned by the post office because the address on the envelope is not decipherable, or a child's published, hardcover book that sits unread on the library shelf because the handwriting is illegible makes clear the importance of legibility. Illegible writing means a failure to communicate, a harsh lesson for a writer!

Teaching Handwriting Through Writing

Handwriting instruction can be taught in two ways, either through direct instruction or incidentally (Farris, 1991). As first-grade teachers introduce manuscript handwriting and third-grade teachers introduce cursive handwriting forms, they use direct instruction, and teachers at other grade levels also use direct instruction to review these handwriting forms (Tompkins & Hoskisson, 1991). As a part of teaching writing, however, teachers often teach handwriting incidentally. This approach supplements the formal instructional program in the primary grades when students are learning the correct formation of each letter in manuscript and cursive forms. In the middle and upper grades, this approach is the more efficient approach because it is individualized. As teachers observe students writing, they identify letters that are formed incorrectly or other handwriting problems which they can work with students to remedy.

Elements of Fluency and Legibility.   The goal of handwriting instruction is for students to develop fluent and legible handwriting. To reach this goal, students must first understand what qualities constitute fluency and legibility and then analyze their own handwriting according to these qualities and work to solve problems. There are six characteristics of fluent and legible handwriting according to the Zaner-Bloser handwriting program (Barbe, Wasylyk, Hackney, and Braun, 1984):

1. *Letter Formation.* Each letter is formed with specific strokes. In manuscript handwriting, letters are composed of vertical, horizontal, and slanted lines plus circles or parts of circles. Cursive letters are composed of slanted lines, loops, and curved lines.
2. *Size and Proportion.* The size of students' handwriting decreases during the elementary grades, and the proportional size between upper- and lowercase letters increases.
3. *Spacing.* Students leave adequate space between letters in words and between words and sentences so their handwriting can be read easily.
4. *Slant.* Letters are consistently parallel. In the manuscript form, letters are vertical. In cursive handwriting, letters slant slightly to the right for right-handed students and are vertical to 45 degrees to the left of vertical for left-handed students.
5. *Alignment.* For proper alignment in both handwriting forms, all letters are uniform in size and consistently touch the baseline.
6. *Line Quality.* Students write at a consistent speed and hold their writing instruments correctly and in a relaxed manner to make steady, unwavering lines of even thickness. These characteristics are summarized in Figure 11-9.

Teachers teach fluency by making sure that students write easily and quickly without excessive muscular discomfort. Some children stop writing periodically, put down their pens or pencils, and shake their arms to relax their muscles. Others complain that their arms hurt when they write. Often these students squeeze their pens or pencils too tightly, causing unnecessary tension. Teachers can talk to students about the problem and ask them to monitor themselves, periodically stopping and remov-

FIGURE 11-9   *Characteristics of Fluent and Legible Handwriting*

Letter Formation

Letters are formed with specific strokes.
Cursive letters are joined carefully.

Size and Proportion

Letter size decreases for middle- and upper-grade students.
Proportion of upper- to lowercase manuscript letters is 2:1.
Proportion of upper- to lowercase cursive letters increases from 2:1 to 3:1.

Spacing

Adequate space is left between letters.
Adequate space is left between words and sentences.
Spacing is consistent.

Slant

Letters are consistently parallel.
Manuscript letters are vertical.
Cursive letters are slanted slightly to the right.

Alignment

Letters are uniform in size.
Letters consistently touch the baseline.

Line Quality

Lines are steady and unwavering.
Lines are of consistent thickness.

ing their writing instruments from their hands. Students should hold the pencil or pen loosely enough that they can easily pull it out of their hands. Also, students who haven't written very much will benefit from daily journal writing or quickwriting to exercise their arm muscles.

Correct letter formation and spacing receive the major focus in handwriting instruction during the elementary grades. While the other four elements usually receive less attention, they too are important in developing legible and fluent handwriting.

Assessing Handwriting Skills.   Students can use the characteristics of the six elements of fluency and legibility in assessing their handwriting skills. Primary grade students, for example, can check to see if they have formed a particular letter correctly, if the round parts of letters are joined neatly, or if slanted letters are joined in sharp points. Older students can examine a piece of handwriting and check to see if their letters are consistently parallel or if the letters touch the baseline consistently.

Checklists for students to use in assessing their own handwriting on final copies of their compositions can be developed from the characteristics of the six elements of legibility and fluency. A sample checklist for assessing manuscript handwriting is presented in Figure 11-10. Checklists can also be developed for cursive handwriting. It is important to involve students in developing the checklists so they can appreciate the need to make their handwriting more legible and fluent.

Handwriting Minilessons. Handwriting can be tied to writing through minilessons in which the teacher introduces or reviews a specific handwriting skill. Students practice the skill immediately in a short teacher-supervised writing activity and later in their own writing projects. One item on the evaluation checklist for the writing project is whether or not the specific handwriting skill is used correctly on the final copy. For example, to review the formation of lowercase cursive *b* and how to connect it to the following letter, the teacher might demonstrate on the chalkboard, as part of the minilesson, how to form the letter and connect it to other letters such as *br, ba, bl,* and *bo.* Then students apply what the teacher presented and practice the letter by working in small groups to create a tongue twister composed of *b* words which they each recopy in their best handwriting.

Left-Handed Writers. Left-handed students have unique handwriting problems, and special adaptations of procedures used for teaching right-handed students are

---

HANDWRITING CHECKLIST

Name _____

	Never	Sometimes	Always
1. Do I form my letters correctly?	☐	☐	☐
☐ Do I start my line letters at the top?			
☐ Do I start my circle letters at 1:00?			
☐ Do I join the round parts of letters neatly?			
☐ Do I join the slanted strokes in sharp points?			
2. Do my lines touch the midline or top line neatly?	☐	☐	☐
3. Do I space evenly between letters?	☐	☐	☐
4. Do I leave enough space between words?	☐	☐	☐
5. Do I make my letters straight up and down?	☐	☐	☐
6. Do I make all my letters sit on the baseline?	☐	☐	☐

FIGURE 11-10 *A Checklist for Assessing Manuscript Handwriting*

necessary (Howell, 1978). In fact, many of the problems that left-handed students have can be made worse by using the procedures designed for right-handed writers (Harrison, 1981). These special adjustments are necessary to allow left-handed students to write legibly, fluently, and with less fatigue.

The basic difference between right- and left-handed writers is physical orientation. Right-handed students pull their hand and arm slightly toward their body as they write, while left-handed writers move the hand and arm away from the body. As left-handed students write, they move their left hand across what has just been written, often covering it. Many children adopt a "hook" position with their wrists to avoid covering and smudging what they have just written.

Because of this different physical orientation, left-handed writers need to make three major adjustments (Howell, 1978). First, left-handed writers should hold pencils or pens an inch or more farther back from the tip than right-handed writers do. This change will help them to see what they have just written and to avoid smearing their writing. Left-handed writers need to work to avoid hooking their wrists. They should keep their wrists straight and elbows close to their bodies to avoid the awkward hooked position.

Second, left-handed students should tilt their writing papers slightly to the right (in contrast to right-handed students, who tilt their papers to the left) to more comfortably form letters without twisting their wrists. Sometimes it is helpful to place a piece of masking tape on the student's desk to indicate the proper amount of tilt.

Third, left-handed students should slant their letters in a way that allows them to write comfortably. Students and their teachers should accept that left-handed students often write cursive letters vertically or even slightly backward, in contrast to right-handed students, who slant cursive letters to the right. The Zaner-Bloser handwriting program (Barbe, Wasylyk, Hackney, & Braun, 1984) recommends that left-handed writers slant cursive letters slightly to the right, as right-handed students do, but other educators, such as Harrison (1981), advise teachers to permit any slant between vertical and 45 degrees to the left of the vertical.

The Handwriting-Writing Connection

Most students use handwriting to record their ideas, and this makes an undeniable connection between handwriting and writing, although this may change as microcomputers with word processing programs become standard equipment in homes and elementary classrooms. This connection raises a number of questions about handwriting and writing: Should young children who have not learned to form the letters of the alphabet be permitted to write? Should students use manuscript or cursive handwriting for writing? Which writing instruments and paper are best? Does handwriting influence teachers' assessment of students' writing?

Young Children's Handwriting.   Preschool children begin writing before they have been taught how to form the letters, and they often develop their own unique ways to form letters in much the same way adults might if they were trying to figure out how to form Chinese or Japanese symbols. Fluency is important, and children should not be stopped from using letters they don't form correctly. Instead, children should be allowed to experiment with writing and gain confidence with using marks on paper to express meaning. Parents and preschool teachers can demonstrate "simpler" ways to form letters when children inhibit their fluency by making letter formation more difficult than it needs to be. It is adequate to simply demonstrate the formation of the letter for the child; handwriting practice sheets are unnecessary. Through experience with writing and by modeling adults' writing, children will learn to form most of the letters. Any problematic letters can be taught in kindergarten or first grade.

Young children's writing often reveals reversed letters such as *d* for *b* and *z* for *s*. These reversals are quite common for children who are learning the alphabet. In fact, it is amazing that more reversals are not made. Also, most reversals are left-right reversals, not top-bottom reversals. Most reversals take care of themselves by the end of first grade, especially if children are not continually reminded of their errors.

Manuscript Versus Cursive Handwriting. Upper-grade students are often faced with a decision when they write: whether to use manuscript or cursive writing. Teachers may require students to use either manuscript or cursive handwriting when they are teaching or reviewing the form, but in general students should write in whatever form they are more comfortable. Handwriting should not interfere with getting ideas down on paper during the drafting stage or with preparing a legible final copy to share.

Writing Instruments and Paper. Students use all sorts of writing instruments on both lined and unlined paper as they write. Special pencils and handwriting paper are often provided for writing activities in the primary grades. Kindergartners and first graders commonly use fat beginner pencils, 13/32 inch in diameter, because it has been assumed that these pencils are easier for young children to hold. However, most children prefer to use the regular-size, 10/32 inch, pencils that older students and adults use. Moreover, regular pencils have erasers! Research now indicates that beginner pencils are not better than regular-size pencils for young children (Lamme & Ayris, 1983). Likewise, there is no evidence that specially shaped pencils and little writing aids that slip onto pencils to improve children's grip are effective.

Many types of paper, both lined and unlined, are used in elementary classrooms. The few research studies that have examined the value of lined paper in general, and paper lined at specific intervals for particular grade levels, offer conflicting results. One study suggests that young children's handwriting is more legible using unlined paper, while older children's handwriting is better using lined paper (Lindsay & McLennan, 1983). Most teachers seem to prefer that students use lined paper for most writing activities, but students easily adjust to whichever type of writing paper is available. Students often use rulers to line their paper when they are given unlined paper, and they may ignore the lines on lined paper if the lines interfere with their drawing or writing.

Impact of Handwriting on Writing. The quality of students' handwriting has been found to influence how teachers assess and grade compositions. Markham (1976) found that both student teachers and experienced elementary classroom teachers consistently graded papers with better handwriting higher than papers with poor handwriting, regardless of the quality of the content. Students in the elementary grades are not too young to learn that poor quality or illegible handwriting may lead to lower grades, and teachers must recognize that it is likely they also have this bias.

MICROCOMPUTERS[1]

Microcomputers are another valuable tool for student writers, and word processing is one of the most important classroom applications for these computers (Daiute, 1985; Hoot & Silvern, 1988; Knapp, 1986; Rodrigues & Rodrigues, 1986; Wrench, 1987). Teachers and researchers have found that students write more and that both their writing and their attitude toward writing improve when they compose on microcomputers. Several reasons for these improvements seem obvious. First of all, it is fun to use a computer. Students can experiment with writing and easily correct errors, thus encouraging risk taking and problem solving. Next, microcomputers allow students to revise and refine their writing without the chore of having to recopy the final draft. In addition, writing looks professional after it is printed out on a printer and graphics can be added.

Word Processing Capabilities

Computers have several capabilities that make the tasks of formatting, revising, and editing mechanically easier.

1. *Typeover.* Word processing programs allow writers to back up and type over mistakes. This process is like using a self-correcting electric typewriter. Undesired letters are simply replaced by the new letters typed during the correcting.
2. *Insert and Delete.* Word processing programs allow writers to insert or delete letters, words, sentences, and paragraphs within the body of the text. These changes require only a few keystrokes. The remainder of the text automatically adjusts to the changes by shifting lines up, down, or over.
3. *Block Move.* The block function allows writers to define a block of text and move it from one location in the text to another. Large amounts of text can be moved in this manner. Writers can also move a block of text back to its original location if they regret a move. Another option is to copy of the block of text or portions of text to another location.
4. *Search and Replace.* Sometimes authors wish to locate every occurrence of a certain word within the text and to replace it with a more appropriate word. For example, writers who find that a word has been consistently misspelled throughout the composition can use the search and replace function to correct the misspell-

---

[1]   Adapted from Smith & Tompkins, 1983

ing. Writers can specify a particular word to be searched for throughout the composition and then identify a word or phrase to replace it.

Word Processing Programs

Many word processing programs that are currently available for use by adults can be used by elementary students, and others have been developed specifically for children. A list of some of these programs is presented in Figure 11-11. Look for the following features when selecting a word processing program for children to use:

1. *The Menu on the Screen.* The menu is displayed across the top of the monitor screen and shows the functions available for students to use.
2. *Commands on the Screen.* Commands continually appear on the screen and are simple, one-keystroke commands. Placing the commands on the screen makes it unnecessary for students memorize lists of commands or to refer to instruction booklets.
3. *Pictures to Depict Word Processing Concepts.* Pictures (called icons) are used to depict word processing tasks graphically. These pictures are easy for students to remember.
4. *Safeguards from Accidental Erasures.* Word processing programs have safeguards to help prevent students from accidentally erasing text. A question or warning appears on the screen before text can be deleted.
5. *Software Tutorials.* Students can learn to use the word processing program on the microcomputer using an on-screen tutorial, rather than reading the manual.

A checklist for evaluating word processing programs for both children and adults is presented in Figure 11-12. Specific requirements are included for each stage of the writing process. For example the revising stage requires that the software has space for reader comments; a way to check sentence and paragraph length; the capacity to insert, delete, and move text; and a search and replace feature.

Auxiliary programs related to word processing include spelling checkers, keyboarding programs, text and graphics programs, and electronic mail. Students use these programs in conjunction with word processing programs.

Spelling Checkers.   Spelling checkers are built into many word processing programs and may also be purchased separately. After students have completed a piece of writing, a spelling checker program is used to search through the composition for misspelled words. A dictionary included on the computer disk usually holds 50,000 words or more, and the words in the student's composition are compared against the words in the dictionary. The two greatest drawbacks of spelling checkers is that they do not recognize inflectional endings of words or homonym errors. For instance, a student may write *their* and spell it correctly, but if the word should be *they're* a spelling checker will not catch the error. Most spelling checkers allow users to add other words to the dictionary, such as classmates' names, content area vocabulary, and slang.

FIGURE 11-11   *Word Processing Programs*

Title	Publisher	Grade Levels
Appleworks	South-Western 5101 Madison Road Cincinnati, OH 45227	Upper
Bank Street Prewriter	Scholastic 730 Broadway New York, NY 10003	Primary
Bank Street Writer III	Broderbund Software 17 Halldrive San Rafael, CA 94901	Middle Upper
FirstWriter	Houghton Mifflin One Beacon Street Boston, MA 02108	Primary
Macmillan Writing Program	Macmillan 866 Third Avenue New York, NY 10022	Middle
MacWrite	Claris 5201 Patrick Henry Drive Santa Clara, CA 95052	Middle Upper
Magic Slate	Sunburst Communications 39 Washington Street Pleasantville, NY 10570	Primary Middle
Quill	DC Heath 125 Spring Street Lexington, MA 02173	Middle Upper
Writing Workshop	Milliken 1100 Research Blvd PO Box 21579 St. Louis, MO 63132	Middle Upper

Betza (1987) lists five suggestions for selecting and using a spelling checker with elementary students:

▼ Find the best spelling checker available for your computer and have students experiment with it and add words to make it better.
▼ Use spelling checkers to involve students with editing.
▼ Keep records of students' spelling progress.
▼ Use spelling checkers selectively.
▼ Reserve the spelling checker for the final draft.

Thesaurus and grammar programs are also available that allow students to highlight specific problems in their compositions and request the computer to supply options. Many teachers, however, feel that the usefulness of these programs is quite limited.

Keyboarding Tutorials. Keyboarding tutorial programs are designed to teach typing skills to children so they can use word processing more effectively. There are two types of tutorials. Comprehensive tutorials teach the correct fingering on the keyboard and include these features:

▼ Students are introduced to the home row of keys first.
▼ Students practice the keys using meaningful letter and word combinations.
▼ Students receive frequent feedback about accuracy and speed.
▼ Students can correct errors while typing.
▼ The program displays upper- and lowercase letters. (Knapp, 1986)

One of the best-known comprehensive keyboarding tutorials is *Microtype: The Wonderful World of Paws* (South-Western Publishing). Other tutorials are presented in a game format, such as *Kids on Keys* (Spinnaker) and *Type Attack* (Sirus Software); these drill programs are better suited for increasing children's typing speed than introducing them to keyboarding. *Type to Learn* (Sunburst Communication) integrates keyboarding with reading and writing.

When students begin to use the microcomputer for word processing, the question of keyboarding arises because familiarity with the location of letters on the keyboard allows students to enter words more easily and faster. Students who don't know the locations of keys on the keyboard use the hunt-and-peck technique to arduously produce their compositions. This ties up the computer longer than necessary, and children can learn bad keyboarding habits that may be hard to break later. The fact is that word processing is already a standard method of writing, and keyboarding is becoming a basic literacy skill. Many educators recommend teaching students basic keyboarding skills as soon as they begin to use microcomputers, while others suggest postponing keyboarding instruction until third or fourth grade, after students have learned manuscript and cursive handwriting skills. Whether or not they have learned the correct fingering on the keyboard, children should not be discouraged from using a computer.

Text and Graphics Programs. Students can use text and graphics programs such as *Newsroom* (Springboard), *Newspaper Maker* (Scholastic), and *Print Shop* (Broderbund) to create class newspapers, literary magazines, signs, and greeting cards. These programs allow students to publish their writing in very professional-looking publications.

Electronic Mail. Students can use the word processor to write notes and letters to classmates, pen pals, and the teacher using an electronic mail program. They write

Name of software _____

Software publisher _____

Address _____

Cost _____ Grade level _____

Type of computer required _____

Type of printer required _____

Number of disk drives needed _____ Recommended _____

Necessary memory capability required for program _____

Extra hardware needed _____

	Excellent	Adequate	Poor
1. Basic Requirements			
The software has:			
• Cataloging capability	_____	_____	_____
• Option to rename files	_____	_____	_____
• Disks that can be copied	_____	_____	_____
• Option to undo previous action	_____	_____	_____
• Familiar terms	_____	_____	_____
• Automatic updating of existing material	_____	_____	_____
• Directions on screen at all times	_____	_____	_____
• Help or aid key	_____	_____	_____
• Mnemonic commands that are logical and easy to use	_____	_____	_____
• Two key commands (control plus one other)	_____	_____	_____
• Displayed characters sufficiently readable for intended audience (40/80 column)	_____	_____	_____
• Easy change from one function to another	_____	_____	_____
• Instructional manual	_____	_____	_____
• Backup disks and manuals available at reduced cost	_____	_____	_____
• Glossary and illustrations in manual	_____	_____	_____
2. Prewriting Requirements			
The software has:			
• Tutorials	_____	_____	_____
• Data disk to accompany tutorial	_____	_____	_____
• Prewriting activities such as brainstorming, prompting, classifying	_____	_____	_____
3. Drafting Requirements			
The software has:			
• Screen warnings before deleting, saving, or quitting	_____	_____	_____
• Single-key capitalization	_____	_____	_____

FIGURE 11-12 *A Checklist for Evaluating Word Processing Programs*
Source: Oklahoma Writing Project, 1986.

- Cursor movement using standard keys and rapid scrolling _____ _____ _____
- Choice of word wrap or hyphenation at end of line _____ _____ _____
- Upper- and lowercase printing and display _____ _____ _____
- Maximum length of document information _____ _____ _____

4. **Revising Requirements**
   The software has:
   - Space for reader comments _____ _____ _____
   - Sentence and paragraph length check _____ _____ _____
   - Capability to insert, delete, and move text _____ _____ _____
   - Search and replace features _____ _____ _____

5. **Editing Requirements**
   The software has:
   - Spelling check _____ _____ _____
   - Mechanics check _____ _____ _____
   - Supplemental editing software available _____ _____ _____

6. **Publishing Requirements**
   The software has:
   - Page number indicators _____ _____ _____
   - Screen display truly representative of printed copy _____ _____ _____
   - Integration of graphics with text _____ _____ _____
   - Print options
     - boldface type _____ _____ _____
     - underlining _____ _____ _____
     - subscript/superscript _____ _____ _____
     - centering _____ _____ _____
     - justified margins _____ _____ _____
     - multiple line spacing _____ _____ _____
     - interrupt or cancel printing process _____ _____ _____
     - variety of print fonts and sizes _____ _____ _____
     - foreign symbols _____ _____ _____
     - page break _____ _____ _____
     - prints specified text _____ _____ _____
     - single or continuous paper feed _____ _____ _____

Comments:

FIGURE 11-12, *continued*

letters on the computer, revise and edit the messages, and then transmit them to another computer using a modem hooked up to the sending and receiving computers. Teachers can also write messages back and forth to students and send announcements and reminders to students through electronic mail (Newman, 1986, 1989). A real advantage of this communication system is that students develop an increased sense of audience (Bruce, Michaels, & Watson-Gegeo, 1985), and when students write back and forth about books they are reading, they share initial reactions and create deeper interpretations (Moore, 1991). One word processing program that includes an electronic mail system, called the "Mailbag," for exchanging messages is D.C. Heath's *QUILL.*

Word Processing in the Elementary Classroom

The first step in using computers for word processing with elementary students is to introduce students to the computer using the tutorial lessons that accompany most word processing programs. Students work through the tutorial lesson in groups of two or three, and then they summarize what they have learned by making word processing reference charts that include general directions on operating the word processing program (e.g., how to access a file, save a file, and print out a hard copy) and a list of commands (e.g., insert, delete, move, search, and replace) and keystrokes that allow students to execute these commands. Students can use their charts for quick reference as they work at the computers.

It is a good idea for the teacher to complete the first writing assignment with the students as a large-group collaboration so all students can review the word processing procedures. A large screen is especially useful for class collaborations and group teaching sessions, but a regular monitor can be used. The next several writing assignments should be short, generally no longer than a paragraph or two. In this way, students can concentrate on working through the word processing procedure.

Often one or two students in each classroom quickly assume an important new status as "computer expert," either because of a special interest or expertise with computers. These experts help other students with word processing tasks, mastering commands, and using the printer. Cochran-Smith and her colleagues (1988) found that the "experts" were often not the smartest or best-behaved students, but they approached the computer more systematically than other children.

Word Processing with Young Children

Computers with word processing programs can be used very effectively to record young children's language experience stories (Barber, 1982; Smith 1985). Teachers may want to sit children on their laps or stand beside them and the computer to model keyboarding. Teachers take children's dictation as they do in traditional language experience activities. After entering the child's dictation, the child and the teacher read the text and make any needed revisions. Next, the text is printed out, and the child can add a drawing. If the child has already drawn a picture, the printout can be cut and taped onto the drawing. The microcomputer simplifies the process of taking children's dictation because teachers can record dictation on a computer more quickly than they can write, the dictation can be revised and edited easily, and a clean copy of the revised writing can be printed out.

Salinger (1988) recommends that the language experience approach be used to introduce young children to word processing, and other educators suggest that young children can use computers themselves for word processing. Daiute (1985) reports that children as young as 6 years old can learn the positions of the keys on the keyboard. They can also use a graphic tablet (a device that attaches to the computer) to draw and handwrite letters and words that appear directly on the screen.

In first and second grade, students can write their own compositions on the word processor. An interesting report of first graders writing on a computer is given in Phenix and Hannan's article, "Word Processing in the Grade One Classroom" (1984). Two teachers describe how their first graders wrote and revised a variety of compositions on computers and "learned that writing does not have to come out right the first time" and "that revising is a normal way writing is done" (p. 812). These are the same process approach generalizations that teachers work toward with students at all grade levels.

The Microcomputer-Writing Connection

In the process approach to writing, students write by developing and refining their compositions. The microcomputer with a word processing program is a useful tool in each of the five stages of the writing process. In prewriting, students use word processing to take notes, to quickwrite, to brainstorm, and for other rehearsal activities. As students pour out and shape their ideas in the drafting stage, the computer is a more efficient tool than pencil and paper. Students who have good typing skills can input text or make changes more quickly than they can write by hand. Even students who have not learned to type very well prefer to write using the word processor (Kane, 1983).

In the revising stage, students print out copies of their rough drafts to use in conferences. After reading and discussing their compositions during a conference, students return to the computer to make substantive revisions that reflect the reactions and suggestions received in the conference. Word processing allows students to revise easily, without cutting and pasting changes in their rough drafts. In fact, students are more willing to revise without the recopying penalty (Moore, 1989).

Microcomputers are especially useful during editing when students correct mechanical errors in their compositions. Students have "clean" texts to proofread, whether they read them on the screen or as a printed copy. After proofreading and editing, students return again to the computer to make their corrections quickly and easily.

After students have completed all corrections, they decide how to format their compositions (e.g., margins, typefaces, spacing, numbering) and print out the final copy to share with an audience. Using word processing relieves students from the tedium of recopying their final copies by hand. The professional-looking final copies often boost students' feeling of accomplishment, especially for students with poor handwriting skills.

Typically, two or three students work together in a buddy system and take turns using the microcomputer. Although this system is often necessitated by the small number of computers available, there is an added benefit: social interaction. Students working together are more inclined to collaborate with each other, providing support, assistance, and feedback as they compose (DeGroff, 1990).

Cochran-Smith and her colleagues (1988) researched the methods used to introduce word processing to students in kindergarten through fourth grade over a 2-year period. They found that students had conceptual "bugs" about word processing and these misconceptions caused problems as they were learning to use word processing programs. One problem was equating keyboard-and-screen with paper-and-pencil. They did not recognize and appreciate the unique capabilities of a microcomputer for formatting, revising, or editing text. A second problem was their inexperience with keyboarding and locating letters on the keyboard.

Many teachers have expressed the hope that microcomputers will encourage students to use a process approach and write and revise a series of drafts. However, Kane (1983) found that students in her study composed the same way on the computer that they composed with pen and paper. In other words, students who normally write single-draft papers or who limit revisions to making minor changes are likely to continue to do so. This finding reinforces the idea that the computer is only a tool, and that good teaching is required for students to learn to write well.

Answering Teachers' Questions About . . . Writers' Tools

1. *I'm concerned that if my students misspell words on rough drafts, they will learn to spell them incorrectly.*

In a single composition—and sometimes in a single sentence—children may spell an unfamiliar word several different ways as they problem-solve for the "best" spelling. Research studies have shown that allowing children to use invented spelling leads to increased, rather than decreased, achievement in spelling. Since learning to spell a word involves much more than simply writing it once or twice, there is little chance that children will internalize the incorrect spelling.

Seeing misspelled words on a composition bothers me, too. I think children's misspellings are a teacher problem, not a student problem. One way to solve the problem is to not look too closely while students are writing rough drafts and sharing them in writing groups. Instead of reading the drafts yourself, ask students to read their rough drafts to you. An overemphasis on correct spelling during writing distracts students from their real purpose in writing—communicating! The time to express concern about student's spelling is during editing.

2. *My students' parents have complained when their children misspell words on work I've sent home. What should I do?*

It is crucial to explain to parents about the role of spelling in the writing process and the emphasis you will place on spelling in your classroom. It is helpful to have a rubber stamp marked "rough draft" for students to stamp on their papers to identify papers in which content counts more than mechanics. Also, even with careful editing, it is likely that children will continue to misspell a few words on their final copies. Spelling is a writer's tool, and it needs to be put in proper perspective.

3. *Many questions deal with grammar on the achievement tests that I am required to administer in my school district. You say that teaching grammar does little good, but I have to prepare my students for the tests. What should I do?*

Of course, you should prepare them for the tests, but don't confuse teaching grammar to prepare students for the achievement test with teaching grammar to improve writing skills. If grammar must be taught, it is probably more effective to have students manipulate sentences taken from their compositions rather than sentences in textbooks. When using their own writing, students are more interested in learning how to combine words into sentences.

4. *I don't want my students to learn bad habits, so I always expect them to use their best handwriting skills. Are you suggesting that it is all right for them to be messy?*

No one uses his or her best handwriting all the time. Think about the last time you scribbled a grocery list or wrote a letter to a friend. Was your handwriting more important on the grocery list or on the letter? There are two purposes for handwriting. When people write for themselves, their writing is private and handwriting is not very important; however, when people write for others, the legibility of handwriting is more important. Students are aware of these differences, and they should be encouraged to think about their purpose and write more legibly when their writing will be shared with others.

5. *I only have one microcomputer in my classroom. How can I use it to teach writing?*

While an ideal situation would be to have a computer available on each student's desk, it is, unfortunately, not yet a reality. When you have only one or two computers in the classroom, students will probably prewrite and write rough drafts with paper and pencil, and then type their compositions on the word processor before revising them. A schedule is needed so that all students can have access to the computer. Expect students to volunteer to collaborate on compositions so they can have more time on the computer. This collaboration will also benefit their writing.

6. *I don't know enough about computer programming to teach my students about word processing.*

It isn't necessary for teachers or students to know computer programming to use word processing programs. These programs are user friendly, and you and your students can learn to use them with several hours of practice and a few basic commands. The programs designed for elementary students are even easier to use than programs for adults. Many word processing programs have on-screen tutorials to teach students (and their teachers) how to use them. Also, in almost every class one or two children will be familiar with computers and word processing programs, and they will quickly become the resident computer experts.

REFERENCES

Anderson, K. F. (1985). The development of spelling ability and linguistic strategies. *The Reading Teacher, 39,* pp. 140–147.

Barbe, W. B., Wasylyk, T. M., Hackney, C. S. & Braun, L. A. (1984). *Zaner-Bloser creative growth in handwriting* (Grades K–8). Columbus, OH: Zaner-Bloser.

Barber, B. (1982). Creating BYTES of language. *Language Arts, 59,* 472–475.

Barron, R. W. (1980). Visual and phonological strategies in reading and spelling. In U. Frith (Ed.), *Cognitive processes in learning to spell.* London: Academic Press.

Beers, J. W., & Henderson, E. H. (1977). A study of developing orthographic concepts among first graders. *Research in the Teaching of English, 11,* 133–148.

Betza, R. E. (1987). Online: Computerized spelling checkers: Freinds or foes? *Language Arts, 64,* 438–443.

Braddock, R., Lloyd-Jones, R., & Schoer, L. (1963). *Research in written composition.* Champaign, IL: National Council of Teachers of English.

Bruce, B., Michaels, S., & Watson-Gegeo, K. (1985). How computers can change the writing process. *Language Arts, 62,* 143–149.

Clarke, L. K. (1988). Invented versus traditional spelling in first graders' writings: Effects on learning to spell and read. *Research in the Teaching of English, 22,* 281–309.

Cochran-Smith, M., Kahan, J., & Pares, C. L. (1988). When word processors come into the classroom. In J. L. Hoot and S. B. Silvern (Eds.), *Writing with computers in the early grades* (pp. 43–74). New York: Teachers College Press.

Cook, G. E., Esposito, M., Gabrielson, T., & Turner, G. (1984). *Spelling for word mastery.* Columbus, OH: Merrill.

Daiute, C. (1985). *Writing and computers.* Reading, MA: Addison-Wesley.

DeGroff, L. (1990). Is there a place for computers in whole language classrooms? *The Reading Teacher, 43,* 568–572.

Elbow, P. (1973). *Writing without teachers.* New York: Oxford University Press.

Elley, W. B., Barham, I. H., Lamb, H., & Wyllie, M. (1976). The role of grammar in a secondary school English curriculum. *Research in the Teaching of English, 10,* 5–21.

Farris, P. J. (1991). Handwriting instruction should not become extinct. *Language Arts, 68,* 312–314.

Fraser, I. S., & Hodson, L. M. (1978). Twenty-one kicks at the grammar horse. *English Journal, 67,* 49–53.

Frith, U. (1980). Unexpected spelling problems. In U. Frith (Ed.), *Cognitive processes in learning to spell.* London: Academic Press.

Gentry, J. R. (1978). Early spelling strategies. *Elementary School Journal, 79,* 88–92.

Gentry, J. R. (1981). Learning to spell developmentally. *The Reading Teacher, 34,* 378–381.

Gentry, J. R. (1982a). An analysis of developmental spellings in *Gyns at wrk. The Reading Teacher, 36,* 192–200.

Gentry, J. R. (1982b). Developmental spelling: Assessment. *Diagnostique, 8,* 52–61.

Graves, D. H. (1983). *Writing: Teachers and writers at work.* Portsmouth, NH: Heinemann.

Haley-James, S. (Ed.). (1981). *Perspectives on writing in grades 1–8.* Urbana, IL: National Council of Teachers of English.

Harrison, S. (1981). Open letter from a left-handed teacher: Some sinistral ideas on the teaching of handwriting. *Teaching Exceptional Children, 13,* 116–120.

Henderson, E. H. (1980a). Developmental concepts of word. In E. H. Henderson & J. W. Beers (Eds.), *Developmental and cognitive aspects of learning to spell: A reflection of word knowledge* (pp. 1–14). Newark, DE: International Reading Association.

Henderson, E. H. (1980b). Word knowledge and reading disability. In E. H. Henderson & J. W. Beers (Eds.), *Developmental and cognitive aspects of learning to spell: A reflection of word knowledge* (pp. 138–148). Newark, DE: International Reading Association.

Hillerich, R. L. (1977). Let's teach spelling—not phonetic misspelling. *Language Arts, 54,* 301–307.

Hoot, J. L., & Silvern, S. B. (Eds.). (1988). *Writing with computers in the early grades.* New York: Teachers College Press.

Horn, E. (1957). Phonetics and spelling. *Elementary School Journal, 57,* 424–432.

Howell, H. (1978). Write on, you sinistrals! *Language Arts, 55,* 852–856.

Hunt, K. W., & O'Donnell, R. C. (1970). *An elementary school curriculum to develop better writing skills.* Washington, DC: US Government Printing Office.

Hutson, B. A. (1980). Moving language around: Helping students become aware of language structure. *Language Arts, 57,* 614–620.

Kane, J. H. (1983). Computers for composing. In *Chameleon in the classroom: Developing roles for computers* (Technical Report No. 22). New York: Bank Street College of Education.

Knapp, L. R. (1986). *The word processor and the writing teacher.* Englewood Cliffs, NJ: Prentice-Hall.

Lamme, L. L., & Ayris, B. M. (1983). Is the handwriting of beginning writers influenced by writing tools? *Journal of Research and Development in Education, 17,* 32–38.

Lawlor, J. (1983). Sentence combining: A sequence for instruction. *The Elementary School Journal, 84,* 53–62.

Lindsay, G. A., & McLennan, D. (1983). Lined paper: its effects on the legibility and creativity of young children's writings. *British Journal of Educational Psychology, 53,* 364–368.

Markham, L. R. (1976). Influences of handwriting quality on teacher evaluation of written work. *American Educational Research Journal, 13,* 277–283.

Marsh G., Friedman, M., Desberg, P., & Welsh, V. (1980). The development of strategies in spelling. In U. Frith (Ed.), *Cognitive processes in learning to spell.* London: Academic Press.

Mellon, J. C. (1969). *Transformational sentence combining: A method of enhancing the development of syntactic fluency in English compositions* (NCTE Research Report No. 10). Urbana, IL: National Council of Teachers of English.

Moore, M. A. (1989). Computers can enhance transactions between readers and writers. *The Reading Teacher, 42,* 608–611.

Moore, M. A. (1991). Electronic dialoguing: An avenue to literacy. *The Reading Teacher, 45,* 280–286.

Newman, J. M. (1986), Online: Electronic mail and newspapers. *Language Arts, 63,* 736–741.

Newman, J. (1989). Online: From far away: *Language Arts, 66,* 791–797.

Noyce, R. M., & Christie, J. F. (1983). Effects of an integrated approach to grammar instruction on third graders' reading and writing. *Elementary School Journal, 84,* 63–69.

O'Hare, F. (1973). *Sentence combining: Improving student writing without formal grammar instruction* (NCTE Research Report No. 15). Urbana, IL: National Council of Teachers of English.

Oklahoma Writing Project. (1986). *Checklist for evaluating word processing software.* Unpublished manuscript. Norman, OK: University of Oklahoma.

Phenix, J., & Hannan, E. (1984). Word processing in the grade one classroom. *Language Arts, 61,* 804–812.

Pooley, R. C. (1974). *The teaching of English usage.* Urbana, IL: National Council of Teachers of English.

Read, C. (1971). Preschool children's knowledge of English phonology. *Harvard Educational Review, 41,* 1–34.

Read, C. (1975). *Children's categorization of speech sounds in English* (NCTE Research Report No. 17). Urbana, IL: National Council of Teachers of English.

Read, C. (1986). *Children's creative spelling.* London: Routledge & Kegan Paul.

Rodrigues, D., & Rodrigues, R. J. (1986). *Teaching writing with a word processor, grades 7–13.* Urbana, IL: ERIC Clearinghouse on Reading and Communication Skills and National Council of Teachers of English.

Salinger, T. S. (1988). Language experience as an introduction to word processing. In J. L. Hoot & S. B. Silvern (Eds.), *Writing with computers in the early grades* (pp. 90–104). New York: Teachers College Press.

Smith, F. (1982). *Writing and the writer.* New York: Holt.

Smith, J. J. (1985). The word processing approach to language experience. *The Reading Teacher, 38,* 556–559.

Smith, P. L., & Tompkins, G. E. (1983). *Computers and writing.* Unpublished manuscript. Norman, OK: University of Oklahoma.

Strong, W. (1986). *Creative approaches to sentence combining.* Urbana, IL: ERIC Clearinghouse on Reading and Communication Skills and National Council of Teachers of English.

Templeton, S. (1979). Spelling first, sound later: The relationship between orthography and higher order phonological knowledge in older students. *Research in the Teaching of English, 13,* 255–265.

Tompkins, G. E., & Hoskisson, K. (1991). *Language arts: Content and teaching strategies* (2nd ed.). New York: Merrill/Macmillan.

VanDeWeghe, R. (1982). Spelling and grammar logs. In C. Carter (Ed.), *Nonnative and nonstandard dialect students: Classroom practices in teaching English, 1982–1983* (pp. 101–105). Urbana, IL: National Council of Teachers of English.

Weaver, C. (1979). *Grammar for teachers: Perspectives and definitions.* Urbana, IL: National Council of Teachers of English.

Wrench, W. (1987). *A practical guide to computer uses in the English/language arts classroom.* Englewood Cliffs, NJ: Prentice-Hall.

Zutell, J. (1979). Spelling strategies of primary grade school children and their relationship to Piaget's concept of decentration. *Research in the Teaching of English, 13,* 69–79.

Assessing Students' Writing

Using Portfolios

In Mrs. Meyers's third-grade classroom, students keep readers' and writers' workshop folders in their desks. They place all the materials they are working on, checklists, and other records in their folders as they work. (They also have math folders and theme cycle folders in their desks.) As they complete a theme study or at the end of a grading period, students organize the materials in these folders, self-evaluate their work, and choose materials from their work-in-progress folders to put into their portfolios.

Portfolios are more than collections of students' work; they are a tool for systematically documenting students' growth as learners. Mrs. Meyers's students assume an important role in keeping track of what they are learning. Each student's portfolio is an accordian file subdivided into three sections: language arts, math, and theme cycles. In each section, students place samples of their work, including process writings that have been revised and edited and informal writings, such as journal entries, quickwrites, clusters, charts, and diagrams.

Mrs. Meyers adds other materials to students' portfolios: anecdotal notes, photos of projects, checklists, and conference notes. In these teacher contributions, Mrs. Meyers focuses on what her students know about writing and what they can do as writers. She also includes comments about goals students are working toward.

During the last week of the fall semester, third-grade Tiffany reviews the work in her portfolio. She selects the following writings for the second grading period:

▼ a photocopy of the final version of her autobiography along with her rough drafts, prewriting clusters, and lifeline
▼ a simulated journal about Eleanor Roosevelt written after reading a biography about the famous first lady
▼ a collection of Christmas poems
▼ her literature log with entries written to classmates about books Tiffany read during readers' workshop
▼ story problems written in math as part of a money unit
▼ a math log for a unit on fractions with quickwrites and drawings
▼ a report about games the Plains Indians played written as part of a theme cycle on Native Americans, with rough drafts and other preliminary writings
▼ a learning log from the theme cycle, including maps, clusters, and quickwrites

As she adds each item to her portfolio, Tiffany writes a reflection, or self-assessment, pointing out her accomplishments and explaining why she selected each item for her portfolio. She clips a reflection to the top of each item. Figure 12-1 presents two of these reflections. The first one is about her autobiography, and her comments reflect her pride in this book. Her parents value it greatly, and Tiffany points out some of her accomplishments, including the table of comments, three chapters, and photo illustrations. The second reflection is about her literature log, which is a series of letters sent back and forth to classmates, in which she remarks about the books she is reading. Previously, Tiffany limited her comments to the name of the book and a sentence describing the book. After a conference with Mrs. Meyers, Tiffany is trying to write longer, more interesting letters. She is writing to a more varied audience and including a question to spur the classmate to respond.

Mrs. Meyers keeps two crates holding students' portfolios on a counter in the classroom; it is accessible to the children at any time. Mrs. Meyers encourages the

FIGURE 12-1   *A Third Grader's Reflections on Two of Her Writings*

students to review their own portfolios and look for ways their writing and their knowledge about written language has developed.

By the end of the year, students' portfolios will be thick with papers that document the activities students have been involved in and each student's development as a reader and writer. During the last week of the school year, students will review their portfolios and remove about half of the materials. The other half will be passed on to the fourth-grade teacher. Students make a take-home portfolio for the materials they remove to document their third-grade year. Mrs. Meyers adds a cover letter for these take-home portfolios, and in this letter she comments on the portfolios, reflects on the class and their year together, and invites parents to celebrate their children's successes as learners as they review the portfolio.

P ortfolio assessment is an innovative way to assess students' learning which shifts assessment from a test or a grade to complete pieces of writing that represent a student's achievements (De Fina, 1992; Wiggins, 1989; Graves & Sunstein, 1992). Portfolios contain a collection of writings selected by students, students' self-assessments of their writings, and teachers' anecdotal notes about students as writers and their writings. The writing portfolio is similar to an artist's portfolio, a collection of exemplary work, gathered over time to document the talents and achievements of the artist (D'Aoust, 1992). The goal of portfolio assessment is to learn how students develop and perform as writers. It is a more authentic form of assessment because entire student papers (usually with rough drafts and prewriting clusters), not just grades, are used to document student learning.

A portfolio is not just a manila folder with a collection of student writing; it is a way of learning about students and how they write; it gives evidence of both the products students create and the process they use (Lucas, 1992). The difference between a writing folder and a portfolio is reflection (D'Aoust, 1992). Reflection requires students to pause and become aware of themselves as writers. Indeed, reflection is part of the writing process itself. Students write, pause, reflect, write some more, reflect, and so on. Many students initially lack the vocabulary to be reflective. They do not know what to say or how to apply writing concepts to themselves as writers.

Portfolio assessment is an integral part of the curriculum. Yetta Goodman (1989) explains that assessment "cannot be divorced from classroom organization, from the relationship between teacher and student; from continuous learning experiences and activities" (p. 4). The important thing to remember is that assessment leads to action—revision, teaching, or future writing. Assessment need never be a dead end.

According to Kenneth Goodman (1989), assessment has five characteristics:

▼ Assessment is holistic, using natural language taken from authentic contexts.
▼ Assessment treats students with respect and reveals their writing competencies.
▼ Assessment is consistent with what researchers have learned about teaching, learning, and language development.
▼ Assessment is innovative, creative, and dynamic.
▼ Assessment is open-ended, allowing for change and individual differences.

These characteristics are embodied in portfolio assessment. According to de Fina (1992), portfolios are systematic, authentic, and meaningful collections of students' writings and other works, and students not only select pieces to be placed in their portfolios but learn to establish criteria for their selections. Because of students' involvement in selecting pieces for their portfolios and reflecting on them, portfolio assessment respects students and their abilities. Portfolios are dynamic and reflect students' day-to-day learning activities. They are open-ended and ongoing, showing the student's progress over a period of time.

While assessing students' learning is important, assessment, whether traditional or holistic, can still have negative consequences. Frank Smith (1988) regards grading as the greatest danger in education today, and he cautions teachers that even when their purpose in grading writing is to benefit the writer, negative consequences are inevitable:

When evaluation and grading are unavoidable, as they so often are, it can be made clear to the student that the "mark" is given for administrative or bureaucratic purposes that have nothing to do with "real world" writing. Grading never taught a writer anything. Writers learn by learning about writing, not by getting letters or numbers put on their efforts and abilities. (p. 30)

Portfolio assessment mitigates some of Smith's concerns, but teachers must be sensitive to the negative consequences of any type of assessment as they assess students' writing.

This chapter focuses on three assessment activities: informal, process, and product. Teachers use informal monitoring or daily observation to keep track of students' progress. Process and product assessment are more formal measures and are appropriate when students use the process approach to writing. In process assessment, teachers monitor the process students use as they write, while product assessment deals with the quality of students' finished compositions. In all three types of assessment, however, the goal is to help students become better writers. The last section of this chapter examines ways to explain portfolio assessment and report the results of assessment to parents.

INFORMAL MONITORING OF STUDENT WRITING

Keeping track of students' progress in each curricular area is one of the more complex responsibilities facing elementary teachers, and this ongoing assessment is more difficult in writing than in other areas. Writing is multidimensional and not adequately measured simply by counting the number or quality of compositions a student has written. Three procedures for daily monitoring of students' progress in writing are observing, conferencing, and collecting writing in folders. These informal procedures allow teachers to interact daily with students and to document the progress students make in writing.

Observing

Careful, focused observation of students as they write (and keeping detailed notes of these observations) is part of good teaching as well as part of assessment in writing classrooms. Teachers watch students as they write, participate in writing groups, revise and proofread their writing, and share their finished compositions with genuine audiences. Teachers observe to learn about students' attitudes toward writing, the writing strategies that students use, how students interact with classmates during writing, and whether classmates seek out particular students for assistance or sharing writing.

While observing, teachers may ask questions (e.g., "Are you having a problem?" "What are you planning to do next?") to clarify what they have observed. Observing is not necessarily time-consuming. Even though teachers watch and interact with students throughout their reading and writing projects, these observations take only a few minutes, and for experienced teachers who know their students well, a single glance may provide the needed information about a student's progress.

In general, the richest source of information will be close attention to students as they read and write. Graves (1983) suggests that teachers should observe the class as a whole during writing as well as spend approximately 5 minutes observing each individual student. This "close-in" observation, as Graves calls it, involves sitting next to or across from students as they write. Graves recommends that teachers tell students why they are observing by saying, "I'm going to watch as you write for a few minutes so that I can help you become a better writer. Pretend that I'm not here, and just continue with what you are doing." Teachers may do this "close-in" observation only once a month as students write for varied purposes and audiences.

Conferencing

As students write, teachers often hold short, informal conferences to talk with them about their writing or to help them solve a problem related to their writing. These conferences can be held at students' desks as the teacher moves around the classroom, at the teacher's desk, or at a special writing conference table. Some occasions for these conferences include the following:

1. *On-the-Spot Conferences.* Teachers visit briefly with students at their desks to monitor some aspect of the writing assignment or to see how the student is progressing. These conferences are brief, with the teacher often spending less than a minute at a student's desk before moving on.
2. *Prewriting Conferences.* The teacher and student make plans for writing in a prewriting conference. They may discuss possible writing topics, how to narrow a broad topic, or how to gather and organize information before writing.
3. *Drafting Conferences.* At these conferences, students bring their rough drafts and talk with the teacher about specific writing trouble spots. Together the teacher and the student discuss the problem and brainstorm ideas for solving it.
4. *Revising Conferences.* A small group of students and the teacher meet together in a revising conference to get specific suggestions about how to revise their compositions. These conferences offer student writers an audience to provide feedback on how well they have communicated.
5. *Editing Conferences.* In these individual or small-group conferences, the teacher reviews students' proofread compositions and helps them to correct spelling, punctuation, capitalization, and other mechanical errors.
6. *Instructional Minilesson Conferences.* In these conferences, teachers meet with individual students or small groups to provide special instruction on a strategy or skill (e.g., writing a lead, using commas in a series) that is particularly troublesome for students.
7. *Assessment Conferences.* In assessment conferences, teachers meet with students after they complete their compositions to talk with them about their growth as writers and their plans for future writing. Teachers ask students to reflect on their writing competencies and to set goals for their next writing assignment.

8. *Portfolio Conferences.* The teacher meets individually with students to review the writing samples and other materials they have placed in their portfolios. Students might explain why they chose to include particular writing samples in the portfolio, or the teacher might read and respond to the self-evaluations attached to each writing sample. As with assessment conferences, teachers and students can use portfolio conferences for setting goals and reflecting on students' growth as writers.

At these conferences, the teacher's role is to be a listener and guide. Teachers can learn a great deal about students and their writing if they listen as students talk about their writing. When students explain a problem they are having to the teacher, teachers are often able to help them decide on a way to work through the problem. A list of questions that teachers can use in conferences to encourage students to talk about their writing is presented in Figure 12-2. Graves (1983) suggests that teachers balance the amount of their talk with the child's talk during the conference, and at the end reflect on what the child told them, what responsibilities the child can take, and whether the child understands what to do next.

FIGURE 12-2   *Questions Teachers Ask in Writing Conferences*

As students begin to write:

What are you going to write about?
How did you choose (or narrow) your topic?
What prewriting activities are you doing?
How are you gathering ideas for writing?
How will you organize your writing?
How will you start writing your rough draft?
What form will your writing take?
Who will be your audience?
What problems do you think you might have?
What do you plan to do next?

As students are drafting:

How is your writing going?
Are you having any problems?
What do you plan to do next?

As students revise their writing:

What questions do you have for your writing group?
What help do you want from your writing group?
What compliments did your writing group give you?

What suggestions did your writing group give you?
How do you plan to revise your writing?
What kinds of revisions did you make?
What do you plan to do next?

As students edit their writing:

What kinds of mechanical errors have you located?
How has your editor helped you proofread?
How can I help you identify (or correct) mechanical errors?
What do you plan to do next?
Are you ready to make your final copy?

After students have completed their compositions:

What audience will you share your writing with?
What did your audience say about your writing?
What do you like best about your writing?
If you were writing the composition again, what changes would you make?
How did you use the writing process in writing this composition?

Collecting Writing Samples

Students keep their current writing in their desks in manila folders called theme studies folders. Students have separate folders for each literature focus unit and theme cycle they are involved in. These folders contain work-in-progress including stories, poems, reports, and other pieces being developed and refined using the writing process. All prewriting activities and drafts should be kept together in order to document the process that students use. Students also keep learning logs, quickwrites, diagrams, clusters, and other informal writing related to ongoing literature study and theme cycles in these folders.

Students select their best pieces of writing from literature studies and theme cycles to place in their portfolios. Writing should be dated, and all pieces related to one project should be clipped together. Many pieces of writing in a student's portfolio should illustrate all stages of the writing process so the student's progress can be tracked month by month. Many aspects of the writing process can be documented through the samples in a student's portfolio, including topics and themes, writing forms, types of revisions, proofreading skills, spelling, and handwriting.

Writing portfolios can also be used for parent conferences and as part of the assessment at the end of each grading period. Parents may need help in understanding what the pieces of writing demonstrate. Rynkofs (1988) recommends that parents and teachers examine portfolios together for what they show children *do* know and apply rather than what they don't know. Also, when portfolios are sent home for parents to examine at the end of a grading period, Rynkofs suggests preparing a cover sheet that describes the types of writing parents will see in the portfolio, the competencies the student demonstrated in the writings, and goals for the upcoming grading period. After viewing the portfolio, parents may make comments or ask questions on the cover sheet and return it to school.

Portfolios can also be passed from teacher to teacher to provide a developmental perspective on students' growth as writers, and the summary sheets written at the end of each grading period will provide useful information for teachers as well as parents. Bingham (1988) explains that writing portfolios are useful because they provide accountability by documenting the writing program and individual students' progress.

In a writing process classroom, students rarely throw away a piece of writing or take it home to stay because part of the record of the child's writing development is lost. Also, these pieces of writing may be used in the classroom for minilessons on specific writing skills and strategies.

Keeping Records

Teachers need to document the data collected through observations and conferences. Simply recording a grade in a grade book does not provide an adequate record of a student's writing progress; instead, teachers should keep a variety of records to document students' writing progress. These records may include copies of students' writing, anecdotal notes from observations and conferences, checklists of strategies and skills taught in minilessons, strategies and skills applied in students' writing, and writing process activities that students participate in while writing.

Anecdotal Records. Teachers make brief anecdotal records as they observe students writing informally—making clusters or writing in journals—and doing process writing projects. Anecdotal notes provide teachers with rich details about students' writing and their knowledge of written language. These notes are a powerful tool for ongoing literacy assessment (Rhodes & Nathenson-Mejia, 1992). As teachers take notes, they describe the specific event and report what they have observed, without evaluating or interpreting the information. Teachers also connect the student's writing behavior with other information about the student. A yearlong collection of these records provides a comprehensive picture of a student's development as a writer. Instead of recording random samples, teachers should choose events that are characteristic of each student's writing.

Several organizational schemes are possible, and teachers should use the format that is most comfortable for them. Some teachers make a card file with dividers for each child and write anecdotes on notecards. They feel comfortable jotting notes on these small notecards or even carrying around a set of cards in their pockets. Other teachers divide a spiral-bound notebook into sections for each child and write the anecdotes in the notebook that they keep on their desks. A third scheme is to write anecdotes on sheets of paper and clip these sheets to the students' writing portfolios. Another possibility is to use self-sticking notes that can be attached to notecards or in notebooks. Like notecards, little pads of these notes are small enough to fit into a pocket.

Teachers need a routine for making anecdotal records. Some teachers identify five students to observe each day, and others concentrate on one small group of students each day. Whatever the arrangement, teachers use notecards, a notebook, or little pads of paper to take notes. Later they transfer the notes to a more permanent file. Periodically, teachers review and analyze the notes they have collected. Rhodes and Nathenson-Mejia (1992) recommend that teachers identify patterns that emerge over time, including similarities and differences, identify strengths and weaknesses, and make inferences about students' writing development. It is important that teachers make time to both record anecdotal notes and analyze them.

An excerpt from an anecdotal record documenting a fifth grader's progress in writing is presented in Figure 12-3. In this excerpt, the teacher has dated each entry and used writing terminology such as *clustering, drafting,* and *compliments.* Each entry provides information about the skills and strategies the child has demonstrated.

Checklists. Teachers can develop a variety of checklists to use in assessing students' progress in writing. Some of the possible checklists include inventories of

▼ writing forms
▼ writing strategies
▼ punctuation marks and other mechanical skills
▼ writing topics or themes

FIGURE 12-3 *Excerpt from an Anecdotal Writing Record*

Name: Matthew   Grade: 5

American Revolution Theme

March 5   Matthew selected Ben Franklin as historical figure for American Rev-
               olution projects.

March 11   Matthew fascinated with information he has found about B. F.
               Brought several sources from home. Is completing B. F.'s lifeline with
               many details.

March 18   Simulated journal. Four entries in four days! Interesting how he
               picked up language style of the period in his journal. Volunteers to
               share daily. I think he enjoys the oral sharing more than the writing.

March 25   Nine simulated journal entries, all illustrated. High level of enthusi-
               asm.

March 29   Conferenced about cluster for B. F. biography. Well developed with
               five rays, many details. Matthew will work on "contributions" ray. He
               recognized it as the least-developed one.

April 2   Three chapters of biography drafted. Talked about "working titles" for
               chapters and choosing more interesting titles after writing that reflect
               the content of the chapters.

April 7   Drafting conference. Matthew has completed all five chapters. He
               and Dustin are competitive, both writing on B. F. They are reading
               each other's chapters and checking the accuracy of information.

April 12   Writing group. Matthew confused Declaration of Independence with
               the Constitution. Chapters longer and more complete since drafting
               conference. Compared with autobiography project, writing is more so-
               phisticated. Longer, too. Reading is influencing writing style, e.g.,
               "Luckily for Ben." He is still somewhat defensive about accepting
               suggestions except from me. He will make 3 revisions—agreed in
               writing group.

April 15   Revisions: (1) eliminated "he" (substitute), (2) resequenced Chapter
               3 (move), and (3) added sentences in Chapter 5 (add).

April 19   Proofread with Dustin. Working hard.

April 23   Editing conference—no major problems. Discussed use of commas
               within sentences, capitalizing proper nouns. Matthew and Dustin
               more task-oriented on this project; I see more motivation and commit-
               ment.

April 29   Final copy of biography completed and shared with class.

▼ writing process activities
▼ misspelled words by category of invented spelling
▼ types of revisions
▼ writing competencies

Three sample checklists are presented in Figure 12-4. Teachers add checkmarks, dates, comments, or other information to complete these checklists. The forms can be clipped inside students' writing portfolios.

PROCESS MEASURES

Until recently, the formal assessment of student writing has focused on the quality of students' finished compositions; however, the writing process and its emphasis on what students actually do as they write has spawned a different approach to writing assessment. Process assessment is designed to probe how students write, the decisions they make as they write, and the strategies they use rather than the quality of their finished products. Three measures for process assessment are writing process checklists, student-teacher assessment conferences, and self-assessment by students. Information from these three measures together with the product assessment measures provides a more complete assessment picture.

Writing Process Checklists

As teachers observe students while they are writing, they can note how students move through the writing process stages: gathering and organizing ideas during prewriting, pouring out and shaping ideas during drafting, meeting in writing groups to get feedback about their writing and then making substantive changes during revising, proofreading and correcting mechanical errors during editing, and publishing and sharing their writing (McKenzie & Tompkins, 1984). The checklist presented in Figure 12-5 lists several characteristic activities for each stage of the writing process. Teachers observe students as they write and participate in other writing process activities, and place checkmarks and add comments as necessary for each observed activity. Students can also use the checklist for self-assessment to help them become aware of the activities involved in the writing process. Temple and his colleagues (1988) advocate periodic process assessments to determine whether students are using the writing process.

The writing process checklist can also be adapted for various types of writing projects. For example, if students are writing autobiographies, items can be added in the prewriting stage about developing a lifeline and clustering ideas for each chapter topic. In the sharing stage, items focusing on adding a table of contents, an illustration for each chapter, and sharing the completed autobiography with at least two other people can be included. Checklists for an autobiography project and for a project on fables are presented in Figure 12-6 (pp. 386–387) to show how the basic writing process checklist can be adapted for two types of writing.

Punctuation Mark Skills Checklist			
Name: _____ Grading Period 1 2 3 4			
Skill	Introduced	Practiced	Applied in Writing
Period at the end of a sentence			
after abbreviations			
after numbers in a list			
after an initial			
Question Mark at the end of a question			
Exclamation Mark after words or sentences showing excitement or strong feeling			
Quotation Marks before/after direct quotations			
around title or a poem, short story, song, or TV program			
Apostrophe in contractions			
to show possession			
Comma to separate words in a series			
between day and year			
between city and state			
after greeting in a friendly letter			

FIGURE 12-4 *Checklists for Monitoring Students' Writing*
Adapted from Faigley & Witte, 1981, pp. 400–414; Tompkins and Friend, 1988, pp. 4–9.

Punctuation Mark Skills Checklist			
Name: _____ Grading Period 1 2 3 4			
Skill	Introduced	Practiced	Applied in Writing
after closing of a letter			
after an initial *yes* or *no*			
after a noun of direct address			
to separate a quote from the speaker			
before the conjunction in a compound sentence			
after a dependent clause at the beginning of a sentence			
Colon before a list			
in writing time			
after the greeting of a business letter			
after an actor's name in a script			
Parentheses to enclose unimportant information			
to enclose stage directions in a script			
Hyphen between parts of a compound number			
to divide a word at the end of a line			
between parts of some compound words			

FIGURE 12-4, *continued*

Writing process checklists can also be used in conjunction with product assessment. Teachers can base a percentage of students' grades on how well they used the writing process and the remaining percentage on the quality of the writing.

Assessment Conferences

Language arts educators such as Nancie Atwell (1988) argue that to encourage students to take risks and experiment in their writing not every piece of writing should be graded. Instead, through assessment conferences teachers meet with individual students, and together they discuss the student's writing, examine papers from the

Revision Checklist				
Name: _____			Grading Period 1 2 3 4	
Type of Change				
Level of Change	1 Add	2 Substitute	3 Delete	4 Move	TOTAL
1 Word					
2 Phrase/ Clause					
3 Sentence					
4 Multi- sentence/ Paragraph					
5 Entire Text					
TOTAL					

FIGURE 12-4, *continued*

writing portfolio, and decide on a grade based on their goals for the writing project or grading period. These discussions may focus on any aspect of the writing process including topic selection, prewriting activities, word choice, writing-group activities, types of revisions, consistency in editing, and degree of effort and involvement in the writing project. These questions encourage students to reflect on their writing:

▼ What was easy (or difficult) about writing this paper?
▼ What did you do well on this writing assignment?
▼ What did you do to gather and organize ideas before writing?
▼ What kinds of help did you get from your writing group?
▼ What kind of revisions did you make?
▼ How do you proofread your papers?

Writing Forms Checklist	
Name: _____ Grading Period 1 2 3 4	
ABC book	learning log
ad/commercial	letter—business
autobiography	letter—friendly
biography	letter—simulated
book/film review	lifeline/timeline
brainstormed list	map
comic strip	myth/legend
chart/diagram/poster	newspaper
cluster	newspaper—simulated
comparison	persuasive essay
cubing	poem
directions	puzzle
fable	research report
greeting card	script
interview	story
journal-dialogue	other
journal-personal	
journal-simulated	

FIGURE 12-4, *continued*

▼ What mechanical errors are easy (or difficult) to locate?
▼ Read your favorite part to me. Why do you like it?

  Through the judicious use of these questions, teachers help students probe their understanding of the writing process and their own competencies. Atwell keeps these conferences brief, spending only 10 minutes with each student, and at the end of the meeting, she and the student develop a set of goals for the following writing project or grading period. This list of goals can be added to the student's writing folder and used to begin the next assessment conference. An upper-grade student's list of goals might include the following:

▼ I will have my rough drafts ready for my writing group on time.
▼ I will write five poems during the next grading period.

Student: _____	Dates					
Prewriting Can the student identify the specific audience to whom he/she will write?						
Does this awareness affect the choices the student makes as he/she writes?						
Can the student identify the purpose of the writing activity?						
Does the student write on a topic that grows out of his/her own experience?						
Does the student engage in rehearsal activities before writing?						
Drafting Does the student write rough drafts?						
Does the student place a greater emphasis on content than on mechanics in the rough drafts?						
Revising Does the student share his/her writing in conferences?						

FIGURE 12-5 *A Writing Process Checklist*
Source: McKenzie & Tompkins, 1984, p. 211.

> ▼ I will locate 75% of my spelling errors when I proofread.
> ▼ I will explain the purpose in the first two paragraphs of the essays I write.

Self-Assessment

Temple and his colleagues (1988) recommend that we teach students to assess their own writing and writing processes. In self-assessment, students assume responsibility for assessing their own writing and for deciding which pieces of writing they will share with the teacher and classmates and place in their portfolios. This ability to reflect on one's own writing promotes organizational skills, self-reliance, independence, and creativity. Furthermore, self-evaluation is a natural part of writing (Stires, 1991).

Students assess their writing throughout the writing process. They assess their rough drafts as well as their finished compositions. Before sharing their writing with classmates in a writing group, for example, students examine their rough drafts and make some preliminary assessments. This self-assessment may deal with the quality of writing; that is, whether or not the writing communicates effectively and how adequately the writing incorporates the requirements for the composition as stipulated

Student: _____	Dates					
Revising Does the student participate in discussions about classmates' writing?						
In revising, does the student make changes to reflect the reactions and comments of both teacher and classmates?						
Between first and final drafts, does the student make substantive or only minor changes?						
Editing Does the student proofread his/her own papers?						
Does the student help proofread classmates' papers?						
Does the student increasingly identify his/her mechanical errors?						
Publishing Does the student publish his/her writing in an appropriate form?						
Does the student share this finished writing with an appropriate audience?						

FIGURE 12-5, *continued*

by the teacher. For example, third graders can check to see that their animal reports answer these questions:

▼ Where does the animal live?
▼ What does the animal eat?
▼ What does the animal look like?
▼ How does the animal protect itself?

Fifth graders who are writing reports on states can check to see that they have included geographic, historical, and economic information as well as other information that the teacher has specified. Teachers can guide students as they assess their writing by listing questions on the chalkboard or developing a checklist for students to complete as they consider their writing. A sample checklist for fifth graders who are writing state reports is presented in Figure 12-7.

After students meet in a writing group, they use self-assessment again as they decide which revisions to make. This assessment is often difficult for students as they

---

Autobiography Checklist

Writer: _____

Prewriting	_____	Created a lifeline
	_____	Brainstormed eight chapter topics
	_____	Chose four topics for chapters
	_____	Clustered each topic for a chapter
Drafting	_____	Wrote a draft of each chapter
	_____	Wrote on every other line and marked papers as a ROUGH DRAFT
Revising	_____	Participated in a writing group
	_____	Made at least three changes in the draft
Editing	_____	Completed an editing checklist with a partner
	_____	Had a conference with the teacher
Publishing	_____	Added a title page and a table of contents
	_____	Recopied the autobiography
	_____	Added an illustration for each chapter
	_____	Shared the autobiography with two other people

1. _____

2. _____

FIGURE 12-6   *Process Checklists for Specific Writing Forms*

struggle to deal with their own egocentricity as well as the sometimes laborious suggestions made by others. They also consider the teacher's revision suggestions but in the end often choose to make a revision suggested by a classmate instead.

Teachers can develop a self-assessment questionnaire for students to complete after sharing their writing. Some questions should deal with the writing process and others with the composition. A self-assessment questionnaire for eighth graders is presented in Figure 12-8. As students gain experience with self-assessment, they can write more sophisticated reflections. Completing the self-assessment questionnaire, sharing their reflections, can be considered as one of the steps in the sharing stage of the writing process.

Students use self-assessment as they select pieces of writing to place in their portfolios. They choose favorite compositions as well as those that demonstrate new competencies or experimentation with new techniques. During evaluation confer-

Fables Project Checklist		Student	Teacher
Writer: _____			
Prewriting	Read 5 fables and took notes in your reading log.	☐	☐
	Drew a story cluster of one fable.	☐	☐
	Copied the list of characteristics of fables that we developed together.	☐	☐
	Listed morals from 10 fables.	☐	☐
	Planned a fable and drew a story cluster.	☐	☐
Drafting	Wrote a rough draft from your story cluster.	☐	☐
Revising	Participated in a writing group and compared your fable with the list of characteristics of fables.	☐	☐
	Made at least one revision.	☐	☐
Editing	Proofread with a partner and corrected spelling and other errors.	☐	☐
	Had a conference with the teacher.	☐	☐
Publishing	Wrote the final copy in your best handwriting.	☐	☐
	Added an illustration.	☐	☐
	Shared with classmates from the author's chair.	☐	☐

FIGURE 12-6, *continued*

ences, teachers help students make selections and talk about how the writing demonstrates the student's growth as a writer. Students also write self-assessments or reflections to attach to compositions that are placed in portfolios. In their reflections, students comment on their reasons for selecting a particular piece of writing.

Self-assessment can also be used for an end-of-the-school-year assessment. Coughlan (1988) asked his seventh-grade students to "show me what you have learned about writing this year" and "explain how you have grown as a written language user, comparing what you knew in September to what you know now" (p. 375). These upper-grade students used a process approach to develop and refine their compositions, and they submitted all drafts with their final copies. Coughlan exam-

Name: _____ State: _____

After you have written the rough draft of your state report, complete this checklist to make sure that you have included all the necessary information.

Yes   No

☐   ☐   Have you written information about the **geography** of the state?

☐   ☐   Have you drawn a **map** of the state?

☐   ☐   Have you written information about the **history** of the state?

☐   ☐   Have you made a **timeline** of the state?

☐   ☐   Have you written information about the **economy** of the state?

☐   ☐   Have you written information about **places to visit** in the state?

☐   ☐   Have you written **something special** about the state?

☐   ☐   Have you included maps and other information that the **state tourist department** sent to you?

FIGURE 12-7   *Self-Assessment Checklist for a Report on a State*

Name _____ Date _____

Title _____

As you publish your writing, reflect on your writing processes and this piece of writing. Please respond briefly to at least three questions in each section.

Part 1: Your Writing Processes

What part of the writing process was most successful for you?

What writing strategies did you use?

What part of the writing process was least successful for you?

What do you need help with?

Part 2: This Piece of Writing

What pleases you most about this piece of writing?

Are you comfortable with this topic and genre?

How did you organize your writing?

Does your lead grab your readers' attention?

Which type of mechanical errors cause you the most trouble?

FIGURE 12-8   *A Self-Assessment Questionnaire*
Source: Tompkins, 1992, p. 246

ined both the content of their compositions and the strategies they used in thinking through the assignment and writing their responses. He found this "test" to be a very worthwhile project because it "forced the students to look within themselves . . . to realize just how much they had learned" (p. 378). Moreover, the students' compositions verified that they had learned about writing and that they could articulate that learning.

PRODUCT MEASURES

Even though assessment of the process students use when writing may be of greater importance in assisting students to improve their writing, it is the finished composition, the product, that parents, teachers, and employers use to judge writing achievement (Bean & Bouffler, 1987). Product assessment focuses on the quality of students' compositions and often is equated with assigning a grade.

Assessing the quality of student writing is one of the most laborious and time-consuming responsibilities of teaching, so much so that some teachers assign very few writing projects in order to avoid assessment. Teachers can decrease the time spent assessing students' writing in two ways. First, teachers teach students to use a process approach to writing. When students use the writing process, assessment is not as difficult because students write better compositions. Second, teachers identify the requirements of the writing project for students as it is assigned; when students understand the requirements of the project *before* they write, the finished compositions are easier to grade because they more closely meet the requirements of the project.

When teachers assess students' writing, they should have specific criteria in mind. These criteria vary according to the writing project and the purpose of the assessment, but they should get to the heart of writing and not focus just on mechanical errors. No matter what type of assessment measure is used, the goal of assessment is to help students improve as writers and feel successful.

The most common way to assess student papers is for teachers to mark mechanical errors, make a few comments, assign a grade, and return the composition to the student. However, writing is a complex cognitive activity, and measuring only one or two dimensions of a student's work, as in this common procedure, is inadequate. Four product measures that provide a broader assessment of writing and address its multiple dimensions are (a) holistic scoring, (b) primary trait scoring, (c) analytic scoring, and (d) error analysis. Each type of measure is discussed below. Also discussed in this section are responding to students' writing and assigning grades.

Holistic Scoring

In holistic scoring, teachers read students' writing for a general or whole impression, and according to this general impression they sort compositions into three, four, five, or six piles from strongest to weakest. Then the compositions in each pile can be awarded a numerical score or letter grade. Every aspect of the composition, both content and mechanical considerations, affects the teacher's response, but none of them are specifically identified or directly addressed using a checklist. Instead, the focus is on overall writing performance.

Holistic scoring is often used for large-scale school district or national writing assessments, and for these assessments, readers are carefully trained. Compositions are typically rated on four- or eight-point numerical scales. Even-number scales are favored so there is no middle number for average compositions. Before the scoring begins, trainers review a small group of compositions to identify anchor papers representative of each point on the scale. All compositions are read by at least two readers, and numerical scores are either averaged or added together for a cumulative score.

The holistic approach is rapid and efficient and is used to judge overall writing performance without emphasis on any particular writing skill. However, it is not an appropriate measure to use when teachers want to assess how well students have used a particular writing form or applied specific writing skills in a composition. The major drawback of this approach in elementary classrooms is that teachers may unknowingly place too much emphasis on mechanical correctness, particularly spelling, grammar/usage, and handwriting, and therefore bias their assessment (Rafoth & Rubin, 1984; Searle & Dillon, 1980).

Primary Trait Scoring

In primary trait scoring teachers focus on specific writing or rhetorical skills in assessing a composition. The most important, or primary, traits will vary depending on the writing form and audience. For example, the primary traits that teachers want to assess in friendly letters written to pen pals will be different from those in business letters written to state departments of tourism. Similarly, the primary traits assessed for tall tales that students write are different from those for myths.

Primary trait assessment is based on two ideas: first, that compositions are written using specific forms for specific functions and audiences, and second, that writing should be judged according to situation-specific criteria. Because the criteria are specific, primary traits differ from one writing project to another, depending on the nature of the assignment. Strong compositions will exemplify the primary traits, and weak compositions will not, no matter how well written the weaker papers may be.

The first step in primary trait scoring is to determine which traits are essential to a specific writing project. These are the traits that will be scored. The next step is to develop a scoring guide with a list of the primary traits to use in assigning scores. Teachers distribute the scoring guide to students before they begin writing so that they know the criteria the teacher will use to assess their finished compositions.

As with holistic scoring, this measure was first used for large-scale writing assessments, but teachers use it when they specify what students are to include in the writing project. For example, if students are writing a research report and they are directed to include the answers to at least three research questions and a bibliography, these are primary traits, and students' compositions can be assessed as to whether each component was included. In large writing assessments, if students include one item, they receive a score of one, a two for two items, and so on. Usually a four-point system is used, but the number of points depends on the number of traits being assessed.

A primary trait scoring guide for reading logs written by fifth graders is presented in Figure 12-9. The criteria are divided into two parts. The reading log must meet the basic criteria presented in the first part before the quality of the entries can be assessed using the criteria in the second part. The criteria in the second part are listed in order of increasing difficulty. For students to receive the highest grade, the entries must exhibit almost all of the criteria.

Analytic Scoring

In analytic scoring teachers score compositions against a range of writing skills. This traditional form of assessment is most appropriate when teachers want to compare students' writing to a standard of excellence. Paul Diederich (1974) developed an analytic scoring system for high school and college students that divided writing performance into two main categories, general merit and mechanics, and he identified several specific traits related to each category. The specific traits for general merit are ideas, organization, wording, and flavor. The specific traits related to mechanics are usage and sentence structure, punctuation and capitalization, spelling, and handwriting and neatness. Diederich's two categories, general merit and mechanics, are comparable to the two categories, content and mechanics, discussed in this book. Perhaps the most significant drawback of this system is that equivalent weight is given to the two categories even though writing educators recommend that greater emphasis be given to content than mechanics.

Reading Log Scoring Guide

Name: _____ Book: _____

Part 1: Required Criteria

_____ Bibliographic information about the book

_____ A list of 20 interesting or new words found in the book

_____ At least 8 entries

_____ A cover with title and illustration

Part 2: Grading Criteria (1 for C; 2 for B; 3 or 4 for A)

_____ Entries include opinions and feelings

_____ Entries include 2 interesting words from the book

_____ Entries make comparisons with other books

_____ Entries make comparisons between the book and the reader's life

---

FIGURE 12-9 *A Primary Trait Scoring Guide*

One analytic scoring system, adapted from Diederich's scale, that can be used to assess the quality of elementary students' compositions is presented in Figure 12-10. In this system, the traits of good writing are divided into four categories: ideas, organization, style, and mechanics. This arrangement emphasizes mechanics less than do some other analytic scoring systems, such as Diederich's. Percentage values can also be assigned to each category to determine a grade. Some teachers may assign 25% to each of the four categories, while other teachers may assign 30% to each of the first three categories and 10% to mechanics.

This factor analysis of writing is more time-consuming than other assessment measures, and it has been criticized for several reasons. Edward White (1985, p. 124)

	Strong	Average	Weak
Ideas			
1. Ideas are creative.	_____	_____	_____
2. Ideas are well developed.	_____	_____	_____
3. Audience and purpose are considered.	_____	_____	_____
Organization			
1. An organizational pattern is used.	_____	_____	_____
2. Ideas are presented in logical order.	_____	_____	_____
3. Topic sentences are clear.	_____	_____	_____
Style			
1. Good choice of words.	_____	_____	_____
2. Use of figurative language.	_____	_____	_____
3. Variety of sentence patterns.	_____	_____	_____
Mechanics			
1. Most words are spelled correctly.	_____	_____	_____
2. Punctuation and capitalization are used correctly.	_____	_____	_____
3. Standard language is used.	_____	_____	_____

Comments:

FIGURE 12-10   An Analytic Scoring System

characterizes this approach as "pedagogically destructive and theoretically bankrupt" even though it is the most commonly used measure in schools today. Analytic scoring is subjective, and the categories may not be appropriate for some writing forms or may not reflect what students are learning about writing, as a primary trait scoring system would. Also, students who are rated high on one trait tend to be rated high on other traits; this is known as the "halo" effect.

Error Analysis

Simply identifying and counting the number of errors in students' compositions is a useless measure of writing quality, but analyzing the types of errors that students make can provide valuable information about students' writing. However, the term *error* has a negative connotation. A better term is *miscue.* Kenneth Goodman (1973) coined the more neutral term *miscue* to describe language errors made by students as they read aloud. A reading miscue is defined as any oral reading response that does not match the text, and specific categories of miscues have been delineated. All readers produce miscues as they read, and categorizing them and analyzing possible patterns provides information about readers' thought processes during reading. Goodman found that good readers' miscues were more often related to meaning than poor readers' miscues, which tended to be related to phonics.

Just as teachers gain a better understanding of students' reading behaviors through a careful analysis of students' oral reading miscues, teachers can gain similar insight into students' development as writers by observing, categorizing, and analyzing writing miscues. In miscue analysis, only those miscues that alter the meaning of the text are considered important because the goal of reading comprehension is meaning. The decision of whether or not to correct a student's miscue depends on how seriously the miscue alters the meaning of what is being read and on the possibility that the student may self-correct the miscue. These same guidelines should apply for writing, and many teachers find it more useful to talk with students about miscues in assessment conferences than to try to guess at the students' reasoning and write a reaction on the compositions. Also, students often self-correct their writing miscues when they reread their compositions.

Teachers can categorize writing miscues and examine the list to discover patterns of error. This information is then used to make instructional decisions. An example is analyzing students' invented spelling errors to understand their stage of spelling development and to plan appropriate writing projects and spelling instruction (see Chapter 11).

Responding to Student Writing

When teachers assess students' compositions, they often feel compelled to respond to the writing with comments. Searle and Dillon (1980) examined the comments middle- and upper-grade teachers made on writing and found that four categories of comments accounted for more than 86% of all written responses made by the teachers in the study. The four categories were (a) grades for content and mechanics, (b) correction of most mechanical errors, (c) comments about sentence, paragraph, and other structural errors, and (d) comments such as "good work" to encourage students. This overwhelming attention to error led the researchers to conclude that the message students receive from these comments is that correctness of form is more important than audience, purpose, and content.

Other researchers have suggested that teachers should not write comments on student writing after it has been completed (Gee, 1971). Donald Graves (1983) and Eileen Tway (1980a, 1980b) recommend that comments about writing be shared with students orally in writing groups and conferences. Tway also recommends that teachers find and encourage the "nuggets" of possibility in students' writing as a way to foster growth in writing. She lists these nuggets:

▼ Original comparisons
▼ Interesting observations
▼ Elaborations
▼ Unusual treatment or twist to a usual idea or expression
▼ Creative spin-off from traditional or popular stories
▼ Word play
▼ Contrived spelling for effect
▼ Spoof on vagaries of life
▼ Vivid impressions
▼ Surprise ending (1980a, p. 304)

She suggests a variety of ways that teachers foster these nuggets, including encouraging students as they write, using questions to probe students' thinking, demonstrating how to support general statements with details, helping students to expand the nucleus of an idea, using literature as a model, and enjoying writing and the empowerment of language with students.

Assigning Grades

"Grading is a fact of life," according to Donald Graves (1983, p. 93), but he adds that teachers should use grades to encourage students as they write, not to hinder their achievement. Teachers gather information to use in grading students' progress in writing from a variety of sources, including observations, checklists, conferences, and the writing in portfolios. An adequate assessment of students' writing should include informal monitoring of student writing and process measures as well as product measures.

When students' writing is graded using product measures, only compositions that students have revised and edited should be graded, and only those papers that students identify as their best papers from all the writing they have done during a grading period should be graded. It is unfair to grade all writing and then average the grades, according to Graves, because "dry periods, slumps, high peaks are the pattern for writers of all abilities" (p. 93). Further, Tom Romano (1987) explains that grades don't teach nearly as much as teachers think, but they do have far-reaching effects on students' attitudes toward writing and on their willingness to write.

REPORTING TO PARENTS

Reporting to parents is crucial in a process-oriented writing program because the approach to language learning is different from what parents experienced in school. It is only natural that they question the rough draft papers that children bring home with unmarked errors, or that, if they visit the classroom, they are surprised by the movement around the classroom and the accompanying noise as students work in writers' workshop. Moreover, parental participation in schooling is a key factor in children's academic achievement according to the United States Department of Education's booklet *What Works: Research About Teaching and Learning* (Office of Educational Research and Improvement, 1986). Four components of a reporting program are explaining the rationale, demonstrating the program, displaying results, and communicating students' achievement through report cards.

Gill Potter (1989) argues that parents should be participants, not just interested parties, in their children's schooling. He points out that there is a subtle difference between *involvement* and *participation,* with the latter term indicating a more in-depth relationship. Educators have articulated hierarchical models of parent participation in schools (Wood, 1974; Petit, 1980) to describe how parents move from attendance at parent-teacher meetings to participation in curriculum planning. At the most basic level, parents monitor school activities by chatting informally with the teacher before and after school or by exchanging informal notes. At the next level, teachers strive to inform parents about the instructional program and their child's achievement through hallway displays, parent-teacher conferences, report cards, and other printed materials distributed by the school. At the third level, parents participate in the instructional program by volunteering in the classroom and providing special expertise for content area instruction. At the highest, most formal level, parents develop the curriculum through participation in curriculum planning committees and textbook selection committees.

Explaining the Rationale

When any new educational program is being implemented, parents will be curious about it, and to the extent that it differs from what they recall from their elementary school experience, they will be more concerned about it. Often parents expect their children to be educated as they were educated.

The process approach to writing and writers' workshop are predicated on a new view of language learning, and introducing parents to a new writing program begins with an overview of psycholinguistic and sociolinguistic theories of learning (Fields, 1988). Comparing how children learn to talk to how they learn to write and describing the type of environment that supports language learning are important components of this overview. Understanding the rationale for the program and the contribution of writing to literacy as well as how writing relates to higher-level thinking skills and learning across the curriculum is important if parents are to accept the new writing program.

Parents will also be interested in some of the specifics of the program. They will want to know about the process approach to writing and the five stages of the writing

NCTE National Council of Teachers of English
1111 Kenyon Road, Urbana, Illinois 61801

How to Help Your Child Become a Better Writer

**Suggestions for Parents
from the National Council of Teachers of English**

Dear Parent:

We're pleased you want to know how to help the NCTE effort to improve the writing of young people. Parents and teachers working together are the best means for assuring that children and youth will become skillful writers.

Because the situation in every home is different, we can't say when the best time is to pursue each of the following suggestions. In any case, please be aware that writing skill develops slowly. For some, it comes early; for others it comes late. Occasionally a child's skill may even seem to go backwards. Nonetheless, with your help and encouragement, the child will certainly progress.

The members of the National Council of Teachers of English welcome your involvement in your child's education in writing. We hope you will enjoy following these suggestions for helping your child become a better writer, both at home and at school.

Sincerely,

Executive Director

Things to Do at Home

1. Build a climate of words at home. Go places and see things with your child, then talk about what has been seen, heard, smelled, tasted, touched. The basis of good writing is good talk, and younger children especially grow into stronger control of language when loving adults—particularly parents—share experiences and rich talk about those experiences.

2. Let children see you write often. You're both a model and a teacher. If children never see adults write, they gain an impression that writing occurs only at school. What you *do* is as important as what you say. Have children see you writing notes to friends, letters to business firms, perhaps stories to share with the children. From time to time, read aloud what you have written and ask your children their opinion of what you've said. If it's not perfect, so much the better. **Making changes** in what you write confirms for the child that revision is a natural part of writing—which it is.

3. Be as helpful as you can in helping children write. Talk through their ideas with them; help them discover what they want to say. When they ask for help with spelling, punctuation, and usage, supply that help. Your most effective role is not as a critic but as a helper. Rejoice in effort, delight in ideas, and resist the temptation to be critical.

4. Provide a suitable place for children to write. A quiet corner is best, the child's own place, if possible. If not, any flat surface with elbow room, a comfortable chair, and a good light will do.

5. Give the child, and encourage others to give, the gifts associated with writing:

—pens of several kinds
—pencils of appropriate size and hardness
—a desk lamp
—pads of paper, stationery, envelopes—even stamps
—a booklet for a diary or daily journal
(Make sure that the booklet is the child's private property; when children want to share, they will.)

—a dictionary appropriate to the child's age and needs. Most dictionary use is for checking spelling, but a good dictionary contains fascinating information on word origins, synonyms, pronunciation, and so forth.

—a thesaurus for older children. This will help in the search for the "right" word.

—a typewriter (even a battered portable will do), allowing for occasional public messages, like neighborhood newspapers, or play scripts.

—erasers or "white-out" liquid for correcting errors that the child wants to repair without rewriting.

6. Encourage (but do not demand) frequent writing. Be patient with reluctance to write. "I have nothing to say" is a perfect excuse. Recognize that the desire to write is a sometime thing. There will be times when a child "burns" to write; others, when the need is cool. But frequency of writing is important to develop the habit of writing.

7. Praise the child's efforts at writing. Forget what happened to you in school and resist the tendency to focus on errors of spelling, punctuation, and other mechanical aspects of writing. Emphasize the child's successes. For every error the child makes, there are dozens of things he or she has done well.

8. Share letters from friends and relatives. Treat such letters as special events. Urge relatives and friends to write notes and letters to the child, no matter how brief. Writing is especially rewarding when the child gets a response. When thank-you notes are in order, after a holiday especially, sit with the child and write your own notes at the same time. Writing ten letters (for ten gifts) is a heavy burden for the child; space the work and be supportive.

9. Encourage the child to write for information, free samples, and travel brochures. For suggestions about where to write and how to write, purchase a copy of the helpful U.S. Postal Service booklet *All about letters* (available from NCTE @ $2.50 per copy; class sets of 20 or more, $1.50 each).

10. Be alert to occasions when the child can be involved in writing, for example, helping with grocery lists, adding notes at the end of parents' letters, sending holiday and birthday cards, taking down telephone messages, writing notes to friends, helping plan trips by writing for information, drafting notes to school for parental signature, writing notes to letter carriers and other service persons, and preparing invitations to family get-togethers.

Writing for real purposes is rewarding, and the daily activities of families present many opportunities for purposeful writing. Involving your child may take some coaxing, but it will be worth your patient effort.

Things to Do for School Writing Programs

1. Ask to see the child's writing, either the writing brought home or the writing kept in folders at school. Encourage the use of writing folders, both at home and at school. Most writing should be kept, not thrown away. Folders are important means for helping both teachers and children see progress in writing skill.

2. Be affirmative about the child's efforts in school writing. Recognize that for every error a child makes, he or she does many things right. Applaud the good things you see. The willingness to write is fragile. Your optimistic attitude toward the child's efforts is vital to strengthening his or her writing habit.

3. Be primarily interested in the content, not the mechanics of expression. It's easy for many adults to spot misspellings, faulty word usage, and shaky punctuation. Perfection in these areas escapes most adults, so don't demand it of children. Sometimes teachers—for the same reason—will mark only a few mechanical errors, leaving others for another time. What matters most in writing is words, sentences, and ideas. Perfection in mechanics develops slowly. Be patient.

4. Find out if children are given writing instruction and practice in writing on a regular basis. Daily writing is the ideal; once a week is not often enough. If classes are too large in your school, understand that it may not be possible for teachers to provide as much writing practice as they or you would like. Insist on smaller classes—no more than 25 in elementary schools and no more than four classes of 25 for secondary school English teachers.

5. Ask if *every* teacher is involved in helping youngsters write better. Worksheets, blank-filling exercises, multiple-choice tests, and similar materials are sometimes used to *avoid* having children write. If children and youth are not being asked to write sentences and paragraphs about science, history, geography, and the other school subjects, they are not being helped to become better writers. *All* teachers have responsibility to help children improve their writing skills.

6. See if youngsters are being asked to write in a variety of forms (letters, essays, stories, etc.) for a variety of purposes (to inform, persuade, describe, etc.), and for a variety of audiences (other students, teachers, friends, strangers, relatives, business firms). Each form, purpose, and audience demands differences of style, tone, approach, and choice of words. A wide variety of writing experiences is critical to developing effective writing.

7. Check to see if there is continuing contact with the imaginative writing of skilled authors. While it's true that we learn to write by writing, we also learn to write by reading. The works of talented authors should be studied not only for ideas but also for the writing skills involved. Good literature is an essential part of any effective writing program.

8. Watch out for "the grammar trap." Some people may try to persuade you that a full understanding of English grammar is needed before students can express themselves well. Some knowledge of grammar *is* useful, but too much time spent on study of grammar steals time from the study of writing. Time is much better spent in writing and conferring with the teacher or other students about each attempt to communicate in writing.

9. Encourage administrators to see that teachers of writing have plenty of supplies—writing paper, teaching materials, duplicating and copying machines, dictionaries, books about writing, and classroom libraries of good books.

10. Work through your PTA and your school board to make writing a high priority. Learn about writing and the ways youngsters learn to write. Encourage publication of good student writing in school newspapers, literary journals, local newspapers, and magazines. See that the high school's best writers are entered into the NCTE Achievement Awards in Writing Program, the Scholastic Writing Awards, or other writing contests. Let everyone know that writing matters to you.

By becoming an active participant in your child's education as a writer, you will serve not only your child but other children and youth as well. You have an important role to play, and we encourage your involvement.

Single copies of this statement are available free upon request, and may be copied without permission from NCTE. Multiple copies are available at a bulk rate of U.S. $7 per 100, prepaid only. Send request to NCTE Order Department, 1111 Kenyon Road, Urbana, IL 61801.

FIGURE 12-11 NCTE Brochure for Parents

process, the types of writing activities involved, how the program will be implemented, and, in particular, how this new emphasis on writing will benefit their children.

One way to describe writers' workshop is by showing videotapes of the program in schools where it has already been implemented. Videotapes of the writing process classrooms that Donald Graves has worked with in New Hampshire ("The Writing and Reading Process: A New Approach to Literacy" developed by Jane Hansen and Donald Graves) and Jerome Harste's series "The Authoring Cycle: Read Better, Write Better, Reason Better" are available from Heinemann Educational Publishers (361 Hanover Street, Portsmouth, NH 03801). Videotapes documenting writing activities in classrooms of teachers who have participated in National Writing Project summer institutes are available from the National Council of Teachers of English (1111 Kenyon Road, Urbana, IL 61801). Videotapes can also be made of classrooms in local schools that have implemented a process approach to writing.

Another way to involve parents is by talking to them about how they can help at home to encourage writing. Just as children need to see their parents reading for enjoyment and for genuine communicative purposes, they need to see them writing in order to appreciate writing as a genuine, functional communicative tool rather than only as something teachers make them do in school. A brochure developed by the National Council of Teachers of English, "How to Help Your Child Become a Better Writer," is presented in Figure 12-11. Copies of this brochure can be ordered from the NCTE and used in a workshop for parents. Knowledge about the writing program their child is involved in and ways they can support that learning empower parents so that they can participate meaningfully in their child's education (Allen & Freitag, 1988).

Parents may feel uncomfortable about the amount of responsibility children assume in writing process classrooms or the fact that skills are not taught in a definite sequence using a workbook. However, taking time to explain the rationale, describe the program, and invite parents to observe the program in action will help to allay their fears.

Demonstrating the Program

Having parents visit in classrooms and observe as students work in a writers' workshop is the best way to demonstrate the program. Students are enthusiastic and more committed to their writing, and as they talk about their writing, they use terms such as *clustering, rough draft, bibliography,* and *proofreading.* Their behavior provides additional evidence of the value of the program. Parents who visit classrooms see their children assuming more responsibility, working cooperatively, and taking risks as they extend their knowledge. When it is not possible for parents to view a classroom during the school day, students can demonstrate a writing group or a class collaboration activity for parents at an evening meeting. Also, writing activities in classrooms can be videotaped and then shown to parents at a later date. A teacher or student can narrate the videotape explaining what parents are seeing and why the activities are useful.

Displaying the Results

The results of a process-oriented writing program can be displayed in many ways. During parent-teacher conferences, parents can examine students' portfolios and the many pieces of writing they contain. Class newspapers and anthologies are two ways to publish student writing and, at the same time, communicate with parents. Also, in class newspapers, students can explain writing projects in progress and enlist parental support. Writing should also be displayed in the hallways and as bound books in the school library. When students write scripts for skits, plays, puppet shows, or commercials they should be performed for parents. Inviting parents to view the presentations is a convincing way to display the results of writing.

After a thorough orientation to the writing process approach, parents will be able to understand why their children don't bring work home every day, why they may need to go to the public library to do research or to check out a book to read, why misspelled words have not been corrected on rough drafts, and that there is an important difference between revising and editing. A summary of ways to encourage parents' participation in a school writing program is presented in Figure 12-12.

FIGURE 12-12   *Ten Ways to Encourage Parents' Participation in a School Writing Program*

1. **Open Houses.** Invite parents to attend open houses to view recently completed writing projects.
2. **Portfolios.** Send portfolios home for parents to review at the end of each grading period.
3. **Videotapes.** Plan viewings of videotapes (either those that are commercially available or made locally) to show the writing process in action.
4. **Professional Library.** Lend books about writing such as Judith Newman's *The Craft of Children's Writing* (1984) from a professional library established in the school.
5. **Newsletters.** Prepare weekly or monthly newsletters for parents that describe the writing program and explain new terminology and activities.
6. **Displays.** Display student writing in school hallways, the public library and other community buildings, and shopping malls.
7. **School Assemblies.** Celebrate writing in weekly assemblies that all students in the school attend and participate in.
8. **Interviews with Community Persons.** Interview community persons with special expertise in various content areas as a part of writing projects.
9. **Anthologies.** Publish an annual anthology of student writing that includes entries written by each student in the school.
10. **Volunteers.** Invite parents to serve as volunteers in the classroom to assist with writing projects.

Communicating Through Report Cards

Report cards remain a part of the school life, and they are probably the most obvious form of communicating with or reporting to parents. Even though teachers change how they teach students when they implement the process approach to writing, the report cards often remain the same with space for a single letter or number grade in language arts or writing. What does change is the way teachers determine these grades. Teachers use informal monitoring procedures, process measures, and product measures to determine grades. Many teachers also insert a sheet describing the informal and formal writing projects students were involved in during the grading period or the specific writing skills that students demonstrated through these projects. Students may also take home their writing portfolios for their parents to review and then return them to school.

Answering Teachers' Questions About...
Assessing Students' Writing

1. *Don't I have to grade every paper my students write?*

No, in a writing process classroom, students write many more papers than teachers can read and critique. As often as possible, students should write for themselves, their classmates, and other genuine audiences rather than for the teacher. Teachers need to ask themselves whether assessing each piece of writing will make their students better writers, and most teachers will admit that such a rigorous critique will not. More likely, grading every composition will clear teachers' conscience about whether they are good teachers; it will not, however, do much to improve students' writing. Teachers should use the informal monitoring procedures and process assessment measures discussed in this chapter as well as grades. Donald Graves (1983) further recommends that teachers grade only the compositions that students identify as their best ones.

2. *There are so many ways to assess writing, I don't know which one to use.*

How you assess a piece of writing depends on the writing project and on your reason for assessing it. Informal monitoring of student writing provides one measure that students are writing and completing assignments. Using process measures can help assess students' use of the writing process and various writing strategies. Process assessment should be used when teachers want to measure how well students are using the writing process. Most teachers are more familiar with product assessment and more inclined to use a product-oriented measure. If the goal of the assessment is to determine the relative merits of one composition over another, then a product measure is appropriate. Over the grading period, teachers should use a variety of assessment measures to have a more complete picture or portfolio of students as writers.

3. *If I don't correct students' errors, how will they learn not to make the errors?*

Children construct their own knowledge of the world through experience, according to Jean Piaget (1975) and other cognitive theorists. The application of this theory to writing instruction is that through experiences with reading and writing, students construct knowledge of writing and mechanical conventions of written English. Writing researchers have documented that students with differing amounts of writing experience make different kinds of writing errors, and that the errors of inexperienced writers are less sophisticated than those made by more experienced writers. Teachers can make a far more important contribution to students' learning by structuring worthwhile writing experiences, providing instruction in writing as it relates to the writing projects that students are involved in, and providing opportunities for students to share their writing with classmates than by correcting students' errors after the writing has been completed.

4. *I just don't agree with you. The mechanics are important—they are the mark of a good writer—and they should receive more importance in grading. I think mechanics should count the most in grading a student's writing.*

I agree that using correct spelling, grammar, and other mechanics is one indication of a good writer, and when the conventions of written English are used correctly, the writing is easier to read. However, literary prizes are not awarded for technically correct writing; they are awarded for writing that exhibits unique content. I would rather read writing that is clever and creative, well organized, or makes me laugh or cry even if it has some mechanical errors than a bland, error-free composition. Think for a moment about book reviews. Are books ever recommended because they don't have mechanical errors, or are they recommended because of their memorable characters or vivid language? The mechanics of writing are important, but they are better dealt with in the editing stage after students have drafted and revised their writing than in the early stages of the writing process when students are concerned with gathering and organizing ideas and finding the words to express those ideas.

REFERENCES

Allen, J. M., & Freitag, K. K. (1988). Parents and students as cooperative learners: A workshop for parents. *The Reading Teacher, 41,* 922–925.

Atwell, N. (1988). *In the middle. Writing, reading, and learning with adolescents.* Portsmouth, NH: Heinemann.

Bean, W., & Bouffler, C. (1987). *Spell by writing.* Rozelle, New South Wales (Australia): Primary English Teaching Association.

Bingham, A. (1988). Using writing folders to document student progress. In T. Newkirk & N. Atwell (Eds.), *Understanding writing: Ways of observing, learning, and teaching K–8* (2nd ed.) (pp. 216–225). Portsmouth, NH: Heinemann.

Coughlan, M. (1988). Let the students show us what they know. *Language Arts, 65,* 375–378.

D'Aoust, C. (1992). Portfolios: Process for students and teachers. In K. B. Yancey (Ed.), *Portfolios in the writing classroom: An introduction* (pp. 39–48). Urbana, IL: National Council of Teachers of English.

De Fina, A. A. (1992). *Portfolio assessment: Getting started.* New York: Scholastic.

Diederich, P. B. (1974). *Measuring growth in English.* Urbana, IL: National Council of Teachers of English.

Faigley, L., & Witte, S. (1981). Analyzing revision. *College Composition and Communication, 32,* 400–414.

Fields, M. V. (1988). Talking and writing: Explaining the whole language approach to parents. *The Reading Teacher, 41,* 898–903.

Gee, T. C. (1971). *The effects of written comment on exposition composition* (Doctoral dissertation, North Texas State University). *Dissertation Abstracts International, 31,* 3412A.

Goodman, K. S. (1973). Windows on the reading process. In K. S. Goodman and O. S. Niles (Eds.), *Miscue Analysis.* Urbana, IL: National Council of Teachers of English.

Goodman, K. S. (1989). Preface. In K. S. Goodman, Y. M. Goodman, & W. J. Hood (Eds.), *The whole language evaluation book* (pp. xi–xv). Portsmouth, NH: Heinemann.

Goodman, Y. M. (1989). Evaluation of teachers: Teachers of evaluation. In K. S. Goodman, Y. M. Goodman, & W. J. Hood (Eds.), *The whole language evaluation book* (pp. 3–14). Portsmouth, NH: Heinemann.

Graves, D. H. (1983). *Writing: Teachers and children at work.* Portsmouth, NH: Heinemann.

Graves, D. H., & Sunstein, B. S. (Eds.). (1992). *Portfolio portraits.* Portsmouth, NH: Heinemann.

Lucas, C. (1992). Introduction: Writing portfolios—changes and challenges. In K. B. Yancey (Ed.), *Portfolios in the writing classroom: An introduction* (pp. 1–11). Urbana, IL: National Council of Teachers of English.

McKenzie, L., & Tompkins, G. E. (1984). Evaluating students' writing: A process approach. *Journal of Teaching Writing, 3,* 201–212.

Newman, J. (1984). *The craft of children's writing.* Portsmouth, NH: Heinemann.

Office of Educational Research and Improvement. (1986). *What works: Research about teaching and learning.* Washington, DC: United States Department of Education.

Petit, D. (1980). *Opening up schools.* Harmondsworth, England: Penguin.

Piaget, J. (1975). *The development of thought: Equilibration of cognitive structures.* New York: Viking.

Potter, G. (1989). Parent participation in the language arts program. *Language Arts, 66,* 21–28.

Rafoth, B. A., & Rubin, D. L. (1984). The impact of content and mechanics on judgments of writing quality. *Written Communication, 1,* 446–458.

Rhodes, L. K., & Nathenson-Mejia, S. (1992). Anecdotal records: A powerful tool for ongoing literacy assessment. *The Reading Teacher, 45,* 502–509.

Romano, T. (1987). *Clearing the way: Working with teenage writers.* Portsmouth, NH: Heinemann.

Rynkofs, J. T. (1988). Send your writing folders home. In T. Newkirk & N. Atwell (Eds.), *Understanding writing: Ways of observing, learning, and Teaching K–8* (2nd ed.), (pp. 226–235). Portsmouth, NH: Heinemann.

Searle, D., & Dillon, D. (1980). Responding to student writing: What is said or how it is said. *Language Arts, 57,* 773–781.

Smith, F. (1988). *Joining the literacy club.* Portsmouth, NH: Heinemann.

Stires, S. (1991). Thinking throughout the process: Self-evaluation in writing. In B. M. Power & R. Hubbard (Eds.), *The Heinemann Reader: Literacy in process* (pp. 295–310). Portsmouth, NH: Heinemann.

Temple, C., Nathan, R., Burris, N., & Temple, F. (1988). *The beginnings of writing* (2nd ed.). Boston: Allyn & Bacon.

Tompkins, G. E. (1992). Assessing the processes students use as writers. *Journal of Reading, 36,* 244–246.

Tompkins, G. E., & Friend, M. (1988). After your students write: What's next? *Teaching Exceptional Children, 20,* 4–9.

Tway, E. (1980a). How to find and encourage the nuggets in children's writing. *Language Arts.* *57,* 299–304.

Tway, E. (1980b). Teacher responses to children's writing. *Language Arts, 57,* 763–772.

White, E. M. (1985). *Teaching and assessing writing.* San Francisco: Jossey-Bass.

Wiggins, G. (1989). A true test: Toward more authentic and equitable assessment. *Phi Delta Kappan, 70,* 703–704.

Wood, A. J. (1974). Some effects of involving parents in the curriculum. *Trends in Education, 35,* 39–45.

APPENDIX

Samples of Students' Poems

Additional samples of formula poems, free-form poems, syllable- and word-count poems, rhymed poems, and model poems are presented in this appendix. Some poems were written by primary grade students; others by middle and upper grade students. Teachers may want to share these poems with their students as part of the instructional strategy presented in Chapter 9.

FORMULA POEMS

"I Wish . . ." Poems

I wish I were an astronaut
I wish the stars were touchable.
I wish I could float.
I wish I could not burn by the sun.
I wish I could go to Planet Pluto.
I wish I could touch the stars.
I wish I were an astronaut.

David, grade 5

I wish I could fly
high in the sky.
I wish I could soar,
fly above the sea.
I wish I were a bald eagle
and eagles were not endangered.
I wish I could fly.

Josh, grade 5

I Wish . . .

I wish
That a magical rain
Would sweep across the earth
Turning war to peace
And nuclear missiles to dust.

Craig, grade 8

I wish
Our heads could pop off
So we could fix our insides
If they were damaged.

Becky, grade 6

Color Poems

Blue Is

Blue is an ice cube
melting in my hand
Blue is a tuba
playing in a band
Blue is a waterbed
that feels like silk
Blue is a blueberry
floating in milk.
Blue is an ocean
crashing on the shore
Blue is a bluejay
coming back for more.

David, grade 4

White

White is my paper
that floats gently
off the corner of my desk.

White is a pampered,
fat, house cat climbing
on the back of the chair

White is the fluffy clouds
hovering over me
for what seems like Eternity.

White is the snow
falling gently to its fate
along the busy highway.

Todd, grade 7

Yellow

Yellow is shiny galoshes
splashing through mud puddles.
Yellow is a street lamp
beaming through a dark, black night.
Yellow is the egg yolk
bubbling in a frying pan.
Yellow is the lemon cake
that makes you pucker your lips.
Yellow is the sunset
and the warm summer breeze.
Yellow is the tingling in your mouth
after a lemon drop melts.

Class collaboration, grade 7

Five Senses Poems

Red

Tastes like hot sauce on a taco
Looks like blood
Feels like when I'm angry
Smells like a red, red rose
Sounds like a fire crackling

Class collaboration, grade 5

Being Heartbroken

Sounds like thunder and lightning
Looks like a carrot going through a blender
Tastes like sour milk
Feels like a splinter in your finger
Smells like dead fish
It must be horrible!

Kim, grade 6

Electricity

Feels like ants crawling over me
Sounds like people running

Tastes like old stale bread
Looks like dancing fire
It's a shocking experience!

Don, grade 6

"If I were . . ." Poems

If I were a pig
I would play in the mud.
I would live at a farm
I would love to eat corn.
And I would lay pork chops.

Kevin, grade 1

If I were . . .

If I were a dragon,
I would breathe fire at people.

If I were a snake,
I would slither around people
and bite them.

If I were a wild horse,
I would buck off people
who tried to ride me.

If I were a mouse,
I would eat all the cheese
and never get caught in a trap.

If I were a baby,
I would squeal
and cry all day long.

If I were a billionaire,
I would spend the money
with my friends.

If I were a pencil,
I would stay dull all the time.

Leslie, grade 4

If I were a glove
I'd catch fly balls all day.
If I were a bat
I wouldn't let a ball cross the plate
If I were a ball
I would fly over the fence

If I were a home-plate
I wouldn't let people step on me.

Devin, grade 5

"*I used to/But now*" *Poems*

I used to be a cat
But now I am a dog.

I used to be a gorilla
But now I am a kangaroo.

I used to be a moon
But now I am a planet

I used to be a person
But now I am a Martian.

I used to be a Martian
But now I am a wallabangoo.

I used to be on earth
But now I live with the fairy folk.

Third-grade class collaboration

Me

I used to be a lightbulb,
But now I am a star.
I used to think the world was a kitten,
But now I know it's a lion.
I used to think I was so large
But now I know I am small.
I used to be a fool,
But now I go to school.
I used to just see myself,
But now I see others.
I used to live in Canada,
But now I live in the USA.
I used to not know who I was,
But now I know I am Cassidy.

Cassidy, grade 6

I used to be a giraffe
Walking high and proud
Touching the sky
Skimming the clouds.

But now I'm a snake
Slithering from place to place.
Everyone's scared.
I've no pride at all.

Kevin, grade 8

Lie Poems

Our Freaky Family

I know a green alien's alphabet.
My baby cousin is old
because his vocabulary is "goo-goo-gaa-gee."
My Mom is rainbow-colored
because she's a gardener.
Our purple and silver dog
had blue and gold kittens.
Our maroon and gold house
is set on a zebra-colored yard.

Amber, grade 4

Me

I live in an orange and pink pepperoni hotdog.
I eat red dogs and purple cats.
I am married to a white raincoat
I work in the middle of yellow Earth to keep it moving.
I play on an orange and black Venus space hockey team.

Eric, grade 4

The Whole Truth and Nothing But the Truth

The world is a square, purple desert.
The year is 2000 in black oil Oklahoma.
I can fly in the blue sky on the beach
Alaska is as hot as the Amazon River is pink.
I'm 556 blue years old.
My brother is sailing on 50 maroon yachts.
I can fly in two silver boats inside a ham.
My room is a small fuchsia morgue.
I drink flourescent pink Scope inside my locker.
Our polka-dotted school is as tiny as a Georgia peanut.

Sixth-grade class collaboration

"_____ *is" Poems*

Thunder is . . .

Thunder is someone bowling.
Thunder is a hot cloud bumping against a cold cloud.
Thunder is someone playing basketball.
Thunder is dynamite blasting.
Thunder is a Brontosaurus sneezing.
Thunder is people moving their furniture.
Thunder is a giant laughing.
Thunder is elephants playing.
Thunder is an army tank.
Thunder is Bugs Bunny chewing his carrots.

Second-grade class collaboration

Sadness Is

Sadness is a dropping tear hitting the ground
Sadness is a dark cloud drifting in the sky
Sadness is a gloomy day just starting

Chelsa, grade 5

What is Misery?

Misery is . . .
Falling in a deep mud hole
Getting sick while eating lunch
Stepping on thin ice
Wrecking your new bike
Eating corned beef and cabbage

Anonymous, grade 7

Preposition Poems

Beside the building I saw a deer.
Near the deer I saw something
above him. It was a fly, flying
around his head.

Before he ran I walked
toward him.
But when I got three feet
from him, he ran away.

Kevin, grade 4

Dear Teacher,

    I know I had it,
    I just know I did.
    It wasss—

Beside my bed
Above the desk
Against the wall
Among the books
Behind the door
Below the table

    Unless—my little brother ate it!
    Oh no!

              Brandon, grade 7

Superman

Within the city
In a phone booth
Into his clothes
Like a bird
In the sky
Through the walls
Until the crime
Among us
   Is defeated!

        Mike, grade 7

Free-Form Poems

The Dinosaur Poem

Millions of years ago
It was breakfast time.
The meat-eating dinosaurs,
Tyrannosaurus and Allosaurus,
   walked on their two legs
   looking for food
   in the swamp where
   they lived.
They found a Brontosaurus

And they ate him,
   clawing and
   hissing—
   Chomp! Chomp!

They spit out a bone
And went home.

John, age 5 (dictated)

Hershey's Kiss

M-M-M
delicious and scrumptious
Hershey's Kisses
When you plop it into your mouth
your tastebuds have a ball.
First you have it—
then it's gone.
When you eat chocolate, you're going to say,
YUM YUM

I love it!

Mark, age 7

Odes

Ode to the American Flag

Oh, American Flag, American Flag,
you have seen the beautiful firecrackers
bursting in the air on the fourth of July.
You have seen the new lands
and the rippling oceans.

Oh, American Flag, American Flag,
you hear jets and airplanes flying overhead.
You hear gunshots during the wars
and best of all, you hear the beautiful song,
the "Star Spangled Banner"
that tells you your country is free.

Oh, American Flag, American Flag,
your country tastes delicious pies
and yummy pizza and fried chicken
that makes your mouth water.
And don't forget your delicious hamburgers.

Oh, American Flag, American Flag,
you smell the fresh spring air

and the sweet smell of flowers
You smell the pine trees that are green
all through the year and the fresh air
that surrounds the pine trees

Oh, American Flag, American Flag,
you have felt sadness when you see
the Americans die and you feel pride
after a war when the Americans win.
You have felt honor when
American citizens are honored.

Oh, American Flag, American Flag,
you love your country so.
You have felt the tears and the pains
of all the USA and your country loves you so.

Jenny, grade 5

Ode to Grass

Oh grass,
Why do you whisper
and call to me?
At times you are short
and other times you are long.
You smell like a pine
in a farm field.
You feel so soft
and so fluffy to me.
Grass, how do you taste?

Sixth-grade class collaboration

Found Poems

(The following poem was written in response to a newspaper article about people forming a human conveyor belt to rescue books from a flooded library storage room.)

A Human Conveyor Belt

Students
Teachers
Parents
Transfer—
A human chain

Anonymous, grade 7

(The following poem was written in response to a movie review of a horror film.)

> An innocent victim, asleep
> only to awake to another
> "Bad Dream."
> I watched with a tide,
> a tide of unease rising
> within me
> shrinking.
>
> *Angela, grade 7*

Acrostics

Jeff

J azzy
E nchanting
F unny
F abulous

Jeff, grade 5

Ghost

G host creeping down the
H all
O h, what's that grabbing my neck?
S h-h-h! It's after me
T hump! It got my neck—
    Oh, heck!

Kelsey, grade 5

Chicago

C ity of
H ardworking people.
I ndustries everywhere,
C onstantly noisy streets, three-story buildings.
A thick cloud of fog covers the city.
G reat things to see,
O verlooking Lake Michigan.

April, grade 6

Mosquito

M ost
O f the time they
S warm
Q uietly above and
U nder your hand
I f
T hey would
O nly leave you alone!

Jeff, grade 7

SYLLABLE- AND WORD-COUNT POEMS

Haiku

Spider web shining
Tangled on the grass with dew
waiting quietly.

Candice, grade 4

A crafty sea gull
Soars through the wind, plunges for prey
Splash, gulp, satisfied.

Amy, grade 5

Icicles

The icicles hang
From the low roof of the house
Like glittering stars

Jason, grade 8

Fall

Multi-colored leaves
covering the cool, brown earth
winter's patchwork quilt

Vickie, grade 8

Tanka

Butterflies

Delicate and quick
Fluttering through the blue sky

In rainbow colors
Darting between the flowers
Gracefully landing on them

Amy, grade 6

The rose seems anxious
For the first spring rain to come
And give her a drink
Of its crystal clear water
So her leaves can breathe again

Tiffany, grade 7

Cinquain

Brother
Fun, pesky
Crying, walking, talking
I love my brother
Jeffrey

Audrey, grade 3

Pool
Fun, hard
Swimming, jumping, diving
You can make friends
Y.M.C.A.

Amanda, grade 3

Raccoon
Fuzzy soft sleek
Climbing crawling drinking
cheerful playful
Black mask

Twister
Dangerous Wind
Moving Destroying Turning
Scary Speeding
Funnel

Josh, grade 5

Abandoned House

Cobwebs
Hanging about
Furniture full of dust
Windows broken from strong winds
Dirty

Jennifer, grade 8

Diamante

PEOPLE
cool, dirty
running, playing, buying
clothes, hat, antenna, spacesuit
talking, walking, running
green, ugly
ALIEN

Gabriel, grade 3

FEET
stinky, sweaty
running, hurting, kicking
shoes, socks, hair, hat
thinking, concentrating, hurting
smart, hard
HEAD

Third-grade class collaboration

ICE
cold solid
Freezing chilling hardening
snow streets stoves camp-outs
burning sizzling frying
hot flames
FIRE

Fourth-grade class

CAT
pretty soft
running jumping eating
whiskers milk bones dirt
running jumping eating
loyal brave
DOG

Russell, grade 5

RHYMED POEMS

Limericks

There once was a thing at the zoo
I think that it's from Kalamazoo
It has a big nose
And ears I suppose
And for dinner, it eats airplane glue.

Jason, grade 6

Mrs. Hobb has a hat with a feather
That can even tell the weather.
It's pink when it's hot
and grey when it's not.
(By the way, it's made of leather.)

Carrie, grade 6

The Egyptian Mummy

There once was an Egyptian mummy
Who found himself next to a dummy.
Said the mummy, "Don't move
While I find a new groove,
For I don't find this situation funny."

Nicole, grade 8

Clerihews

Albert Einstein
His genius did shine.
Of relativity and energy did he dream
And scientists today hold him in high esteem.

Heather, grade 6

Mickey Mouse
Lives in a paper house
With a comical wife
In a cartoon life.

Carrie, grade 8

Clint Eastwood
All his movies, really good
I would gladly pay to hear him say,
"C'mon punk, make my day!"

Bobby, grade 8

MODEL POEMS

Apologies

Oh cookie jar,
oh cookie jar,
will you ever forgive me?
I opened your mouth
and put my hand
down your tonsils
to get some cookies.
Please, oh please,
forgive me
and my hand.
Soon I will fill you up
   again
      and again
         and again
            Krystal, grade 4

Dear Chair,

I'm so-oo-oo sorry
Day after day
I sit on you.
I didn't know
I weighed 72 pounds
until just this morning.
Please,
I beg you,
please forgive me.
        Tony, grade 5

The Truck

Dad,
I'm sorry
that I took
the truck
out for
a spin.
I knew it
was wrong.

But . . .
The exhilarating
motion was
AWESOME!

Jeff, grade 7

Invitations

My Place

Come take a ride on my seagull's back.
To a magical land where the color is pink
and love is extreme.
Come study the twinkle in the cold, blue stars.
Come wade on the clear water's waves.
Come sit under the green lacy trees.
Come to this island where the meadows are cool,
and people are everything.

B. J., grade 7

Come with Me

Come with me and fly above
    the shores of hope, the sea of love.
And land where people know no pain
    where no one's selfish, no one's vain.
Where mountains greet you with a colorful view,
    and seagulls and bluebirds are singing to you.
A place where animals roam about free,
    a place where everyone longs to be.

Amy, grade 7

Prayers from the Ark

The Kangaroo's Prayer

Dear Lord,
I thank you for making me live in Australia.
I thank you for giving me a pouch for my joey.
I forgive you for making me so ugly.
I forgive you for making my arms so short.
I thank you for making the grass so fresh.
Oh, I almost forgot, thank you very much
for giving me such powerful legs for jumping
so high and so far.

Chad, grade 2

The Mouse's Prayer

Dear Lord,
I am glad I am a mouse.
Thank you for making me quiet
and giving me sharp teeth.
I can sneak up on a cat and bite his tail.
I can also chew holes in the walls.
And thank you very much for the cheese.
I love cheese!

Jason, grade 2

Elephant's Prayer

Dear God,

I am the elephant.
Why did you make me so fat?
The ground moans when I walk.
Yet I thank you for keeping the grass
sweet and green so I can be strong.
Thank you for keeping the mud puddles soft.
I ask you one favor.
Could you keep me with this fine herd
for as long as I live?

Mattson, grade 6

If I Were in Charge of the World

If I Were in Charge of the World

I would make a law that everyone over five could drive.
I would be rich.
I would make it hot all the time, even if it snows.
I would put Alaska and Hawaii very close to the main United States.
I would let no one die.
I would make it so that kids could boss adults around.
I would make everyone look like Cookie Monster.
I would let all the animals go free.
I would get rid of people who tease people.
I would build no more schools.
I would make spring break three weeks long.
I would make people know everything when they were born
so they didn't have to go to school.
I would make people not smoke, drink, or get hooked on drugs.

I would make kids their own boss.
That's what I would do
If I were in charge of the world.

Fourth-grade class collaboration

If I were in charge of the world, I . . .
    would make it where you didn't have to miss recess
    and where you wouldn't get in trouble.
If I were in charge of the world, I . . .
    would make it where cake was a fruit
    and broccoli wasn't anything to do with food.
If I were in charge of the world, I . . .
    would make it where anyone over ten could drive a car
    and your parents would have to buy you the car you wanted.
That's what I would do
If I were in charge of the world.

Jack, grade 5

If I Were in Charge of the World

If I were in charge of the world,
there wouldn't be Brussels sprouts,
there wouldn't be quiet,
there wouldn't be homework, and
there would be more recess.

There wouldn't be long lunch lines,
there wouldn't be any days but Saturday and Sunday,
there wouldn't be chores for kids, and
there would be desserts instead of full meals.

There wouldn't be any certain bed times,
there wouldn't be cooked carrots,
there wouldn't be prunes, and
that's almost all there would be
if I were in charge of the world!

Tracy, grade 5

Title and Author Index

Subject Index

About the Author

Gail E. Tompkins is a Professor of Literacy and Early Education at California State University, Fresno, where she teaches courses in reading and language arts for both preservice and inservice teachers. She also codirects the San Joaquin Valley Writing Project. Formerly she taught at the University of Oklahoma and directed the Oklahoma Writing Project. *Teaching Writing* grew out of Dr. Tompkins's experiences working side by side with kindergarten through eighth-grade teachers in Oklahoma and California, sharing her strategies for teaching writing and giving demonstration lessons in their classrooms.

Teaching Writing is one of three textbooks Dr. Tompkins has written, all published by Macmillan. She is coauthor of *Language Arts: Content and Teaching Strategies* (second edition) with Kenneth Hoskisson and *Teaching Reading with Literature* with Lea M. McGee. In addition, Dr. Tompkins has written more than 25 articles on topics related to writing, reading, and language arts which have been published in *Language Arts, The Reading Teacher,* and other professional journals. She also regularly speaks to teachers at local district meetings and professional conferences across the United States and in Canada and Europe.

Dr. Tompkins recalls that she always wanted to be an author. She wrote her first books as an elementary student and continues to enjoy writing today. It is her creative outlet, and she has plans for other textbooks and maybe even a novel. When she is not writing, Dr. Tompkins enjoys working with her husband in the garden, playing with her Cairn and Westie puppies, swimming to keep cool in the heat of summer, and traveling in California and Europe.

ISBN 0-02-420843-4